Lab Manual for
A+ Guide to Managing and Maintaining Your PC

Fifth Edition

Jean Andrews, Ph.D.

THOMSON

COURSE TECHNOLOGY

Australia • Canada • Mexico • Singapore • Spain • United Kingdom • United States

THOMSON

COURSE TECHNOLOGY

**Lab Manual for A+ Guide to Managing and Maintaining
Your PC, Fifth Edition**

is published by Course Technology.

Senior Editor:
Lisa Egan

Senior Editor:
Will Pitkin III

Product Manager:
Manya Chylinski

Associate Product Managers:
Mirella Misiaszek
David Rivera

Editorial Assistant:
Amanda Piantedosi

Senior Marketing Manager:
Jason Sakos

Development Editor:
Amanda Brodkin

Production Editor:
Pamela Elizian

Executive Editor:
Mac Mendelsohn

Composition:
GEX Publishing Services

Text Designer:
GEX Publishing Services

Manuscript Quality Engineer:
Marianne Snow

Manufacturing:
Trevor Kallop

Cover Designer:
Abby Scholz

Disclaimer
Course Technology reserves the right to revise this publication and make changes from time to time in its content without notice.

ISBN 0-619-21344-2

Contents

Preface

This Lab Manual is designed to be the very best tool on the market to enable you get the hands-on practical experience needed to learn to troubleshoot and repair personal computers and operating systems. It contains more than 150 labs, each of which targets a very practical problem you are likely to face in the "real world" when troubleshooting PCs. We have made every attempt to write labs that allow you to use generic hardware devices. A specific hardware configuration is not necessary to complete the labs. In learning to install, support, and troubleshoot operating systems, you will learn to use the command prompt and learn to support Windows 98, Windows NT Professional, Windows 2000 Professional, and Windows XP Professional. Each chapter contains labs that are designed to provide the structure needed by the novice, as well as labs that challenge the experienced and inquisitive student.

This book helps prepare you for the two revised A+ Upgrade Certification exams offered through the Computer Technology Industry Association (CompTIA): The A+ Core Hardware Service Technician examination and the Operating System Technologies examination. Because the popularity of this certification credential is quickly growing among employers, obtaining certification increases your ability to gain employment, improve your salary, and enhance your career. To find more information about A+ Upgrade Certification and its sponsoring organization, CompTIA, go to the CompTIA Web site at *www.comptia.org*.

Whether your goal is to become an A+ certified technician or to become a PC support technician, the *Lab Manual for A+ Guide to Managing and Maintaining Your PC, Fifth Edition*, along with Jean Andrews's textbooks, will take you there!

Features

To ensure a successful experience for both instructors and students, this book includes the following pedagogical features:

- **Objectives**—Every lab opens with learning objectives that set the stage for students to absorb the lessons of the lab.

- **Materials Required**—This feature outlines all the materials students need to complete the lab successfully.

- **Activity Background**—A brief discussion at the beginning of each lab provides important background information.

- **Estimated Completion Time**—To help students plan their work, each lab includes an estimate of the total amount of time required to complete the activity.

Activity—Detailed, numbered steps walk students through the lab. These steps are divided into manageable sections, with explanatory material between each section.

- **Figures**—Where appropriate, photographs of hardware or screenshots of software are provided to increase student mastery of the lab topic.
- **Review Questions**—Exercises at the end of each lab help students test their understanding of the lab material.
- **Web Site**—For updates to this book and information about other A+ and PC Repair products, go to *www.course.com/pcrepair.*

ACKNOWLEDGMENTS

I would like to give special thanks to Amanda Brodkin, for her patience and her undying commitment to excellence throughout this entire project.

I would also like to extend my sincere appreciation to Lisa Egan, Manya Chylinski, Pamela Elizian, and all the Course Technology staff for their instrumental roles in the development of this Lab Manual.

Many thanks to Nadine Schreiter of Lakeshore Technical College and Michael Lehrfeld of Brevard Community College, who served as technical editors of previous editions of the manual and still had an impact on this edition. Thank you to Scott Johns for your invaluable experience and for help in developing many of the labs. And I especially want to thank Jill West whose patience, support, and careful attention to detail made my life so much easier. This book is dedicated to the covenant of God with man on the earth.

—Jean Andrews, Ph.D.

USING THIS BOOK

This Lab Manual is designed to accompany *A+ Guide to Managing and Maintaining Your PC, Fifth Edition, Comprehensive*, *A+ Guide to Hardware, Third Edition*, and *A+ Guide to Software, Third Edition*. Lab activities in this book are designed specifically to correlate with chapters in each of these three books. Guidance on using this Lab Manual with each of these books follows.

A+ Guide to Managing and Maintaining Your PC, Fifth Edition, Comprehensive

Chapters correspond directly to chapters in this Lab Manual—Chapter 1 corresponds directly to the labs in Chapter 1 in this Lab Manual, Chapter 2 corresponds directly to the labs in Chapter 2, and so on.

A+ Guide to Software, Third Edition

- Chapter 1   Labs 3.1, 23.6, 23.7, 23.8, and 23.11
- Chapter 2   Labs 1.3, 2.1, 2.2, 2.3, 2.4, and 2.5
- Chapter 3   Labs 3.3, 3.4, 3.5, 3.6, and 5.1
- Chapter 4   Labs 12.1, 12.2, 12.3, 12.4, 12.5, 12.6, 12.7, 12.8, 12.9, 12.10, and 12.11
- Chapter 5   Labs 13.1, 13.2, 13.3, 13.4, 13.5, 13.6, 13.7, 13.8, and 13.9
- Chapter 6   Labs 8.4, 14.1, 14.2, 14.3, 14.4, and 14.5
- Chapter 7   Labs 15.1, 15.2, 15.3, 15.4, and 15.5
- Chapter 8   Labs 16.1, 16.2, 16.3, 16.4, 16.5, 16.6, and 16.7
- Chapter 9   Labs 6.5 and 6.6,
- Chapter 10   Labs 7.5, 9.1, 9.2, 9.3, and 9.4
- Chapter 11   Labs 18.6, 18.7, 18.8, and 18.9
- Chapter 12   Labs 19.1, 19.2, 19.3, 19.4, and 19.5
- Chapter 13   Labs 20.6, 21.1, 21.2, 21.3, 21.5, 23.9, 23.10, 23.12, 23.13, and 23.14

A+ Guide to Hardware, Third Edition

- Chapter 1   Labs 1.1, 1.2, 1.3, 1.4, and 1.5
- Chapter 2   Labs 2.1, 2.2, 2.3, 3.2, and 3.3
- Chapter 3   Labs 4.1, 4.2, 4.3, 4.4, 4.5, and 20.6
- Chapter 4   Labs 5.1, 5.2, 5.3, 5.4, and 5.5
- Chapter 5   Labs 6.1, 6.2, 6.3, 6.4, and 6.5
- Chapter 6   Labs 7.1, 7.2, 7.3, and 7.4
- Chapter 7   Labs 8.1, 8.2, 8.3, 8.5, 9.5, and 9.6
- Chapter 8   Labs 10.1, 10.2, 10.3, 10.4, 10.5, and 10.6
- Chapter 9   Labs 11.1, 11.2, 11.3, 11.4, 11.5, and 11.6
- Chapter 10   Labs 17.1, 17.2, 17.3, 17.4, and 17.5
- Chapter 11   Labs 18.1, 18.2, 18.3, 18.4, and 18.5
- Chapter 12   Labs 20.1, 20.2, 20.3, and 20.4
- Chapter 13   Labs 21.1, 21.3, 21.4, and 21.5
- Chapter 14   Labs 22.1, 22.2, 22.3, 22.4, and 22.5
- Chapter 15   Labs 23.1, 23.2, 23.3, 23.4, and 23.5
- Chapter 16   Labs 9.3, 24.1, 24.2, 24.3, 24.4, and 24.5

CLASSROOM SETUP

Lab activities have been designed to explore many different hardware setup and troubleshooting problems while attempting to keep the requirements for specific hardware to a minimum. Other lab activities have been designed to progressively explore several operating systems so that you can install and use Windows 98, followed by Windows NT Professional, Windows 2000 Professional, and Windows XP.

Most labs take 30 to 45 minutes; a few may take a little longer. For several of the labs, your classroom should be networked and provide access to the Internet. When access to the Windows setup files is required, these files can be provided on the Windows installation CD or on a network drive made available to the PC.

When the particular OS is not of concern, the minimum hardware requirements are:

- 90 MHz or better Pentium-compatible computer
- 24 MB of RAM
- 540-MB hard drive
- A PC toolkit with ground bracelet (ESD strap)

The minimum hardware requirements for Windows 98 are:

- 90 MHz or better Pentium-compatible computer
- 24 MB of RAM
- 195-MB hard drive

The minimum hardware requirements for Windows NT Workstation are:

- 90 MHz or better Pentium-compatible computer
- 16 MB of RAM
- 125-MB hard drive

Additional setup notes on Windows NT Workstation:

- Install Windows NT Workstation on a FAT partition and provide an additional NTFS partition for data
- You will need a user account with administrative privileges

The minimum hardware requirements for Windows 2000 Professional are:

- 133 MHz or better Pentium-compatible computer
- 64 MB of RAM
- 2-GB hard drive

Additional setup notes on Windows 2000 Professional:

- You will need a user account with administrative privileges
- An NTFS partition that might be the partition where Windows 2000 is installed

The minimum hardware requirements for Windows XP are:

- 233 MHz or better Pentium-compatible computer (300 MHz preferred)
- 64 MB of RAM (128 MB preferred)
- 1.5-GB hard drive (2-GB preferred)

Additional setup notes on Windows XP Professional:

- You will need a user account with administrative privileges

A few of the labs focus on special hardware. For example, one lab requires that a CD-ROM drive, sound card, and speakers be installed, and another lab uses a PC camera, a sound card, microphone, and speakers. Two labs require a multimeter. Also, one lab requires a modem and a working phone line, and another lab requires a parallel cable.

LAB SETUP INSTRUCTIONS

Configuration Type and Operating Systems

Each lab begins with a list of required materials. Before beginning a lab activity, verify that each student workgroup or individual has access to the needed materials. Then, make sure that the proper operating system is installed and in good health. Note that in some cases, it is not necessary that an operating system be installed. When needed, the Windows setup files can be provided on the Windows CD, on a network drive, or, in some cases, on the local hard drive. In some labs, device drivers are needed. Students will be able to work more efficiently if these drivers are available on floppy disk or on a network drive prior to beginning the lab.

Protect Data

In several labs, it is possible that data on the hard drive might get lost or corrupted. For this reason, it is important that valuable data stored on the hard drive is backed up to another media.

Access to the Internet

Several labs require access to the Internet. In these labs, if necessary, you can use one computer to search the Internet to download software or documentation and another computer for performing the lab procedures. If the lab does not have Internet access, you can download the needed software or documentation prior to lab and bring the files to lab stored on floppy disk.

THE TECHNICIAN'S WORK AREA

When opening a computer case, it is important to have the proper tools and be properly grounded to ensure that you don't cause more damage than you repair. Now, let's take a look at the components of an ideal technician's work area:

- Grounding mat (with grounding wire properly grounded)
- Grounding wrist strap (attached to the grounding mat)
- Non-carpet flooring
- A clean work area (no clutter)
- A set of screwdrivers
- ¼" Torx bit screwdriver
- ⅛" Torx bit screwdriver
- Needle-nose pliers
- A PLCC (Plastic Leadless Chip Carrier)
- Pen light (flashlight)
- Several new antistatic bags (for transporting and storing hardware)

At minimum, you must have at least two key items. The first is a ground strap. If a grounding mat isn't available, you can attach the ground strap to the computer's chassis and, in most cases, provide sufficient grounding for handling hardware components inside the computer case. The second key item is, of course, a screwdriver. You won't be able to open most chassis without some type of screwdriver.

PROTECT YOURSELF, YOUR HARDWARE, AND YOUR SOFTWARE

When you work on a computer, it is possible to harm both the computer and yourself. The most common accident that happens when attempting to fix a computer problem is erasing software or data. Experimenting without knowing what you are doing can cause damage. To prevent these sorts of accidents, as well as the physically dangerous ones, take a few safety precautions. The following text describes the potential sources of damage to computers and how to protect against them.

Power to the Computer

To protect both yourself and the equipment when working inside a computer, turn off the power, unplug the computer, and always use a grounding bracelet. Consider the monitor and the power supply to be "black boxes." Never remove the cover or put your hands inside this equipment unless you know about the hazards of charged capacitors. Both the power supply and the monitor can hold a dangerous level of electricity even after they are turned off and disconnected from a power source.

Static Electricity, or ESD

Electrostatic discharge (ESD), commonly known as static electricity, is an electrical charge at rest. A static charge can build up on the surface of a nongrounded conductor and on non-conductive surfaces such as clothing or plastic. When two objects with dissimilar electrical charges touch, static electricity passes between them until the dissimilar charges are made equal. To see how this works, turn off the lights in a room, scuff your feet on the carpet, and touch another person. Occasionally you may see and feel the charge in your fingers. If you can feel the charge, then you discharged at least 3,000 volts of static electricity. If you hear the discharge, then you released at least 6,000 volts. If you see the discharge, then you released at least 8,000 volts of ESD. A charge of less than 3,000 volts can damage most electronic components. You can touch a chip on an expansion card or system board and damage the chip with ESD and never feel, hear, or see the discharge.

ESD can cause two types of damage in an electronic component: catastrophic failures and upset failures. A catastrophic failure destroys the component beyond use. An upset failure damages the component so that it does not perform well, even though it may still function to some degree. Upset failures are the most difficult to detect because they are not easily observed.

Protect Against ESD

To protect the computer against ESD, always ground yourself before touching electronic components, including the hard drive, system board, expansion cards, processors, and memory modules. Ground yourself and the computer parts, using one or more of the following static control devices or methods:

- *Ground bracelet or static strap:* A ground bracelet is a strap you wear around your wrist. The other end is attached to a grounded conductor such as the computer case or a ground mat, or it can plug into a wall outlet. (Only the ground prong makes a connection!)

- *Grounding mats:* Ground mats can come equipped with a cord to plug into a wall outlet to provide a grounded surface on which to work. Remember, if you lift the component off the mat, it is no longer grounded and is susceptible to ESD.

- *Static shielding bags:* New components come shipped in static shielding bags. Save the bags to store other devices that are not currently installed in a PC.

The best way to protect against ESD is to use a ground bracelet together with a ground mat. Consider a ground bracelet to be essential equipment when working on a computer. However, if you find yourself in a situation where you must work without one, touch the computer case before you touch a component. When passing a chip to another person, ground yourself. Leave components inside their protective bags until ready to use. Work on hard floors, not carpet, or use antistatic spray on the carpets.

Besides using a grounding mat, you can also create a ground for the computer case by leaving the power cord to the case plugged into the wall outlet. This is safe enough because the power is turned off when you work inside the case. However, if you happen to touch an exposed area of the power switch inside the case, it is possible to get a shock. Because of this risk, in this book, you are directed to unplug the power cord to the PC before you work inside the case.

There is an exception to the ground-yourself rule. Inside a monitor case, the electricity stored in capacitors poses a substantial danger. When working inside a monitor, you *don't* want to be grounded, as you would provide a conduit for the voltage to discharge through your body. In this situation, be careful *not* to ground yourself.

When handling system boards and expansion cards, don't touch the chips on the boards. Don't stack boards on top of each other, which could accidentally dislodge a chip. Hold cards by the edges, but don't touch the edge connections on the card.

After you unpack a new device or software that has been wrapped in cellophane, remove the cellophane from the work area quickly. Don't allow anyone who is not properly grounded to touch components. Do not store expansion cards within one foot of a monitor, because the monitor can discharge as much as 29,000 volts of ESD onto the screen.

Hold an expansion card by the edges. Don't touch any of the soldered components on a card. If you need to put an electronic device down, place it on a grounded mat or on a static shielding bag. Keep components away from your hair and clothing.

Protect Hard Drives and Disks

Always turn off a computer before moving it to protect the hard drive, which is always spinning when the computer is turned on (unless the drive has a sleep mode). Never jar a computer while the hard disk is running. Avoid placing a PC on the floor, where the user can accidentally kick it.

Follow the usual precautions to protect disks. Keep them away from magnetic fields, heat, and extreme cold. Don't open the floppy shuttle window or touch the surface of the disk inside the housing. Treat disks with care and they'll generally last for years.

CHAPTER ONE

INTRODUCING HARDWARE

Labs included in this chapter

➤ Lab 1.1 Gather and Record System Information

➤ Lab 1.2 Identify Computer Parts

➤ Lab 1.3 Use Shareware to Examine a Computer

➤ Lab 1.4 Compare Costs

➤ Lab 1.5 Plan an Ideal System

The following grid shows the correlation between the labs in this chapter and the A+ Guides to Hardware and Software.

A+ Guide to Managing and Maintaining Your PC, Fifth Edition	A+ Guide to Hardware, Third Edition	A+ Guide to Software, Third Edition
Lab 1.1 Gather and Record System Information	Chapter 1	
Lab 1.2 Identify Computer Parts	Chapter 1	
Lab 1.3 Use Shareware to Examine a Computer	Chapter 1	Chapter 2
Lab 1.4 Compare Costs	Chapter 1	
Lab 1.5 Plan an Ideal System	Chapter 1	

LAB 1.1 GATHER AND RECORD SYSTEM INFORMATION

Objectives

The goal of this lab is to use a system's physical characteristics and other sources to determine how the system is configured. After completing this lab, you will be able to:

➤ Gather system information by observing a system

➤ Use available tools to access specific system information

Materials Required

This lab will require the following:

➤ Windows 98, Windows 2000, or Windows XP

➤ Workgroup of 2–4 students

Activity Background

When working with a computer system, it is a good idea to know what components are installed on the system. This lab will help you identify some of these components as you gather information by observing the system and by using system tools.

> Estimated completion time: **15 minutes**

ACTIVITY

Observe the physical characteristics of your system and answer the following questions:

1. Does the system have any identification on it indicating manufacturer, model, or component information? If so, list them.

   _____

   _____

2. How many floppy drives does your system have?

   _____

3. Describe the shape of the connection used by your mouse. How many pins does the connection have?

   _____

1

4. Does your system have CD or DVD drives? If so, how many?

_____

5. How many internal hard drives does your system have? Explain how you got your answer.

_____

_____

_____

Like other versions of Windows, Windows XP can be customized by the user to behave and to display information to that user's taste. Windows XP also has the ability to mimic the way previous versions of Windows presented menus and settings for users who are more comfortable with those methods. To help ensure that the step-by-step instructions for Windows XP exercises are easy for you to follow, complete these steps to restore Windows XP defaults to your system.

1. Boot your system and log in if necessary, then select **Control Panel** from the Start menu. The Control Panel window will open.

2. Under the Control Panel section on the left side of the Control Panel window, click **Switch to Category View** if Classic View has been enabled. See Figure 1-1.

Figure 1-1   Windows XP Control Panel in Classic View

3. With the Category View of Control Panel enabled, click the **Appearance and Themes** category. The Appearance and Themes window appears.

4. From the Appearance and Themes window, select the **Folder Options Control Panel** icon. The Folder Options dialog box appears.

5. On the General tab of the Folder Options dialog box, click the **Restore Defaults** button, then click **Apply**, as shown in Figure 1-2.

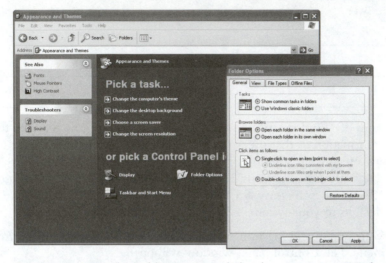

Figure 1-2   Use the Folder Options dialog box to restore Windows XP defaults to a folder

6. Select the **View** tab in the Folder Options dialog box. On the View tab, click the **Restore Defaults** button, then click **OK** to apply the settings and close the dialog box. See Figure 1-3.

Figure 1-3   View tab of the Folder Options dialog box

7. From the Appearance and Themes window, select the **Taskbar and Start Menu** icon. The Taskbar and Start Menu dialog box appears.

8. On the Taskbar tab of the Taskbar and Start Menu dialog box, verify that all boxes are checked except for Auto-hide the taskbar and Show Quick Launch boxes under the Taskbar appearance section. Click **Apply** if any changes were made. See Figure 1-4.

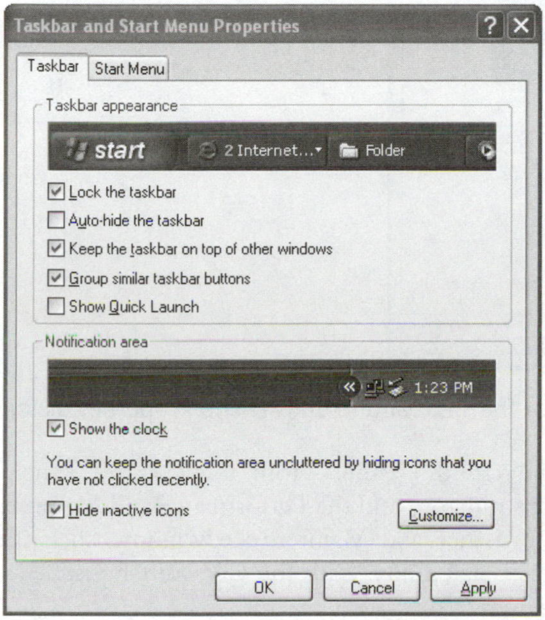

Figure 1-4   Use the Taskbar and Start Menu Properties dialog box to control how the taskbar appears and functions

9. Select the **Start Menu** tab in the Taskbar and Start Menu dialog box. On the Start Menu tab, verify that the radio button next to Start Menu is selected, then click **OK** to apply the settings and close the dialog box. See Figure 1-5. Close the Appearance and Themes window.

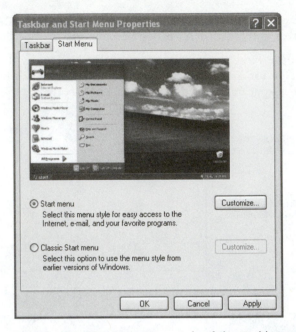

Figure 1-5   The Start Menu tab of the Taskbar and Start Menu Properties dialog box

From the Start menu, open the Control Panel. From the Control Panel, click the
Performance and Maintenance category and the Performance and Maintenance window will appear. From the Performance and Maintenance window, click the **System**
icon to open the System Properties dialog box. With the General tab visible as shown in
Figure 1-6, record the following:

1. Which OS is installed?

   _____

2. What is the version number of your operating system?

   _____

3. Who is the system registered to?

   _____

4. What type of CPU is your system built around?

   _____

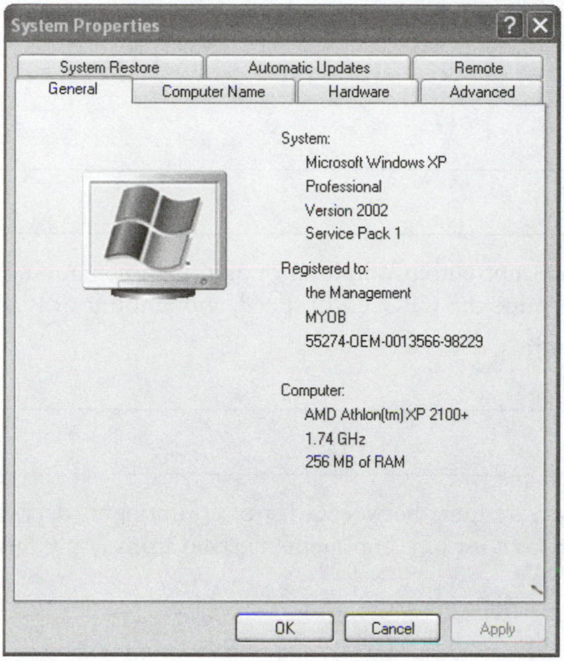

Figure 1-6   The System Properties dialog box

5. How much RAM is installed in your system?

_____

Close the System applet. Close the Performance and Maintenance window.

From the Start menu, open My Computer and locate the following information:

1. How many floppy disk drives appear and which drive letters are assigned to them?

_____

2. How many other local drives appear and which drive letters are assigned to them?

_____

3. How many network drives appear and what are their names?

_____

4. What System Tasks are listed in the left of the My Computer window?

_____

_____

_____

Review Questions

1. List two other ways to get to the System Properties applet besides using the Control Panel.

   _____

   _____

2. What is one other place, not within Windows or any documentation, where you would be able to determine the CPU, CPU speed, and amount of RAM installed on your system?

   _____

   _____

3. What differences, if any, are there between a list of components derived from a physical inspection versus a list of components derived from My Computer and System Properties?

   _____

   _____

4. How might a user, unfamiliar with how Windows XP presents menus and maintenance utilities, improve their ease and efficiency while using Windows XP?

   _____

   _____

LAB 1.2 IDENTIFY COMPUTER PARTS

Objectives

The goal of this lab is to examine your computer to identify the parts inside and outside the case. After completing this lab, you will be able to:

➤ Identify computer components outside the case

➤ Identify computer components inside the case

Materials Required

This lab will require the following:

➤ Working computer

➤ Phillips head screwdriver

➤ Anti-static bracelet

➤ Workgroup of 2–4 students

➤ A display of four or more unknown computer parts prepared by the instructor

Activity Background

When working with a computer system, you must be able to identify the hardware components, both inside and outside the case. Components are not always adequately labeled, especially those inside the case. This lab helps you learn to recognize these components.

Estimated completion time: **30 minutes**

ACTIVITY

Observe the physical characteristics of your system and answer the following questions:

1. What size monitor do you have? Measure the diagonal on the monitor screen.

   _____

2. How many keys are on your keyboard?

   _____

3. Are there any switches on the sides or bottom of the keyboard? If so, how are these switches labeled?

   _____

4. What other external components does your PC have (speakers, printer, and so forth)? Describe each component with as much detail as you can.

   _____

   _____

   _____

5. Look at the back of your PC and list all cables and cords connected to ports and other connections. Fill in the following table:

Describe the port or connector the cable or cord is connected to	Purpose of the cable or cord
1.	
2.	
3.	
4.	
5.	
6.	

6. What other ports on the PC are not being used? List them here:

_____

_____

_____

_____

Now you will open the PC case and examine the components inside. As you work, it is very important that you *not* touch anything inside the case unless you are wearing an anti-static bracelet. Follow these directions:

To remove the cover from a desktop PC, follow these steps:

1. Power down the PC and unplug it. Next, unplug the monitor, printer, and any other device that has its own external power supply. Do not disconnect any cables or cords connected to the back of the PC case.

2. Locate and remove the screws on the back of the case. Look for the screws in each corner and one in the top, as shown in Figure 1-7. Be careful that you don't unscrew any other screws besides these. (These other screws probably are holding the power supply in place, as illustrated in Figure 1-8.)

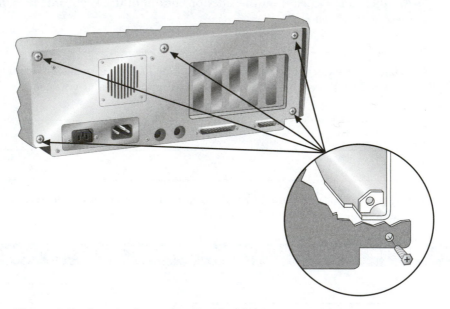

Figure 1-7   Locate the screws that hold the cover in place

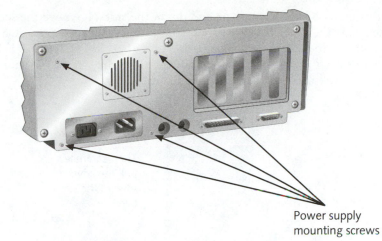

Power supply
mounting screws

Figure 1-8   Power supply mounting screws

3. After you remove the cover screws, slide the cover forward and up to remove it from the case, as shown in Figure 1-9.

Remove screws   Pull cover back, then up, to remove

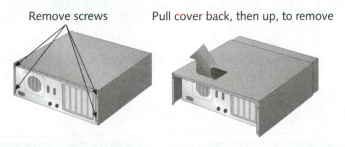

Figure 1-9   Removing a desktop cover

To remove the cover from a tower PC, follow these steps:

1. Power down the PC and unplug it from its power outlet. Next, unplug from the power outlet the monitor and any other device that has an external power source.

2. Look for screws in all four corners and down the sides. Remove the screws and then slide the cover back slightly before lifting it up to remove it. See Figure 1-10. Some tower cases have panels on either side of the case held in place with screws on the back of the case. Remove the screws and slide each panel toward the rear and then lift it off the case.

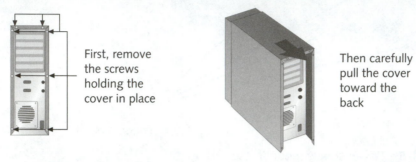

First, remove the screws holding the cover in place

Then carefully pull the cover toward the back

Figure 1-10 Removing a tower cover

With the cover removed, you are ready to look for some components. As you complete the following, refer to drawings in Chapters 3 and 4 of the textbook *A+ Guide to Hardware* or in Chapters 4 and 5 of the textbook *A+ Guide to Managing and Maintaining Your PC*, as necessary.

1. Put on your anti-static bracelet and connect the clip to the side of the computer case.

2. Identify and describe the following major components. List any other components found inside the case. Fill in the table:

Component	Description (include size, location, what it connects to, and what is connected to it in the system)
Power supply	
Floppy disk drive	
Hard drive	
Motherboard	
CPU	
Cooling fan (not inside the power supply)	
CD-ROM drive	
Video card	
Network card	
Sound card	

Challenge Activity

If your instructor has prepared the display of four assorted computer parts, fill in the following table:

Identify the part	Describe how you determined your answer
1.	
2.	
3.	
4.	

Review Questions

1. Describe how you determined which expansion card was the video card.

   _____

2. If your system has a CD-ROM drive, describe how you determined which drive was the CD-ROM drive.

   _____

3. Describe how you identified the type of CPU you have.

   _____

4. How did you know that you were or were not connected to a network?

   _____

5. Does your system have much room for adding new components? Explain your answer.

   _____

6. If you were adding one other component to the inside of the computer case, what would it be and where would you install it?

   _____

LAB 1.3 USE SHAREWARE TO EXAMINE A COMPUTER

Objectives

The goal of this lab is to use SANDRA, Standard version to examine your system. After completing this lab, you will be able to:

➤ Download a file from the Internet

➤ Install SANDRA

➤ Use SANDRA to examine your system

Materials Required

This lab will require the following:

➤ Windows 98, Windows 2000, or Windows XP

➤ Internet access

➤ If using Windows 98 or Windows 2000, software such as WinZip to uncompress a zipped file

Activity Background

Good PC support people are always good investigators. This lab is designed to help you learn how to conduct an investigation via the Internet. As you will see, the Internet offers a wealth of resources to those who take the time to search, download, and investigate the possible uses of software available there. This exercise is designed to help you learn to be such an investigator. Follow these directions to find and download a shareware utility that you can use to diagnose PC problems. Then you will print a report from the downloaded software about the hardware and software on your computer.

Estimated completion time: **30 minutes**

ACTIVITY

1. Open your browser and go to *www.sisoftware.co.uk*.

2. Click the **Downloads** link.

3. Follow one of the links pointing to a location that offers the SANDRA download.

4. Follow the instructions on the site that you selected to begin the download process.

5. When the File Download dialog box appears, save the file to your PC desktop. You can then disconnect from the Internet. What is the name of the downloaded file?

Note that if the Sisoft Web site is unavailable, you can use a search engine to locate the shareware.

Next, you can install SANDRA on your PC. Follow these steps:

1. If the file has a .zip file extension, double-click it to uncompress the SANDRA zip file and extract the setup file.

2. Run the setup program by double-clicking the executable file, which has an .exe file extension. (This might be the downloaded file or the extracted file.) Within the installation wizard, use English as the language selection, accept the EULA, and accept the default settings throughout. The SANDRA installation creates a new program in your Program Group and adds an icon to your desktop.

3. When you finish the installation, SANDRA will launch. Read the Tip of the Day, clear the checkbox next to Show Tips on Start-up, and then click **OK** to close. If you are using Windows XP, you should see a screen similar to the one shown in Figure 1-11.

Figure 1-11 SiSoftware Sandra main window installed under Windows XP

The screens for Windows 98 and Windows 2000 look similar, but, as shown in Figure 1-12, they do not group the icons under headings.

Figure 1-12   SiSoft Sandra main window installed under Windows 2000 or
Windows 98

You can execute each of the utilities, in turn, by double-clicking the icons, or you can create a composite report of the results of each selection. To learn more, complete the following:

1. Double-click the **System Summary** icon. The System Summary utility launches and gathers information about your system before displaying it in a format similar to Device Manager, with devices listed by type.

2. Click the red X at the bottom of the System Summary utility or press Esc on your keyboard to close the System Summary utility.

3. Open the **Windows Information** utility. Scroll down and note the information types that are listed. According to this utility, which version of Windows are you using?

_____

4. What is the path to the Temporary Folder on your system?

_____

5. Click the red X at the bottom of the Windows Information utility or press Esc on your keyboard to close the Windows Information utility.

1

6. Open the **Drives Information** utility. The utility begins to gather information regarding your drives. Do not move the mouse or touch the keyboard while this is in progress. How much Total Space does the hard drive contain? How much Free Space does the hard drive contain? What type of File System does the hard drive use?

_____

_____

7. Click the red X at the bottom of the Drives Information utility or press Esc on your keyboard to close the Drives Information utility.

8. Open the **DMA Settings** utility. Why are you unable to view the DMA Settings information?

_____

_____

9. Close the DMA Settings utility.

You can create a composite report of your system using SANDRA. To learn more, follow these steps:

1. From the SiSoft SANDRA menu bar, click **File** and then click **Create a Report Wizard…**.

2. In the wizard introduction window, click **Next** (right-pointing arrow in a green circle).

3. In the Step 1 of 9 window, accept the default **Make choices and generate report** from the drop-down menu. Click **Next** to continue.

4. In the Step 2 of 9 window, click the **Clear All** (red X over a box) button. Check the boxes next to both Mainboard Information and Windows Memory Information, and then click **Next** to continue.

5. In the Step 3 of 9 window, click the **Clear All** button and then click **Next** to continue.

6. In the Step 4 of 9 window, click the **Clear All** button and then click **Next** to continue.

7. In the Step 5 of 9 window, click **Next** to continue.

8. In the Step 6 of 9 window, add any comments that you desire and click **Next** to continue.

9. In the Step 7 of 9 window, select the **Print or Fax** option from the drop-down menu and then click Next to continue.

10. In the Print dialog box, click **OK** for Windows 98 or **Print** for Windows 2000 or Windows XP. Click the **Exit** (red X) to close the wizard and then collect your report from the printer.

11. Continue to explore each utility in SANDRA, and then close SANDRA. You will use SANDRA again in later chapters, so don't uninstall it.

In this lab, you downloaded SANDRA from the SiSoft Web site. But many popular utilities are available from multiple sources on the Internet. To see for yourself, follow these steps:

1. Attempt to find SANDRA at www.zdnet.com.

2. Is the program available through this avenue as well? Print the Web page or pages to support your answer.

_____

Review Questions

1. What URL can you use to find a link to download SANDRA?

_____

2. Is SANDRA capable of hardware diagnostics only?

_____

3. Which two of the four system resources are you *not* able to view with the version of SANDRA you downloaded and why?

_____

_____

_____

4. What type of software is SANDRA?

_____

LAB 1.4 COMPARE COSTS

Objectives

The objective of this lab is to compare a pre-assembled system and the components that could be assembled to build a comparable system. After completing this lab, you will be able to:

➤ Identify the key components of a pre-assembled system

➤ Locate prices for components needed to assemble a comparable system

➤ Compare the cost of a pre-assembled system and a self-assembled system

Materials Required

This lab will require the following:

➤ Internet access and/or access to a computer publication such as *Computer Shopper*

Activity Background

In this lab you will compare the cost of a brand name system with the cost of a system with the same specifications assembled from individual components. If you can't find an exact match for components, find the closest possible substitute. Use the Internet and available computer-related publications as your sources for information.

Estimated completion time: **45 minutes**

ACTIVITY

1. Find an advertisement for a complete, pre-assembled system similar to the one shown in Figure 1-13.

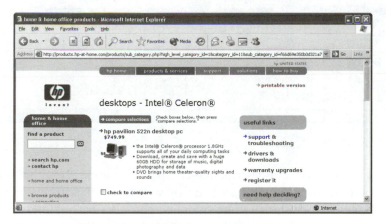

Figure 1-13   Complete, pre-assembled system

2. Study the advertisement and list the following specifications:

■ Processor/MHz:—————————————————————

■ RAM:—————————————————————

■ OS:—————————————————————

■ HDD capacity:—————————————————————

- Monitor: _____
- Sound/Speakers: _____
- Other Drives: _____
- Bonus Items: _____
- Bundled Software: _____
- Total Price: _____

3. Find advertisements similar to those shown in Figure 1-14. Notice that the items are grouped by component type.

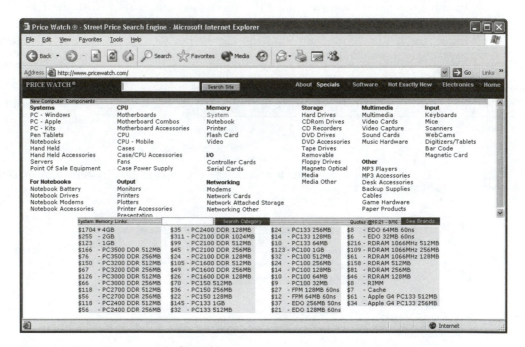

Figure 1-14   Components for sale

Using the following table, list and describe the comparable components, their individual prices, and the source of your information. You may wish to check several sources to find the best price. Remember, most mail order or online purchases have shipping costs associated with them. If you can determine an exact shipping price for each particular component, include this as part of the component's price. If you cannot find the exact shipping price, include a 10 percent fee as part of the price for each shipped component. You might have to include tax, depending on the state-to-state taxing laws that apply. Sometimes the shipping cost is offset by not having to pay state sales taxes on an item.

Component	Description	Source	Price
Processor/MHz			
Motherboard			
RAM			
Case and power supply			
OS			
HDD capacity			
Monitor			
Sound/speakers			
CD-ROM drive			
Other drives			
Bonus items			
Bundled software			
TOTAL SYSTEM PRICE			

Review Questions

1. Which approach to acquiring a system seems to be less expensive?

   _____

   _____

2. What is the single most expensive component of a system built from individual components?

   _____

3. What was the estimated cost of shipping (if any) associated with the component-built system?

   _____

4. What are some potential pitfalls of building your own PC? Rewards?

   _____

   _____

Note: As you continue with this course, you will be better able to answer this last question based on your own experiences in the course.

LAB 1.5 PLAN AN IDEAL SYSTEM

Objectives

The objective of this lab is to plan and price your own ideal system within a budget. After completing this lab, you will be able to:

➤ Describe what you want your system to be able to do

➤ Pick components that best meet your goal

➤ Stay within a budget

Materials Required

This lab will require the following:

➤ Internet access and/or access to a computer publication such as *Computer Shopper*

Activity Background

In the future you may be in a position to build a system to your specifications from individual components. Within a budget of $1200, what system would you put together? In this activity, you determine the answer based on your current knowledge and experience. Expect that your opinions will most likely change as you continue in this course.

Estimated completion time: **30 minutes**

ACTIVITY

1. On a separate piece of paper, make a table similar to the one used in Lab 1.4. Use the table to list the components that you would like to include in your system, the cost of each component, and the source for each component. To begin, list everything you want and do not worry about price.

2. Once you have determined the total price of all the components you want to include in your ideal system, add up the prices and see if you are within your $1200 budget.

3. If you are under budget, consider including additional components in your system or better versions of components you are already including. If you are over budget, determine what components you need to exclude or whether you need to use less expensive versions of some components. Either way, record what components you choose. Also, note how you altered your ideal system to meet your budget.

Review Questions

1. What is the goal of your system? In other words, how do you plan to use your system? Explain your choices for components.

   _____

   _____

   _____

2. How would you change your choices if you were to use this computer at a corporate office as a business workstation?

   _____

   _____

   _____

3. What single change would you make if you had an extra $200 in the budget?

   _____

   _____

4. How might you change your design if your budget was only $1000?

   _____

   _____

Keep your responses to this lab for later reference. As you learn more about PCs in this course, you can look back at these responses and see where you might change your mind based on new information you have learned.

How an Operating System Works with Hardware and Other Software

---

Labs included in this chapter

➤ Lab 2.1 Examine System Resources with Device Manager

➤ Lab 2.2 Create and Examine a Windows 98 Startup Disk

➤ Lab 2.3 Use Microsoft Diagnostics with Windows

➤ Lab 2.4 Install Windows Components

➤ Lab 2.5 Convert Numbers

The following grid shows the correlation between the labs in this chapter and the A+ Guides to Hardware and Software.

A+ Guide to Managing and Maintaining Your PC, Fifth Edition	A+ Guide to Hardware, Third Edition	A+ Guide to Software, Third Edition
Lab 2.1 Examine System Resources with Device Manager	Chapter 2	Chapter 2
Lab 2.2 Create and Examine a Windows 98 Startup Disk	Chapter 2	Chapter 2
Lab 2.3 Use Microsoft Diagnostics with Windows	Chapter 2	Chapter 2
Lab 2.4 Install Windows Components		Chapter 2
Lab 2.5 Convert Numbers		Chapter 2

LAB 2.1 EXAMINE SYSTEM RESOURCES WITH DEVICE MANAGER

Objectives

In this lab, you will learn about Device Manager. After completing this lab, you will be able to use Device Manager to:

➤ Determine what components are installed on a system

➤ Examine system resource allocation

➤ Print a system summary

Materials Required

This lab will require the following:

➤ Windows 98, Windows 2000, or Windows XP

Activity Background

Windows 98, Windows 2000, and Windows XP provide a powerful configuration tool called Device Manager, which you can use to view and print a system's hardware configuration. Windows NT does not have Device Manager. Device Manager is more powerful than MSD, but not quite as good as some third-party utilities. (You examined one of these third-party utilities in Lab 1.3.) Note that Windows 98 and Windows 2000/XP offer slightly different Device Managers, so as you complete this lab be sure to follow the directions for your version.

> Estimated completion time: **30 minutes**

ACTIVITY

To access Device Manager in Windows 98, follow these steps:

1. Click the **Start** button on the taskbar, point to **Settings**, and then click **Control Panel**. The Control Panel window opens.

2. Double-click the **System** icon.

3. In the System Properties dialog box, click the **Device Manager** tab.

To access Device Manager in Windows 2000, follow these steps:

1. Click the **Start** button on the taskbar, click **Settings**, and then click **Control Panel**. The Control Panel window opens.

2. Double-click the **System** icon.

3. In the System Properties dialog box, click the **Hardware** tab, and then click the **Device Manager** button.

2

4. Device Manager opens. If a message dialog box appears, read and close it. According to this message, what must you do in order to actually make changes in Device Manager?

To access Device Manager in Windows XP, follow these steps:

1. Click the **Start** button on the taskbar and then click **Control Panel**. The Control Panel window opens. Click **Performance and Maintenance**.

2. Click the **System** Control Panel icon. The System Properties dialog box appears.

3. In the System Properties dialog box select the **Hardware** tab.

4. In the Device Manager section of the System Properties dialog box, click the **Device Manager** button. The Device Manager window appears.

5. If a message dialog box appears, click **OK** to continue. Why did you receive the prompt?

In both Windows 2000 and Windows XP, Device Manager appears similar to Figure 2-1. You can right-click an item in the list and then select Properties from the shortcut menu to view information about that item, or you can view the item's Properties by double-clicking the item. When you click the + sign to the left of an item, a list of the installed devices for that item appears beneath the item. To see how this works, follow these steps:

Figure 2-1   Windows 2000 and Windows XP Device manager can be accessed from the System Properties window

1. Click the **plus sign** next to Network adapters.
2. Double-click a device listed under Network adapters. A Properties dialog box opens.
3. Click the **Resources** tab. This tab shows all resources used by the selected device.

Use the Resources tab in the Properties dialog box to complete the following:

1. What IRQ is assigned to the network adapter?

   _____

2. What is the I/O range of the network adapter?

   _____

3. What Memory Addresses are available to the network adapter?

   _____

4. Close the Properties window.

Device Manager in Windows 2000 and Windows XP hides some resources from initial view. To view hidden devices in Windows 2000 and Windows XP:

1. List the device types that are currently displayed.

   _____

   _____

   _____

2. From the menu bar, click **View** and then click **Show hidden devices**.
3. How many additional devices appeared?

   _____

4. Expand **Non-Plug and Play Drivers**.
5. Explore the properties of several drivers and note some of the differences between the Driver tabs of Non-Plug and Play Drivers and non-hidden devices.

   _____

   _____

2

Device Manager also enables you to view resources in other ways.

To view resources in Windows 98:

1. In Device Manager, click the **View resources by connection** option button and observe that the groupings change.

2. Click the **plus sign** next to Plug and Play BIOS to view the devices managed by the Plug and Play BIOS.

To view resources in Windows XP:

1. Click **View** on the Device Manager menu bar and then click **Resources by type**. Note that information is now grouped into four categories.

2. Click the **plus sign** next to Interrupt request (IRQ) to see which device is assigned to each IRQ line.

Device Manager enables you to print information about individual devices or device categories. You can also print a system summary. To print a system summary, follow the directions for your version of Windows.

To print a system summary for Windows 98:

1. Click the **Print** button.

2. Click the **System summary** option button and click **OK**.

To print a system summary for Windows 2000:

1. Click **View** on the Device Manager menu bar and then click **Print**.

2. Click the **System summary** option button and then click **Print**.

To print a system summary for Windows XP:

1. Click the **Print** button.

2. Click the **System summary** option button and then click **Print**.

Review Questions

1. For each entry below, list the tab on a device's Properties box in Device Manager where you would be able to perform the action or find the information.

   - Start a troubleshooting wizard:_____
   - Determine the IRQ setting:_____
   - Disable or enable the device:_____
   - Allow the device to bring the system out of standby:_____
   - Find conflict information:_____

2. How do you display individual devices under the group headings?

_____

3. What are two ways to access a device Properties box in Device Manager?

_____

_____

4. What types of additional devices appeared when you chose to display hidden devices?

_____

_____

5. What three options are available for printing in Device Manager?

_____

_____

_____

LAB 2.2 CREATE AND EXAMINE A WINDOWS 98 STARTUP DISK

Objectives

The objective of this lab is to learn how a Windows 98 startup disk is made and used. After completing this lab, you will be able to:

➤ Create a Windows 98 startup disk

➤ Describe the steps in booting from a startup disk

Materials Required

This lab will require the following:

➤ Windows 98 operating system

➤ Blank floppy disk

➤ Workgroup of 2–4 students

Activity Background

From within Windows 98, you can create a startup disk, which is a great tool for troubleshooting and setup. A startup disk is a bootable disk that also contains several helpful utilities and drivers. In this activity, you will create and experiment with a startup disk.

> Estimated completion time: **30 minutes**

ACTIVITY

1. Open the Control Panel and double-click the **Add/Remove Programs** icon.

2. In the Add/Remove Programs applet, click the **Startup Disk** tab.

3. In the Startup Disk tab, click the **Create Disk** button and follow the prompts to create the startup disk.

4. When the process is complete, close the Add/Remove Programs applet.

Answer the following questions about the startup disk:

1. What two files on the startup disk end in the ".bat" extension?

   _____

2. What are the purposes of these files?

   _____

   _____

3. What kind of information is provided in the README.TXT file?

   _____

   _____

With the startup disk in the drive, reboot your computer and answer these questions:

1. What prompt do you see while the system boots?

   _____

2. What type of drive is set up during the boot process?

   _____

3. Why do you think this drive is set up?

   _____

To continue exploring the startup disk, follow these steps:

1. Using the command prompt provided by the startup disk, access the hard drive by entering the following command: **C:**

2. Your prompt should now be the C prompt. Write the prompt here.

_____

3. Use the DIR command to view the contents of the root directory of the **C** drive.

4. Keeping in mind that filenames usually describe the file's function, record the names of the files listed as a result of the DIR command. Explain what you think the purpose of each file is.

_____

_____

_____

Keep your startup disk to use in later labs.

Review Questions

1. Why might you want to use a startup disk?

_____

_____

2. What icon in the Control Panel do you use to create a startup disk?

_____

3. Why would you need CD-ROM support when using the startup disk?

_____

_____

4. If you wanted to examine the files on the CD-ROM drive, what command(s) would you execute at the command prompt?

_____

5. What three files must be on the startup disk to make the disk bootable?

_____

2

LAB 2.3 USE MICROSOFT DIAGNOSTICS WITH WINDOWS

Objectives

The goal of this lab is to observe the boot process. After completing this lab, you will be able to:

➤ Use the Microsoft Diagnostics (MSD) utility to examine your system

➤ Compare results of MSD using real mode and protected mode

Materials Required

This lab will require the following:

➤ Windows 98 operating system

➤ Bootable floppy disk from Lab 2.2 or startup disk from Lab 2.2

➤ Path to Windows 98 setup files as provided by your instructor

Activity Background

The Microsoft Diagnostics (MSD) utility, which is included with both DOS and all versions of Windows, examines your system and displays useful information about ports, devices, memory, and the like. The program file for Microsoft Diagnostics, MSD.EXE, is located in the Tools/OldMSDOS directory on your Windows 98 installation CD. In this lab you will install and use MSD.

Estimated completion time: **30 minutes**

ACTIVITY

Before you can begin using MSD, you need to copy the program file to your hard disk.

1. Insert the Windows 98 installation CD into your CD-ROM drive or access the setup files at the location provided by your instructor.

2. Copy the file **MSD.EXE** from the Windows 98 Tools/OldMSDOS directory to your hard drive, storing it in a folder named **Tools**.

Now that you have copied the necessary program file to your hard disk, you can launch MSD. Follow these steps to use MSD in a real mode environment:

1. Reboot your computer using the bootable floppy disk from Lab 2.2 or a Windows 98 startup disk from Lab 2.2, which will boot your PC into real mode and provide a command prompt. Or you can point to Start, click Shut Down, and then click "Restart Computer in MS-DOS mode."

2. At the command prompt, type **C:\TOOLS\MSD.EXE** and then press **Enter**. Note that this is a way to execute a program file located in a different directory from the one you are working in. You told the computer the exact path, called an absolute path, to the file you wanted to execute. At this point, your screen should look similar to Figure 2-2.

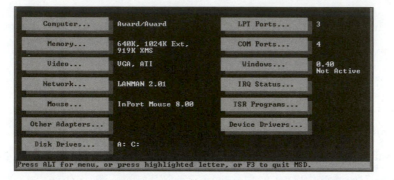

```
  Computer...      Award/Award        LPT Ports...    3

   Memory...       640K, 1024K Ext,   COM Ports...    4
                   919K XMS

   Video...        VGA, ATI           Windows...      0.40
                                                      Not Active

  Network...       LANMAN 2.01        IRQ Status...

   Mouse...        InPort Mouse 8.00  TSR Programs...

Other Adapters...                     Device Drivers...

 Disk Drives...    A: C:

Press ALT for menu, or press highlighted letter, or F3 to quit MSD.
```

Figure 2-2   The MSD utility

Study all the MSD menu options and answer the following questions about your system:

1. What categories of information are available in MSD?

_____

_____

2. What version of the operating system are you running?

_____

3. What COM ports are available on the system?

_____

4. What IRQ and Port Address are associated with COM1?

_____

5. How far does the MEMORY map extend?

_____

6. What is the Address Range at 1024K?

_____

Save the information you noted so that you can compare it with the information you will obtain from MSD in the next set of steps. Now you are ready to close MSD.

1. Click **File** on the MSD menu bar and then click **Exit**.

2. Remove the floppy disk and reboot your PC to the Windows desktop.

3. Using Windows Explorer, double-click the **MSD.EXE** file to start it again.

With MSD open, answer the following questions again:

1. What categories of information are available in MSD?

   _____

   _____

2. What version of the operating system are you running?

   _____

3. What COM ports are available on the system?

   _____

4. What IRQ and Port Address are associated with COM1?

   _____

5. How far does the MEMORY map extend?

   _____

6. What is the Address Range at 1024K?

   _____

Compare the information obtained the first time you used MSD with the information you obtained the second time, and then answer these questions:

1. How does your first set of answers compare to your second set of answers?

   _____

   _____

2. How do you explain the differences?

_____

_____

3. What key can you press to exit MSD?

_____

You are finished with MSD now, so you can close it.

Review Questions

1. In what categories would you look to find information on COM ports?

_____

2. What message did you see when you started MSD from within Windows?

_____

3. Which category gives information on the type of network installed?

_____

4. What is an advantage of saving MSD.EXE to the hard drive?

_____

5. What is the absolute path to MSD.EXE on the Windows 98 setup CD?

_____

6. What Windows tool is similar to MSD?

_____

7. As a PC repair technician, when would you use MSD?

_____

_____

2

LAB 2.4 INSTALL WINDOWS COMPONENTS

Objectives

The objective of this lab is to add an optional component to Windows. After completing this lab, you will be able to:

➤ Use the Add/Remove Programs utility

➤ Install desktop wallpaper

➤ Select a wallpaper for your desktop

Materials Required

This lab will require the following:

➤ Windows 98 operating system

➤ Path to the Windows 98 setup files as provided by your instructor

Activity Background

Windows includes many optional features that can be installed either when you install the operating system itself, or at some later time, after the operating system has already been installed. In this lab you will install optional desktop wallpapers on a computer that already has Windows 98 installed.

Estimated completion time: **30 minutes**

ACTIVITY

1. Open the Control Panel and double-click the **Add/Remove Programs** icon.

2. Click the **Windows Setup** tab. In the Components field you should see several categories of Windows components listed.

3. Click **Accessories** and then click the **Details** button. A window opens displaying Windows components in the Accessory category.

4. Select the **Desktop Wallpaper** checkbox and then click **OK** to close the window.

5. Click **Apply**.

6. When prompted, click **OK**, type the path to the Windows setup files and then click **OK** again.

7. Windows installs the files containing the new desktop wallpaper. When the installation is complete, click **OK** to exit the Add/Remove Programs utility.

8. In the Control Panel, double-click the **Display** icon.

9. Click the **Background** tab and then browse through the various wallpapers. Experiment with the Tile, Center, and Stretch options in the drop-down menu. Observe the preview of your wallpaper selections in the Background tab.

10. Select a background combination you like, click **Apply**, and then click **OK** to close the Display utility.

11. Close any other open windows and observe your new desktop wallpaper.

Review Questions

1. What collection of files is necessary to install a new Windows component?

_____

2. Which utility is used to install new Windows components?

_____

3. What category of components is Desktop Wallpaper part of?

_____

4. What utility did you use to select a wallpaper for your system?

_____

5. Is it necessary to apply the Display properties before you see what a wallpaper will look like?

_____

LAB 2.5 CONVERT NUMBERS

Objectives

The objective of this lab is to practice converting numbers between decimal, binary, and hexadecimal forms. After completing this lab, you will be able to:

➤ Convert decimal numbers to hexadecimal and binary form

➤ Convert hexadecimal numbers to binary and decimal form

➤ Convert binary numbers to decimal and hexadecimal form

2

Materials Required

This lab will require the following:

➤ Pencil and paper and/or Windows Calculator

➤ Appendix C (The Hexadecimal Number System and Memory Addressing) from the textbook *A+ Guide to Software* or from the textbook *A+ Guide to Managing and Maintaining Your PC*

➤ Windows 98, Windows 2000, or Windows XP

Activity Background

You will sometimes want to know what resources are being reserved for a device. This information is often displayed on a computer in hexadecimal (or hex) numbers, which is shorthand for the binary numbers that computers actually use. Often, you will want to convert these into the more familiar decimal numbers. This will give you a better picture about which resources are reserved for a device.

> Estimated completion time: **60 minutes**

ACTIVITY

1. Convert the following decimal numbers to binary numbers using either a calculator or the instructions provided in Appendix C (The Hexadecimal Number System and Memory Addressing) from the textbook *A+ Guide to Software* or from the textbook *A+ Guide to Managing and Maintaining Your PC*. (To access the Windows Calculator, click **Start** on the taskbar, point to **Programs**, point to **Accessories**, and then click **Calculator**.)

   ■ 14 = _____

   ■ 77 = _____

   ■ 128 = _____

   ■ 223 = _____

   ■ 255 = _____

2. Convert the following decimal numbers to hexadecimal notation:

   ■ 13 = _____

   ■ 240 = _____

   ■ 255 = _____

   ■ 58880 = _____

   ■ 65535 = _____

3. Convert the following binary numbers to hexadecimal notation:
   - 100 = _____
   - 1011 = _____
   - 111101 = _____
   - 11111000 = _____
   - 10110011 = _____
   - 00000001 =_____

4. Hexadecimal numbers are often preceded with "0x." Convert the following hex numbers to binary numbers:
   - 0x0016 = _____
   - 0x00F8 = _____
   - 0x00B2B = _____
   - 0x005A = _____
   - 0x1234 = _____

5. For Windows 98, click the **Start** button on the taskbar, click **Run**, type **winipcfg** and click **OK**. In the IP Configuration window, click the **More Info** button. [For Windows 2000/XP, to open a Command window, click **Start** on the taskbar, point to **Programs** (for Windows XP, **All Programs**), point to **Accessories**, and then click **Command Prompt**. At the command prompt, type **ipconfig /all**.] A network card is assigned an address that identifies the card on the network. For Windows 98, the address is called the Adapter Address, and for Windows 2000/XP, the address is called the Physical Address. Either way, the address assigned to the network card is expressed in a series of paired hexadecimal numbers separated by dashes. Convert each pair to a binary number.

   - Adapter address in hexadecimal form: _____
   - Adapter address in binary pairs: _____

6. Convert the following hexadecimal numbers to decimal:
   - 0x0013 = _____
   - 0x00AB = _____
   - 0x01CE = _____
   - 0x812A = _____

7. Referring to Figure 2–3, convert the numbers in the network adapter's memory range and determine how many bytes, expressed in a decimal number, are in its memory address range.

   _____

2

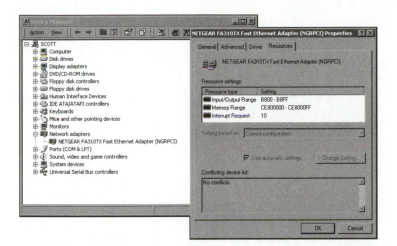

Figure 2-3   Memory Range and Input/Output Range expressed as hex numbers

8. Convert the following binary numbers to decimal:

- 1011 = _____
- 11011 = _____
- 10101010 = _____
- 111110100 = _____
- 10111011101 = _____
- 11111000001111 = _____

Review Questions

1. Computers actually work with _____ numbers.

2. Computers often express numbers in _____ format, which is a base-sixteen number system.

3. Most people are more comfortable when working within a _____, or base-ten number system.

4. In hex, what decimal value does the letter A represent?

   _____

5. Hexadecimal numbers are often preceded by _____ so that a value containing only numerals is not mistaken for a decimal number.

UNDERSTANDING THE BOOT PROCESS AND MS-DOS MODE

Labs included in this chapter

➤ Lab 3.1 Examine Files and Directories

➤ Lab 3.2 Observe the Boot Process

➤ Lab 3.3 Modify Configuration Files and Observe the Results

➤ Lab 3.4 Learn to Work from the Command Line

➤ Lab 3.5 Examine Windows Configuration Files

➤ Lab 3.6 Learn File Naming Conventions

The following grid shows the correlation between the labs in this chapter and the A+ Guides to Hardware and Software.

A+ Guide to Managing and Maintaining Your PC, Fifth Edition	A+ Guide to Hardware, Third Edition	A+ Guide to Software, Third Edition
Lab 3.1 Examine Files and Directories		Chapter 1
Lab 3.2 Observe the Boot Process	Chapter 2	
Lab 3.3 Modify Configuration Files and Observe the Results	Chapter 2	Chapter 3
Lab 3.4 Learn to Work from the Command Line		Chapter 3
Lab 3.5 Examine Windows Configuration Files		Chapter 3
Lab 3.6 Learn File Naming Conventions		Chapter 3

LAB 3.1 EXAMINE FILES AND DIRECTORIES

Objectives

The goal of this lab is to use different methods to examine files and directories. After completing this lab, you will be able to:

➤ Use the command line to view information about files and directories

➤ Use My Computer to view information about files and directories

➤ Display information about files and directories in other ways

Materials Required

This lab will require the following:

➤ Windows 9x, Windows 2000, or Windows XP operating system

Activity Background

You can access information about the file structure of a PC in several ways. From the command line, you can use the DIR command to list files and directories. In Windows, you can use Explorer or My Computer to view the same information. In the following activity, you will practice using the DIR command and My Computer.

Estimated completion time: **30 minutes**

ACTIVITY

Follow these steps to access file information via the command line:

1. For Windows 9x, click the **Start** button on the taskbar, point to **Programs**, and then click **MS-DOS Prompt**. (For Windows 2000/XP, click the **Start** button on the taskbar, point to **Programs** (or **All Programs** for Windows XP), point to **Accessories**, and then click **Command Prompt**.)

2. The command-line window opens with the current directory indicated by the prompt. Type **DIR** and press **Enter**.

3. A detailed list of files and directories within the current directory appears. If there are many files and directories, only the last several will be visible on the screen. Try these variations of the DIR command and explain how the information is displayed:

DIR/P

DIR/W

3

4. Examine the results of the DIR command. The results vary with versions of Windows, but each listing should include the following information:

- The date and time the file was created

- The directory markers. Directories do not include an extension. Instead, they are indicated by a <DIR> tag.

- The size of the file, in bytes

- The name of a file or directory. Most files have an extension.

- A summary including the number of files and directories within that directory, the number of bytes used by those files, and the number of bytes of free space on the drive.

To print this file information, you can copy the contents of the Command Prompt window to the Windows Clipboard, open the Notepad program, paste the file information into Notepad, and then use Notepad's Print command. To try that technique now, follow these steps:

1. Click the MS–DOS Prompt icon (for Windows 9x) or the Command Prompt icon (for Windows 2000/XP) located on the title bar.

2. Point to **Edit**, and then click **Mark**. A blinking cursor will appear at the top of your command-line window.

3. Left–click and drag over the information you would like to copy to the clipboard; you will notice the information is highlighted. It may be necessary for you to scroll the window to capture all necessary information.

4. Once you have highlighted all the information you wish to copy, click the MS-DOS Prompt icon (for Windows 9x) or the Command Prompt icon (for Windows 2000/XP) located on the title bar again.

5. Point to **Edit**, and then click **Copy**.

6. Click **Start**, point to **Programs**, and then point to **Accessories** and select **Notepad**.

7. Click **Edit**, and then click **Paste**.

8. Click **File**, and then click **Print**. Use the print options to print your document.

9. Close the Command Prompt window and Notepad without saving the file.

In addition to the Command Prompt window, you can also use My Computer to examine files and directories. My Computer can display information in a variety of ways. Before you view files and directories using this tool, you'll first change some settings to control how the information is displayed. In Windows 9x, follow these steps:

1. From the Windows 9x desktop, double-click the **My Computer** icon. The My Computer window opens.

2. Click **View** on the menu bar, and then click **Folder Options**. The Folder Options window opens.

3. Click the **General** tab (if necessary), click the **Custom, based on settings you choose** option button, and then click the **Settings** button.

4. In the "Browse Folders as Follows" section, click the **Open each folder in its own window** option button and then click **OK**. The Custom Settings window closes.

5. Click **Apply** and then click **OK** to close the Folder Options window.

To change settings in Windows 2000/XP, follow these steps:

1. From the Windows 2000 desktop, double-click the **My Computer** icon. For Windows XP, click **Start** and then click **My Computer**. The My Computer window opens.

2. Click **Tools** on the menu bar and then click **Folder Options**. The **Folder Options** dialog box opens.

3. In the Folder Options window, click the **View** tab (if necessary), check **Show hidden files and folders**, and uncheck **Hide file extensions for known file types**.

4. Click **Apply** and then click **OK** to close the Folder Options window.

Now that you have changed the way information is displayed, you are ready to use My Computer to access specific information about your system's files and directories. Complete the following for both Windows 9x and Windows 2000/XP:

1. Maximize the My Computer window and then click the icon representing drive C.

2. How much free space is available?

   _____

3. How much space is used?

   _____

4. Double-click the icon for drive C. How are folders represented in this window?

   _____

   _____

5. Windows uses a different icon for different types of files. Describe three different icons and the files they represent.

_____

_____

_____

6. Click **View** on the My Computer menu bar and then click **Details**. Notice
that this command displays the same information as the DIR command.

7. Close all open windows.

Review Questions

1. What command displays a list of files and directories at the command line?

_____

2. Does Windows display file extensions by default?

_____

3. How can you change the way Windows displays file extensions?

_____

_____

4. What tool other than My Computer can you use to explore a file structure
graphically?

_____

5. In My Computer, what type of graphic displays information about a drive?

_____

6. How does Windows graphically distinguish between different file types?

_____

LAB 3.2 OBSERVE THE BOOT PROCESS

Objectives

In this lab you will observe the sequence of events in a PC's boot process. After completing this lab, you will be able to:

➤ Describe the boot process in detail

➤ Halt the boot process

➤ Diagnose problems in the boot process

Materials Required

This lab will require the following:

➤ Lab PC designated for disassembly

➤ Windows 9x or Windows 2000/XP operating system

➤ Blank floppy disk

➤ Workgroup of 2–4 students

Activity Background

This lab will familiarize you with the boot process and give you some practice recognizing when the boot process halts and observing the resulting information displayed on the monitor. Working in teams, you will begin by observing a PC booting up and noting every step, from turning on the power to the appearance of the Windows desktop. Once you are familiar with all the steps in the boot process, your workgroup will intentionally introduce problems that will cause the boot process to fail on your PC and observe the results. Then you will introduce one problem on your PC and your workgroup will switch PCs with another workgroup's PC and attempt to figure out why that workgroup's PC failed to boot.

Estimated completion time: **30 minutes**

ACTIVITY

1. Boot your team's PC and then, using the information displayed on the monitor as a guide, record every step in the process. (List this information on a separate piece of paper.) For example, you are looking for RAM initialization, display of CPU speed, a list of devices that are detected, what happens when the screen turns from black to another color, and other similar events. You may have to boot the PC several times in order to record all of the steps.

Perform each of the following steps to introduce a problem in the boot process of your team's PC. For each problem, boot the PC and describe the problem as a user unfamiliar with PC technology might describe it. List any error messages that you see.

1. Insert a blank floppy disk into the floppy drive.
   - Describe the problem as a user sees it, including error messages.

   _____

   _____

2. Unplug the keyboard.
   - Describe the problem. Does the computer still boot into Windows?

   _____

   _____

3. Unplug the mouse.
   - Describe the problem. Does the computer still boot into Windows?

   _____

   _____

4. Unplug the monitor.
   - Describe the problem.

   _____

5. After a minute, plug the monitor in. Did the system boot correctly?

   _____

6. Now cause one problem in the list above and switch places with another team. Do not tell the other team what problem you caused.

7. Detect, diagnose, and remedy the problem on the other team's PC.

Review Questions

1. What is the first message displayed on the monitor after you turn on the power?

   _____

   _____

2. What devices are detected during the boot process?

   _____

   _____

3. Of all the problems you studied during the activity, which halts the boot process earliest in the process?

_____

_____

4. Which problem results in messages about the operating system not being present?

_____

_____

5. Why do you think it is useful to be familiar with all the different steps in the boot process?

_____

_____

LAB 3.3 MODIFY CONFIGURATION FILES AND OBSERVE THE RESULTS

Objectives

The objective of this lab is to learn to use configuration files that affect the MS-DOS command-line environment. Specifically, you will load drivers that make it possible to use a mouse in the command-line environment. You will also learn to use utilities executed at the commandline. After completing this lab, you will be able to:

➤ Create a bootable floppy disk

➤ Copy files to a floppy disk

➤ Modify configuration files

Materials Required

This lab will require the following:

➤ Windows 9x operating system

➤ File provided by your instructor needed to load a 16-bit generic mouse driver (for example, Mouse.com or Mouse.sys)

➤ Location provided by your instructor of the Windows and DOS utility programs Msd.exe and Edit.com.

➤ Blank floppy disk

3

Activity Background

In this lab you will boot to a command prompt by using a bootable floppy disk. As you will see, normally a command prompt environment does not allow you to use the mouse. Once the PC is booted, you will use Microsoft Diagnostics utility (MSD), a program that displays information about the hardware environment, to verify that the PC does not provide mouse support. Then you will add mouse support by adding to your system a configuration file that loads a mouse driver. The mouse driver file normally comes on a floppy disk bundled with a mouse, but your instructor might provide an alternate location. Finally, you will reboot the PC, run MSD again, and verify that mouse support has indeed been enabled.

> Estimated completion time: **30 minutes**

ACTIVITY

Follow these steps on a Windows 9x PC to create a bootable floppy disk and to copy a file to the disk.

1. Click **Start** on the taskbar, point to **Programs**, and then click **MS-DOS Prompt**.

2. Insert a blank floppy disk.

3. Type **FORMAT A: /S** and press **Enter**.

4. The following prompt appears: "Insert new diskette for drive A: and press Enter when ready." Press **Enter** to start formatting the disk.

5. Watch as the floppy disk is formatted and the system files are transferred to the floppy disk.

6. When prompted, type a volume name if you wish and press **Enter** (or simply press **Enter** to bypass this step entirely).

7. When asked if you want to format another disk, type **N** and then press **Enter**. (Note that if your disk was already formatted, you could have used the SYS A: command to copy system files to the disk.)

Now that you have created a boot disk, follow these steps to copy some configuration files to the boot disk.

1. Insert the Windows 9x CD into the CD drive, type **Copy D:\tools\ oldmsdos\msd.exe A:**, and then press **Enter**. (If you don't have access to the Windows 9x CD, your instructor might give you an alternate location for the file. If your CD has a drive letter other than D, substitute the appropriate drive letter.)

2. Repeat Step 1 for the mouse driver file and the text editor, Edit.com, in the location specified by your instructor. The mouse driver file will be named Mouse.com, Mouse.sys or a similar name.

3. Close the Command Prompt window and shut down the system.

At this stage, the boot disk contains the necessary configuration files. Next, you will boot the PC using the boot disk and verify that the mouse is not available.

1. With the floppy disk still in the drive, boot the system. An A prompt displays on your screen.

2. To use the Microsoft Diagnostic Utility, at the command prompt, type **MSD.EXE** and then press **Enter**.

3. Move the mouse around. Does the mouse work as you would expect?

_____

4. Press **F3** to exit MSD.

You will now use the Edit program to create and edit an Autoexec.bat file.

1. At the A prompt, type **Edit Autoexec.bat**. The Edit window opens and the Autoexec.bat file is created.

2. Enter the command to load the mouse driver, using the filename of the driver, such as Mouse.com.

3. To exit the editor and save your changes, press the **Alt** key, and use your arrow keys to select **Exit** from the Exit menu.

4. When asked if you want to save your changes to the file, select **Yes**.

Now you will test your floppy disk to see if it provides mouse support.

1. With the boot disk still in the floppy drive, reboot.

2. Run the MSD program. Did you observe any change when you moved the mouse?

_____

3. Click **Exit** from the **File** menu to close MSD. Remove the floppy disk and reboot the PC.

Review Questions

1. When formatting a disk, what command can you use to make the floppy disk a boot disk?

_____

2. If you have a formatted floppy, what command other than **Format a: /s** can you use to transfer the system files to the floppy disk?

_____

3. Which configuration file did you modify to cause the mouse to be automatically supported?

_____

4. Did you notice a difference in the boot process after you changed a configuration file?

_____

5. When booting from a floppy disk, how would you automatically load a program to provide support for your CD-ROM drive?

_____

_____

LAB 3.4 LEARN TO WORK FROM THE COMMAND LINE

Objectives

The goal of this lab is to introduce you to some commands used when working from the command line. You will change and examine directories and drives, and you will perform a copy operation. You will also learn to use the DOS Help feature and how to read the Help information. In later labs, you will learn to perform more advanced operations from the command line. After completing this lab, you will be able to:

➤ Create a file and folder with Notepad and My Computer

➤ Examine directories

➤ Switch drives and directories

➤ Use various commands at the command prompt

Materials Required

This lab will require the following:

➤ Windows 9x, Windows 2000, or Windows XP operating system

➤ Blank formatted floppy disk

Activity Background

In Lab 2.2 you were introduced to the command-line environment when you used the DIR command to explore file structure. Most people work from the command line only when troubleshooting or performing some specific task. For most tasks, you'll rely on a graphical interface, such as My Computer, in Windows. In this lab, you will use My Computer to create a new folder and a new file. Then, you will delete that file from the command line. In this lab it is assumed that Windows is installed on drive C. If your installation is on a different drive, substitute that drive letter in the following steps.

Estimated completion time: **30 minutes**

ACTIVITY

To create a new folder and text file from within My Computer, follow these steps:

1. From the Windows desktop, double-click **My Computer**, and then double-click the drive C icon. Note that if you are using Windows XP, the My Computer icon might not be on the desktop. In this case, click **Start** and click **My Computer**.

2. Right-click anywhere in the blank area of the drive C window, select **New** in the shortcut menu, and then click **Folder**. A new folder icon appears with "New Folder" highlighted, ready for you to rename it.

3. Type **Tools** and press **Enter** to rename the folder "Tools."

4. To create a file in the Tools folder, double-click the **Tools** folder icon and then right-click anywhere in the blank area of the Tools window. Select **New** in the shortcut menu, and then click **Text Document**. A new file icon appears in the Tools window with "New Text Document.txt" highlighted, ready for you to rename it.

5. Double-click the **New Text Document.txt** icon in \Tools. The file opens in Notepad.

6. Click **File** in the Notepad menu bar, and then click **Save As...**.

7. In the Save As dialog box, name the file **Deleteme**, and make sure the **Save as type:** is **Text Documents**. Click **Save** to save the file.

8. Close Notepad.

9. Right-click **New Text Document.txt** and then click **Delete** in the Shortcut menu. Click **Yes** to confirm the deletion. The file is deleted.

10. Close all open windows.

To practice using the command-line environment, perform these steps:

1. To open the command-line window in Windows 9x, click **Start** on the taskbar, point to **Programs**, and then click **MS-DOS Prompt**. To open the command-line window in Windows 2000, click **Start** on the taskbar, point to **Programs**, point to **Accessories**, and then click **Command Prompt**. To open the command-line window in Windows XP, click **Start** on the taskbar, point to **All Programs**, point to **Accessories**, and then click **Command Prompt**.

2. A command-line window opens. The title bar of this window differs with different versions of Windows. Below the title bar, a command prompt like the following appears in Windows 9x:

C:\WINDOWS>

3

In Windows 2000, the following command prompt appears instead:

C:\>

The Windows XP command prompt depends on the user name of the person currently logged in, for example:

C:\Documents and Settings\Jean Andrews>

The command prompt indicates the working drive (drive C) and working directory (either the \Windows directory, the root directory indicated by the backslash, or the Documents and Settings directory of the current user). Commands issued from this prompt apply to this folder unless you indicate otherwise.

3. Type **DIR** and press **Enter**. Remember that DIR is the command used to list the contents of a directory. You should see a list of files and directories in the command-line window. The list may be too large to fit within one screen, in which case you will see only the last entries. This list contains the names of both files and directories. For example, Config.sys is a single file. Entries with the label <DIR> indicate that they are directories (folders), which can contain files or other directories. Also listed for each entry is the time and date it was created and the number of bytes it contains. (This information will appear differently depending on which version of Windows you are using.) The last two lines in the list give a summary of the number of files and directories in the current directory, as well as the space consumed and the free space available on the drive.

As you'll see in the next set of steps, there are two ways to view any files that are not displayed due to the length of the list and the size of the window. To learn more about displaying lists of files in the command-line environment, perform the following steps:

1. Type **DIR /?** and then press **Enter** to display Help information for the directory command. You can obtain Help information for any command by entering the command followed by the **/? switch**.

2. Type **DIR /W** and then press **Enter**. What happened?

_____

_____

3. Type **DIR /P** and then press **Enter**. What happened?

_____

_____

4. Type **DIR /OS** and then press **Enter**. What happened?

_____

_____

5. Type **DIR /O–S** and then press **Enter**. What happened? What do you think the hyphen between O and S accomplishes?

_____

_____

6. Insert a blank disk into the floppy drive. Type **A:** and then press **Enter**. The resulting prompt should look like this: A:\>. What does the A: indicate?

_____

7. What do you think you would see if you executed the DIR command at this prompt?

_____

_____

8. Type **DIR** and press **Enter**. Did you see what you were expecting?

_____

9. Change back to the C drive by typing **C:** and pressing **Enter**.

10. Type **DIR C:\Tools** and press **Enter**. This tells the computer to display a list of the contents of a specific directory without actually changing to that directory. In the resulting file list, you should see the file you created earlier, Deleteme.txt.

11. Type **DEL Deleteme.txt** and press **Enter** to instruct the computer to delete that file. You will see a message indicating that the file could not be found. This is because the system assumes commands refer to the working directory unless a specific path is given. What command do you think you could use to delete the file without changing to that directory?

_____

_____

12. Type **CD** and press **Enter**. The resulting prompt is C:\> for Windows 9x, Windows 2000, and Windows XP. The \ in the command you typed indicates the root directory.

13. Type **CD Tools** and then press **Enter**. The prompt now ends with "Tools>," (indicating that Tools is the current working directory).

3

14. Now type **DEL Deleteme.txt /p** and press **Enter**. You will be prompted to type in "**Y**" for **Yes** or "**N**" for **No**. If you do not enter the **/p switch** to **Prompt for Verification**, the file is deleted automatically without a confirmation message. It is a good practice to use the **Prompt for Verification switch**, especially when deleting multiple files with wildcard characters. Also, when you delete a file from the command line, the file does not go to the Recycle Bin, like it would if you deleted it from Windows Explorer or My Computer, therefore making it more difficult to recover accidentally deleted files.

15. Type **Y** to delete the Deleteme.txt file. You are returned to the Tools directory.

To display certain files in a directory, you can use an asterisk (*) or a question mark (?) as wildcard characters. Wildcard characters are placeholder characters that represent other unspecified characters. The asterisk can represent one or more characters. The question mark represents any single character. The asterisk is the most useful wildcard, and for that reason it is the one you'll encounter most often. To learn more, follow these steps:

1. Return to the root directory. What command did you use?

_____

2. Type **DIR *.*** and press **Enter**. How many files are displayed?

_____

3. Type **DIR C*.*** and press **Enter**. How many files are displayed?

_____

4. Explain why the results differed in the previous two commands.

_____

_____

CRITICAL THINKING (additional 30 minutes)

Do the following to practice using additional commands at the command prompt:

1. Copy the program file **notepad.exe** from the \Windows directory in Windows 98 (or the \WINNT or \Windows directory in Windows 2000/XP) to the **\Tools** directory. What command did you use?

_____

2. Rename the file in the \Tools directory as **Newfile.exe**. What command did you use?

_____

3. Change the attributes of **Newfile.exe** to make it a hidden file. What command did you use?

_____

4. Type **DIR** and then press **Enter**. Is the Newfile.exe file being displayed?

_____

5. Unhide **Newfile.exe**. What command did you use?

_____

6. List all files in the \Windows or \WINNT directory that have an .exe file extension. What command did you use?

_____

_____

7. Create a new directory named **\New** in \Windows or \WINNT and copy **Newfile.exe** to the \New directory. What commands did you use?

_____

_____

8. Using the /p switch to prompt for verification, delete the **\New** directory. What commands did you use?

_____

_____

Review Questions

1. What command/switch can you use to view Help information for the DIR command?

_____

2. What do you add to the DIR command to list the contents of a directory that is not the current working directory?

_____

3. What command can you use to change directories?

_____

4. What command can you use to delete a file?

_____

5. What command can you use to switch from drive A to drive C?

_____

LAB 3.5 EXAMINE WINDOWS CONFIGURATION FILES

Objectives

The goal of this lab is to introduce you to the Autoexec.bat and Config.sys configuration files. After completing this lab, you will be able to:

➤ Use Windows Explorer to examine your system's file structure

➤ Locate configuration files

➤ View configuration files using Notepad

Materials Required

This lab will require the following:

➤ Windows 9x or Windows 2000/XP operating system

➤ Windows 9x startup disk

Activity Background

Two files in DOS and Windows 9x that can be used to configure a system each time it boots are Autoexec.bat and Config.sys. These files are used to load real-mode programs and drivers and to set environmental variables. In this lab, you will examine these files using Windows Explorer to locate the files on the startup disk and examine their contents.

Windows Explorer is a good tool for browsing through a system's file structure. Whenever you are instructed to find a file in this manual, the instructions assume that you are using Windows Explorer unless otherwise specified. Although there are other ways to browse for files, such as in the My Computer window, Windows Explorer has some key advantages. In Windows Explorer, the left pane shows a hierarchical view of the file structure. If you click a folder in this pane, the contents of the folder are then displayed in the right pane.

Estimated completion time: **15 minutes**

ACTIVITY

To use Windows Explorer to open the Autoexec.bat and Config.sys files, follow these steps:

1. Click the **Start** button on the taskbar, point to **Programs**, and then click **Windows Explorer** (or right-click the **Start** button on the taskbar and then click **Explore**).

2. Insert the startup disk.

3. In the left pane of Windows Explorer, click the icon for **drive A**. The drive is highlighted in the left pane, and the right pane displays a list of folders and files stored on the floppy disk.

4. If necessary, scroll down the right pane until you can see the Autoexec.bat file.

5. Right-click **Autoexec.bat**, and then click **Edit** in the shortcut menu. The file opens in a text editor (usually Notepad by default), ready for you to modify it. Autoexec.bat is a batch file that contains a list of commands for tasks that you want the system to execute each time it starts up. Your system might contain other batch files, but only Autoexec.bat is run by default each time the system boots.

6. Look for entries in the Autoexec.bat file (similar to the entry shown in Figure 3-1) that instruct the OS where to look for executable files. Virus protection software and any drivers that are loaded for DOS compatibility can also be referenced in Autoexec.bat.

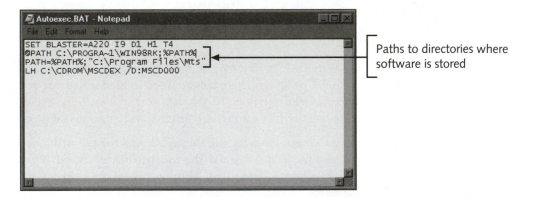

Figure 3-1   The Autoexec.bat file tells the OS where to look for executable files, virus protection software, and DOS-compatible drivers

7. Close the file. If you had made any changes, you would be asked whether you wanted to save them. Do *not* save any changes at this time.

8. In Windows Explorer, locate the Config.sys file on the A drive, right–click **Config.sys**, and then click **Open With...** in the shortcut menu. The Open With dialog box appears.

9. In the Open With dialog box, scroll down and select **Notepad**, clear the **Always use this program to open this file** check box and then click **OK**. Config.sys opens in Notepad.

10. Note that the Config.sys file contains configuration instructions as well. An example is shown in Figure 3–2. Yours may have instructions for loading device drivers to high memory to free up conventional memory for DOS applications.

3

Figure 3-2   A Config.sys file

11. Close Config.sys. If you made any changes, do *not* save them.

Review Questions

1. What is the purpose of configuration files?

_____

_____

2. On either a startup disk or on a hard drive, in what directory are Autoexec.bat and Config.sys located?

_____

3. Are other batch files besides Autoexec.bat automatically processed during the boot process?

_____

4. Which configuration file can contain a path statement?

_____

5. Which configuration file can instruct DOS drivers to load in high memory?

_____

LAB 3.6 LEARN FILE NAMING CONVENTIONS

Objectives

The goal of this lab is to teach you about file naming conventions. After completing this lab, you will be able to:

➤ Describe the 8.3 convention

➤ Describe long filenames

➤ Observe long filename conversion in an 8.3 environment

Materials Required

This lab will require the following:

➤ Windows 9x operating system

Activity Background

In Windows 9x, you can use filenames of up to 255 characters. DOS, however, only recognizes filenames that use the 8.3 convention—that is, filenames that are up to eight characters long, followed by a period, followed by up to three characters. The last three characters after the period are referred to as the file extension. The file extension usually defines the file type; for instance, the extension "txt" indicates a text file. If you use DOS on your Windows 9x computer, DOS will convert any long filenames to the 8.3 format. In this lab you will create several files within Windows, assigning them filenames of various lengths. Then you will display these filenames at the command prompt (that is, from within DOS) and note any changes to the long filenames.

Estimated completion time: **30 minutes**

ACTIVITY

By default, file extensions are not displayed within Windows. So before you can examine file extensions in Explorer, you need to display them. Follow these steps:

1. Open Windows Explorer, click **Tools** on the menu bar, and then click **Folder Options**.

2. On the View tab, deselect the **Hide file extensions for known file types** check box, click **Apply**, and then click **OK**. The Folder Options dialog box closes.

3. In Explorer, browse through several folders and note the file extensions. Table 3-1 lists common file extensions with their corresponding file types. Note that in Windows, files with the same extension are represented by the same icon.

Table 3-1   File Extensions with Corresponding File Types

File Extension	File Type
.txt	Text
.exe	Executable
.com	Command
.sys	System
.cab	Cabinet (contains compressed installation or setup files)

Now you will use a DOS command window (DOS box) to create a directory on the hard drive and store a file in it using the DOS naming convention. Follow these steps:

1. Open a command prompt window. Change directories to the root of the C drive.

2. Type **MD Test** and press **Enter**. The MD command instructs the system to make a directory, in this case one called Test.

3. Use the **DIR /AD /P** command to verify that this new directory exists.

4. Type **CD Test** to change to the Test directory.

5. Type **Edit Test.txt** and press **Enter**. This edit command opens a DOS text editor called Edit, and creates a file named Test.txt. Using this program, you can create and edit text files.

6. Type **This is a test. This file was created with Edit.**

7. Press **ALT+F+S** to save the file.

8. Press **ALT+F+X** to exit Edit. Leave the command window open.

Now that you have created a file using the DOS naming convention, you will use Notepad to create a file with a long filename. Follow these steps:

1. In Windows Explorer, find the Test folder and double-click **Test.txt**. (Note that this fairly short filename is identical in Explorer and in the command prompt environment.) The file opens in Notepad, which is the default text editor for Windows.

2. In Notepad, click **File** on the menu bar and then click **New**. Type **This is a test. This file was created in Notepad with a long filename.**

3. Click **File** on the menu bar, click **Save as...**, name the file **Longnametest.txt**, and then click **Save**. Do *not* close Notepad.

4. Look at the filename in Explorer. Note that the name appears exactly as you typed it in the Save As dialog box. Note also that the file is represented by the same icon as the Test.txt file. Next, you will see how DOS displays the long filename.

5. Return to the DOS command window, which should still have \Test as the current working directory. Type **DIR** and record the short names and long names of the files listed.

_____

_____

6. Now you're ready to create another file with a long filename. In Notepad, amend the text to read **This is the second file created in Notepad with a long filename.** and save this file as **Longnametestagain.txt**, using the same procedure as in Step 3.

7. In the command prompt window, execute another DIR command. You should now see two files other than Test.txt. These files are named Longna~1.txt and Longna~2.txt. As you can see, DOS changes long filenames to the 8.3 format by leaving the first six characters and adding a ~ (tilde) and a number indicating the alphabetical instance (beyond the sixth character) of that file. Compare the way the file Longnametest.txt was displayed earlier, when it was the only file other than Test.txt, and the way it is displayed now.

In DOS, directory names that are longer than eight characters are automatically abbreviated in the same way as long filenames. It is possible, however, to use long directory names in DOS in some situations. To learn more, perform these steps:

1. At the command prompt, make the C root the current directory and then type **DIR /O /P**. Note the way DOS lists the Program Files directory, which does not follow the 8.3 DOS naming convention for files and directories. The directory is listed by DOS as Progra~1.

2. From the C:\> prompt, type **CD Progra~1** and press **Enter**. This makes the Progra~1 directory the current directory.

3. If you want to use a long (that is, unabbreviated) directory name with the CD command, you need to enclose the directory name in quotation marks. To try this now, first type **CD** and then press **Enter**. This makes the C root the current directory.

4. Type **CD "Program Files"** (including the quotation marks) and press **Enter**. Program Files is now the current directory.

Review Questions

1. What does 8.3 mean in the context of naming conventions?

_____

_____

2. How does Windows graphically depict file types?

_____

_____

3. What type of file ends in .exe?

_____

4. How is a long filename represented at the DOS prompt?

_____

_____

5. How can you use long names at the DOS prompt?

_____

_____

3

4

ELECTRICITY AND POWER SUPPLIES

Labs included in this chapter

➤ Lab 4.1 Take a Computer Apart and Put It Back Together

➤ Lab 4.2 Find Documentation on the Internet

➤ Lab 4.3 Learn PC Power Supply Facts

➤ Lab 4.4 Measure the Output of Your Power Supply

➤ Lab 4.5 Replace a Power Supply

The following grid shows the correlation between the labs in this chapter and the A+ Guides to Hardware and Software.

A+ Guide to Managing and Maintaining Your PC, Fifth Edition	A+ Guide to Hardware, Third Edition	A+ Guide to Software, Third Edition
Lab 4.1 Take a Computer Apart and Put It Back Together	Chapter 3	
Lab 4.2 Find Documentation on the Internet	Chapter 3	
Lab 4.3 Learn PC Power Supply Facts	Chapter 3	
Lab 4.4 Measure the Output of Your Power Supply	Chapter 3	
Lab 4.5 Replace a Power Supply	Chapter 3	

LAB 4.1 TAKE A COMPUTER APART AND PUT IT BACK TOGETHER

Objectives

The goal of this lab is to help you get comfortable working inside a computer case. After completing this lab, you will be able to:

➤ Take a computer apart

➤ Recognize components

➤ Reassemble the computer

Materials Required

This lab will require the following:

➤ Computer designated for disassembly

➤ PC toolkit

➤ Ground strap and static mat

Activity Background

If you follow directions and take your time, there is no reason to be intimidated by working inside a computer case. This lab will take you step by step through the process of disassembling and reassembling a PC. Follow your computer lab's posted safety procedures when disassembling and reassembling a PC and remember to always wear your ground strap. Also, never force a component to fit into its slot.

You will begin this lab by removing the cover of your PC. Then you will remove the components inside. Next you will reassemble the components and replace the cover. This lab includes steps for working with a desktop PC and a tower PC. Follow the steps that apply to your situation.

Also, in this lab, you are instructed to disassemble your PC in this order: remove the expansion cards, interior cables and cords, power supply, case fans, motherboard, and drives. Because some systems are designed so that the disassembly order should be different from the one above, your instructor might change this order. For example, you might not be able to get to the power supply to remove it until drives or the motherboard are out of the way. Be sure to follow any specific directions from your instructor.

Estimated completion time: **45 minutes**

ACTIVITY

Follow the procedure outlined below to remove the case cover and expansion cards. (If you are working with a tower case, lay it on its side so that the motherboard is on the bottom.)

4

1. Remove the cover from your desktop PC.

2. To make reassembly easier, take notes or make a sketch of the current placement of boards and cables and identify each board and each cable. You can mark the location of a cable on an expansion card with a marker if you like. Note the orientation of the cable on the card. Each cable for the floppy disk drive, hard drive, or CD-ROM drive has a colored marking on one side of the cable called the edge color. This color marks pin 1 of the cable. On the board, pin 1 is marked either with the number 1 or 2 beside the pin or with a square soldering pad on the back side of the board. (See Figure 4-1.) You might not be able to see this soldering pad now.

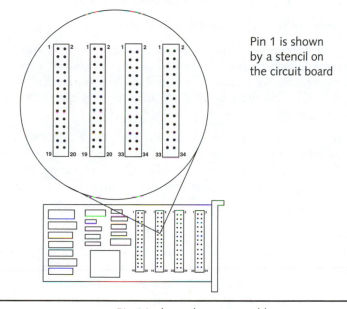

Pin 1 is shown
by a stencil on
the circuit board

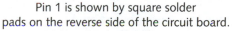

Pin 1 is shown by square solder
pads on the reverse side of the circuit board.

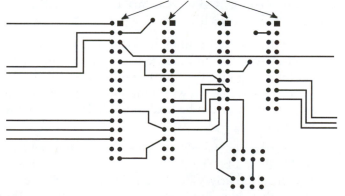

Figure 4-1   How to find pin 1 on an expansion card

3. Remove the cables from the expansion cards. There is no need to remove the other end of the cable from its component (floppy disk drive, hard drive, or CD-ROM drive). Lay the cable over the top of the component or case.

4. Remove the screw holding the card to the case. If for some reason you aren't wearing a ground strap, touch the case before you touch the card.

5. Grasp the card with both hands and remove it by lifting straight up and rocking the card from end to end (not side to side). Rocking the card from side to side might spread the slot opening and weaken the connection.

6. If the card had a cable attached, examine the card connector for the cable. Can you identify pin 1? Lay the card aside on a flat surface.

7. Remove any other expansion cards in the same way.

8. In some proprietary systems, an expansion card assembly attaches to the motherboard, with each card attached to the assembly. If your system has this arrangement, remove it now. It is probably held in place by screws or clips and may or may not have a rail guide that you can use to locate the assembly within the case.

9. To remove the power supply, first remove the power cables to the motherboard, case fans, other remaining components, and the power switch if necessary. Make notes about which cable attaches to what. Once the cables are removed, support the power supply with one hand and remove the screws attaching it to the case.

10. Remove any case fans.

In some systems, it is easier to remove the drives first and then the motherboard. In other systems, it is easier to remove the motherboard first. In these instructions, in order to not risk your dropping a drive on the motherboard when removing the drive, you are directed to first remove the motherboard and then the drives. Your instructor, however, might prefer you first remove the drives, then the motherboard.

1. Begin removing the motherboard by removing any power cables connected to any case or component fans. Be sure to make notes or label the cables so that you can reinstall them correctly.

2. Finish removing the motherboard by removing the screws holding the board to the stand-offs. Usually six to nine screws attach the motherboard to the case. Be careful not to gouge the board or otherwise damage components with the screwdriver. Because the screws on the motherboard are often located between components, they can be hard to reach. Be very careful not to damage the motherboard.

3. To remove drives, remove the ribbon cable if it is still attached. Many cases have a removable drive bay. The drives are attached to this bay and the bay may be removed with all the drives attached. This allows easier access to drive mounting screws than from inside the case. If your case has a removable drive bay, this is the preferred method of removal. Otherwise remove each drive separately. Be careful not to jar the drive as you remove it from the case.

4. If your system has a removable drive bay, it is likely that the floppy drive came out with the removable bay. If the floppy drive is still in the system, remove the screws holding the drive in place and slide the drive out of the case.

5. Remove any CD-ROM, DVD, or tape drives from the case. These drives are usually in the 5-inch drive bays and are held in place by four to eight screws. Once the screws are removed, the drive will slide out the front of the case.

6. Remove any other components.

Now that you have removed all the components, you are ready to reassemble the PC. Replace each component carefully. Take care to install each component firmly without over-tightening the screws. Do not force components to fit. If a component will not easily fit the way it should, look for some obstruction preventing it from falling into place. Look carefully for the reason the component will not fit correctly and make any small adjustments as necessary. The following steps outline the necessary procedure, which is essentially the reverse of the disassembly procedure:

1. Install the drives in their bays and then install the motherboard, unless your instructor prefers you install the motherboard first.

2. Place each card in its slot (it doesn't have to be the same slot, just the same bus) and replace the screw. Don't place a PCI or ISA video card near the power supply; otherwise, EMI from the power supply might affect the video picture.

3. Replace the cables, being sure to align the colored edge with pin 1. (In some cases it might work better to connect the cable to the card before you put the card in the expansion slot.)

4. Check to make sure that no cables are interfering with any fan's ability to turn. A common cause for an overheated system is a fan that can't move air because a cable is preventing it from spinning.

5. When all components are installed, you should have refitted all of the screws that you removed earlier. If some screws are missing, it is particularly important to turn the case upside down and *gently* shake the case to dislodge any wayward screws. Any screw lying on a board has the potential to short out that board when power is applied. Do not use a magnet to try and find missing screws in the case because you might damage the data on hard drives and floppy disks left in the floppy disk drives.

6. Plug in the keyboard, monitor, and mouse.

7. In a classroom environment, have the instructor check your work before you power up.

8. Turn on the power and check that the PC is working properly before you replace the cover. Don't touch the inside of the case while the power is on.

9. If all is well, turn off the PC and replace the cover and its screws. If the PC does not work, don't panic. Turn off the power and then go back and check each cable connection and each expansion card. You probably have not solidly seated a card in the slot. After you have double-checked everything, try again.

Review Questions

1. When removing the cover, why should you take care only to remove the screws that hold the cover on?

_____

_____

2. How should you rock a card to remove it from its slot? Why is it important to know how to properly rock a card?

_____

_____

_____

3. What should you do to help you remember which components connect to which cables?

_____

4. What marking on a ribbon cable identifies pin 1?

_____

5. What component(s) defines the system's form factor?

_____

_____

6. What form factor does your PC use?

_____

7. Why would a PC technician ever have to change out a computer's motherboard?

_____

4

LAB 4.2 FIND DOCUMENTATION ON THE INTERNET

Objectives

The goal of this lab is to show you how to locate documentation on the Internet in order to determine how much power a component uses. After completing this lab, you will be able to:

➤ Find the manufacturer and model of a component

➤ Search for a product's documentation or manual

➤ Download and view a product manual

Materials Required

This lab will require the following:

➤ Computer designated for disassembly

➤ Internet access

➤ Adobe Acrobat Reader

➤ PC toolkit with ground strap

Activity Background

Often the power specifications for a component are not labeled on the component itself but are included in the documentation. When working with PCs, it is very common to encounter a component for which you have no documentation on hand. In this exercise, you will learn to find the make and model of a component and, if possible, find online documentation for it.

Estimated completion time: **30 minutes**

ACTIVITY

1. Open the PC's case and locate the component assigned to you by your instructor (or randomly select a component). If you are working with a team, each person on your team should be assigned a different component.

2. Examine the component until you find a sticker or stenciled label identifying its manufacturer and model number.

The manufacturer and model are not clearly marked on every component. If you're having trouble finding this information on a component, such as a video card, try researching according to the component's chipset. The information identifying the chip is usually stenciled on the chip. If you need to find out how much power an unlabeled component will use, it's sometimes helpful to consult the documentation for similar components.

3. Take your notes to a computer that has Internet access.

4. If you already know the manufacturer's URL, go to that site and try to find documentation in these locations:

- The Support section of the site, as shown in Figure 4-2
- The Downloads section
- The Customer Service section

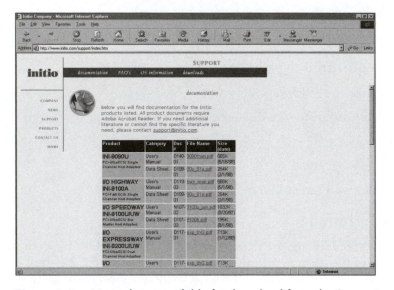

Figure 4-2   Manuals are available for download from the Support section of a manufacturer's Web site

If you are not sure of the manufacturer's URL, try searching for the manufacturer or model number using a good search engine. In fact, searching by model number will often get you to the information in the fewest steps. Keep in mind that most documentation is provided in PDF format, which means you may need Adobe Acrobat Reader or a browser plug-in to view the documentation.

5. Print out or save the documentation, and file it as a reference for when you need information about that component.

6. What CPU does your system use?

_____

7. Go to the manufacturer's Web site and find and print the Web page showing the power consumption of your CPU expressed in watts.

Review Questions

1. How is a component commonly marked for identification?

   _____

   _____

2. In what sections of a Web site are manuals commonly found?

   _____

3. In what format are manuals commonly provided?

   _____

4. What software do you need to view a PDF document?

   _____

5. Why would a PC repair technician need to know the power consumption of a peripheral?

   _____

   _____

Lab 4.3 Learn PC Power Supply Facts

Objectives

The goal of this lab is to determine if a PC's power supply is adequate for the PC's components. After completing this lab, you will be able to:

➤ Examine documentation and estimate the peak power consumption (in watts) required by the system components

➤ Examine a power supply to determine if it meets the system's needs

Materials Required

This lab will require the following:

➤ Lab computer designated for disassembly

➤ Documentation for system components that includes information about electrical requirements

➤ Access to the Internet

➤ PC toolkit with ground strap

➤ Workgroup of 2–4 students

Activity Background

A power supply must be able to provide adequate power for all devices in a system at peak consumption. If the power supply's maximum rated wattage (peak wattage) is not greater than the sum of the peak consumption of all components, the system may crash or spontaneously reboot (or worse) during heavy use. Furthermore, an inadequate power supply might run well during light use, but then fail when the system is stressed. You can prevent such problems by using documentation to determine whether a power supply is adequate for the demands of a particular system. In this activity, you'll learn more about your system's power supply.

Estimated completion time: **30 minutes**

ACTIVITY

Remove the cover from your PC and answer the following questions:

1. How many watts are supplied by your power supply? (This information is usually printed on the label on the top of the power supply.)

   _____

2. How many cables are supplied by your power supply?

   _____

3. Where does each cable lead?

   _____

   _____

4. Does the power supply provide adequate power for the estimated peak consumption of the system? Fill in the following table:

Component	Wattage
Hard drive	
Floppy drive	
CD-ROM drive	
DVD drive	
Zip drive	
Other drive	
Motherboard	
CPU	

4

5. Determining the power consumption of the motherboard and CPU can be difficult without adequate documentation. If you were able to locate that documentation in the previous lab, calculate the total wattage requirements for the system. Otherwise, this might not be possible.

   Total wattage requirements for all components: _____

6. Suppose your power supply stops working, and you must buy a replacement. Search the Internet for a comparable power supply. The cost of power supplies varies greatly. For example, a 400–watt power supply can cost from $15 to $75. The difference in quality can be judged partly by the weight of the power supply because, in general, the heavier it is, the more transistors and the more heavy duty the transistors are, which, in turn, makes for a better power supply. Print two Web pages showing a high-end and a low-end power supply that would meet your system's needs. Which power supply would you recommend be purchased for your system and why?

   _____

Review Questions

1. Where can you usually find electrical information about your power supply?

   _____

2. What can happen if the power supply does not meet the electrical demands of the system?

   _____

   _____

3. When would a system approach its peak power consumption?

   _____

   _____

4. How can you estimate a system's peak power consumption?

_____

_____

5. Will a system with an inadequate power supply always fail immediately when it is powered up? Why or why not?

_____

6. What is one way to determine if a power supply is of good quality or not of good quality?

_____

LAB 4.4 MEASURE THE OUTPUT OF YOUR POWER SUPPLY

Objectives

The goal of this lab is to use a multimeter to measure the various voltages supplied by a power supply. After completing this lab, you will be able to:

➤ Use a multimeter

➤ Measure voltage supplied by a power supply

Materials Required

This lab will require the following:

➤ Lab computer designated for this exercise

➤ PC toolkit with ground strap

➤ Multimeter

➤ Workgroup of 2-4 students

Activity Background

In most situations, if you suspect a problem with a power supply, you would simply exchange it for a known-good one. But in a few instances, you might want to measure the output of your power supply using a multimeter.

A multimeter is an electrical tool that performs multiple tests. It can typically measure continuity, resistance, amperage, and voltage. It may have a digital or analog meter that displays output. It will also have two leads used to contact the component you are testing. The various models of multimeters work slightly differently. Follow the appropriate procedure for your specific multimeter. In this lab you will measure the electrical voltage supplied to the motherboard and floppy drive. Follow your computer lab's posted safety procedures when completing this activity.

Estimated completion time: **30 minutes**

ACTIVITY

Caution: Be sure you have your multimeter set to measure voltage and not current (amps). If the multimeter is set to measure current, you might damage the power supply, the motherboard, or both.

Using your multimeter, measure the power output to your system's motherboard and to the floppy drive, and then fill in two of the three tables below. Note that the column headings "Red Lead" and "Black Lead" refer to the color of the probes.

Detailed directions for using a multimeter can be found in Chapter 3 of the textbook *A+ Guide to Hardware*. Be very careful as you work inside the computer case with the power on. Don't touch any components other than those described below. The following steps outline the basic procedure for using a multimeter:

1. Remove the cover from the computer case.

2. Set the multimeter to measure voltage in a range of 20 volts and set the AC/DC switch to DC. Insert the black probe into the meter's – jack and the red probe into the meter's + jack.

3. Turn on the multimeter and turn on the computer.

4. Measure each circuit by placing a red probe on the lead and a black probe on ground (see Figure 4–3). Use the leads listed in the table on the next page. Write the voltage measurement for each connection in the "Voltage Measure" column.

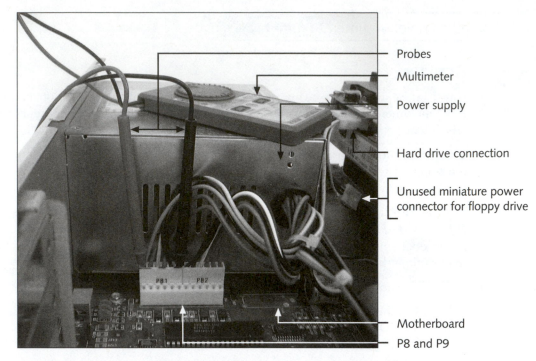

Figure 4-3   Multimeter measuring voltage on an AT motherboard

     5. Turn off the PC and replace the cover.

Complete the following table for the AT motherboard:

Red Lead	Black Lead	Voltage Measure
3	5	
3	6	
3	7	
3	8	
4	Ground	
9	Ground	
10	Ground	
11	Ground	
12	Ground	

Complete the following table for the ATX motherboard:

Red Lead	Black Lead	Voltage Measure
10	7	
10	5	
10	3	
10	17	
10	16	
10	15	
10	13	
9	Ground	
6	Ground	
4	Ground	
2	Ground	
1	Ground	
20	Ground	
19	Ground	
18	Ground	
12	Ground	
11	Ground	

Complete the following table for the floppy drive:

Red Lead	Black Lead	Voltage Measure
1	3	
4	2	

Review Questions

1. What is the electrical voltage from the house outlet to the power supply?

   _____

2. What voltages are supplied by the power supply on your system?

   _____

3. What model of multimeter are you using?

   _____

4. List the steps to set this multimeter to measure resistance.

_____

_____

_____

5. Besides voltage and resistance, what else can this multimeter measure?

_____

LAB 4.5 REPLACE A POWER SUPPLY

Objectives

The goal of this lab is to give you experience replacing a power supply. After completing this lab, you will be able to:

➤ Identify the power supply

➤ Remove the power supply from the case

➤ Install a new power supply and new cabling

Materials Required

This lab will require the following:

➤ Lab PC designated for this exercise

➤ PC toolkit with anti-static ground strap

➤ Workgroup of 2-4 students

Activity Background

This exercise will test your ability to remove and replace a power supply. Power supplies, as a rule, are considered Field Replaceable Units (FRU). This means that because of the danger of working inside power supplies and as a time saver, a PC technician does not repair them. If you find that a power supply is faulty, replace it with a compatible power supply, then send the original off to be reconditioned or recycled.

Estimated completion time: **30 minutes**

ACTIVITY

1. Disconnect the power and all peripherals and remove the case cover.

   _____

2. Examine the power supply and record the number and type of connectors needed, and estimate the peak power requirements for the system (which you learned how to do in Lab 4.3). If the components required more power than the power supply could provide, this could have contributed to its failure.

   _____

3. What type of power connector to the motherboard does the power supply provide?

   _____

4. What is the form factor of the power supply?

   _____

5. Remove the cabling and the power supply. Usually the power supply is held in place by four screws in the back of the case. Some proprietary systems may use other methods of securing the power supply.

6. Examine the power supply designated by your instructor, or swap your power supply with your neighbor's.

7. What is the form factor of this new power supply?

   _____

8. What is the power rating of this new power supply?

   _____

9. Will this new power supply satisfy the needs of your system?

   _____

10. Install the new power supply.

11. Close the case, reattach the peripherals, and test the system.

4

Review Questions

1. How many connectors linked your original power supply to the motherboard?

   _____

2. How many watts of peak power could the original power supply provide?

   _____

3. Why should you calculate the peak power required for all components?

   _____

   _____

4. What are two reasons that PC technicians do not usually repair a power supply?

   _____

   _____

5. What term is used to refer to components that are commonly replaced but not repaired?

   _____

6. What is the most efficient way to determine if your power supply is bad?

   _____

THE MOTHERBOARD

Labs included in this chapter

➤ Lab 5.1 Examine and Adjust CMOS Settings

➤ Lab 5.2 Use a Motherboard Diagnostic Utility

➤ Lab 5.3 Identify a Motherboard and Find Documentation on the Internet

➤ Lab 5.4 Remove and Replace the Motherboard

➤ Lab 5.5 Identify Motherboard Components and Form Factors

The following grid shows the correlation between the labs in this chapter and the A+ Guides to Hardware and Software.

A+ Guide to Managing and Maintaining Your PC, Fifth Edition	A+ Guide to Hardware, Third Edition	A+ Guide to Software, Third Edition
Lab 5.1 Examine and Adjust CMOS Settings	Chapter 4	Chapter 3
Lab 5.2 Use a Motherboard Diagnostic Utility	Chapter 4	
Lab 5.3 Identify a Motherboard and Find Documentation on the Internet	Chapter 4	
Lab 5.4 Remove and Replace the Motherboard	Chapter 4	
Lab 5.5 Identify Motherboard Components and Form Factors	Chapter 4	

LAB 5.1 EXAMINE AND ADJUST CMOS SETTINGS

Objectives

The goal of this lab is to help you explore and modify CMOS settings. After completing this lab, you will be able to:

➤ Enter the CMOS setup utility

➤ Navigate the CMOS setup utility

➤ Examine some setup options

➤ Save changes to setup options

Materials Required

This lab will require the following:

➤ Lab PC designated for this lab

➤ SANDRA, Standard version, installed in Lab 1.3

Activity Background

When a system is powered up, the startup process is managed by a set of instructions called the BIOS. The BIOS, in turn, relies on a set of configuration information stored in CMOS that is continuously refreshed by battery power when the system is off. You can access and modify the CMOS setup information via the CMOS setup utility included in the BIOS. In this lab, you will examine the CMOS setup utility, make some changes, and observe the effects of your changes.

Setup utilities vary slightly in appearance and function, depending on manufacturer and version. The steps in this activity are based on the common Award Modular design. You might have to perform different steps to access and use the CMOS utility on your computer.

Estimated completion time: **30 minutes**

ACTIVITY

Before you access the BIOS on your computer, you will record the exact date and time as indicated by your computer's internal clock. (You will use this information later, to confirm that you have indeed changed some CMOS settings.) After you record the date and time, you will determine which version of the BIOS is installed on your computer. To do this, you will use the SANDRA utility, which you installed in Lab 1.3. Follow these steps:

1. Using Windows, double-click the clock on the taskbar and record the time and date.

_____

_____

2. Close the Date/Time Properties window.

3. Start **SANDRA**, and then double-click the **CPU & BIOS Information** icon.

4. Select **System BIOS** in the **Device** field.

5. Record the manufacturer and version information for your BIOS.

_____

6. Close SANDRA.

Now that you know what BIOS your computer runs, you can determine how to enter the setup utility. In general, to start the setup utility, you need to press a key or key combination as the computer is booting up. To learn more about entering the setup utility on your particular computer, follow these steps:

1. Using the information recorded in Step 5, consult Table 5-1 to find out how to enter your system's setup utility. (Alternatively, when you first turn on the PC look for a message on your screen, which might read something like "Press F2 to access setup.")

Table 5-1   Methods for entering CMOS setup utilities, by BIOS

BIOS	Method for entering CMOS setup
AMI BIOS	Boot the computer, and then press the Delete key.
Award BIOS	Boot the computer, and then press the Delete key.
Older Phoenix BIOS	Boot the computer, and then press the Ctrl + Alt + Esc or Ctrl + Alt + S key combination.
Newer Phoenix BIOS	Boot the computer, and then press the F2 or F1 key.
Dell Computers with Phoenix BIOS	Boot the computer, and then press the Ctrl + Alt + Enter key combination.
Older Compaq computers like the Deskpro 286 or 386	Place the diagnostics disk in the drive, reboot the system, and choose Computer Setup from the menu.
Newer Compaq computers like the Prolinea, Deskpro, DeskproXL, Deskpro LE, or Presario	Boot the computer, wait for two beeps, then, when the cursor is in the upper-right corner of the screen, press the F10 key.
All other older computers	Use the setup program on the floppy disk that came with the PC. If the floppy disk is lost, contact the motherboard manufacturer to obtain a replacement.

Note: For Compaq computers, the CMOS setup program is stored on the hard drive in a small, non-DOS partition of about 3MB. If this partition becomes corrupted or the computer is an older model, you must run setup from a diagnostic disk. If you cannot run setup by pressing F10 at startup, it's likely that a damaged partition or a virus is taking up space in conventional memory.

Now you are ready to enter the CMOS setup utility included in your BIOS. Follow these steps:

1. If a floppy disk is necessary to enter the CMOS setup utility, insert it now.

2. Restart the computer.

3. When the system restarts, enter the setup utility using the correct method for your computer.

4. Notice that the CMOS utility groups settings by function. For example, all the power management features will be grouped together in a Power Management window.

5. The main screen usually has a Help section that describes how to make selections and exit the utility. Typically, you can use the arrow keys or Tab key to highlight options. Once you have highlighted your selection, you usually need to press the Enter key, Page Down key, or the spacebar. The main screen might display a short summary of the highlighted category. Look for and select a category called something like **Standard CMOS Setup**.

6. In the Standard CMOS Setup screen, you should see some or all of the following settings. List the current setting for each of the following:

   - Date: _____

   - Time: _____

   - For IDE hard drives, a table listing drive size and mode of operation, cylinder, head, and sector information:

     _____

     _____

   - Floppy drive setup information, including drive letter and type:

     _____

   - Halt on error setup (the type of error that will halt the boot process):

     _____

   - Memory summary (summary of system memory divisions):

     _____

   - Boot sequence (drives the BIOS searches for an OS):

     _____

7. Exit the Standard CMOS setup screen and return to the main page. Select a section called something like **Chipset Features Setup**.

8. Record settings for the following, as well as any other settings in this section:

   - RAM setup options:

     _____

     _____

- AGP setup options:

  _____

  _____

- CPU–specific setup options:

  _____

  _____

- Settings for serial and parallel ports:

  _____

  _____

- Provisions for enabling/disabling onboard drive controllers and other embedded devices:

  _____

  _____

  _____

  _____

Note: Most of the CMOS settings never need changing, so it isn't necessary to understand every setting.

9. Exit to the CMOS setup main screen. You may see options for loading CMOS defaults (which restores factory settings and can be helpful in troubleshooting) as well as options for exiting with or without saving changes. There might be an option to set user and supervisor passwords as well as a utility to automatically detect IDE hard disk drives.

Now that you are familiar with the way the CMOS setup utility works, you will change the date and time settings. Then you will reboot the computer, confirm that the changes are reflected in the operating system, and return the CMOS date and time to the correct settings.

1. Return to the Standard CMOS setup screen.

2. Highlight the time field(s) and set the time ahead one hour.

3. Move to the date field(s) and set the date ahead one year.

4. Return to the main CMOS setup screen and select an option named something like **Save Settings and Exit**. If prompted, verify that you do wish to save the settings.

5. Wait while the system reboots. Allow Windows to load.

6. At the desktop, check the time and date. Are your CMOS setup changes reflected in Windows?

_____

7. Reboot the computer, return to CMOS setup, and set the correct time and date.

8. Verify that the changes are again reflected in Windows.

Critical Thinking (additional 30 minutes)

Working with your team, do the following to practice troubleshooting problems with CMOS.

1. Propose a change that you could make to CMOS setup that would prevent a computer from booting successfully. What change do you propose?

_____

2. Have your instructor approve the change, because some changes might cause information written to the hard drive to be lost, making it difficult to recover from the problem without reloading the hard drive. Did your instructor approve the change?

_____

3. Now go to another team's computer and make the change to CMOS setup while they make a change to your system.

4. Return to your computer and troubleshoot the problem. Describe the problem as a user would describe it.

_____

_____

5. What steps did you go through to discover the source of the problem and fix it?

_____

_____

6. If you were to encounter this same problem in the future, what might you do differently to troubleshoot it?

_____

_____

Review Questions

1. Do all systems use the same method to enter CMOS setup? Can you enter CMOS setup after the system has booted?

   _____

2. How are settings usually grouped in the CMOS setup utility?

   _____

3. In what section will you usually find time and date setup located in the CMOS setup utility?

   _____

   _____

4. What types of options are shown on the CMOS setup main screen?

   _____

5. What automatically happens after you exit CMOS setup?

   _____

6. What tool in SANDRA can you use to find information on your version of the BIOS?

   _____

   _____

7. Why does a computer need CMOS?

   _____

   _____

8. When troubleshooting a computer, when might you have to enter CMOS setup? List at least three reasons.

   _____

   _____

   _____

LAB 5.2 USE A MOTHERBOARD DIAGNOSTIC UTILITY

Objectives

The goal of this lab is to help you learn how to use a motherboard diagnostic utility. After completing this lab, you will be able to:

➤ Download and install the AMIDiag utility

➤ Use the AMIDiag utility to examine your motherboard

Materials Required

This lab will require the following:

➤ Windows 9x operating system

➤ Internet access

Activity Background

AMIDiag, distributed by American Megatrends, Inc., is a well-known diagnostic utility that you can use to solve a variety of computer problems. The utility is DOS-based and works under both DOS and Windows 9x. In this activity, you will download a demonstration version of AMIDiag from the Internet and then learn how to use it.

Estimated completion time: **30 minutes**

ACTIVITY

1. Use your favorite search engine, such as *www.google.com*, to search for Diagdemo.zip, which is an archive (a collection of compressed files) containing the files necessary to install the demo version of AMIDiag 4.5, a shareware version of AMIDiag for PC diagnostics. Look for this version, rather than later versions that don't have as much functionality, by searching for "AMIDiag 4.5".

2. Download Diagdemo.zip to your PC. Your instructor might ask you to save the file to a specific folder on your hard drive. If so, what is the name of the folder?

_____

3. Close your browser, open Explorer, and then expand the file **Diagdemo.zip** by double-clicking it.

4. Open a command-prompt window, and then switch to the directory where the demo software files are stored.

5. At the command prompt, type **amidiag**, and then press **Enter**. The screen shown in Figure 5-1 appears.

Figure 5-1   AMIDiag opening menu

Many times a support technician is not given step-by-step directions when using utility software, but must discover how to use the software by exploring menus and using the software's help functions. The following exercise gives you practice in doing that. Use the AMIDiag software to answer these questions:

1. Perform the test of processor speed. What is the detected speed?

2. On the Memory menu, perform all the tests that this demonstration version of the software allows. Record any errors detected.

3. On the Misc. menu, perform the serial port test. Write down any error messages that appear. If you get an unexpected error, perform the test more than once. Do you get the same results each time?

4. On the Option menu, select **System Information**. If you received errors in Step 3, this program might lock up, and you might need to reboot. If you completed the information check successfully, record the results:

5. On the System board menu, select **DMA Controller Test**. Why does this test not work?

6. Exit the program, and then close the command prompt window.

Challenge Activity (additional 15 minutes)

Copy the AMIDiag software to a Windows 9x startup disk and execute the software from the startup disk on a Windows 2000/XP computer.

1. Describe how the software works using this method.

_____

2. When might this method be useful?

_____

Review Questions

1. Does the AMIDiag utility run with a GUI interface?

_____

2. What menu in AMIDiag contains the serial port test?

_____

3. What are some tests included in the shareware version of AMIDiag?

_____

4. What menu in AMIDiag contains the System Information program?

_____

5. At what points in the test process did you receive error messages? What do these error messages tell you about your computer?

_____

In the following table, list at least three situations where you think it would be appropriate to use AMIDiag for troubleshooting. Describe the problem as the user would describe it to you. For example, "My serial mouse does not work." Then write the suspected source of the problem and the appropriate AMIDiag test. The table includes one example to help you get started.

Description of problem as the user sees it	Suspected source of the problem	AMIDiag test
"My serial mouse does not work."	Serial port does not work	Serial port test

Lab 5.3 Identify a Motherboard and Find Documentation on the Internet

Objectives

The goal of this lab is to learn to identify a motherboard and find online documentation for it. After completing this lab, you will be able to:

➤ Physically examine a motherboard

➤ Determine a motherboard's manufacturer and model

➤ Search the Internet for motherboard documentation

Materials Required

This lab will require the following:

➤ PC designated for disassembly

➤ Internet access

➤ Adobe Acrobat

➤ PC toolkit with ground strap

Activity Background

You may often be asked to repair a PC for which the documentation is lost or not available. Fortunately, you can almost always find documentation for a device online as long as you have the device's manufacturer name and model number. In this lab, you will learn to find the manufacturer's name and model number on a motherboard. Then you will locate documentation for that device on the Internet.

Estimated completion time: **30 minutes**

Activity

1. Boot the PC and use SANDRA, which you installed in Chapter 1, Lab 1.3, to learn the type of CPU installed on your computer. Record that information:

_____

2. Following safety precautions, including using a ground strap, remove the PC's case cover and then remove any components obscuring your view of the motherboard. In some cases you may have to remove the motherboard itself, but this is usually unnecessary.

3. Look for a stenciled or silkscreened label printed on the circuit board itself that indicates the manufacturer and model. Note that other components sometimes have labels printed on a sticker affixed to the component. On a motherboard, the label is generally printed directly on the circuit board itself. Common motherboard manufacturers include Abit, Asus, and Intel.

Also, note that the manufacturer name is often printed in much larger type than the model number. Model numbers often include both letters and numbers and many contain a version number as well. Figure 5-2 shows an example of a motherboard label.

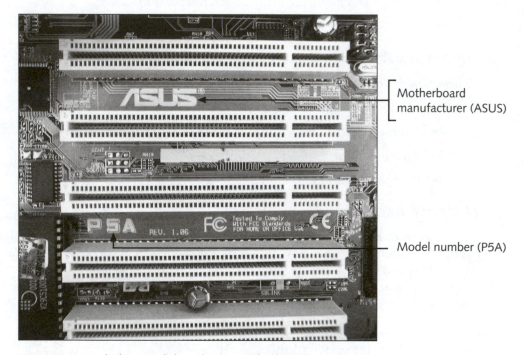

Motherboard manufacturer (ASUS)

Model number (P5A)

Figure 5-2   Label printed directly on motherboard

4. Record the information on the motherboard label.

5. Take your information to a PC with Internet access and open a browser.

6. If you know the URL of the manufacturer, go directly to the Web site. (Table 5-2 shows the URLs for some motherboard manufacturers.) If you do not know the URL of the manufacturer's site, search for the manufacturer or model with your favorite search engine, as shown in Figure 5-3. In the search results, click a link that is associated with the manufacturer. If this link does not take you directly to the documentation, it will usually get you within two or three links away. Continue until you find the manufacturer's Web site.

Table 5-2   URLs for major motherboard manufacturers

Manufacturer	URL
motherboards.com	www.motherboards.com
American Megatrends, Inc.	www.megatrends.com
ASUS	www.asus.com
Dell	www.dell.com
Diamond Multimedia	www.diamondmm.com
First International Computer, Inc.	www.fica.com
Gateway	www.gateway.com
Giga-Byte Technology Co., Ltd.	www.giga-byte.com
IBM	www.ibm.com
Intel Corporation	www.intel.com
Supermicro Computer, Inc.	www.supermicro.com
Tyan Computer Corporation	www.tyan.com

Figure 5-3   Search results using manufacturer name and model number

7. When you have found the site of your motherboard's manufacturer, look for a link for service or support. Click this link, and, if necessary, select the appropriate product category and model number. Sometimes knowing the type of CPU the board supports can be useful in finding the right board.

8. Continue working your way through the site until you find the motherboard documentation. The documentation may include a variety of documents covering technical specification and installation instructions. The documentation will probably also include a basic manual, which is usually a combination of technical and installation specifications.

9. When you find the documentation, you might also find a link to updated dri-vers. If you see such a link, click it and note the release date of these drivers. If they are newer than the current drivers, it is often advisable to update these as well. If possible, record the release dates for the updated drivers:

_____

10. Return to the main documentation page, and, if it is available, select the manual. If it is not available, select the installation instructions.

11. The manual is probably in PDF format, so you will need to have a copy of Adobe Acrobat Reader installed. If you have the browser plug-in, you can open the document from the source location, or you can download the manual to your computer and then open it. Using your preferred method, open the docu-ment and print the motherboard documentation. Save this documentation for use in Lab 5.4.

Review Questions

1. How is the label usually applied to a motherboard? How is it most often applied to other components?

_____

2. On the label of a motherboard or other component, how can the manufac-turer often be differentiated from the model number?

_____

3. What type of link on a manufacturer's Web site will usually lead you to manu-als and other documentation?

_____

4. What other information about your motherboard might you want to examine on the manufacturer's Web site?

_____

5. In what format is documentation most often available for download?

_____

6. What other information, such as BIOS update and drivers, can be obtained besides motherboard documentation at this site?

_____

LAB 5.4 REMOVE AND REPLACE THE MOTHERBOARD

Objectives

The goal of this lab is to familiarize you with the process of replacing an old or faulty motherboard. After completing this lab, you will be able to:

➤ Use SANDRA to determine the specifications of your CPU

➤ Remove a motherboard

➤ Configure a new motherboard according to its documentation

➤ Install a replacement motherboard

Materials Required

This lab will require the following:

➤ A computer designated for this lab

➤ SANDRA, Standard version, installed in Lab 1.3

➤ Workgroup of 2-4 students

➤ PC toolkit with ground strap

Activity Background

In this lab you will exchange a motherboard with another workgroup to simulate the process of replacing a faulty motherboard. When you install the new motherboard, you must configure it for your system by adjusting jumper and CMOS settings according to the documentation printed in Lab 5.3. Then you will install the replacement motherboard.

Estimated completion time: **45 minutes**

ACTIVITY

In this activity, follow safety precautions as you work to remove the motherboard. Be sure to use a ground strap.

1. Launch SANDRA (which you installed in Chapter 1, Lab 1.3) and use the CPU & BIOS information utility to examine the CPU in your system. Record the information listed in the Processor section.

_____

_____

_____

2. Power the system down, unplug everything, and remove the case cover. Then remove the cabling and expansion cards from the motherboard. Take all necessary precautions (including using a ground strap), and make a sketch of cabling and component placement.

3. Six screws usually attach the motherboard to the case via spacers. The spacers prevent the printed circuitry from shorting out on the metal case and provide space for air circulation. Remove the screws attaching the motherboard, and set them aside in a cup, bag, or bowl so that you don't lose them.

4. Carefully lift the motherboard out of the case. You may have to tilt the board to clear the drive bays and power supply. In some cases you may have to remove the drives to get the motherboard out.

5. Exchange the motherboard and the motherboard documentation with that of another team. You might also exchange the CPU and memory, depending on whether your current CPU and memory modules are compatible with the new motherboard. Follow directions given by your instructor as to what to exchange. Be sure you have the new motherboard's documentation, which should have been found on the Internet in Lab 5.3.

Critical Thinking

Your instructor might ask you to remove jumpers and reset DIP switches on your motherboard before passing it to the other team. These modifications will make the other team's configuration more challenging. As an alternative, your instructor might have a display motherboard somewhere in the lab that uses jumpers and DIP switches for part of its configuration.

1. With the new motherboard in front of you, consult the new board's documentation and find any jumpers that must be configured to match your system. Older boards use jumpers to adjust clock multipliers and memory speeds, as well as to clear the CMOS settings. Unless otherwise instructed, *do not* remove the jumper to clear CMOS settings. Note that newer boards are often "jumperless," with all configuration settings done within CMOS setup. The only jumper these boards will have is the one to clear CMOS settings. Remove and replace the jumpers in the configuration specified to match your processor information.

2. Install the motherboard, cabling, and expansion cards, and any other components you removed.

3. Boot the system and enter the CMOS setup utility. For jumperless motherboards, make any adjustments specified in the motherboard's documentation.

4. Save settings and exit CMOS setup.

5. Reboot the system and verify that the system is functioning correctly. Describe any error messages:

_____

6. What steps do you plan to take to troubleshoot this error?

_____

Critical Thinking (additional 30 minutes)

To learn more about motherboards, do the following:

1. Once the PC is working, ask your instructor to configure a startup password on your computer.

2. Without knowing the password, boot the computer.

3. List the steps required to accomplish this.

_____

_____

_____

Review Questions

1. How many screws usually attach the motherboard to the computer case?

_____

2. What is the purpose of spacers?

_____

3. A jumperless motherboard is likely to have one jumper. Which jumper is it?

_____

4. Where can you access the configuration settings for a jumperless motherboard?

_____

LAB 5.5 IDENTIFY MOTHERBOARD COMPONENTS AND FORM FACTORS

Objectives

The goal of this lab is to help you learn to identify motherboard form factors and components. After completing this lab, you will be able to:

➤ Identify a motherboard's CPU type

➤ Identify connectors

➤ Identify the form factor based on component type and placement

Materials Required

Instructors are encouraged to supply a variety of motherboards, some common and others not so common. At the very least, this lab will require the following:

➤ Three different motherboards

Note: If three motherboards are not available, look on the Web sites of the motherboard manufacturers listed in Lab 5.3 for three boards.

Activity Background

As a PC technician, you should be able to look at a motherboard and determine what type of CPU, RAM, and form factor you are working with. You should also be able to recognize any unusual components the board might have. In this lab, you will examine various motherboards and note some important information about them.

> Estimated completion time: **30 minutes**

ACTIVITY

Fill in the following table for your assigned motherboards. If you have more than three motherboards, use additional paper. When the entry in the Item column includes a question mark (such as "PCI Bus?") write a yes or no answer.

Item	Motherboard 1	Motherboard 2	Motherboard 3
Manufacturer/model			
BIOS manufacturer			
CPU type			
Chipset			
RAM type/pins			
PCI bus?			
ISA bus?			
AGP bus?			
SCSI controller?			
IDE controller?			
Embedded audio, video, etc.			
Jumperless?			
Form factor			
Describe any unusual components			

5

1. How can you determine if a motherboard is an AT board or an ATX board based on the location of the CPU in relation to the expansion slots?

   _____

   _____

2. Of the motherboards you examined, which do you think is the oldest? Why?

   _____

   _____

   _____

3. Which motherboard best supports old and new technology? Why?

_____

_____

_____

4. Which motherboard appears to provide the best possibility for expansion? Why?

_____

_____

_____

5. Which motherboard is most likely the easiest to configure? Why?

_____

6. Which motherboard do you think is the most expensive? Why?

_____

7. What are some considerations that a motherboard manufacturer has to contend with when designing a motherboard? (For example, consider room for large CPUs and cooling fans, where the power supply is located in relationship to the power connector, new technologies and so forth.)

_____

_____

CHAPTER SIX

MANAGING MEMORY

Labs included in this chapter

➤ Lab 6.1 Research RAM on the Internet

➤ Lab 6.2 Explore the Kingston Web Site

➤ Lab 6.3 Upgrade RAM

➤ Lab 6.4 Troubleshoot Memory Problems

➤ Lab 6.5 Use Himem.sys

➤ Lab 6.6 Manage Virtual Memory

The following grid shows the correlation between the labs in this chapter and the A+ Guides to Hardware and Software.

A+ Guide to Managing and Maintaining Your PC, Fifth Edition	A+ Guide to Hardware, Third Edition	A+ Guide to Software, Third Edition
Lab 6.1 Research RAM on the Internet	Chapter 5	
Lab 6.2 Explore the Kingston Web Site	Chapter 5	
Lab 6.3 Upgrade RAM	Chapter 5	
Lab 6.4 Troubleshooting Memory Problems	Chapter 5	
Lab 6.5 Use Himem.sys	Chapter 5	Chapter 9
Lab 6.6 Manage Virtual Memory		Chapter 9

LAB 6.1 RESEARCH RAM ON THE INTERNET

Objectives

The goal of this lab is to help you learn how to find important information about RAM that you will need when upgrading memory. After completing this lab, you will be able to:

➤ Find documentation on your system's motherboard

➤ Read documentation for your system's RAM specifications

➤ Search the Internet for RAM prices and availability

Materials Required

This lab will require the following:

➤ Windows 98 or Windows 2000/XP operating system

➤ Internet access

Activity Background

At one time, RAM was literally worth more than its weight in gold. When building a system back then, most people made do with the minimum amount of RAM required for adequate performance. These days RAM is much cheaper, which means you can probably buy all the RAM you need to make your system perform at top speed. Graphics editing software, in particular, benefits from additional RAM. In this lab, you will research how to optimize RAM on a graphics workstation with a memory upgrade budget of $150.

Estimated completion time: **30 minutes**

ACTIVITY

1. Use My Computer to determine the amount of RAM currently installed. Record the amount of RAM here:

   _____

2. Using skills learned in Lab 5.3, determine the manufacturer and model of your motherboard. (If you don't have the motherboard documentation available, search for it on the Web and print it.)

Use the documentation for your motherboard to answer these questions:

1. What type (or types) of memory does your motherboard support? Be as specific as the motherboard documentation is.

_____

_____

2. How many slots for memory modules are included on your motherboard?

_____

3. How many memory slots on your motherboard are used and how much RAM is installed in each slot?

_____

_____

4. What is the maximum amount of memory that your motherboard supports?

_____

5. What size and how many memory modules will be needed to upgrade your system to the maximum amount of supported memory?

_____

Now that you have the necessary information about your system's memory, go to a local computer store that sells memory or, using the Internet, go to *Pricewatch.com* or a similar Web site, and complete the following:

1. What is the price of the memory modules required to configure your system for maximum memory?

_____

2. Will your budget enable you to install the maximum supported amount of RAM?

_____

3. Can you use the existing memory modules to upgrade to the maximum amount of supported memory?

_____

4. What is the most additional memory that you could install and still stay within your budget? (Assume you will use the existing memory modules.)

_____

Explore other types of memory on *Pricewatch.com* or a similar Web site and answer the following questions:

1. On average, what is the least expensive type of memory per MB that you can find? What is its price?

_____

_____

2. On average, what is the most expensive type of memory per MB that you can find? What is its price?

_____

3. Is SO-DIMM memory for a notebook computer more or less expensive than the equivalent amount of Rambus memory for a desktop PC? Give specific information to support your answer.

_____

_____

Review Questions

1. Why might you want to upgrade RAM on a system?

_____

_____

2. How many pins are found on a DIMM? How many on a RIMM?

_____

_____

3. Which is more expensive, DIMM or RIMM?

_____

4. What is a disadvantage of using two 64MB modules instead of a single 128MB module in a system with three slots for memory modules?

_____

_____

5. What are two disadvantages of using only one 256MB module rather than two 128MB modules?

_____

_____

_____

LAB 6.2 EXPLORE THE KINGSTON WEB SITE

6

Objectives

The goal of this lab is to use the Kingston Web site to learn about RAM. After completing this lab, you will be able to:

➤ Identify types of RAM

➤ Determine appropriate memory types for a given system

Materials Required

➤ Internet access

Activity Background

RAM comes in a variety of shapes, sizes, and speeds. Not every type of RAM works with every system. In this lab you will use the Web site of Kingston Technology, a major RAM manufacturer, to learn about RAM and to learn how to make sure you have the right memory module to upgrade your system.

Estimated completion time: **30 minutes**

ACTIVITY

Do the following to begin learning about system memory:

1. Open your browser and go to the Web site *www.kingston.com*.

2. Notice that the Memory Search section of the site allows you to search for memory based on the type of system you have. What other three ways can you search for memory?

_____

_____

_____

When you search the site based on your system, results of the search include a list of compatible memory types with prices, maximum memory supported by your system, processors supported, and number of expansion slots on your system for memory modules. Do the following to find information about a memory upgrade for a motherboard:

1. Select one of the motherboards from the table in Chapter 5, Lab 5.5. Which motherboard did you select?

_____

2. Perform a Memory Search on the Kingston site for information on this motherboard. Answer the following questions:

   ■ What are the types of memory module this board can use?

   _____

   _____

   _____

   ■ What types of processor does the board support?

   _____

   _____

   _____

   ■ How many memory slots are on the board?

   _____

   ■ What is the maximum amount of memory the board supports?

   _____

Now continue exploring the Kingston site. Do the following:

1. Return to the Kingston home page.

2. Click the Memory Tools link. A drop-down menu appears displaying several tools, one being the Memory Assessor. Selecting this link begins a process whereby you can specify which OS you are researching and Kingston will give you a recommended amount of physical RAM based on usage criteria.

3. Using these tools, and perhaps other areas of the site, answer the following questions:

   ■ In general, do the operating systems for desktops and workstations require more or less memory than the operating systems for servers?

   _____

   _____

- How wide is the data path on a 168-pin DIMM?

_____

- DDR is an extension of what older memory technology?

_____

_____

- What does the SO in SO-DIMM represent?

_____

- What is an advantage of loading applications entirely into RAM rather than loading part of an application into virtual memory (a page file)?

_____

_____

_____

- What is another term for a page file, and why are page files used?

_____

_____

- How many bits of information does a single cell of a memory chip on a 256MB PC2700 DDR module hold?

_____

- Why would you have problems with a system in which you installed three known-good RIMMs?

_____

_____

_____

- A relatively new memory technology uses only a 16-bit path. What acronym defines this type of memory?

_____

- What type of material is used to make a memory "chip?"

_____

_____

6

■ What function(s) does the aluminum plate on a RIMM serve?

_____

_____

■ Why might you not mind using slower memory (in MHz) if faster memory is available for a marginal price difference?

_____

_____

■ What are some possible ramifications of installing modules in a way that does not comply with the system's bank schema?

_____

_____

■ What is a memory performance measurement in which the lower the number, the better the performance?

_____

■ What memory technology achieves better performance by using both the rising and falling sides of the clock cycle?

_____

_____

■ List five things to consider when upgrading memory.

_____

_____

_____

_____

_____

■ In a situation where a motherboard would support either SDRAM or EDO, which would give better performance?

_____

- What memory technology uses a heat spreader?

_____

- What types of memory do notebook computers typically use?

_____

- Name two certain characteristics of a system using RAMBUS licensed memory.

_____

_____

6

Review Questions

1. Is a DIMM or a RIMM more expensive given that they both hold the same amount of memory? Why do you think this is the case?

_____

_____

2. Summarize why adding RAM offers a performance advantage.

_____

_____

3. Which tool on the Kingston Web site could you use to find Kingston modules for your system if you know the model number of your system's motherboard?

_____

4. If you were planning to buy a new system, would you choose a motherboard that uses DIMMs or RIMMs? Why?

_____

_____

LAB 6.3 UPGRADE RAM

Objectives

The goal of this lab is to learn to plan an upgrade of memory and then perform the upgrade. After completing this lab, you will be able to:

➤ Estimate how much free memory your system has available during typical and stressed use

➤ Determine how much and what kind of memory is needed for an upgrade

➤ Upgrade RAM in your system

Materials Required

This lab will require the following:

➤ SANDRA, Standard version, installed in Lab 1.3

➤ Internet access

➤ PC toolkit and anti-static bracelet

➤ Additional memory module compatible with your system

Activity Background

In this lab you will examine your system, gather information on its memory sub-system, and establish a memory usage baseline. Using this information, you will determine through further research whether the system will support a RAM upgrade required to run a CAD application. Finally, you will install an additional memory module, re-examine your system, and compare against the baseline.

> Estimated completion time: **45 minutes**

ACTIVITY

Use SANDRA to answer the following questions about your system:

1. What OS are you running?

_____

2. What type of processor is your system using?

_____

3. What is the manufacturer/model of your motherboard?

_____

4. How many MB of RAM are currently installed?

_____

5. What type of memory modules are installed? Be as specific as you can.

_____

6. At what speed does the memory bus operate?

_____

To establish a memory usage baseline, follow these steps:

1. Leaving SANDRA open, launch one instance each of Windows Explorer, Paint, and Internet Explorer.

2. Use the Windows Memory Information tool in SANDRA and record the amount of free physical memory. This is your memory baseline. How much memory is free?

_____

3. Launch six additional instances of Internet Explorer, browsing to a different site on each. Try to locate and view or listen to a movie trailer or video, because this activity is memory intensive compared with displaying a static Web page.

4. Refresh the information in the Windows Memory Information tool by clicking the blue arrow. Record the free physical memory. How much memory is now free?

_____

The change is the result of the demands of running and displaying six additional Web pages.

Suppose that the engineering department of your employer is interested in deploying a CAD program that requires 1 GB of RAM over and above the OS's memory requirements. Use your investigating skills to document whether your system is able to support the additional RAM required. Do the following:

1. Will your system currently support the CAD program?

_____

2. If your system will not support it, can you upgrade RAM to meet the requirements? How much memory must be added?

_____

3. In the space provided, record how you arrived at your answers to the last two questions. Include where you found the information.

_____

_____

_____

_____

4. If an upgrade will support the CAD program, what is the retail price of the necessary modules required to meet specifications?

_____

Next you will simulate making the upgrade. Do the following:

1. Shut down your system and remove all exterior cabling.

2. Be sure you are wearing your anti-static bracelet. Open the system case and locate the slots for memory modules.

3. Remove any data cabling and other devices preventing you from getting at the slots. Answer the following questions:

   ■ How many modules are currently installed? Are there any empty slots in which to install an additional module?

   _____

   ■ At what point during boot-up might you be able to determine how many modules are in use?

   _____

4. Notice that the slots have a retaining mechanism at each end to secure the modules in the slot. These mechanisms are typically plastic levers that you spread outward to unseat and remove modules. These modules are inserted and removed straight up and down. Spread the plastic levers apart before inserting or removing the memory modules.

5. Examine an empty slot and note that there are raised ridges that line up with notches on the pin edge of the memory module. Because modules are designed to be inserted in only one orientation, these ridges prevent them from being inserted incorrectly.

6. With the module correctly oriented, insert the module and gently but firmly push it in.

7. Reassemble your system.

Though it is extremely rare to purchase a bad memory module, it is a good idea to give the system every opportunity to detect faulty memory. BIOS tests your physical memory each time the system is booted. If a module is drastically flawed, the system usually will not boot. Instead, the system will issue a beep code indicating memory problems. Assuming that the module is in relatively good shape and the video has initialized, the system BIOS's POST routine will typically display a memory count in bytes as it tests memory.

Most POST routines will run through the test three times before proceeding. You can skip this redundant testing by enabling a "Quick" POST in CMOS setup. Quick POST is great to cut down boot-up time during normal use, but when installing new RAM, it is best to give the system every opportunity to detect a problem. Therefore, you should disable Quick POST until you are confident that the module has no obvious problem. With this in mind, follow these steps to verify that the system properly recognizes the upgrade:

1. Boot the system and enter CMOS setup.

2. Verify that any Quick POST is disabled, and, if necessary, specify that you have installed additional memory. (Telling CMOS about new memory is not necessary unless you have a very old motherboard.)

3. Save your settings and reboot. Record below whether the additional memory was recognized, and how many times it was tested.

_____

4. Being careful to duplicate the steps, perform the same baseline tests that you did earlier in this lab. Record the results here:

   ■ Amount of free memory with SANDRA, Windows Explorer, Paint, and Internet Explorer open:

   _____

   ■ Amount of free memory with the system heavily used:

   _____

5. When you have finished, remove the additional memory and return the system to its previous configuration.

Review Questions

1. What is the minimum memory requirement for the OS your system is running?

_____

2. What are at least two ways you can determine how much RAM is installed?

_____

_____

3. What SANDRA module(s) can be used to display information about system memory?

_____

_____

4. What feature is employed on memory slots and modules to prevent modules from being inserted incorrectly?

_____

5. In what situation might you wish to disable a Quick POST and why?

_____

_____

LAB 6.4 TROUBLESHOOT MEMORY PROBLEMS

Objectives

The goal of this lab is to provide you with hands-on experience troubleshooting memory problems. After completing this lab, you will be able to:

➤ Identify some symptoms that indicate memory problems

➤ Identify a faulty module

➤ Use DocMemory to test installed RAM

Materials Required

This lab will require the following:

➤ Internet connection

➤ Windows 9x

➤ SANDRA, Standard version, installed in Lab 1.3

➤ Printer

➤ Compression utility such as WinZip

➤ Blank floppy disk

➤ Acrobat Reader

➤ PC toolkit and anti-static bracelet

Activity Background

The symptoms of faulty RAM are many and varied. Faulty memory can cause a complete failure to boot, fatal exception errors while working with an application, or catastrophic data loss. But sometimes faulty memory presents itself only as annoying interruptions as you work. RAM that is outright dead is fairly easy to identify. If the dead module is the only module installed, the system will not boot. If it is one of several modules, you will notice the system reports less memory than you expected.

However, it is not common for a module to fail absolutely. More often a module will develop intermittent problems that cause data corruption, applications to hang at unexpected times, or Windows NT/2000/XP to hang and display the Blue Screen of Death. In this lab, you will learn how to detect and isolate faulty memory modules to prevent these situations.

Estimated completion time: **60 minutes**

ACTIVITY

Reliable memory function is essential to system operation. Therefore, when the system is booted, if memory is not detected or has major problems, the startup BIOS will begin emitting a beep code defining a general or particular memory problem. If memory is found adequate by startup BIOS, during POST startup BIOS does a thorough test of physical memory, which is usually repeated three times before the system summary is displayed and boot continues. Then, while Windows is loading, Windows tests all memory above 1MB.

These tests are well and good at startup, but often modules that are partially corrupted will not show a problem until they are running at certain temperatures. Because these faults show up only at certain times and temperatures, they are referred to as thermal intermittents. Although these problems are extremely difficult to nail down and document absolutely, they are actually fairly easy to remedy if the fault is on the memory module instead of on the motherboard.

DocMemory is a utility that allows either a quick test or a "burn in" test that runs until an error is encountered or there is human intervention. This "burn in" is particularly useful in discovering a thermal intermittent fault.

In the following steps, you will use DocMemory to test installed RAM. Note that you can create a boot disk on a Windows 9x machine and then use that bootable floppy disk to boot a PC and test memory on that PC, even if Windows NT/2000/XP is installed. Do the following:

1. On a Windows 9x computer, search the Web for a file called DocMem1_45a.exe and its accompanying documentation named docguide.pdf. This utility can be found at *www.dewassoc.com/performance/memory/diag_memory_2.htm*. DocMem1_45a.exe is the program that is used to create a boot disk that runs the diagnostic routine.

2. Open and print the file Docguide.pdf (the documentation file) for later use.

3. Download and run DocMem1_45a.exe. A dialog box containing support contact information opens. Click **OK** to continue.

4. DocMemory then opens in a command-prompt window. Use the arrow keys and the Enter key or use the mouse to select **Make Boot Disk**. A license agreement appears.

5. Scroll down and accept the license agreement. The license agreement disappears, revealing a prompt to insert a blank disk. Insert the disk and press **Enter**.

6. The formating process begins and ends automatically, transferring system files. Then the utility and Autoexec.bat are added to the disk. When the files have been copied, a message is displayed, indicating that the process is complete. Press any key and the command-prompt window closes. Close the installation window as well.

7. The disk is now ready to be used on any Windows system. For the purpose of this lab, leave the disk in the system and reboot.

8. The system boots into the DocMemory utility. Purchase information is displayed and then disappears, revealing a Select Type of Test dialog box with options to run the Burn-in Test, Quick Test, or Cancel. To test for a thermal intermittent, the Burn-in Test is the best choice. However, in the interest of time, for this lab select the **Quick test**.

9. The test begins and the status is displayed in the upper-left side of the screen. Your processor and RAM are identified in the upper-right side. The bottom of the screen displays pass/fail results. This portion of the lab varies in time due to differences in the amount of RAM and the processor speeds of various systems.

10. While waiting for the test to finish, consult the documentation and answer the following questions.

   ▪ What two things happen when a fault is detected?

   _____

   _____

   ▪ What two areas can DocMemory test?

   _____

   _____

   ▪ What type of fault is the Walk Data "0" & "1" test designed to uncover?

   _____

   _____

11. When the test ends or errors are found, record the results below.

   _____

   _____

   _____

Follow these steps to observe the effects of a faulty memory module and interpret beep codes:

1. Use SANDRA to determine the BIOS manufacturer for your system and record it here.

   _____

2. Search documentation or the Internet for a list of beep codes for that manu-facturer.

3. Shut down the system and remove all external cabling.

4. Put on your anti-static bracelet, open the case, remove all memory modules, and set them aside in an anti-static bag.

5. Reassemble the system, leaving out memory.

6. Power up the system and describe the outcome, including any beep codes, below.

   _____

   _____

   _____

7. If you heard beep codes, using the documentation obtained in Step 2, interpret their meaning below.

   _____

   _____

8. Shut down the system, disassemble it, install the RAM, and reassemble.

9. Boot the system to verify that the system is functional.

Using the documentation for DocMemory, summarize the process of using a known-good memory module to provide strong evidence that a particular memory module is faulty.

_____

_____

_____

_____

Review Questions

1. What are some common symptoms of a thermal intermittent?

_____

_____

2. How many times does POST usually test memory?

_____

3. Why can't a Windows NT–based machine be used to create a DocMemory disk?

_____

_____

4. Describe the symptoms created by a dead memory module.

_____

_____

_____

5. Which DocMemory test would be ideal for diagnosing a thermal intermittent?

_____

LAB 6.5 USE HIMEM.SYS

Objectives

The goal of this lab is to help you investigate ways memory can be used by observing the effects of Himem.sys. After completing this lab, you will be able to:

➤ Configure Himem.sys

➤ Configure Msdos.sys to stay in text mode throughout the boot

➤ Observe the effects Himem.sys has on the system

Materials Required

This lab will require the following:

➤ Windows 98

➤ Two blank floppy disks

➤ Windows 98 setup CD or setup files located in a place provided by your instructor

Activity Background

If you have the need frequently to run programs in MS-DOS mode, setting up Config.sys and Autoexec.bat is important because they help set environmental variables in MS-DOS mode. Himem.sys is necessary to use many DOS utilities. Another key function of Himem.sys is that it independently tests RAM during boot. By observing the effects of changing how the system employs Himem.sys, you can get an idea of its various functions. In this lab, you will configure and observe Himem.sys.

> Estimated completion time: **30 minutes**

ACTIVITY

To configure your system to remain in text mode throughout boot-up, complete the following steps:

1. Using Windows Explorer, right-click **Msdos.sys** in the root directory of the system partition. Select **Properties** from the shortcut menu. The Msdos.sys Properties dialog box opens.

2. In the Attributes section, clear the box indicating that the file is read-only. Click **OK** to apply your change and close the dialog box.

3. Again, right-click **Msdos.sys**, this time selecting **Open with...** from the shortcut menu. The Open with dialog box opens.

4. In the field Choose the program you want to use:, select **NOTEPAD**. If necessary, clear the **Always use this program to open this type of file** check box and click **OK**. Notepad opens displaying the entries in Msdos.sys.

5. Under the [Options] heading add the line **Logo=0**. (Be sure to type a zero and not a capital "O".) Using the File menu, save the changes and close Notepad.

6. Reboot the computer and record any messages you see concerning Himem.sys. Notice that the Windows logo screen never appears during startup. This allows you to observe the entire text-based boot sequence, which can be useful in observing and diagnosing boot problems.

_____

_____

_____

In DOS and Windows 3.x, Himem.sys was always loaded using a Device= command line in Config.sys. Himem.sys is automatically loaded by Windows 9x, even if a Config.sys file is not present. However, you can use Config.sys under Windows 9x to load Himem.sys to configure how Himem.sys loads. To do this, you would create a Config.sys file and add the Himem.sys command line to it with appropriate switches. To configure Himem.sys and watch it load, follow these steps:

1. In the root of the system partition, right-click **Config.sys**. Select **Open with...** from the shortcut menu. The Open with dialog box opens.

2. In the field Choose the program you want to use:, select **NOTEPAD**. If necessary, clear the **Always use this program to open this type of file** check box and click **OK**. Notepad opens, displaying the entries in Config.sys.

3. In Config.sys, add the line **Device=C:\Windows\himem.sys**. Using the File menu, save your changes and close Notepad.

4. Reboot the computer, recording any messages you see concerning Himem.sys.

   _____

   _____

   _____

5. Following Steps 1–4, add the switch **/V** (be sure to type a capital V) to the Device= line. The resulting line should appear as Device=C:\Windows\ Himem.sys /V, with a space before the switch. "V" stands for verbose or descriptive. This means that text will be displayed to keep you informed of its progress. Reboot the system, if necessary more than once, and answer the following questions:

   ■ How much high memory did Himem.sys report available?

   _____

   ■ What version of Himem.sys is loaded?

   _____

6. Following the previous process to edit Config.sys, add the switch /TestMem:ON. Reboot and record any changes.

   _____

   _____

   _____

Now you will create a Windows 98 startup disk using the Add/Remove Programs applet in the Control Panel. Then you will use Scandisk on the startup disk to scan your hard drive for errors, which will be a first step in demonstrating why loading Himem.sys from Config.sys is important. Do the following:

1. From Control Panel, launch the **Add/Remove Programs** dialog box.

2. When the dialog box opens, select the **Startup disk** tab.

3. Click the **Create Disk** button and, if prompted, provide the location of the Windows setup files.

4. Insert the floppy disk when prompted, and click **OK** to continue and create a startup disk.

5. When the startup disk is complete, examine its contents in Windows Explorer. Does the startup disk contain both Config.sys and Himem.sys? Open the Config.sys file and write the command line that loads Himem.sys.

   _____

6. With the startup disk in the drive, reboot the computer.

7. When prompted, select the option to start the computer without CD-ROM support.

8. When you arrive at the command prompt, type **Scandisk C:** and press **Enter** to scan the hard drive for errors.

9. Observe as Scandisk performs a data scan on drive C. When prompted, do not perform a surface scan. Press **X** to return to the command prompt.

10. Remove the startup disk and reboot the system.

Now you will create a bootable disk and copy the Scandisk utility to it. Then you will attempt to use Scandisk without having Himem.sys loaded. Do the following:

1. In Windows Explorer, insert the second blank floppy disk and right-click drive **A**.

2. Select **Format** from the shortcut menu. The Format dialog box appears.

3. In the Format dialog box, select both **Quick (erase)** and **Copy system files** and click the **Start** button.

4. When the summary appears, click **Close** and then click **Close** again to exit. You have created a bootable disk. Using Windows Explorer, examine the disk and list the files on the disk:

   _____

   _____

   _____

5. Now copy Scandisk.exe from the C:\Windows\Command folder to the bootable disk.

6. Reboot the system with the bootable disk in the drive. When you arrive at the command prompt, type **Scandisk C:** to again attempt to scan the hard drive for errors. Describe what happens.

_____

_____

_____

7. What two files must be put on the bootable disk for Scandisk to work?

_____

Review Questions

1. Other than providing access to memory, what other valuable function does Himem.sys provide?

_____

2. What system file is modified to make text messages during startup easier to view?

_____

3. In a command line, when more than one switch is being used, what should come before each switch?

_____

4. Based on the knowledge you have gained in this lab, name three configuration files that can be used to alter the way an OS loads.

_____

5. Name one MS-DOS utility that requires Himem.sys to be loaded for the utility to run. What does Himem.sys do for this utility?

_____

_____

Lab 6.6 Manage Virtual Memory

Objectives

The goal of this lab is to learn to manage virtual memory. After completing this lab, you will be able to:

➤ Locate the Windows tool that allows you to adjust virtual memory settings

➤ Change the size of the paging file

➤ Move the location of the paging file

Materials Required

This lab will require the following:

➤ Windows 2000 or Windows XP operating system

➤ Internet access

➤ Printer

Activity Background

Virtual memory allows the OS to make use of a HDD (hard drive) to simulate RAM. This can be useful when, for instance, the OS is running a number of applications and each requires an allocation of RAM reserved for its use. Ideally, the Virtual Memory Manager will protect actual RAM for the applications that are most active by moving the data used by other applications to a swap file on the hard drive. Windows 2000 and Windows XP call the swap file a paging file. The virtual memory default settings allow Windows to manage the paging file as it sees fit, increasing or decreasing its size as needed.

In most situations, allowing Windows to manage virtual memory with default settings works just fine, but this practice can cause pauses in application response time when the OS switches to an application that has its data stored in the paging file. This delay is caused by the relatively long access time of reading from a drive compared to reading from RAM. This is especially true if the file is on the boot partition or any other partition that is subject to heavy use. In cases where performance has become a problem, you might wish to manually specify virtual memory settings.

Estimated completion time: **30 minutes**

ACTIVITY

Log on to your computer using an account with administrative privileges. Complete the following steps to gather information about your system:

For Windows 2000:

1. Click the **Start** button on the taskbar, point to Settings and then click **Control Panel**. The Control Panel window opens.

2. Double-click the **System** icon in Control Panel. The System Properties dialog box opens.

3. Review the information on the General tab and note how much RAM is installed. Click **OK** to close the System Properties dialog box.

4. Double-click the **Administrative Tools** icon in Control Panel. The Control Panel window changes to Administrative Tools.

5. Double-click the **Computer Management** shortcut in Administrative Tools. The Computer Management snap-in appears in an MMC.

6. In the left pane of Computer Management, click **Disk Management** and review the information displayed in the right pane. List below the required information, then close the MMC and Administrative Tools.

   ■ RAM installed:_____

   ■ Disks installed:_____

   ■ Partitions and letters assigned:_____

   ■ Partition designated as the system partition:_____

   ■ Disk with unallocated space:_____

For Windows XP:

1. Click the **Start** button on the taskbar, then click **Control Panel**. The Control Panel window opens.

2. In the Pick a category section of Control Panel, click **Performance and Maintenance**. The Control Panel changes to Performance and Maintenance.

3. Click the **System** icon in Performance and Maintenance. The System Properties dialog box opens.

4. Review the information on the General tab and list in step 7 how much RAM is installed. Click **OK** to close the System Properties dialog box.

5. Click the **Administrative Tools** icon in Performance and Maintenance. Performance and Maintenance changes to Administrative Tools.

6. Double-click the **Computer Management** shortcut in Administrative Tools. The Computer Management console opens.

7. In the left pane of Computer Management, click **Disk Management** and review the information displayed in the right pane. List the required information, then close the Computer Management console and Administrative Tools applet.

   ■ RAM installed:_____

   ■ Disks installed:_____

   ■ Partitions and letters assigned:_____

   ■ Partition designated as the system partition:_____

   ■ Disk with unallocated space:_____

Visit the Microsoft Web site at *support.microsoft.com* and search the Knowledge Base for the following articles:

- Article 123747: Moving the Windows Default Paging and Spool File
- Article 197379: Configuring Page Files for Optimization and Recovery
- Article 314482: How to Configure Paging Files for Optimization and Recovery in Windows XP
- Article 307886: How to Move the Paging File in Windows XP

Print and read these articles and answer the following questions:

1. What is the default/recommended size of the paging file?

   _____

2. What is a disadvantage of totally removing the paging file from the boot partition?

   _____

   _____

3. What performance-degrading issue will the paging file be subject to if moved to a partition that also contains data?

   _____

   _____

4. What additional benefit is there to setting up a paging file on multiple hard drives?

   _____

   _____

5. According to Article 307886, how do you select the partition on which you wish to modify paging file settings?

   _____

   _____

6. What is the minimum size of the paging file required to allow a memory dump in the event of a STOP error?

   _____

Now you will work with the Virtual Memory dialog box to view and record the paging file settings. The official information may not be clear about the recommended maximum size of the paging file. As you record your settings, notice that the maximum size is the same as the recommended size.

For Windows 2000:

1. Click the **Start** button on the taskbar, point to **Settings**, then click **Control Panel**. The Control Panel window opens.

2. Double-click the **System** icon in Control Panel. The System Properties dialog box opens.

3. In System Properties, select the **Advanced** tab.

4. In the Performance section of the Advanced tab, click **Performance Options**. The Performance Options dialog box opens, as shown in Figure 6-1.

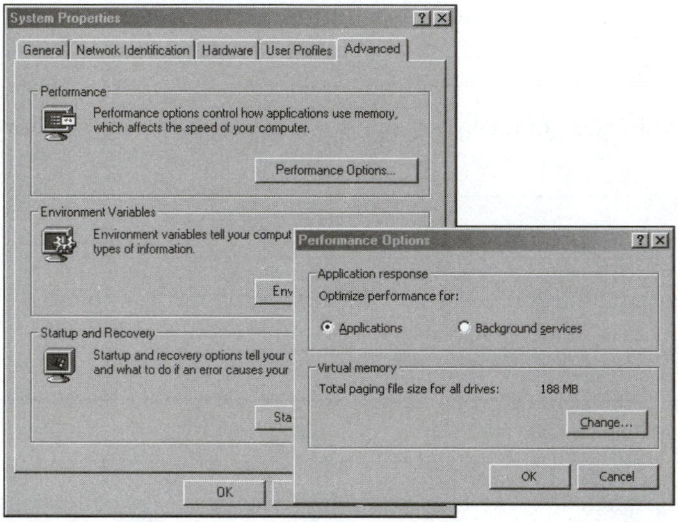

Figure 6-1   Use the Performance Options dialog box in Windows 2000 to access information on your computer's paging file

5. In the Performance Options dialog box, click **Change**. The Virtual Memory dialog box opens, as shown in Figure 6-2. List the current settings.

- Does your computer have multiple paging files?_____

- Drive(s) where located:_____

- Current size:_____

- How is it managed (circle one): Custom *or* System-managed size *or* No paging file

- Minimum allowed:_____

- Recommended:_____

- Currently allocated:_____

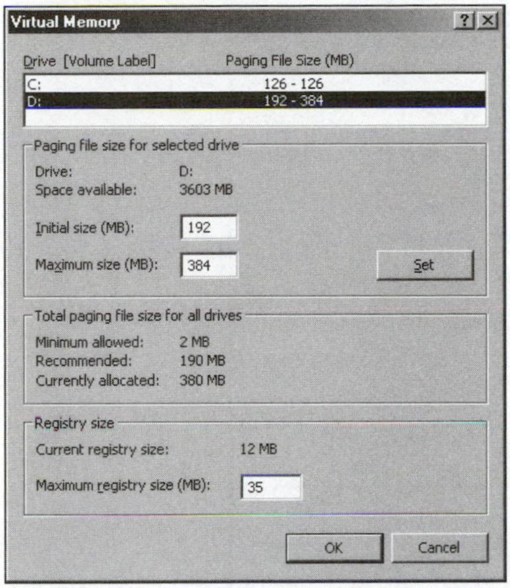

Figure 6-2   The Virtual Memory dialog box for Windows 2000

For Windows XP:

1. Click the **Start** button on the taskbar, then click **Control Panel**. The Control Panel window opens.

2. In the Pick a category section of Control Panel, click **Performance and Maintenance**. The Control Panel changes to Performance and Maintenance.

3. Click the **System** icon in Performance and Maintenance. The System Properties dialog box opens.

4. In System Properties, select the **Advanced** tab.

5. In the Performance section of the Advanced tab, click **Settings**. The Performance Options dialog box opens, as shown in Figure 6-3.

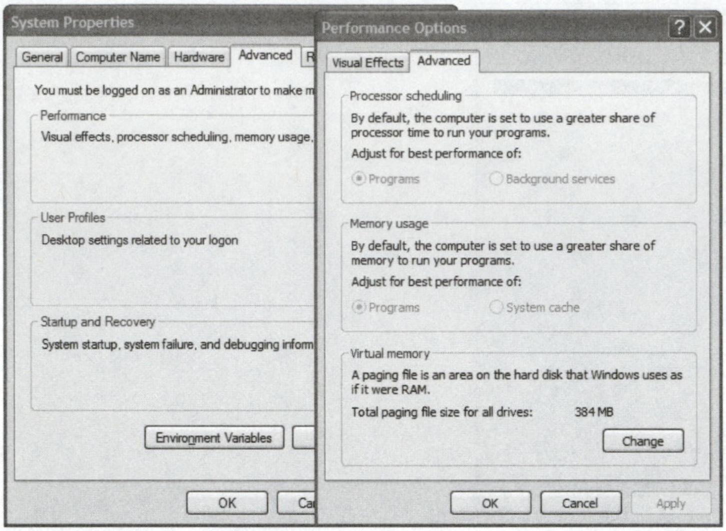

System Properties

General | Computer Name | Hardware | Advanced | R

You must be logged on as an Administrator to make m

Performance

Visual effects, processor scheduling, memory usage.

User Profiles

Desktop settings related to your logon

Startup and Recovery

System startup, system failure, and debugging inform

Environment Variables

OK   Ca

Performance Options   ? X

Visual Effects | Advanced

Processor scheduling

By default, the computer is set to use a greater share of processor time to run your programs.

Adjust for best performance of:

⦿ Programs   ○ Background services

Memory usage

By default, the computer is set to use a greater share of memory to run your programs.

Adjust for best performance of:

⦿ Programs   ○ System cache

Virtual memory

A paging file is an area on the hard disk that Windows uses as if it were RAM.

Total paging file size for all drives: 384 MB

Change

OK   Cancel   Apply

Figure 6-3   Use the Performance Options dialog box in Windows XP to access information on your computer's paging file

6. In the Performance Options dialog box, select the **Advanced** tab.

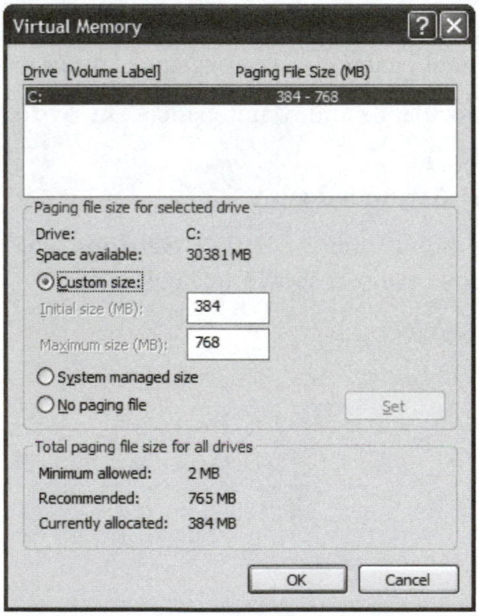

Virtual Memory   ? X

Drive [Volume Label]   Paging File Size (MB)

C: 384 - 768

Paging file size for selected drive

Drive: C:
Space available: 30381 MB

⦿ Custom size:

Initial size (MB):   384

Maximum size (MB):   768

○ System managed size
○ No paging file   Set

Total paging file size for all drives

Minimum allowed: 2 MB
Recommended: 765 MB
Currently allocated: 384 MB

OK   Cancel

Figure 6-4   The Virtual Memory dialog box for Windows XP

7. In the Virtual memory section of the Advanced tab, click **Change**. The Virtual Memory dialog box opens, as shown in Figure 6-4. List the current settings.

- Does your computer have multiple paging files?_____
- Drive(s) where located:_____
- Current size:_____
- How is it managed (circle one): Custom *or* System-managed size *or* No paging file
- Minimum allowed:_____
- Recommended:_____
- Currently allocated:_____

Based on the information in the Knowledge Base articles and the data you have collected about your computer, answer the following questions:

1. Is your computer's paging file set for optimal performance based on its current physical configuration? Explain.

_____

_____

2. What actions and paging file settings would you recommend to maximize performance? Explain.

_____

_____

3. Consider a computer with the following configuration:

- 512MB RAM
- HDD0 C: (system) 17GB NTFS 2.8GB unallocated disk space
- HDD1 D: (general storage) 20GB NTFS no unallocated disk space
- Paging file located on C with Custom size of 384MB initial and 786MB maximum

Based on what you have learned so far, what would be your recommendation to maximize virtual memory performance while allowing the use of debugging information?

_____

_____

_____

_____

Review Questions

1. What is meant by the term "virtual memory"?

_____

_____

2. What does Windows XP call the swap file?

_____

3. Why would you want to move the paging file off of the boot partition?

_____

_____

4. When could fragmentation of the paging file occur?

_____

_____

5. What is the predominant reason for slight pauses in an application when retrieving information from the paging file?

_____

_____

BONUS: Because Microsoft acknowledges a performance advantage to locating the paging file off of the boot partition, what is the main reason that the boot partition is its default location?

_____

_____

CHAPTER SEVEN

FLOPPY DRIVES

Labs included in this chapter

➤ Lab 7.1 Install and Troubleshoot a Floppy Drive

➤ Lab 7.2 Use TestDrive to Test a Floppy Drive

➤ Lab 7.3 Format a Floppy Disk

➤ Lab 7.4 Use the Diskcopy and Xcopy Commands

➤ Lab 7.5 Critical Thinking: Use Debug to Examine Disk Information

---

The following grid shows the correlation between the labs in this chapter and the A+ Guides to Hardware and Software.

A+ Guide to Managing and Maintaining Your PC, Fifth Edition	A+ Guide to Hardware, Third Edition	A+ Guide to Software, Third Edition
Lab 7.1 Install and Troubleshoot a Floppy Drive	Chapter 6	
Lab 7.2 Use TestDrive to Test a Floppy Drive	Chapter 6	
Lab 7.3 Format a Floppy Disk	Chapter 6	
Lab 7.4 Use the Diskcopy and Xcopy Commands	Chapter 6	
Lab 7.5 Critical Thinking: Use Debug to Examine Disk Infomation		Chapter 10

Lab 7.1 Install and Troubleshoot a Floppy Drive

Objectives

The goal of this lab is to give you practice installing a second floppy drive. After completing this lab, you will be able to:

➤ Install a floppy drive

➤ Verify that a floppy drive is working correctly

➤ Troubleshoot problems related to installing a floppy drive

Materials Required

This lab will require the following:

➤ Windows 98 or Windows 2000/XP operating system

➤ System with one floppy drive installed and an empty 3.5-inch drive bay or empty 5-inch drive bay with mounting adapter for a second floppy drive

➤ PC toolkit

➤ A second floppy drive ready for installation

➤ Bootable disk

Activity Background

If you are in a position where you need to duplicate several floppy disks, having a second floppy drive will speed the process significantly. In this lab you will install and test a second floppy drive. But first, you will experiment with an installed floppy drive to become familiar with the correct orientation of the data cable. This activity will also give you an opportunity to verify that the installed floppy drive is working correctly, something that you should always do before installing a new drive so that you know your starting point. After the installation, if the first drive does not work, you will know that the problem did not previously exist and was introduced during the installation process. When making changes to a system, always know your starting point.

Estimated completion time: **45 minutes**

Activity

To experiment with the cable orientation on an installed floppy drive:

1. Verify that you can boot from drive A with a bootable disk.

2. Turn off the computer, open the case and examine the data cable to drive A. Look for the twist in the cable. Verify that the cable is connected to the drive so that the twist is between the drive and the motherboard.

3. Adjust the cable to remove the twist between the drive and the controller. Turn on the PC and try to boot from drive A again. Describe what happens.

_____

_____

4. Turn off the computer, and restore the cable to its original position.

5. Verify that you can again boot from drive A with a bootable disk.

6. Reverse the orientation of the connection between the floppy drive cable and the floppy drive controller so that the edge connector is not aligned with pin 1.

7. Boot the PC. What problem occurs? Describe the problem as a user would describe it.

_____

_____

8. Turn off the computer, and restore the cable to its correct orientation.

9. Verify that you can boot from drive A again with a bootable disk.

In the following steps you will install and test a second floppy drive:

1. Turn off the computer.

2. Install a second floppy drive in your PC. Install the cable so that the connector without the twist is attached to the new drive. (Your instructor might tell you to remove a floppy drive from another PC to install as a second drive in this PC.)

3. Boot the system and enter the CMOS setup utility. What keys do you press at startup to enter CMOS setup?

_____

4. Use the Standard CMOS Setup option (or a similar option) to find the fields on the CMOS setup screen that are used to configure floppy drives. Find the field to enable the B drive. This is the default drive letter assigned to a second floppy drive, the drive that does not require a twist in the floppy drive cable.

5. According to your setup utility, does the ROM BIOS for your computer support an extra–high density 3.5-inch floppy disk drive? List the drive types it does support.

_____

_____

_____

6. Select the option for 1.44MB (or extra-high density 3.5-inch drive) as the drive type for the new drive B just installed.

7. Save CMOS settings and exit the CMOS setup utility. List the steps required to save your settings and exit the utility.

_____

_____

8. Allow the system to reboot from the floppy disk in drive A. Watch the new drive to see if the activity LED comes on. This will be the first indication that the drive has been installed properly.

9. When the system has reached the command prompt, remove the floppy disk from drive A and insert it in drive B.

10. Type **DIR B:** and press **Enter**. Did the drive read the floppy disk as expected?

_____

11. Verify that you can change the default drive to drive B by typing **B:** and pressing **Enter**. What is the new command prompt?

_____

12. Shut down the system.

13. Reverse the drive cabling so that drive A is B and drive B is the new A. Then test by booting from the new drive A.

14. Return the drives to their original assignments, and verify that both function as expected.

15. Change the floppy drive type in CMOS setup to an incorrect setting. (Make sure you don't change the hard drive type accidentally.)

16. Reboot. What error did you see?

_____

17. Now correct the setting and reboot to make sure all components work again.

18. Remove the second floppy drive from your system, and change the CMOS setup to disable drive B so that the BIOS expects to see only a single drive A.

19. Verify that the original drive is functioning correctly. How did you go about verifying that the drive is working properly?

_____

_____

Review Questions

1. Why is it important to verify that original drives already installed in a system are functioning correctly before installing a new drive?

   _____

   _____

2. Which drive should be attached to the connector that has a twist in the cable?

   _____

3. What letter is assigned to any second floppy drive that does not have the twist?

   _____

4. What is the capacity of an extra-high density floppy disk?

   _____

5. What is one advantage of having two floppy drives on a system?

   _____

LAB 7.2 USE TESTDRIVE TO TEST A FLOPPY DRIVE

Objectives

The goal of this lab is to familiarize you with floppy drive diagnostic software. After completing this lab, you will be able to:

➤ Use TestDrive to examine and diagnose problems with floppy drives and floppy disks

➤ Describe errors reported by TestDrive

Materials Required

This lab will require the following:

➤ Windows 98 operating system

➤ Internet access

➤ A floppy disk

Activity Background

MicroSystems Development provides a diagnostic program called TestDrive for examining and diagnosing problems with floppy drives and floppy disks. You will learn to use some functions of this utility in this lab. You will begin by downloading a demo version from the company's Web site. Note that most of the options on the TestDrive menu require that you have a DDD (digital diagnostic disk) for testing the drive, but you can perform a few tests without one.

> Estimated completion time: **30 minutes**

ACTIVITY

To download and install a demo copy of TestDrive:

1. Open your browser and go to *www.msd.com/diags/*.

2. Download the TestDrive software.

3. Insert a disk containing no important data into the floppy drive. Open a command prompt window and switch to the directory containing the Testdriv.exe program. Type **testdriv.exe** and press **Enter** to launch the program. When the program launches, press any key to continue.

Now that you have installed the TestDrive software, you can begin using it. Note that the main window, shown in Figure 7-1, tells you which function key to press to perform various tasks. Follow these steps:

```
┌─────────────────────────────────────────────────────────┐
│ ─                    TESTDRIV                      ▼  ▲   │
├─────────────────────────────────────────────────────────┤
│                                                          │
│            T E S T   D R I V E  (tm)                     │
│                                                          │
│         F1    General Test           *                   │
│         F2    Alignment Test         *                   │
│         F3    Spindle Speed                              │
│         F4    Write/Read Test                            │
│         F5    Hysteresis Test        *                   │
│         F6    Head Azimuth Test      *                   │
│         F7    Hub Centering          *                   │
│         F8    Continuous Alignment   *                   │
│         F9    Cleaning Utility                           │
│         F10   Program Information                        │
│         Esc   Exit TEST DRIVE                            │
│                                                          │
│         A     Select Drive A: 1.44MB  * Requires DDD     │
│                                         Press F10 for    │
│                                         Information       │
│                                                          │
│            ══  Selected Drive is A:  ══                  │
│                                                          │
│    Copyright (C) Microsystems Development  1987, 1988.   │
└─────────────────────────────────────────────────────────┘
```

Figure 7-1   TestDrive main menu

1. Press the **F4** key to perform the Write/Read test. The warning box shown in Figure 7-2 appears.

```
┌─────────────────────── TESTDRIV ───────────────── ▼ ▲ ┐
│ Drive A:          TEST DRIVE  Write / Read Test        5/31/97 │
│ 1.44MB                                                          │
│           Sector ┐   Track ──>                                  │
│                  1   0 - - - 19  - - - 39 - - - 59 - - - 79    │
│                  1 -                                            │
│                  2 -                                            │
│ ■ = Sector OK    3 -                                            │
│                  4 -                                            │
│                  5 -                                            │
│ ▯ = Write Error  6 -                                            │
│                  ┌──────────── ***** Warning ***** ────────┐ad │
│ ▯ =              │  This test requires a formatted 1.44MB scratch disk │0 │
│ ▯ =              │                                          │   │
│                  │    All data will be lost, proceed? <Y/N>_│   │
│ Last             └──────────────────────────────────────────┘   │
│ Total Errors =    0   15 -                                       │
│                       16 -                                       │
│                       17 -        ▶                              │
│                       18 -                                       │
├───────────────┤ Test interrupted, press any key to continue ├──┤
└────────────────────────────────────────────────────────────────┘
```

Figure 7-2   TestDrive Write/Read test

2. Press **Y** to continue. While the test is running, answer these questions:

   ■ In what order are these components of the floppy disk tested: heads, tracks, and sectors.

   _____

   _____

   ■ Did you get any errors? If so, describe each error.

   _____

   _____

3. If you got a significant number of errors, try another disk. Do you see any consistency in errors when switching from one disk to another? If you get a pattern of errors when using several disks, the problem is most likely with the drive. If the errors are isolated to only one disk, the problem is most likely with the disk and not the drive.

   _____

4. Press any key to return to the Main Menu.

5. Select the Spindle speed test, and record the spindle speed below. What is the acceptable range for spindle speed?

   _____

6. Press any key to return to the Main Menu.

7. Select Program Information and answer the following questions:

   ■ What type of disk do most of the TestDrive tests require?

   _____

7

■ What is one function of the software that is not a test?

_____

■ What type of disk is required for this function?

_____

■ What five measurements of floppy disks can be diagnosed by TestDrive?

_____

_____

Review Questions

1. What type of drive is TestDrive designed to test?

_____

2. What are the only two tests that can be run without a special disk?

_____

3. What is the symbol that TestDrive uses to indicate a write error?

_____

4. Suppose you run the Write/Read test with several floppy disks and receive the same errors with each of the disks. What might you conclude?

_____

_____

5. Why do you think TestDrive allows you to try some free tests before you must purchase the software?

_____

_____

LAB 7.3 FORMAT A FLOPPY DISK

Objectives

The goal of this lab is to help you use various formatting options available from the command prompt and in Windows Explorer. After completing this lab, you will be able to:

➤ Use switches for different formatting options

➤ Format a floppy disk using Windows Explorer

Materials Required

This lab will require the following:

➤ Windows 98 or Windows 2000/XP operating system

➤ Blank, unformatted floppy disk

Activity Background

Floppy disks must be formatted before you can use them. These days, floppy disks usually come preformatted from the factory. But you may often be required to reformat a used disk. The formatting process defines track and sector spacing so that data can be written to a known location. Formatting also creates the File Allocation Table, or FAT, which lists the locations of files on the disk. You can format a disk from within Windows Explorer or from the command line. When formatting disks from the command line, you can use switches to make decisions about exactly how the disk will be formatted. These switches allow you to cut some corners to speed the formatting process or to streamline the process of making a bootable disk. In this lab, you will format a floppy disk in several different ways.

> Estimated completion time: **45 minutes**

ACTIVITY

To practice formatting a floppy disk from the command prompt, follow these steps:

For Windows 98:

1. Insert a blank, unformatted floppy disk into drive A.

2. Open a command-prompt window. Use the **Dir** command to examine drive A. Describe what you see on the screen.

_____

_____

3. The system cannot provide information about the contents of the disk because the disk has not yet been formatted. Type **Format /?**, and press **Enter**. This command displays a list of 11 switches that you can use to modify the Format command. What is the correct syntax for a Format command to test clusters on the disk in drive A that are currently marked as bad?

_____

4. To format the disk, type **Format A:**, then press **Enter**.

5. When prompted, press **Enter**. The formatting process begins. Throughout the process, you see a message indicating the percent completed.

6. When the formatting reaches 100%, the system gives you the opportunity to name the volume. Name the volume **FTEST**, then press **Enter**.

7. Next the system displays the formatting summary and prompts you to format another.

8. Type **n**, and press **Enter**.

9. Use the **Dir** command to examine drive A. Now the system is able to give you information about the floppy disk because it has been formatted.

10. A quick format does not write track and sector markings on the disk and is a quick way to reformat a previously formatted disk. To do a quick format, type **Format A: /q** and press **Enter**. Compare the time it took to do a quick format to the time it took to do a full format.

_____

11. Again, use the **Dir** command to examine drive A. Is there a difference between the outcome of the quick format and that of the full format?

_____

For Windows 2000:

1. Insert a blank, unformatted floppy disk into drive A.

2. Open a command-prompt window. Use the **Dir** command to examine drive A. Describe what you see on the screen.

_____

_____

3. The system cannot provide information about the contents of the disk because the disk has not yet been formatted. Type **Format /?** and press **Enter**. This command displays a list of 12 switches that you can use to modify the Format command. What is the correct syntax for a Format command to format only one side of a disk?

_____

_____

4. To format the disk, type **Format A:**, then press **Enter**.

5. When prompted, press **Enter**. The formatting process begins. Throughout the process, you see a message indicating the percent completed.

6. When the formatting reaches 100%, the system gives you the opportunity to name the volume. Name the volume **FTEST**, then press **Enter**.

7. Next the system displays the formatting summary and prompts you to format another.

8. Type **n**, and press **Enter**.

9. Use the **Dir** command to examine drive A. Now the system is able to give you information about the floppy disk because it has been formatted.

10. A quick format does not write track and sector markings on the disk and is a quick way to reformat a previously formatted disk. To do a quick format, type **Format A: /q**, and press **Enter**. Continue through the formatting procedure. Compare the time it took to do a quick format to the time it took to do a full format.

_____

_____

11. Again, use the **Dir** command to examine drive A. Is there a difference between the outcome of the quick format and that of the full format?

_____

_____

For Windows XP:

1. Insert a blank, unformatted floppy disk into drive A.

2. Open a command-prompt window. Use the **Dir** command to examine drive A. Describe what you see on the screen.

_____

_____

3. The system cannot provide information about the contents of the disk because the disk has not yet been formatted. Type **Format /?** and press **Enter**. This command displays a list of nine switches that you can use to modify the Format command. What is the correct syntax for a Format command to format a 1.2-MB floppy disk?

_____

_____

4. To format the disk, type **Format A:**, and then press **Enter**.

5. When prompted, press **Enter**. The formatting process begins. Throughout the process, you see a message indicating the percent completed.

6. When the formatting reaches 100%, the system gives you the opportunity to name the volume. Name the volume **FTEST**, then press **Enter**.

7. Next, the system displays the formatting summary and prompts you to format another.

8. Type **n**, and press **Enter**.

9. Use the **Dir** command to examine drive A. Now the system is able to give you information about the floppy disk because it has been formatted.

10. A quick format does not write track and sector markings on the disk and is a quick way to reformat a previously formatted disk. To do a quick format, type **Format A: /q**, and press **Enter**. Continue through the formatting procedure. Compare the time it took to do a quick format to the time it took to do a full format.

11. Again, use the **Dir** command to examine drive A. Is there a difference between the outcome of the quick format and that of the full format?

Suppose that you wished to make a bootable floppy disks so that you could add utilities and use it for troubleshooting. You can use more than one switch at a time with most commands. To demonstrate this fact with the Format command, complete the following steps:

For Windows 98:

1. Type **Format a: /q /s**, then press **Enter**. This command instructs the system to do a quick format and then to copy the system files required to make the disk bootable.

2. Describe the format process.

   _____

   _____

   _____

   _____

3. How many bytes of free space are now included on the disk? What command did you use to get your answer?

   _____

   _____

4. Close the command-prompt window.

For Windows 2000:

1. Type **Format a: /q /s**, then press **Enter**. This command instructs the system to do a quick format and then to copy the system files required to make the disk bootable.

2. What message did you receive? Suppose that you have a copy of a bootable floppy disk. What command might you use to create another bootable floppy disk using the one that you already have?

3. Now type **Format a: /q/A:512**, and press **Enter**.

4. Describe the format process.

5. How many bytes of free space are now included on the disk? What command did you use to get your answer?

6. Close the command-prompt window.

For Windows XP:

1. Type **Format a: /q /s**, then press **Enter**. This command instructs the system to do a quick format and then to copy the system files required to make the disk bootable.

2. What message did you receive about creating a Windows XP bootable floppy disk?

3. Now type **Format a: /q/A:512,** and press **Enter**.

4. Describe the formatting process.

5. How many bytes of free space are now included on the disk? What command did you use to get your answer?

6. Close the command-prompt window.

To practice formatting a floppy disk from within Windows Explorer, follow these steps:

1. Open Windows Explorer.

2. With the floppy disk inserted in drive A, right-click drive A, then click **Format** in the shortcut menu. The Format window opens.

3. Observe the layout of the Format window, and describe the options provided by the Format window.

_____

Review Questions

1. Suppose you formatted a floppy disk on a Windows 98 system. Would you then be able to reformat the same disk using the /q switch on another Windows 98 system? Why or why not?

_____

_____

2. Suppose you want to format a disk in drive B, making it a bootable disk. What command would you use in Windows 98?

_____

3. In general, what difference did you see in a disk's directory listing after formatting the disk with the /s switch?

_____

_____

4. Why might it be less important for Windows 2000 and Windows XP to provide a switch for creating a bootable floppy disk?

_____

5. What is the difference between a Windows 98 startup disk and a boot disk created using the Format A: /S command?

_____

_____

_____

LAB 7.4 USE THE DISKCOPY AND XCOPY COMMANDS

Objectives

The goal of this lab is to help you observe differences in the Diskcopy and Xcopy commands. After completing this lab, you will be able to:

> ➤ Copy files and folders using the Xcopy command

> ➤ Duplicate a disk using the Diskcopy command

> ➤ Explain when to use Xcopy and when to use Diskcopy when copying files and folders

Materials Required

This lab will require the following:

> ➤ Windows 98 operating system

> ➤ Two blank floppy disks

> ➤ Safety pin

> ➤ Windows 2000/XP operating system (optional)

Activity Background

The Copy command allows you to copy files from one folder to another folder. Using a single Xcopy command, you can copy files from multiple folders, duplicating an entire file structure in another location. The Diskcopy command allows you to make an exact copy of a floppy disk. You will learn to appreciate the differences between these commands in this lab.

Estimated completion time: **45 minutes**

ACTIVITY

Before you begin using the Xcopy and Diskcopy commands, you need to create a test directory to use when copying files. Follow these steps:

1. Open a command-prompt window, and make the root of drive C the current directory. Note that the quickest way to change to the root of a drive is to type **X:** (where **X** is the drive letter), then press **Enter**.

2. Make a directory in the drive C root called **copytest**.

Now you can begin experimenting with the Xcopy command. Follow these steps:

1. Type **Xcopy /?** and press **Enter**. Xcopy Help information appears. Notice all the switches that you can use to modify the Xcopy command. In particular, you can use the /e switch to instruct Xcopy to copy all files and all subdirectories in a directory, including the empty subdirectories, to a new location.

2. Type **Xcopy C:\"program files"\"internet explorer" C:\copytest /e** and then press **Enter**. You will see a list of files scroll by as they are copied from the C:\program files\internet explorer folder to the C:\copytest folder. Notice that in the command line, you had to use quotation marks to surround a folder name that contains spaces.

3. When the copy operation is complete, check the copytest directory to see that the files have been copied and the subdirectories created.

4. Insert a blank floppy disk into drive A, type **md A:\copytest**, then press **Enter**. This creates a directory named copytest on drive A.

5. To copy all the files in the Copytest directory on the hard drive to the Copytest directory on drive A, type the command **Xcopy C:\"program files"\ "internet explorer" A:\copytest**, then press **Enter**.

6. The system begins copying files, but the floppy disk lacks the capacity needed to hold the entire \Internet Explorer directory. As a result, the system displays a message indicating that the disk is out of space and asking you to insert another disk. What is the exact error message?

_____

_____

7. In this case, you do not really want to copy the entire directory to the floppy disk, so you need to stop the copying process. To do that, hold down the **Ctrl** key, then press the **Pause/Break** key. You return to the command prompt.

You have used the Xcopy command to copy some files to a floppy disk. Next, you will use the Diskcopy command to make an exact copy of that floppy disk, which is referred to as the source disk. (The disk you copy files to is known as the target disk.) You'll begin by writing down a list of the files and directories on the source disk. Later, you will compare this list to the list of files actually copied to the target disk. Follow these steps:

1. Display a directory listing for the A:\copytest directory.

2. Write the complete summary of files, directories, and space on the A drive:

_____

_____

_____

_____

3. Verify that the floppy disk you used in the preceding set of steps is inserted in drive A, then type **Diskcopy A: A:** and press **Enter**. This instructs the system to copy files from one floppy disk to another using a single floppy disk drive. (If your system contained a drive B, you could copy files from a disk in drive A to a disk in drive B or vice versa.)

4. Press **Enter** to begin copying.

5. Because you are copying from drive A to drive A, the system prompts you to remove the source disk and to insert the target disk. When prompted, insert a blank floppy disk and press **Enter**.

6. When the copy operation finishes, a message appears asking if you want to copy another disk. Type **n** and press **Enter** to indicate that you do not wish to copy another disk. (When using Windows 98, you must also indicate that you do not wish to make another duplicate.)

7. With the target disk still in drive A, use the **Dir** command to compare the newly copied files with the file list from the source disk, which you recorded in step 2. The disks should be identical.

CRITICAL THINKING (additional 30 minutes)

1. Format one floppy disk. Use any method from Lab 7.3 to format the disk.

2. Use a safety pin to damage one of the floppy disks created in this lab by sliding back the disk's protective guard and punching a small hole about ½ inch from the edge of the disk.

3. Attempt to copy the files on the damaged disk to the newly formatted disk using Xcopy by first copying them to a folder on the hard drive. List the steps you used to do this and describe the outcome.

_____

_____

_____

4. Attempt to recover from the damaged disk the files that the system could not copy. Explain how you were able to do this.

_____

_____

5. Run TestDrive on the damaged disk and describe the outcome.

_____

_____

CRITICAL THINKING (additional 15 minutes)

Do the following to create and use a Windows 2000/XP bootable floppy disk:

➤ Using Explorer on a Windows 2000/XP computer, format a floppy disk.

➤ Copy Ntldr, Ntdetect.com, and Boot.ini from the root of drive C to the root of the floppy disk.

➤ Use the bootable floppy disk to boot the system. What appears on your screen after the boot?

➤ How might this bootable floppy disk be useful to you in troubleshooting?

Review Questions

1. Can a single Copy command copy files from more than one directory?

_____

2. What switch can you use with Xcopy to copy subdirectories?

_____

3. What is the complete Diskcopy command required to copy files on a disk in drive A to a disk in drive B?

_____

4. What is one disadvantage of using the Diskcopy command with only one floppy disk drive?

_____

5. Which Xcopy switch suppresses overwrite confirmation?

_____

LAB 7.5 CRITICAL THINKING: USE DEBUG TO EXAMINE DISK INFORMATION

Objectives

The goal of this lab is to help you use the Debug utility to examine the beginning of a floppy drive. After completing this lab, you will be able to:

➤ Use Debug commands

➤ Explain how Debug displays information

➤ Examine the boot record on a floppy disk

Materials Required

This lab will require the following:

➤ Windows 98 operating system

➤ Windows 98 startup disk

Activity Background

In this lab, you will use the Debug tool to examine the boot record of a floppy disk (specifically, a floppy disk that is configured as a startup disk). The file system on a floppy disk is similar to that of a hard drive, so what you learn here about floppy disks can be applied to hard drives.

It's important to know how to use Debug, because it's available on every computer that runs DOS or Windows 9x. Using Debug, you can see, at the "grassroots level," the contents of a disk. This will help you gain the strong technical insight that you need to take advantage of more user-friendly data recovery software, and to be confident that you understand how such products work. The better you understand how data is constructed on the disk and exactly what problems can arise, the better your chances of recovering lost or damaged data.

Estimated completion time: 45 minutes

ACTIVITY

Follow these steps to examine the boot record of a startup disk:

1. Boot the PC using the startup disk. At the Startup menu, select the **Start Without CD Support** option.

2. The system boots and a RAM drive is created. After the system has booted, examine the text above the command prompt to determine the drive letter of the RAM drive. (A RAM drive provides a place to write files into memory and allows that memory to behave like a logical drive. The Windows 98 Startup disk compresses various useful utilities that would not fit on the floppy disk in an uncompressed state. To be useful, these files must be uncompressed. Normally, compressed files are expanded and written to a hard drive. Because the Windows 98 Startup disk is often used to troubleshoot a malfunctioning system, its designers assumed that the hard drive might not be available for this purpose. Therefore, they designed the startup disk to expand these files to a RAM drive instead.)

3. Change to the RAM drive, type **Debug**, and press **Enter**. The Debug utility runs, and the prompt changes to a dash (-).

Next, you will use the D command (which stands for "dump") to view memory contents expressed in hex values. Then you will learn to read the results of this Debug command. Follow these steps:

1. To view information starting at memory address 0000:0C00, type **D0000:0C00** and press **Enter**.

2. Observe the output of the D command, which shows the contents of memory beginning with memory address 0000:0C00. (See Figure 7-3.) Note that this command displays memory 128 bytes at a time. The information is presented in

lines of 16 bytes each, with the start address on the left side of the window, the hex value of each byte in the middle of the window, and the ASCII interpretation (if any) of each byte on the right side of the window.

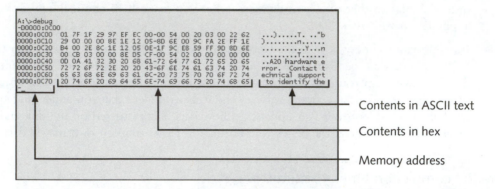

Contents in ASCII text

Contents in hex

Memory address

Figure 7-3   Results of the Debug D command showing contents of 128 bytes of memory

3. If the contents of memory is not ASCII text, then the attempt to display the ASCII interpretation of the contents will appear as gibberish in that ASCII section. Some of the code at these particular memory addresses should be readable in ASCII. What does the code at these memory addresses pertain to?

_____

_____

The Debug utility can be used as an editor to examine and change the contents of memory, a floppy disk, or some other drive. To examine the startup disk, you will copy the boot record to memory.

You will first find an unused area of memory in which you can work. Then you will copy the boot sector to this area of memory. Follow these steps:

1. You need 512 bytes of unused memory. Because the Debug command loads 128 bytes at a time, you will actually look for three consecutive 128 bytes of unused memory. You'll first try memory address 5000:0000. Type **D5000:0000** and press **Enter**. Is the area clear (as indicated by all zeroes)?

_____

2. If the area is not clear, keep trying new memory addresses until you find a clear area. What memory address will you use as your first clear memory address?

_____

3. Now check two more consecutive memory dumps, keeping in mind that you must work with three consecutive memory dumps. (A memory dump displays or "dumps" the contents of memory onto the screen.) Each time you dump

memory, the pointer in memory moves to the next group of 128 bytes. By using successive dump commands, you can move through memory consecutively dumping 128 bytes of memory to the screen. Type **D** and press **Enter** two times to verify that two more successive groups of 128 bytes of memory are empty, making a total of 512 bytes of unused memory addresses.

4. Once you have verified that these 512 consecutive bytes of memory are unused, the next step is to copy, or load, the boot record into this memory. Type **L5000:0000 0 0 1** and press **Enter**. (If you are using some other memory address than 5000:0000, substitute that address in the command line.) You should hear the floppy drive run. Answer these questions to decipher the command:

- What does "L" stand for?

  _____

- What does "5000:0000" indicate?

  _____

- What does the first 0 in "0 0 1" indicate?

  _____

- What does the second 0 in "0 0 1" indicate?

  _____

- What does the 1 in "0 0 1" indicate?

  _____

5. The information from this sector of the floppy disk is now loaded in system memory. To view this information, type **D5000:0000** and press **Enter**. Can you see any indication of with which file system the floppy disk is formatted? Explain.

   _____

   _____

6. Figure 7-4 shows a result of this Dump command for a startup disk formatted using DOS. Compare it to your dump and note the differences. What differences do you see? Table 7-1 lists the items in a boot record to help you with your comparisons.

   _____

   _____

   _____

   _____

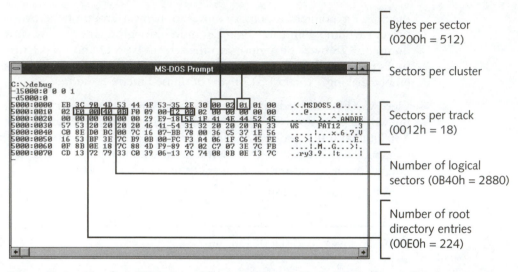

Figure 7-4   The first 128 bytes of the boot record of a 3.5-inch floppy disk formatted with DOS

Table 7-1   Layout of the boot record of a floppy disk or hard drive

Description	Number of bytes
Machine code	11
Bytes per sector	2
Sectors per cluster	1
Reserved	2
Number of FATs	1
Number of root directory entries	2
Number of logical sectors	2
Medium descriptor byte	1
Sectors per FAT	2
Sectors per track	2
Heads	2
Number of hidden sectors	2
Total sectors in logical volume	4
Physical drive number	1
Reserved	1
Extended boot signature record	1
32-bit binary volume ID	4
Volume label	11
Type of file system (FAT12, FAT16, or FAT32)	8
Program to load operating system (bootstrap loader)	Remainder of the sector

7. To exit Debug, type **Q** and press **Enter**. You return to the prompt for your RAM drive.

Review Questions

1. What special feature, created by the Windows 98 startup disk, allows compressed troubleshooting utilities contained on the floppy disk to be expanded to a useful state, even if there is no working hard drive in the system?

   _____

   _____

2. What Debug command dumps data contained at the very beginning of the memory address space?

   _____

3. What command loads two sectors from the C drive, starting at the sixth sector?

   _____

   _____

4. Debug displays data _____ bytes at a time.

5. Why do you think it is important to be very responsible and careful when tinkering with the Debug command?

   _____

   _____

UNDERSTANDING AND INSTALLING HARD DRIVES

Labs included in this chapter

➤ Lab 8.1 Install and Partition a Hard Drive

➤ Lab 8.2 Format a Drive and Test It with ScanDisk

➤ Lab 8.3 Test Hard Drive Performance Using SANDRA

➤ Lab 8.4 Use Disk Management

➤ Lab 8.5 Use Hard Drive Utilities

The following grid shows the correlation between the labs in this chapter and the A+ Guides to Hardware and Software.

A+ Guide to Managing and Maintaining Your PC, Fifth Edition	A+ Guide to Hardware, Third Edition	A+ Guide to Software, Third Edition
Lab 8.1 Install and Partition a Hard Drive	Chapter 7	
Lab 8.2 Format a Drive and Test it with ScanDisk	Chapter 7	
Lab 8.3 Test Hard Drive Performance Using SANDRA	Chapter 7	
Lab 8.4 Use Disk Management		Chapter 6
Lab 8.5 Use Hard Drive Utilities	Chapter 7	

Lab 8.1 Install and Partition a Hard Drive

Objectives

The goal of this lab is to help you master the process of installing a hard drive in a computer. After completing this lab, you will be able to:

➤ Physically install a drive

➤ Set CMOS to recognize the drive

➤ Partition the drive

Materials Required

This lab will require the following:

➤ Windows 9x startup disk

➤ Hard drive with unpartitioned drive space

Activity Background

As a technician, you definitely need to know how to install a hard drive in a computer. You might have to replace a failed drive with a new one, or, if you have a hard drive that is running out of storage space, you might need to install an additional drive. In either case, you need to know the steps involved in installing a new hard drive.

In this lab you will install and partition a new hard drive. Ideally, you would install a second hard drive in a system that already has a working drive. However, this lab also gives you the option of removing the hard drive from your system, trading your hard drive for another student's hard drive, and then installing the traded hard drive in your computer. Ask your instructor which procedure you should perform. Because the steps in this lab allow for both possibilities, you need to read the steps carefully to make sure you are performing the right steps for your particular situation.

In any case, after you install the hard drive, you will have to partition it. If you are installing a hard drive that has been used as a boot device, the drive will already have a primary DOS partition. In that case, you need to verify that the drive contains at least some unpartitioned space. If it does contain unpartitioned space, you can add an extended partition to the drive. Again, ask your instructor for specific directions.

Estimated completion time: **45 minutes**

Activity

Do the following to physically install the drive in the computer case:

1. Remove the case cover. Remove the hard drive and exchange it for another student's hard drive. (If your instructor has provided you with a second hard drive to install in your system, simply open the case cover.)

2. Examine the case and decide where to place the drive. Consider whether to place the drive on the primary or secondary IDE channel and if you will need a bay kit to fit a 3.5-inch drive into a 5-inch drive bay. In most cases, you should use the primary channel for your hard drive and, if possible, it should be the only drive on that channel.

3. Place the drive in or near the bay to test its position. Make sure that all cables will reach in that position. If the cables won't reach, try a different bay or obtain longer cables.

4. When you are satisfied everything will fit, remove the drive and set the jumpers to their proper setting. If the drive is to be the only drive on an IDE channel, set it to single. If it is sharing the IDE cable with another drive, set it to master and set the other drive to slave. If the jumpers are not marked on the drive, consult the drive documentation for jumper configuration. You might have to search the Web site of the drive manufacturer for information on the drive.

5. Install the drive in the bay, and secure it with screws on each side of the drive.

6. Attach the power cord and data cable and close the case.

Now that you have physically installed your hard drive, you need to configure CMOS to recognize the new hard drive. Follow these steps:

1. Attach the keyboard, monitor, and mouse.

2. Boot your computer and enter the CMOS setup utility.

3. If IDE hard drive autodetect is not enabled, enable it now. In CMOS, what is the name of this entry? If you have just enabled autodetect, reboot the system so the drive can now be detected.

_____

4. Check the drive parameters that were set by autodetect, and change them if they were not detected correctly. If your system does not have autodetect, set the drive parameters now. When in doubt use Logical Block Addressing (LBA) or consult the drive documentation. What are the drive parameters in CMOS?

_____

5. Save and exit CMOS setup. The system reboots.

6. While the system boots, watch for the drive to appear during POST.

Now that the drive has been recognized, use the Fdisk utility to create or delete partitions. The following sections show you how to create and delete the primary partition, an extended partition, and a logical DOS drive.

8

Enter Fdisk by following these steps:

1. Insert a Windows 98 startup disk in drive A, and reboot the computer.

2. When you get a command prompt, type **Fdisk** and then press **Enter**.

3. Select **Y** and then press **Enter** to enable Large Disk Support. Large Disk Support uses FAT32 to enable partition sizes above 2GB. The Fdisk Options menu appears as shown in Figure 8-1.

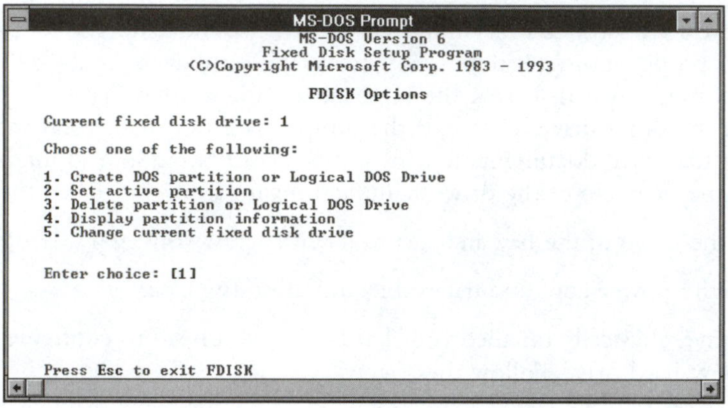

```
┌─────────────────────────────────────────────────────────────┐
│ ──                    MS-DOS Prompt                    ▼  ▲  │
│                     MS-DOS Version 6                         │
│                   Fixed Disk Setup Program                   │
│              (C)Copyright Microsoft Corp. 1983 - 1993        │
│                                                              │
│                       FDISK Options                          │
│                                                              │
│    Current fixed disk drive: 1                               │
│                                                              │
│    Choose one of the following:                              │
│                                                              │
│    1. Create DOS partition or Logical DOS Drive              │
│    2. Set active partition                                   │
│    3. Delete partition or Logical DOS Drive                  │
│    4. Display partition information                          │
│    5. Change current fixed disk drive                        │
│                                                              │
│                                                              │
│    Enter choice: [1]                                         │
│                                                              │
│                                                              │
│                                                              │
│    Press Esc to exit FDISK                                   │
│ ←│                                                        │→ │
└─────────────────────────────────────────────────────────────┘
```

Figure 8-1   Fixed Disk Setup Program (FDISK) menu

On the Fdisk screen, the current fixed disk drive is drive 1. If you are installing a second hard drive, you must first change to drive 2 using the following steps. (If you are installing the only drive in the system, skip these steps and go to the next section, where you will determine what types of partition currently exist on your newly installed drive.)

1. Select option **5** on the menu, then press **Enter**. A list of drives appears.

2. Select drive **2**, then press **Enter**. You return to the Fdisk Options menu shown earlier in Figure 8-1.

Now that you have the correct drive selected, you need to find out what kinds of partition currently exist on the drive. Whether you are installing the only drive on the system or a second drive, follow these steps:

1. To display partition information, select option **4** on the menu, then press **Enter**. Answer these questions about your drive:

   ■ What is the total disk space reported?

   _____

   ■ What is the available disk space reported?

   _____

- Do any partitions currently exist?

- If partitions exist, what kind of partitions are they?

---

2. Press **Escape** to return to the Fdisk Options menu.

If the drive does not already have a primary DOS partition, the next step is to create one. If you are installing a second hard drive on your system, you need to create a primary DOS partition on the second hard drive by using the following steps. (If you have only one hard drive installed or if your second hard drive has a primary partition containing an operating system, skip these steps and move on to the next section, where you will create an extended partition.)

1. To select the second hard drive, from the Fdisk options menu, select option **5** on the menu, then press **Enter**.

2. To select the second hard drive, select option **2** on the menu, then press **Enter**. You return to the Fdisk Options menu.

3. To create a DOS partition, select option **1** on the menu from the Fdisk Options menu, then press **Enter**. The Create DOS Partition or Logical DOS Drive menu appears.

4. To create a primary DOS partition, select option **1** from the Fdisk Options menu, then press **Enter**.

5. The system verifies disk space and displays a progress update. When space on the drive has been verified, Fdisk prompts you to use the maximum available space for the primary DOS partition. Type **N**, then press **Enter**.

6. Fdisk again verifies disk space and prompts for the amount of disk space that you want to use for the primary partition. Type a numerical value that is half of the total available space, then press **Enter**.

7. Fdisk tells you that the primary DOS partition has been created. It displays a summary of the new partition and assigns the partition a drive letter. Record the summary.

Note that Fdisk may slightly increase the partition size to accommodate the disk's geometry. You might also see an error message saying that you do not yet have an active partition.

8. Press **Escape** to return to the Fdisk Options menu.

With a primary partition in place, you are ready to install an extended partition on the last part of the drive. Follow these steps to create an extended partition and one logical DOS drive within that extended partition:

1. In the Fdisk Options Menu, select option **1**, then press **Enter**.

2. To create an extended DOS partition, select option **2**, then press **Enter**.

3. Fdisk verifies disk space and prompts you to enter the amount of disk space to use for the extended partition. Press **Enter** to use the remaining disk space to create the extended partition. Fdisk displays a summary of the extended partition. Note that the extended partition has no drive letter assigned.

4. Press **Escape**. A message appears indicating that no logical drives are defined, and Fdisk again verifies disk space.

5. Fdisk prompts you to enter the amount of space to use for a logical drive. Press **Enter** to use the maximum amount of disk space to create a logical drive.

6. Fdisk assigns a drive letter and displays a summary. Press **Escape** to return to the Fdisk Options menu.

7. Select option **4**, then press **Enter** to display the disk summary. Note that the system column displays Unknown because the drive has not been formatted.

8. Press **Escape** to return to the Fdisk Options menu.

You will now practice deleting partitions. Fdisk is particular about the order in which you create and delete partitions. To delete a primary partition, you must delete an extended partition, and to delete an extended partition, you must delete all the logical DOS drives in the extended partition. A word of warning: If you have an operating system installed on the drive and you have only a single hard drive, *do not delete the primary partition*. Doing so will destroy the operating system installed on the drive.

To delete the extended partition you just created, you must first delete the logical DOS drive in that partition. Follow these steps:

1. From the Fdisk Options menu, select option **3**, then press **Enter**.

2. On the next screen, select option **3**, then press **Enter** to indicate that you are about to delete a logical DOS drive.

3. Type the drive letter assigned to the logical DOS drive, then press **Enter** to confirm that you wish to delete that drive.

4. Enter the volume label (or leave it blank), then press **Enter**. Select **Y** and then press **Enter** to confirm that you wish to delete the drive. Fdisk confirms that the drive has been deleted.

5. Press **Escape** once. The No Logical Drive Defined message appears.

6. Press **Escape** to return to the Fdisk Options menu.

Now that you have deleted the logical DOS drive, you can delete the extended partition. Follow these steps:

1. From the Fdisk Options menu select option **3**, then press **Enter**.

2. On the next screen, select option **2**, then press **Enter** to delete an extended partition.

3. Type **Y**, then press **Enter** to confirm that you want to delete an extended partition. Fdisk confirms that the partition has been deleted.

4. Press **Escape** to return to the Fdisk Options Menu.

If you are working with a second hard drive, you can now delete the primary partition. (Remember, do not delete the primary partition if you are working with a single hard drive.) Follow these steps:

1. From the Fdisk Options menu, select option **3**, then press **Enter**.

2. On the next screen, for the first partition select option **1**, then press **Enter**.

3. Enter the volume label (or leave it blank if there is no volume label), then press **Enter**.

4. Select **Y**, then press **Enter** to confirm that you wish to delete the partition. Fdisk confirms that the drive or partition has been deleted.

5. Press **Escape** to return to the Fdisk Options menu.

   Based on what you have learned, re-create a partition using half of the total disk space. If you have only a single hard drive, create an extended partition. If you have a second hard drive, create only a primary partition, thus leaving half of the drive space unused. Answer these questions:

   - What kind of partition did you create (primary or extended)?

     _____

   - How much space did you use for your partition?

     _____

   - What drive letter was assigned to the logical drive on the new partition?

     _____

To exit the Fdisk utility, follow these steps:

1. With the Fdisk Options menu displayed, press **Escape**.

2. A message is displayed indicating that the system must be rebooted for the changes to take effect. Reboot the system while pressing the **Ctrl** key.

3. Select **Command Prompt Only**.

4. To confirm that the drive is set up correctly, type the drive letter followed by a colon, then press **Enter**. The command prompt now includes the drive's letter.

Review Questions

1. When physically installing a hard drive, what steps should you take before you permanently fix the drive in place with screws?

_____

_____

2. What CMOS setup tool can you use to recognize your hard drive?

_____

_____

3. What are two types of partition?

_____

_____

4. What must you do before you can delete an extended partition?

_____

_____

5. What must you do before you can delete a primary partition?

_____

_____

6. What would prevent your partitions from being recognized after you exit Fdisk?

_____

_____

LAB 8.2 FORMAT A DRIVE AND TEST IT WITH SCANDISK

Objectives

The goal of this lab is to help you prepare a partitioned drive for use. After completing this lab, you will be able to:

➤ Format a drive

➤ Use ScanDisk to test the drive's condition

Materials Required

This lab will require the following:

➤ Windows 98 operating system

➤ Floppy disk containing no essential data

8

Activity Background

Before your computer can read from and write to a drive, you must format the drive. It is also a good idea to test a drive to ensure that it is in working order before you put it to use. In this lab, you will format and test your newly partitioned drive. You will begin by creating a bootable floppy disk and adding some important utility files to it. Then you will use the disk to boot your computer and then format and test your drive. The utility files you will include are:

➤ Scandisk.exe, which is used to detect and repair hard drive errors

➤ Himem.sys, which is used to manage memory above 1 MB

➤ Format.com, which is used to format a drive

You will also include the system file, Config.sys, which contains configuration settings.

Estimated completion time: **30 minutes**

ACTIVITY

Follow these steps to create a bootable disk, then copy the necessary files to it:

1. Create a bootable floppy disk. If you need help, see Lab 2.2.

2. Copy the file named **Scandisk.exe** from **C:\Windows\Command** to the bootable floppy disk.

3. Copy the file named **Himem.sys** from **C:\Windows** to the bootable floppy disk. Himem.sys is necessary to run Scandisk on a hard drive.

4. Copy the file named **Format.com** from **C:\Windows\Command** to the bootable floppy disk.

5. Edit or create the **Config.sys** file on your floppy disk. Add the line **Device=A:\himem.sys**. (Note that if you fail to edit the config.sys file on your boot disk, when you attempt to start ScanDisk you will receive a message indicating it is necessary to do so.)

Now that you have prepared a bootable disk, follow these steps to format your new drive:

1. Boot your system from the floppy disk.

2. At the command prompt, type **Format *x*:** (where *x* is the drive letter assigned to the partition you created in Lab 8.1), then press **Enter**.

3. The system warns you that all data will be lost and prompts you to continue. Type **Y**, then press **Enter** to confirm that you want to format this drive.

4. The system begins formatting the drive. When the formatting process is complete, you are prompted to enter a volume label. You will name the volume New. Type **New** and then press **Enter**.

5. At the command prompt, type the drive letter followed by a colon, then press **Enter**. The newly formatted drive is now the current directory.

6. Use the DIR command to view the drive summary. Record the summary information:

_____

_____

_____

_____

_____

Now that the drive has been formatted, you can use ScanDisk to check the condition of the drive. Follow these steps:

1. Type **A:\Scandisk *x*:** (where *x* is the drive letter of the volume named New).

2. ScanDisk begins checking the following:

- Media descriptor
- File Allocation table
- Directory structure
- File system
- Free space

3. If ScanDisk finds any file fragments or errors, it prompts you to correct the problem. If no errors are found (or after all errors are corrected), ScanDisk displays a summary and prompts you to run a surface scan.

4. A surface scan is a lengthy process in which the disk is scanned block by block until the surface condition of each platter has been checked. Type **Y** to begin a surface scan.

5. ScanDisk begins the surface scan and displays an illustration of the process. While the surface scan continues examining the disk, answer the following questions. ScanDisk can take a long time to complete. For the purposes of this lab, you can cancel the surface scan after you have answered the following questions.

   ■ How many total clusters does the disk contain?

   _____

   ■ How many clusters does each block represent?

   _____

   ■ What symbol indicates a bad cluster?

   _____

Review Questions

1. Write the command you would use to format drive D.

   _____

2. When is Himem.sys required to run ScanDisk?

   _____

3. By default, does ScanDisk run a surface scan automatically?

   _____

4. Why should you run a surface scan?

   _____

5. What happens when ScanDisk finds errors during its automatic check?

   _____

LAB 8.3 TEST HARD DRIVE PERFORMANCE USING SANDRA

Objectives

The goal of this lab is to help you use SANDRA to compare the performance of your system's drives against similar drives. After completing this lab, you will be able to:

➤ Use SANDRA to test your drive's performance

➤ Use SANDRA to compare your system's drives with similar drives

Materials Required

This lab will require the following:

➤ Windows 9x operating system

➤ SiSoft SANDRA, Standard version, installed in Lab 1.3

Activity Background

You can use SANDRA to run a routine of several tests on your drive, report the results, and compare your drive to a selection of comparable drives. This activity will give you an indication of how your drive is performing and whether another product is available that better meets your performance needs. Some tasks, such as video editing, are very demanding on the drive where the files are stored; a faster drive can increase productivity. When making an upgrade decision, it's helpful to compare results reported by SANDRA to information on other hard drives. In this lab you will use SANDRA to test your drive.

Estimated completion time: **30 minutes**

ACTIVITY

Follow these directions to test your drive:

1. Start SANDRA.

2. Double-click the **Drives Benchmark** icon. The Drives Benchmark window opens. (If you don't see the Drives Benchmark icon, you installed the wrong version of SANDRA. You should be using the Standard version.)

3. Click the **Select Drive** list arrow, then select the letter of the drive you are testing from the drop-down menu. What message appeared after you selected drive C?

_____

_____

4. Wait until SANDRA has finished testing your drive before moving your mouse or doing anything else with the system. After the test is finished, a summary appears. Use the summary to answer the following questions:

   ▪ In the Current Drive field, what drive index is reported?

   _____

   ▪ What drives were compared to the Current Drive?

   _____

   _____

5. Click the drop-down menu of one of the compared drives to view it. Note that you can compare your drive against several drives.

6. One by one, select each of the drives, and note their performance ratings. List those drives with a lower performance rating than the current drive:

   _____

   _____

7. List the size and rpm of the two drives with the lowest performance.

   _____

   _____

8. Use the bottom field of the Drives Benchmark window to complete the following table. (Scroll down as necessary to display the information you need.)

Category	Value
Drive Class	
Total Space	
Sequential Read	
Random Read	
Buffered Write	
Sequential Write	
Random Write	
Average Access Time	

8

Review Questions

1. Why might you want to test your drive with SANDRA?

   _____

   _____

2. Based on the drive ratings information you got from SANDRA, do you think a drive performs better if it spins faster or slower?

   _____

3. Based on the drive ratings information you got from SANDRA, do you think a drive performs better if it reads data randomly or sequentially?

   _____

4. Why shouldn't you use the system when SANDRA is testing a drive?

   _____

   _____

LAB 8.4 USE DISK MANAGEMENT

Objectives

The goal of this lab is to help you use Disk Management to work with local hard drives. After completing this lab, you will be able to:

➤ Create a partition from unused disk space

➤ Specify a file system

➤ Format a partition

➤ Delete a partition

Materials Required

This lab will require the following:

➤ Windows 2000 Professional or Windows XP operating system

➤ Printer

➤ Windows 2000 or Windows XP installation files on CD

➤ Unallocated disk space

Activity Background

Disk Management is a Microsoft Management Console snap-in and an administrative tool installed in the Computer Management console by default. To start Disk Management, you first need to start Computer Management. Unlike Fdisk, Disk Management allows you to partition and format disk space from within Windows. In this lab, you will create and delete two different partitions using unallocated disk space.

Estimated completion time: **30 minutes**

ACTIVITY

To work with your local hard drive using Disk Management, follow these steps:

1. Log on using an administrator account. For Windows 2000, open the Control Panel, then double-click the **Administrative Tools** icon. For Windows XP, from Control Panel click **Performance and Maintenance**, then click **Administrative Tools**. The Administrative Tools window opens.

2. Double-click **Computer Management**. The Computer Management snap-in opens in an MMC. In the left pane, click **Disk Management**. The Disk Management interface opens in the right pane. Figure 8-2 shows the interface in Windows 2000.

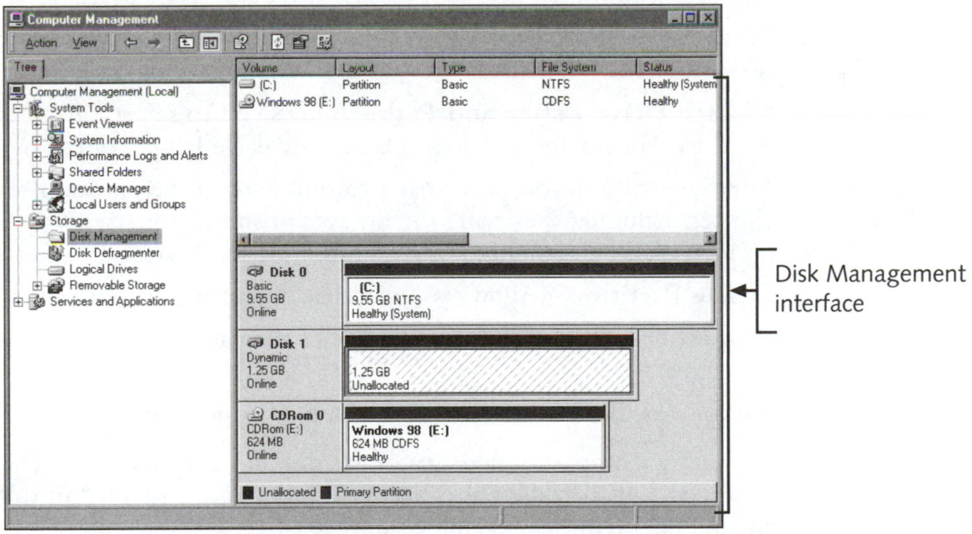

8

Disk Management interface

Figure 8-2   Use Windows 2000 Disk Management to manage hard drives

3. Use the information in the top of the right pane to complete the following table:

Volume	Layout	Type	File System	Status	Capacity

4. Information about each physical drive is displayed in the bottom section of the right pane. In addition, a graphic illustrates each drive's space distribution. Note that drives are labeled with numbers (0, 1, and so forth) in a gray space and that logical drives or volumes are labeled with letters (C, D, E, and so forth) in white space. If a hard drive has just been installed and not yet partitioned, the graphic will show all unallocated (unpartitioned) space, as in Figure 8-2. What drive letters are used on your system?

_____

5. Right-click the right side (white space) of the C drive space in the bottom-right part of the window. A shortcut menu opens with the following options:

- **Open**—Displays the contents of the drive in a window similar to a My Computer window.

- **Explore**—Displays contents of the drive in a window similar to a Windows Explorer window.

- **Mark Active Partition**—Marks the current partition as the partition from which Windows is loaded.

- **Change Drive Letter and Path**—Allows you to select a new letter for the drive. For instance, you can change the drive letter from C to F.

- **Format**—Allows you to format a partition and make partition-related choices, including specifying the file system and sector size. (Windows XP protects itself by disabling Format on the (System) partition.)

- **Delete Partition**—Allows you to delete an entire partition and all contents.

- **Properties**—Displays information about the partition, such as how it is formatted.

- **Help**—Provides information about Disk Management.

6. Right-click the unpartitioned area of the disk drive, which is labeled Unallocated. List the differences between the options provided in this shortcut menu and the menu you examined in Step 5.

_____

_____

In the next set of steps you will create a new partition from unpartitioned space. Note that the partition you are creating should only use *currently unpartitioned* space. Follow these steps:

1. Using *only unpartitioned space*, create a new partition; format the partition using the FAT32 file system and drive letter S. List the steps required to perform this task:

   _____

   _____

   _____

   _____

2. Print a screen shot of the Disk Management window showing the FAT32 drive S.

3. Delete the partition you just created. List the steps required to perform this task:

   _____

   _____

4. Using *only unpartitioned space*, create and format a new NTFS partition using the drive letter H. List the steps required to perform this task:

   _____

   _____

   _____

5. Print a screen shot of the Disk Management window showing the NTFS drive H.

6. Close the Computer Management window.

CRITICAL THINKING: MANAGING PARTITIONS FROM THE RECOVERY CONSOLE (additional 60 minutes)

Do the following to practice managing partitions from the Recovery Console:

1. Access the Windows 2000/XP Recovery Console. List the steps required to perform this task:

   _____

   _____

   _____

2. Open Help and display information about the Diskpart command, including possible command-line options. List the steps required to perform this task:

_____

_____

_____

3. Delete the partition created earlier using Disk Management. List the steps required to perform this task:

_____

_____

_____

4. Create and format a new NTFS partition, using the drive letter R. List the steps required to perform this task:

_____

_____

_____

5. Delete the newly created partition. List the steps required to perform this task:

_____

_____

_____

Review Questions

1. Name an advantage that Disk Management has over Fdisk.

_____

2. What happens to all the information in a partition if you delete the partition?

_____

_____

3. What feature opens if you choose **Explore** from a shortcut menu in Disk Management?

_____

4. Is it possible to create two partitions, using different file systems, out of one area of unallocated disk space? Explain.

_____

_____

_____

5. List the steps involved in removing two empty partitions and creating one single NTFS partition that is assigned the drive letter T.

_____

_____

_____

_____

_____

_____

_____

8

LAB 8.5 USE HARD DRIVE UTILITIES

Objectives

The goal of this lab is to let you work with utilities from hard drive manufacturers that examine and diagnose hard drive problems. After completing this lab, you will be able to:

➤ Identify your hard drive manufacturer

➤ Evaluate utilities provided by hard drive manufacturers for their drives

➤ Test for hard drive problems

Materials Required

➤ Windows 9x is preferred, but other versions of Windows can be used

➤ Internet access

➤ File compression software such as WinZip

➤ Acrobat Reader

➤ Printer access

➤ Blank floppy disk

Activity Background

Hard drive problems can manifest themselves in different ways. The drive may experience immediate and total failure so that it does not operate at all. If failure is due to a problem with the platters, you might not be able to boot at all if the area where system files are stored is affected. If system files are not affected, you may be able to boot and work normally but experience file loss or file corruption. Then again, your may never realize you have a hard drive problem if your hard drive has bad sectors because data might not be saved to that particular physical area of the disk. More often, though, once a disk begins to fail, you notice errors. One tool you can use to diagnose hard drive problems is diagnostic software provided by your hard drive manufacturer. In this lab you will identify your drive manufacturer and use its software to examine your drive. You will also use a generic hard drive utility, Hard Drive Mechanic, which will work as diagnostic software for any manufacturer's hard drive.

Estimated completion time: **60 minutes**

ACTIVITY

The utilities that you will use in this lab require that you boot from a floppy disk. You cannot use a Windows 9x startup disk for this purpose because there is not enough room on the disk for the hard drive utilities. Use the following steps to create a bootable floppy disk:

1. Insert a blank floppy disk into the drive.

2. From Windows Explorer or My Computer, right-click **drive A:** and select **Format** from the shortcut menu. A Format dialog box appears.

3. In the Format type section of the dialog box, select the **Quick (erase)** option. In the Other options section of the dialog box select the **Display summary when finished** and the **Copy system files** options.

4. Click **Start** in the upper-right corner of the dialog box to format and copy files to make the disk bootable. A summary is displayed after the operation is complete. How much space is available?

_____

5. Click **Close** to close the summary, and click **Close** to exit the Format dialog box.

The next thing to do is to identify your hard drive's manufacturer. To do that, you will use a utility for that purpose from Seagate. Follow these steps to identify your drive:

1. Using your Web browser, navigate to *www.seagate.com/support/seatools/index.html*.

2. Look for the section under the heading SeaTools Online, and follow the links to **Online Drive Self Test**. This will open a new window displaying the SeaTools Online testing options.

3. In the new window, follow the **Online Drive Self Test** link to do a quick test of your drive. You might receive a warning about trusting content from Seagate or Ontrack. If you receive this prompt, click **Yes** to receive their content. By following this link, you are allowing a short program to be downloaded onto your PC and executed to identify your drive.

4. A window now displays your drive information. Record the drive information, as it is presented. If you have more than one hard drive, all the drives in your system are listed. Included in the list is the hard drive manufacturer. You will use the drive manufacturer information later in the lab.

_____

_____

5. To select the drive to test, check the box to the left of your drive information, then click the **Next** button at the bottom of the window. A list of tests appears in the next window.

6. Select the **Run short Drive Self Test**, and click **Next** at the bottom of the window. This will begin the test in the same window. The test might take a few minutes. When it is done, record the results of the test.

_____

_____

_____

_____

_____

8

7. When you have recorded your results, close this last window by clicking the **X** in the Title bar. A message appears informing you that you might not want to navigate away from the site. Click **OK** to close the window and continue the lab.

Now you will download generic hard drive diagnostic software that should work on any type of hard drive. To download Hard Drive Mechanic, do the following:

1. In your Web browser, navigate to ***www.highergroundsoftware.com***.

2. Search the Higher Ground Software site for information on Hard Drive Mechanic (HDM). Answer the following questions:

   ▪ What version of Hard Drive Mechanic is available for download in demo form?

   _____

   ▪ Which operating systems does this version of HDM support?

   _____

   ▪ Will HDM run inside or outside of Windows?

   _____

   ▪ What files must *not* be present on the boot disk?

   _____

3. Find and follow the link to download HDM. The File Download dialog box appears.

4. Click **Save** and download the file **hdmdemo.zip** to its own folder. You can create a folder from the Save As dialog box. What is the path to the down-loaded file?

   _____

Now you will test your hard drive with Hard Drive Mechanic (HDM). Follow these instructions to test any manufacturer's drive:

1. In Windows Explorer or My Computer, browse to the location where you downloaded **hdmdemo.zip** and double-click to extract it.

2. When all the files are extracted, copy them, except for the manual, to your bootable floppy disk. You can do this via the drag-and-drop method.

3. Double-click the **Manual.pdf** file to open it in Acrobat Reader, and then print the manual. This manual will be used to give guidance in how to answer the many questions that might be prompted by HDM.

4. Close all programs and restart your computer with the floppy disk in the drive.

5. The computer will boot and settle at the command prompt. At the prompt type **hdmdemo.exe** and press **Enter**. The HDM splash screen appears, and a graphical menu appears horizontally in the upper-left area of the screen. This menu indicates which key to select to choose an option, which is indicated by a blue letter.

6. To begin diagnosing your drive, press the **D** key to open the diagnostics section. A second menu, this time vertically arranged below the first, appears.

7. On the new menu you will see four diagnostic options and an Okay option to exit. These options should be performed from in order top to bottom to test your drive. Consult the manual that you printed as to how to answer the questions. Your instructor may provide you with the correct answers if they are not evident.

8. Did HDM discover any problems with your drive? If so, describe them below:

   _____

   _____

   _____

Now you will find out about hard drive utilities that are supplied by several hard drive manufacturers.

Maxtor offers Maxdiag to support its hard drives. Do the following to find out about this software:

1. In your Web browser, navigate to ***www.maxtor.co.jp/technology/technotes/20007.html***, and locate the link to download the MAXDIAG utility with the filename hddutil.exe.

2. Examine the information on the page and answer these questions:

   ■ With what types of drive will this utility work?

   _____

   _____

   ■ What types of problem will the software identify?

   _____

   _____

   _____

8

3. If you have a Maxtor drive, click the link to download hddutil.exe and save it in its own folder. What is the path to the file?

_____

IBM provides Drive Fitness Test for its hard drives. Do the following to find out about this software:

1. In your Web browser, navigate to **_www.storage.ibm.com/hdd/support/ download.htm_**, and find the link to download the Windows version of the software.

2. Search the information provided about the product, and answer the following questions:

   ■ What types of drive are supported and what two types are expressly not supported?

   _____

   _____

   ■ What types of analysis are performed by the software?

   _____

   _____

   ■ What other OS version (besides Windows) is available to download?

   _____

3. If you have an IBM drive, click the link to download the Drive Fitness Test utility and save it in its own folder. What is the path to the file?

_____

Western Digital provides Data Lifeguard. Do the following to find out about this software:

1. In your Web browser, navigate to _support.wdc.com/download_, and locate the link to download Data Lifeguard 2.8 under the Data Lifeguard Tools (Archived) section.

2. Examine the information provided and answer these questions:

   ■ What size limitation is placed on this software?

   _____

   ■ What would you _not_ be able to do if you were using Windows NT, Windows 2000, or Windows XP instead of Windows 98?

   _____

3. If you have a Western Digital drive, click the link and save it to its own folder. What is the path to the file?

_____

Seagate offers Data Lifeguard. Do the following to find out about this software:

1. In your Web browser, navigate to ***www.seagate.com/support/seatools/index.html***, and locate the link to download SeaTools Desktop.

2. Examine the information provided and answer these questions:

   ■ In what languages is SeaTools available?

   _____

   ■ What type of OS is required?

   _____

3. If you have a Seagate drive, click the link and save the file to its own folder. What is the path to the file?

_____

Now you will use a manufacturer's utility to test your drive. Do the following:

1. If your drive is from one of the previous manufacturers, follow the instructions provided on your drive manufacturer's Web site and perform the test for your hard drive.

2. Summarize the process and results.

_____

_____

_____

_____

If your hard drive is not made by one of the previous manufacturers, go to the Web site of your manufacturer and search for diagnostic software.

   ■ What software did you find?

_____

Review Questions

1. What are some symptoms of hard drive problems listed on the hard drive manufacturers' Web sites? List three in order of seriousness.

_____

_____

_____

2. Which hard drive manufacturer's Web site was the most informative and easiest to use? Why?

_____

_____

_____

3. Which utility from a hard drive manufacturer seemed to be the most powerful? Why?

_____

_____

_____

4. What was the most common method used to run the utilities?

_____

CHAPTER NINE

OPTIMIZING AND PROTECTING HARD DRIVES

➤ Lab 9.1 Perform Hard Drive Routine Maintenance

➤ Lab 9.2 Back Up and Restore Files in Windows 2000/XP

➤ Lab 9.3 Research Data Recovery Services

➤ Lab 9.4 Use Do-It-Yourself Data Recovery Software

➤ Lab 9.5 Troubleshoot Hard Drives

➤ Lab 9.6 Critical Thinking: Sabotage and Repair a Hard Drive Subsystem

The following grid shows the correlation between the labs in this chapter and the A+ Guides to Hardware and Software.

A+ Guide to Managing and Maintaining Your PC, Fifth Edition	A+ Guide to Hardware, Third Edition	A+ Guide to Software, Third Edition
Lab 9.1 Perform Hard Drive Routine Maintenance		Chapter 10
Lab 9.2 Back Up and Restore Files in Windows 2000/XP		Chapter 10
Lab 9.3 Research Data Recovery Services	Chapter 16	Chapter 10
Lab 9.4 Use Do-It-Yourself Data Recovery Software		Chapter 10
Lab 9.5 Troubleshoot Hard Drives	Chapter 7	
Lab 9.6 Critical Thinking: Sabotage and Repair a Hard Drive Subsystem	Chapter 7	

LAB 9.1 PERFORM HARD DRIVE ROUTINE MAINTENANCE

Objectives

The goal of this lab is to help you perform routine maintenance on a hard drive. After completing this lab, you will be able to:

➤ Delete unneeded files on a hard drive

➤ Defragment a hard drive

➤ Scan a hard drive for errors

Materials Required

This lab will require the following:

➤ Windows 98 operating system

➤ Windows 2000/XP operating system (optional)

Activity Background

To ensure that your hard drive operates in peak condition, you should regularly perform some routine maintenance tasks. For starters, you need to ensure that your hard drive includes enough unused space (which it requires to operate efficiently). In other words, you should regularly remove unnecessary files from the drive.

In addition, files on a hard drive sometimes become fragmented over time; defragmenting the drive can improve performance. Other routine maintenance tasks include scanning the hard drive for errors and repairing them. In this lab, you will learn about three tools that you can use to perform important disk maintenance tasks. You should use these tools regularly, in the order given in this lab, to keep your hard drive error-free and performing well.

Estimated completion time: **30 minutes**

Follow these steps to delete unnecessary files on your hard drive:

1. Close all open applications.

2. Click **Start** on the taskbar, point to **Programs**, point to **Accessories**, point to **System Tools**, and then click **Disk Cleanup**. The Select Drive dialog box appears.

3. Select the drive that you want to clean up from the drop-down menu and click **OK**. The Select Drive dialog box closes. The Disk Cleanup dialog box opens.

4. Here you need to select the types of files you want Disk Cleanup to delete. Select all of the possible options. Depending on your system, these options might include Downloaded Program Files, Recycle Bin, Temporary files, and Temporary Internet files.

■ How much disk space does each group of files take up?

_____

_____

■ Based on information given on the Disk Cleanup dialog box, what is the purpose of each group of files?

_____

_____

_____

_____

■ What is the total amount of disk space you would gain by deleting these files?

_____

9

5. Click **OK** to delete the selected groups of files.

6. When asked to confirm the deletion, click **Yes**. The Disk Cleanup dialog box closes, and a progress indicator appears while the cleanup is underway. The progress indicator closes when cleanup is complete, returning you to the desktop.

The next step in routine maintenance is to use ScanDisk to examine the hard drive and repair errors. Follow these steps:

1. Close all open applications.

2. Click **Start** on the taskbar, point to **Programs**, point to **Accessories**, point to **System Tools**, and then click **ScanDisk**. The ScanDisk window opens.

3. ScanDisk offers two options, Standard and Thorough. The Standard option checks for errors in files and repairs them. The Thorough option does the same and, in addition, scans the hard drive surface for problems that might cause future errors. If a segment of the disk surface appears to be damaged in some way, ScanDisk marks that segment so it won't be used in the future. The Thorough option takes longer, but you should use it to get the best benefit from ScanDisk. Select **Thorough** and click **Start**.

4. If ScanDisk finds an error, it asks if you want to repair it. Click **OK** to repair any errors.

5. When the process is completed, ScanDisk reports what it found and corrected. Click **Close** in the report window. What errors, if any, did ScanDisk find?

_____

_____

_____

The last step in routine hard drive maintenance is to use the Disk Defragmenter tool to locate fragmented files and rewrite them to the hard drive in contiguous segments. Follow these steps:

1. Close all open applications.

2. Click **Start**, point to **Programs**, point to **Accessories**, point to **System Tools**, and then click **Disk Defragmenter**. The Disk Defragmenter window opens.

3. Select the drive you want to defragment and click **OK**. Disk Defragmenter begins defragmenting the drive, displaying a progress indicator as it works.

4. Click **Show Details** to expand Disk Defragmenter to a full screen. The Details view of Disk Defragmenter allows you to observe a graphical representation of the defragmentation process.

5. Open Microsoft Word or another program, use the following space to describe what happens, and then close the program and allow Disk Defragmenter to continue.

_____

_____

_____

_____

6. When defragmentation is complete, you are asked if you want to exit Disk Defragmenter. Click **Yes**.

Note that fully defragmenting your hard drive can take half an hour or more, depending on how fragmented your drive is. If you do not have time to wait, you can stop the process by clicking **Stop** and then clicking **Exit** on the confirmation dialog box.

Additional Activity (additional 30 minutes)

Using Windows 2000 or Windows XP, perform the following hard drive routine mainte-nance tasks, which are all accomplished using the Properties window of drive C:

➤ Use Disk Cleanup on the General tab of the drive Properties window to delete unnecessary files on your hard drive.

➤ Use the Error-checking pane under the Tools tab of the drive Properties window to check the volume for errors.

➤ Use the Defragmentation pane under the Tools tab of the drive Properties window to defragment files on the volume.

To access the drive Properties window, using Windows Explorer, right-click the drive, and select **Properties** from the shortcut menu.

Review Questions

1. Why do you think you need to begin your hard disk maintenance chores with Disk Cleanup?

   _____

2. Why do you think you should finish with Disk Defragmenter?

   _____

3. What type of information does the Details view of Disk Defragmenter display?

   _____

   _____

4. What happened when you tried to run another program while Disk Defragmenter was running? Why do you think this happened?

   _____

   _____

   _____

5. What is the disadvantage of deleting temporary Internet files?

   _____

   _____

9

LAB 9.2 BACK UP AND RESTORE FILES IN WINDOWS 2000/XP

Objectives

The goal of this lab is to help you use the Windows 2000 Backup and Recovery Tools to back up and recover lost files. After completing this lab, you will be able to:

➤ Back up files

➤ Delete files

➤ Recover deleted files

Materials Required

This lab will require the following:

➤ Windows 2000 or Windows XP operating system

Activity Background

Windows 2000/XP provides the Windows 2000/XP Backup and Recovery Tools to help you safeguard data in Windows system files. Using these tools, you can back up a single file or even an entire drive from either the local or remote computer. Backups, compressed into a single file, can be saved to a location of your choice, without the need for a dedicated backup device such as a tape drive. In this lab, you will back up, delete, and restore data files using the Windows 2000/XP Backup and Recovery Tools.

Estimated completion time: **45 minutes**

ACTIVITY

Follow these steps to select the files or folders that you wish to back up:

1. Log on to an account that is part of the Power Users group.

2. Create the folders **C:\Backups** and **C:\BackMeUp**, and then create several text files in the C:\BackMeUp folder.

3. Click **Start** on the taskbar, point to **Programs** (for Windows XP, **All Programs**), point to **Accessories**, point to **System Tools**, and then click **Backup**. For Windows XP, click **Advanced Mode**. The Windows 2000/XP Backup and Recovery Tools utility opens. What three options are available on the Welcome tab?

_____

_____

_____

4. Click the **Backup** tab and then in the left pane, click the plus sign next to drive C. The right pane displays all the items that you can back up.

5. First, you will back up an entire folder. Click the box beside the **BackMeUp** folder in the right pane. This indicates that you want to back up the entire contents of that folder.

6. Instruct the system to back up the entire contents of the Documents and Settings folder. Explain how you performed this task.

_____

_____

_____

7. In addition to the folders you just selected for backup, you will select a single file, DSKProbe.exe, for backup. Double-click the **Program Files** folder in the right pane. The Program Files folder is highlighted in the left pane and its contents are displayed in the right pane.

8. Double-click the **Support Tools** folder in either pane. The contents of the Support Tools folder are displayed in the right pane.

9. Check the box next to **DSKProbe.exe**. This indicates that you want to back up this file. (If Support Tools has not been installed on your PC, in this lab, you can substitute Notepad.exe in the C:\Windows folder in place of DSKProbe.exe.)

10. In the Backup media or file name field, type **C:\Backups\Lab11.bkf**. This specifies the name and location of the backup file you will create.

Follow these steps to start the backup process:

1. Click **Start Backup** on the Backup tab. The Backup Job Information dialog box opens. Notice that the Backup description text box displays date and time information about this backup. This information will appear later to help you identify the backup during a recovery process. If you are ever in a situation where you need to perform many backup operations (and therefore have to keep track of multiple backup sets), you should always use this field to describe the files contained in this set. Alternatively, you might wish to keep a backup log book and refer to an entry number in the log book that describes in detail what is contained in this backup set. Because this is your initial backup, you can ignore the other sections of the dialog box and click **Start Backup**.

2. The Backup Schedule dialog box briefly opens and then closes. Next, the Backup Progress dialog box opens. Quickly click **Cancel** in this dialog box.

3. The Backup dialog box opens and displays a message asking if you wish to complete the backup. Click the title bar of the Backup dialog box and drag it

aside so that you can view the Backup Progress dialog box. Answer these questions about the Backup Progress dialog box:

- What three things are provided to give you an idea of how the backup is progressing?

  _____

  _____

  _____

- Can you tell how many files must be backed up?

  _____

- Can you tell which files have already been completed or are currently being processed?

  _____

- What information continues to change even when the backup process is paused?

  _____

4. Click **Yes** on the Backup dialog box to indicate that you wish to continue the backup, and watch as the backup process completes.

5. When the backup is complete, click **Report** on the Backup Progress dialog box to open the Backup Log in Notepad.

6. Print and examine the report. What errors and causes are reported?

   _____

   _____

   _____

Follow these steps to delete files and observe the effects:

1. Log off and log on as a different user, and then right-click the **Recycle Bin** on the desktop. Select **Empty Recycle Bin** from the shortcut menu. Click **Yes** to confirm that you want to empty the Recycle Bin.

2. Open a command window. At the command prompt, type **DEL C:\BackMeUp*.***, and then press **Enter** to delete all files in the C:\BackMeUp directory. Confirm the deletion when prompted. Close the command window.

3. Delete **DSKProbe.exe** in the \Programs Files\Support Tools folder using Windows Explorer.

4. Double-click the **Recycle Bin** and note which files are displayed.

   ▪ Of the files that you deleted, which ones are not displayed in the Recycle Bin?

   _____

   _____

   ▪ Why do you think these files are missing?

   _____

   _____

   ▪ Of the files that you deleted, which files can you restore without using your backups and why?

   _____

   _____

5. Empty the Recycle Bin again and then, using Windows Explorer, look for your text files in C:\BackMeUp to confirm that they are gone.

6. Click **Start** on the taskbar, point to **Programs**, point to **Windows 2000 Support Tools**, point to **Tools**, and then click **DSKProbe.exe**. Record the results below, and then click **Cancel** to close the dialog box.

   _____

   _____

Follow these steps to restore the deleted files:

1. Log off and log on as an administrator. (Power Users do not have permission to restore files.)

2. Click **Start** on the taskbar, point to **Programs**, point to **Accessories**, point to **System Tools**, and then click **Backup**. The Backup window opens.

3. Click the **Restore** tab. In the left pane, click the plus sign to expand the file symbol and then expand the **Media Created *Date and Time*** symbol. Now attempt to expand the **"?"** folder on drive C. This opens the Backup File Name dialog box.

4. In the Backup File Name dialog box, click **Browse**.

5. Select **Lab11.bkf** from the **C:\Backups** folder and then click **Open**. The Select File to Catalog dialog box closes and the Backup Filename dialog box opens with the Operations Status dialog box beneath it.

6. Click **OK** on the Backup Filename dialog box. The Operations Status dialog box, which appeared previously, closes when the cataloging process is completed. Your backup will appear in the left pane of the Restore tab.

7. To restore files and folders, select the necessary check boxes and then click **Start Restore**. Do you think you could choose to restore only part of the information? If so, how?

_____

_____

8. The Confirm Restore dialog box opens. Click **OK** to continue.

9. The Enter Backup Filename dialog box opens and displays your backup file. Click **OK** to continue.

10. The Restore Progress dialog box opens. When the restore operation is complete, click **Close** to exit the Restore Progress dialog box.

11. To confirm that the restore is complete, look for your text files and launch **DSKProbe.exe** from the Start menu.

CRITICAL THINKING (additional 15 minutes)

Assign a Power User to a specific group (not the Administrators group), which will result in a reduction in the errors you encountered during the backup. Log in as this user and perform a backup called **Lab11b.bkf**, and then view and print the backup file. Are the members of the group to which you assigned the Power User allowed to restore files? How could you tell?

_____

_____

_____

Review Questions

1. Is it more important to back up Windows 2000/XP system files or data files? Why?

_____

_____

2. What is the Start menu shortcut for launching Windows 2000/XP Backup and Restore Tools?

_____

3. What feature (or features) do the Windows 2000/XP Backup and Restore Tools provide to help you if you are unfamiliar with the backup/restore process?

_____

_____

4. What will the Backup Job Information dialog box allow you to define? Why is this useful?

_____

_____

_____

5. If time were a factor when restoring critical data files, what could you specify (or decline to specify) in the left pane of the Restore tab to speed up the restoration?

_____

_____

9

LAB 9.3 RESEARCH DATA RECOVERY SERVICES

Objectives

The goal of this lab is to help you research data recovery services. After completing this lab, you will be able to:

➤ Find tips on how to make recovery services less necessary

➤ Explain how to minimize data loss

➤ Describe some recovery options

Materials Required

This lab will require the following:

➤ Internet access

Activity Background

You've probably experienced the feeling that comes with accidentally deleting or over-writing an important file. To make matters worse, you probably couldn't replace the file unless you had backed it up previously. Now imagine if the lost file consisted of financial information that could affect the success or failure of a business employing 100 employees or the lost file contained a creative work that took months to produce. You would certainly try to recover the data yourself, but if you were unable to, you might decide to seek the help of a professional data recovery service. In this lab, you will research sites offering such services.

Estimated completion time: **45 minutes**

ACTIVITY

Use your favorite search engine to research data recovery services. Alternatively, search these Web sites and answer the following questions:

➤ www.datarecoveryclinic.com

➤ www.savemyfiles.com

➤ www.drivesavers.com

➤ www.adv-data.com

➤ www.atl-datarecovery.com

1. Name two Web sites that offer a do-it-yourself data recovery option in addition to professional recovery services.

_____

_____

2. Give an example of a service that offers recovery of data in a Linux operating environment.

_____

3. Give two examples of services that recover data from striped sets or volume sets.

_____

_____

4. From what type or types of media can files be recovered? Circle the correct answer(s):

   a. Tape

   b. CD-ROM

   c. Zip disk

   d. Floppy disk

   e. Hard disk

5. Give two examples of companies that will not charge you if they are unable to recover your important data.

   _____

   _____

6. List two general levels of turn-around time for data recovery.

   _____

   _____

7. What measures are taken when recovering ultrasensitive (secure) data?

   _____

   _____

   _____

8. Besides natural disaster and mechanical failure, what are four other common causes of data loss?

   _____

   _____

   _____

   _____

9. If you learn that you have lost data on drive D, what things should you absolutely not do? Circle the correct answer(s):

   a. Install recovery software on drive C

   b. Defragment drive D

   c. Restore objects in the Recycle Bin

   d. Install recovery software on drive D

9

10. Give two examples of services designed to proactively prevent data loss.

_____

_____

11. List some reasons why it might be impossible to recover some data.

_____

_____

_____

12. Will you always be able to recover all the data that you lose? Why or why not?

_____

_____

_____

13. Why is it important to perform hard drive data recovery in a clean room?

_____

_____

_____

14. What class of clean room should be used for data recovery?

_____

15. In what ways can your recovered data be returned to you?

_____

_____

_____

16. Give one example of a company that specializes in recovery from optical media.

_____

17. What Web site (or sites) includes a "museum" of interesting recovery projects they have undertaken?

_____

_____

18. What circumstances might require that the data recovery service perform a recovery attempt at your site?

_____

_____

19. List two companies that recover data from Flash cards or memory sticks.

_____

_____

20. Pick two of the companies you researched and list some of the other services and products they offer.

_____

_____

Review Questions

1. Based on your research, what impression do you get about how expensive data recovery services are? Explain your answer.

_____

_____

2. Based on your research, do you think individuals or companies would be more interested in using data recovery services? Why?

_____

_____

3. In general, do companies specialize in recovery from specific types of media or do they tend to provide data recovery for all types of media?

_____

_____

4. Based on your research, what three factors would affect the price you might pay for recovery services from a specific provider?

_____

_____

LAB 9.4 USE DO-IT-YOURSELF DATA RECOVERY SOFTWARE

Objectives

The goal of this lab is to help you explore options for recovering data from a malfunctioning hard drive. After completing this lab, you will be able to:

➤ Search the Internet for recovery services

➤ Search *www.ontrack.com* to learn about data recovery

➤ Use EasyRecovery to locate files for possible recovery

Materials Required

This lab will require the following:

➤ Windows 98, Windows 2000, or Windows XP operating system

➤ Internet access

Activity Background

Probably nothing makes a computer user panic more than the prospect of losing important data. As a technician, you have to be prepared to recover data from a variety of storage media; most often, however, you will be asked to recover it from a hard drive. Data on a hard drive may be lost for a variety of reasons ranging from human error to a natural disaster that renders the drive inoperable. In this lab, you will investigate various data recovery options and learn to use one of them.

Estimated completion time: **60 minutes**

Note that if you are using a modem and phone line to connect to the Internet, the time required to download software might increase the time required for this lab.

ACTIVITY

When you need to find information on the Internet, it's often helpful to start with a broad search using a search engine such as Google (*www.google.com*) or AltaVista (*www.altavista.com*). To learn more, follow these steps:

1. Open your browser and go to your favorite search site on the Internet.

2. Search for information on data recovery services.

3. Explore as many links as you have time for. Then, list five Web sites that offer data recovery services:

_____

_____

_____

_____

_____

One major data recovery company is called Ontrack. You'll explore the Ontrack Web site in the following steps:

1. Open your Internet browser and go to *www.ontrack.com*.

2. Answer the following questions, using the links on the Ontrack Web site. If you cannot obtain all the answers from this site, supplement it with information from one or more of the sites you found in your earlier search process. Print pages supporting all of your answers.

   ■ According to the information you printed, what are the two top causes of data loss?

   _____

   _____

   ■ What data recovery options are available?

   _____

   _____

   _____

   ■ What solutions will work with your operating system?

   _____

9

- What should you do if a hardware malfunction is detected?

  _____

  _____

- Is Internet access necessary for this recovery option?

  _____

- Will this option work if you cannot boot from the hard drive?

  _____

3. Return to the Ontrack home page.

4. Locate and follow the link that leads to information about EasyRecovery DataRecovery software.

5. Using information on the EasyRecovery DataRecovery page, answer the following questions.

   - Does this software need to be installed prior to the data loss?

     _____

   - Does this software require that your system be healthy enough to boot from the hard drive?

     _____

   - Can this product recover data from a deleted partition? Print the Web page supporting your answer.

     _____

   - Can this product recover data from removable media? If so, what types?

     _____

     _____

     _____

   Now you will download and use the EasyRecovery Professional Trial edition software, but be aware that Web sites change often, so the links might not read exactly as described in the following steps. Do the following:

1. Create a folder on your hard drive named C:\Downloads. Under this folder, create a folder named C:\Downloads\EasyRecovery. If you put all downloaded files into folders under C:\Downloads, it is easy to find downloaded files and to know their purpose.

2. On the EasyRecovery DataRecovery Web page, under the description of EasyRecovery Professional Trial edition, click the link **Download Trial edition**. The Ontrack Login page appears.

3. Click the link to **Create My Profile**. The New User page appears.

4. Enter your information to create your profile and click **Continue**. The Download page and the File Download dialog box appear.

5. Download the file **Er.exe**, saving it to C:\Downloads\EasyRecovery.

6. Close all open windows and open Windows Explorer. Double-click the **Er.exe** icon. The EasyRecovery window opens.

7. To continue installing EasyRecovery, select **English** as the language. The InstallShield Wizard launches to complete the installation process.

8. Accept the End-User License Agreement (EULA).

   Note that installing the EasyRecovery software on the partition containing the data you want to recover may in fact overwrite the lost data. To avoid this problem, you should install EasyRecovery on a separate partition or PC and then create an EasyRecovery emergency boot disk. For the purpose of this lab, however, it's okay to install on your current PC.

9. Click **Next** several times to continue through each window of the installation process using the default settings.

10. When prompted, select **Yes, I want to restart my computer now** and click **Finish** to complete the EasyRecovery installation. Your PC will restart.

The EasyRecovery Professional shortcut now appears on your desktop. Follow these steps to use the software:

1. Double-click the **EasyRecovery Professional** shortcut on your desktop. An EasyRecovery notice opens and informs you that the edition can identify recoverable files but that you must purchase the full version to recover files. Click **OK** to close the notice. The Ontrack EasyRecovery Professional application launches.

2. Select the **Data Recovery** button and then the **Advanced Recovery Option**. A warning message is displayed suggesting that you copy recovered data to a different media such as a Zip drive or floppy disk if you suspect all partitions on your hard drive might be damaged. Click **OK** to close the notice. The Data Recovery window appears. See Figure 9-1.

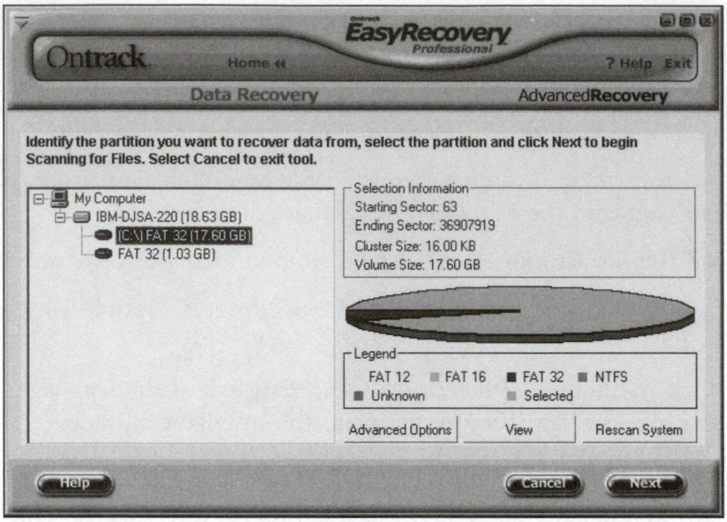

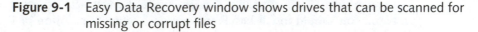

Figure 9-1   Easy Data Recovery window shows drives that can be scanned for missing or corrupt files

3. A list of drives on your system is displayed in the window. Notice that EasyRecovery graphically displays partition information along with a legend defining partition information and use. Select drive C and answer the following questions:

- What is the starting sector for drive C?

   _____

- What is the ending sector for drive C?

   _____

- What is the cluster size for drive C?

   _____

- What file system does drive C use?

   _____

4. Click **Next** to begin scanning for files that the software might recover. The process might take some time as the software searches the entire drive C. You can cancel the process at any time by clicking **Cancel** on the Scanning for Files dialog box. If you cancel the process, a question appears asking, "Would you like to save the state of your recovery to resume at a later time?" Click **No**.

5. A warning message appears stating that the version cannot recover files. Click **OK** to close the notice.

6. A list of files that the software can recover appears. A Condition status appears for each file. Status options are G, D, X, S, B, and N. Click the **Filter Options** button and interpret each of these statuses:

   ■ The status G means: _____

   ■ The status D means: _____

   ■ The status X means: _____

   ■ The status S means: _____

   ■ The status B means: _____

   ■ The status N means: _____

7. Click **OK** to close the Filter Options window.

8. On the Data Recovery window, in the left pane, a hierarchical list of folders is displayed. The right pane shows recoverable files within those folders. You can select folders to search for a corrupted or lost file you are trying to recover. Open a folder on drive C and select a file in that folder. Click **View File** to view the contents of the file. Viewing the contents of a file can often help in locating just the right file.

9. If you were using the purchased version of the software, once you had located the files to recover, you would click **Next** and then specify a destination for the files. These files would then be copied from their current location to the specified destination. Notice that Next is grayed out because you are using the trial version of the software.

10. Click **Cancel** to return to the main window. A message appears asking if you would like to save the state of your recovery. Click **No**.

11. Besides the AdvancedRecovery option on the main window, five other options, which are listed below, are available under Data Recovery. Give a brief explanation of each option:

    ■ DeletedRecovery

    _____

    _____

    ■ FormatRecovery

    _____

    _____

    ■ RawRecovery

    _____

    _____

- ResumeRecovery

  _____

  _____

- EmergencyDiskette

  _____

  _____

12. Using procedures listed in earlier labs, print a screen shot of this EasyRecovery window.

13. Close the EasyRecovery window.

14. Your instructor might tell you to uninstall the EasyRecovery software. If so, uninstall the software using Add/Remove Programs applet in Control Panel.

Review Questions

1. What are three causes of data loss?

   _____

   _____

2. Which of these causes would Remote Data Recovery and EasyRecovery fail to overcome?

   _____

3. Is it normally possible to recover lost data that has been overwritten by other data? Explain.

   _____

   _____

4. What are some symptoms of a hardware malfunction that would result in data loss?

   _____

   _____

5. List some steps to prevent mechanical drive failure.

   _____

   _____

LAB 9.5 TROUBLESHOOT HARD DRIVES

Objectives

The goal of this lab is to help you troubleshoot common hard drive problems. After completing this lab, you will be able to:

➤ Simulate common hard drive problems

➤ Diagnose and repair common hard drive problems

➤ Document the process

Materials Required

This lab will require the following:

➤ A computer with a hard drive subsystem that you can sabotage

➤ Bootable disk

➤ PC toolkit with ground strap

➤ Workgroup of 2–4 students

Activity Background

This lab will give you practice diagnosing and remedying common hard drive problems.

Estimated completion time: **60 minutes**

ACTIVITY

1. Verify that your hard drive is working by using a command prompt or Windows Explorer to display files on the drive.

2. Switch computers with another team.

3. Sabotage the other team's computer by doing one of the following:

   ▪ Remove or incorrectly configure the drive jumpers

   ▪ Remove the power connector from the drive

   ▪ Switch data cables to place devices on incorrect IDE channels

   ▪ Disable IDE controllers in CMOS setup

   ▪ If allowed by your instructor, delete partitions on the hard drive

4. Return to your computer and examine it for any symptoms of a problem.

5. On a separate piece of paper, answer the following questions relating to the problem's symptoms:

   - What symptoms would a user notice? (Describe the symptoms as the user might describe them.)

   - Does the system boot from the hard drive?

   - Does POST display the hard drive?

   - Can you boot from a floppy disk and change to the drive in question?

   - Does the CMOS HDD Autodetect option detect the hard drive?

6. On a separate piece of paper, before you actually begin your investigation, state your initial diagnosis.

7. Diagnose and repair the problem.

8. On a separate piece of paper, list the steps required to confirm your diagnosis and solve the problem.

9. Answer the following questions relating to your final conclusions:

   - What was the problem?

   _____

   - What did you do to correct the problem?

   _____

   _____

   _____

   - Was your preliminary diagnosis correct?

   _____

10. Repeat steps 1–9, choosing actions at random from the list in step 3, until your team has performed all the items listed in step 3. Be sure to write down the relevant information (as instructed in the steps) for each problem.

Review Questions

1. What was the first indication that the power was disconnected from your drive?

_____

_____

2. In what incorrect drive configuration would you be able to access files on the hard drive by booting from the floppy drive?

_____

_____

3. What incorrect configurations have similar symptoms?

_____

_____

4. What problem resulted in no drives being detected except for the floppy drive?

_____

_____

5. List the steps required to use a drive whose partitions have been deleted.

_____

_____

_____

_____

_____

LAB 9.6 CRITICAL THINKING: SABOTAGE AND REPAIR A HARD DRIVE SUBSYSTEM

Objectives

The goal of this lab is to learn to troubleshoot a hard drive by repairing a sabotaged system.

Materials Required

This lab will require the following:

➤ A PC designated for a sabotage (containing no important data)

➤ Workgroup of 2–4 students

Activity Background

You have learned about several tools and methods for troubleshooting and recovering from a hard drive failure. This lab gives you the opportunity to use these skills in a troubleshooting situation. Your group will work with another group to sabotage a system first and then recover your own sabotaged system.

Estimated completion time: **45 minutes**

ACTIVITY

1. If your system's hard drive contains important data, back up that data to another media. Is there anything else you would like to back up before the system is sabotaged by another group?

_____

2. Trade systems with another group and sabotage the other group's system while they sabotage your system. Do one thing that will cause the hard drive to fail to work or give errors after the boot. Use any of the problems suggested in Lab 9.5, or you can introduce a new problem. (Do *not* alter the operating system files.) What did you do to sabotage the other team's system?

_____

_____

3. Return to your system and troubleshoot it.

4. Describe the problem as a user would describe it to you if you were working at a help desk.

_____

_____

5. What is your first guess as to the source of the problem?

_____

6. List the steps you took in the troubleshooting process.

_____

_____

_____

_____

_____

_____

7. What did you do that finally solved the problem and returned the system to good working order?

_____

_____

Review Questions

1. Now that you have been through the previous troubleshooting experience, what would you do differently the next time the same symptoms present themselves?

_____

2. What software utilities did you use or could have used to solve the problem?

_____

3. What third-party software utility might have been useful in solving this problem?

_____

4. In a real-life situation, what might happen that would cause this problem to occur? List three things.

_____

_____

_____

9

SUPPORTING I/O DEVICES

The following grid shows the correlation between the labs in this chapter and the A+ Guides to Hardware and Software.

A+ Guide to Managing and Maintaining Your PC, Fifth Edition	A+ Guide to Hardware, Third Edition	A+ Guide to Software, Third Edition
Lab 10.1 Gather Information on Your System		Chapter 8
Lab 10.2 Identify Hardware Conflicts Using Device Manager		Chapter 8
Lab 10.3 Diagnose Simple Hardware Problems		Chapter 8
Lab 10.4 Plan and Design a Null Modem Cable		Chapter 8
Lab 10.5 Use a Multimeter to Inspect Cables		Chapter 8
Lab 10.6 Critical Thinking: Sabotage and Repair a System		Chapter 8

LAB 10.1 GATHER INFORMATION ON YOUR SYSTEM

Objectives

The goal of this lab is to teach you how to use SANDRA, the Control Panel, and other sources to compile information on your system specifications. After completing this lab, you will be able to:

➤ Use various SANDRA modules to get information about your system

➤ Use Control Panel applets to get information about your system

➤ Compile a documentation notebook

Materials Required

This lab will require the following:

➤ Windows 98 or Windows 2000/XP operating system

➤ Documentation that you collected about your computer in Lab 4.2

➤ SANDRA, Standard version, installed in Lab 1.3

Activity Background

As you continue to work with different kinds of computers, you will find it extremely useful to maintain a report listing the components installed on each computer. This is especially important if you are responsible for a large number of computers. In this lab, you will create such a document. (Note that you will need to refer to this document in future labs.) You will use SANDRA in this lab, which you installed earlier.

Estimated completion time: **45 minutes**

ACTIVITY

Fill in the following charts, which will become part of the total documentation that you will keep about your PC. When necessary, refer to the documentation about your computer that you collected in Lab 4.2 or use the SANDRA software. After you have finished the charts, make copies of them and place them in your computer's documentation notebook. If you are not sure which menus and applets to use in SANDRA, experiment to find the necessary information. Some information can be found in more than one place.

Table 10-1   Computer Fact Sheet

Location of computer	
Owner	
Date purchased	
Date warranty expires	
Size and speed of CPU	
Type of motherboard	
Amount of RAM	
Type of monitor	
Type of video card	
Hard drive type and size	
Size of disk drive A	
Size of disk drive B (if present)	

Table 10-2   Software Installed

Software install name	Version	Installed by	Date

Table 10-3   Other Devices

Name of device	IRQ	I/O address	DMA channel device	Driver filename
Serial port 1				
Serial port 2				
Parallel port				
Mouse				
Modem				
CD-ROM drive				
Display adapter				
Network card				

Create a documentation notebook or binder for your computer that includes copies of these charts, as well as any other documentation that you have collected about your computer. Save space for troubleshooting steps that you will learn in future labs. You will need this notebook in future labs.

Review Questions

1. How did you determine the CPU type?

   _____

   _____

2. How did you determine the driver used by your display adapter?

   _____

   _____

3. List two ways to determine the amount of RAM installed on a system.

   _____

   _____

4. Why would it be important for a PC technician to keep documentation on the computers for which he or she is responsible?

   _____

   _____

LAB 10.2 IDENTIFY HARDWARE CONFLICTS USING DEVICE MANAGER

Objectives

The goal of this lab is to help you learn to use Device Manager to identify hardware conflicts. After completing this lab, you will be able to:

➤ Use Device Manager to investigate your system specifications

➤ Detect hardware conflicts using Device Manager

➤ Use Device Properties to determine which resources are causing a conflict

Materials Required

This lab will require the following:

➤ Windows 98 or Windows 2000/XP operating system

➤ Workstation with no hardware resource conflicts

➤ Hardware device that you can install to create a hardware resource conflict

➤ Access to the Windows installation CD or the setup files stored at another location

Activity Background

Device Manager is an excellent tool for finding information about your hardware specifications. You can also use it to diagnose problems with hardware devices, including those caused by two or more devices attempting to use the same system resources (a situation called a hardware resource conflict). Among other things, Device Manager can identify faulty or disabled devices, conflicting devices, and resources currently in use. This lab will teach you how to use Device Manager to discover this information. You will start by examining your system and verifying that no hardware resource conflicts currently exist on your system. Then you will install a device that creates a resource conflict and observe the effects.

> **Estimated completion time: 30 minutes**

ACTIVITY

You can use Device Manager to print a report about your system. It is a good idea to print such a report when your system is working correctly. You can then use that report later as a baseline comparison when troubleshooting conflicts or other problems.

1. Open Device Manager and print a report that provides information on all devices and also provides a system summary. If you are using a lab PC that does not have access to a printer, you can save the report to a floppy disk and go to another computer to print it.

2. Answer the following:

   - What were the steps you used to print the report?

     _____

     _____

   - How many pages are included in the report?

     _____

   - In one or two sentences, describe the type of information included on the report.

     _____

     _____

     _____

   - List two items in the report that are not displayed in the Device Manager windows.

     _____

3. Put the Device Manager report in your documentation notebook (which you created in Lab 10.1).

Now you will use Device Manager to verify that there are no hardware conflicts.

1. Using Device Manager, check for conflicts among devices. If any conflicts exist, they will be identified by a yellow triangle with an exclamation point. (Note that if a device has been disabled and is not working at all, a red circle with a slash through it will appear over the yellow triangle and exclamation point.)

2. Shut down the system and install the component and its drivers provided by your instructor, which should conflict with another component already installed on the system. If you don't have a device that will cause a conflict, remove a nonessential device such as a modem card or sound card, which will at least cause Device Manager to report an error.

3. Reboot and install drivers if prompted. You might be asked to provide access to the Windows setup files. Did you see a message indicating a conflict or other error? If so, record the message here:

_____

_____

4. Open Device Manager. Does Device Manager report any conflicting devices? Describe the problem as Device Manager reports it, listing all problematic devices:

_____

_____

5. For each device reporting a conflict, access the device's Properties window by right-clicking the device and selecting **Properties** from the shortcut menu. What messages do you see in the Device Status field?

_____

_____

6. Still using the device's Properties window in Device Manager, click the **Resource** tab. What message do you see in the Conflicting Device field?

_____

7. Examine the Resource Type and Settings field. What resources is the device using?

_____

_____

8. Does it appear that you may be able to change the settings for this device?

_____

9. Close the device Properties window.

CRITICAL THINKING (additional 15 minutes)

While the two devices are in conflict, use Device Manager to print a report on your system. Remember that, if your PC is not connected to a printer, you can save the report to a floppy disk and print it from another computer. Compare the report created when the system was working properly to the report created when conflicts existed. Note the differences in the two reports.

Now that you have observed two devices in conflict, you'll remove one of the conflicting devices. When you remove a device, you should first uninstall it in Device Manager. If you don't first uninstall the device before removing it from your system, later, when you want to install a similar or the same device, you will end up with two of them installed under Device Manager, which can cause the new device to not work.

Follow these steps to uninstall the device under Windows and then remove it:

1. For Windows 98, highlight the problem device in Device Manager and click **Remove**. For Windows 2000/XP, right-click the device and then click **Uninstall** in the shortcut menu. If prompted to restart the computer, click **No**.

2. Close Device Manager and shut down the system.

3. Remove the device you installed earlier.

4. Restart the computer, open Device Manager and verify that no conflicts exist.

Review Questions

1. What symbol in Device Manager indicates a component is not working properly?

_____

2. What two devices in your system were in conflict?

_____

3. What resource(s) was causing a conflict?

_____

_____

4. Before physically removing a device from a system, what should you do first?

_____

10

5. What would happen if you did not uninstall the device before removing it from your system?

LAB 10.3 DIAGNOSE SIMPLE HARDWARE PROBLEMS

Objectives

The goal of this lab is to give you practice diagnosing and repairing simple hardware problems. After completing this lab, you will be able to:

➤ Start with a functioning PC, introduce a problem, and remedy the problem

➤ Diagnose a problem caused by someone else

➤ Record the troubleshooting process

Materials Required

This lab will require the following:

➤ Windows 98, Windows 2000, or Windows XP operating system

➤ PC toolkit including screwdrivers and ground strap

➤ Pen and paper

➤ Documentation notebook that you began creating in Lab 10.1

➤ Workgroup of 2–4 students

Activity Background

If you ever work in a shop dealing with the general public, about half of the problems you see will be the result of an inexperienced person making a slight mistake when configuring a system and lacking the knowledge to diagnose and remedy the problem. Unless you are very good and very lucky, you yourself will make many of the same mistakes from time to time. Your advantage is that you will have the experience to narrow down and identify the problem and then to fix it. This lab provides experience troubleshooting and repairing simple problems. Before you begin this lab, team up with another workgroup in your class. Your team will work with this other group throughout the lab.

Estimated completion time: **60 minutes**

ACTIVITY

1. Verify that your team's system is working correctly. Also, verify that you have the completed charts for your system from Lab 10.1.

2. Make one of the following changes to your team's system:

   ■ Remove the power cable from the hard drive on the primary interface or highest SCSI ID

   ■ Reverse the data cable for the floppy drive

   ■ Remove the RAM and place it safely inside the case so the other team cannot see it

   ■ Disable IDE, SCSI, or Serial ATA controllers in CMOS

   ■ Remove the power-on wire from the motherboard connection

   ■ Partially remove the data cable from the hard drive

   ■ For IDE drives, swap master/slave jumper assignments or set both drives to the same setting

3. Switch places with the other team, and then diagnose and remedy the problem on your team's PC. Record the troubleshooting process on a separate sheet of paper.

   ■ Describe the problem as a user would describe it to you if you were working at a Help desk.

   _____

   ■ What is your first guess as to the source of the problem?

   _____

   ■ What did you do that solved the problem and returned the system to good working order?

   _____

4. Repeat Steps 1 through 3, choosing items at random from the list in step 2. Continue until your team has made all the changes listed in step 2.

CRITICAL THINKING (additional 30 minutes)

If time permits, try introducing two changes at a time. This can prove to be a much more difficult situation.

Review Questions

1. What problems resulted in a "non-system disk" error?

   _____

   _____

2. What was typically the first indication that RAM had been removed?

   _____

   _____

3. What was the first indication of a problem with drive assignments?

_____

_____

4. Name three problems resulting in symptoms similar to those related to a problem with the primary slave drive.

_____

_____

_____

5. What was the first indication of a floppy drive problem?

_____

_____

LAB 10.4 PLAN AND DESIGN A NULL MODEM CABLE

Objectives

The goal of this lab is to help you practice visualizing cable and pin-out arrangements by planning a null modem cable. After completing this lab, you will be able to:

➤ Plan a 25-pin null modem cable

➤ Use the Internet to find information on a 9-pin null modem cable

➤ Plan a 9-pin null modem cable

Materials Required

This lab will require the following:

➤ Internet access

Activity Background

A null modem cable can be used for file transfers between PCs. Such a cable is slow compared to the cables used on a modern network, but it will do in a pinch. This lab explains how to plan the pin-outs for a null modem cable.

Estimated completion time: **30 minutes**

ACTIVITY

1. Complete the drawing in Figure 10-1 to illustrate how pins on a 25-pin null modem cable connect. Draw lines between a pin on the left and its corresponding pin on the right. Use the information in Table 10-4 to complete the drawing.

Table 10-4   Connections on a 25-pin null modem cable

Pin number on the left connector	Pin number on the right connector	How the wire connecting the two pins is used
2	3	Data sent by one computer is received by the other.
3	2	Data received by one computer is sent by the other.
6	20	One end says to the other end, "I'm able to talk."
20	6	One end hears the other end say, "I'm able to talk."
4	5	One end says to the other, "I'm ready to talk."
5	4	One end hears the other say, "I'm ready to talk."
7	7	Both ends are grounded.

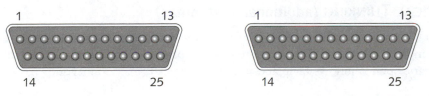

Figure 10-1   Complete the drawing by connecting each pin on the left to a pin on the right that is used by a 25-pin null modem cable

2. Search the Internet for the pin-out specification for a 9-pin null modem cable and complete Table 10-5.

Table 10-5 Connections on a 9-pin null modem cable

Pin number on one connector	Pin number of the other connector	How the wire connecting the two pins is used

3. Use the information entered in Table 10-5 to complete Figure 10-2, which shows how pins on a 9-pin null modem cable connect.

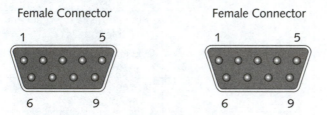

Figure 10-2   Complete the drawing by connecting each pin on the left to a pin on the right that is used by a 9-pin null modem cable

CRITICAL THINKING (additional 30 minutes)

If you have access to a null modem cable, use it to network two PCs and pass files between them in both directions. On a separate piece of paper, list the steps you used to do this. If necessary, open Windows Help and search on Direct Cable Connection.

Review Questions

1. Should a null modem cable be used in place of a modern network connection, if a network connection is available? Why or why not?

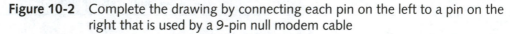

2. How many pins are normally found on a serial connector on the PC itself? Is it male or female?

_____

_____

3. With what industry standard should serial cables comply?

_____

_____

4. Describe a situation in which it is appropriate to use a null modem cable that has a 9-pin connector on one end and a 25-pin connector on the other.

_____

_____

CRITICAL THINKING (additional 15 minutes)

Draw a diagram showing the pin-outs for a 9-pin to 25-pin null modem cable.

10

LAB 10.5 USE A MULTIMETER TO INSPECT CABLES

Objectives

The goal of this lab is to teach you how to use a multimeter to test cables. After completing this lab, you will be able to:

➤ Set up a multimeter to measure resistance

➤ Test cables for resistance to determine pin arrangements

➤ Test cables for broken connections

➤ Measure resistance in a resistor

Materials Required

This lab will require the following:

➤ A multimeter

➤ Three assorted cables

➤ Assorted resistors

➤ Pin-out specifications for cables from Lab 10.4

➤ Internet access (optional)

➤ Workgroup of 2-4 students

Activity Background

One of the multimeter's many uses is to determine if a cable is good or bad. You can also use a multimeter to determine the cable's pin arrangement. All of this is done by measuring resistance in the cable. Resistance is measured in Ohms, with infinite resistance indicating that no electricity can flow. A measure of zero Ohms or zero resistance means that electricity can flow (a state referred to as continuity). A resistor is a device that resists or controls the flow of electricity in a circuit, and a multimeter can be used to measure a resistor. You will begin the lab by setting up and testing your multimeter. Then you will measure resistance in cables and resistors.

Estimated completion time: **45 minutes**

ACTIVITY

To set up and test your multimeter:

1. Set the multimeter to measure resistance.

2. With the probes not in contact with anything, observe the reading on the meter. The reading should be infinity, or 99999.99999, or similar.

3. With the probes touching each other, observe the reading on the meter. The reading should be 0 or similar.

Now that you have verified that your multimeter is working properly, you can use it to measure the resistance or continuity in a cable. Examine cables provided by your instructor. In the following steps you will use your multimeter to discover the pin-outs for each cable:

1. On a separate piece of paper, create a table (similar to Table 10-4) for each cable indicating the cable's pin-outs. Can you identify the cable from your table and your knowledge of cables?

2. For Cable 1, complete the following:

   ■ Description of cable connectors: _____

   ■ Number of pins on each end of the cable: _____

   ■ Number of pins on each end of the cable that are used: _____

   ■ Type of cable: _____

3. For Cable 2, complete the following:

   ■ Description of cable connectors: _____

   ■ Number of pins on each end of the cable: _____

- Number of pins on each end of the cable that are used: _____
- Type of cable: _____

4. For Cable 3, complete the following:
   - Description of cable connectors: _____
   - Number of pins on each end of the cable: _____
   - Number of pins on each end of the cable that are used: _____
   - Type of cable: _____

Suppose a user comes to you with a problem. He has a cable that connects his computer's serial port to a serial printer. He needs to order more of the same cables, but he does not know if this cable is a regular serial cable or a specialized cable made specifically for this printer. One connector on the cable is 9-pin and the other connector is 25-pin. Using this information, answer the following:

1. Describe how to determine what kind of cable he needs to order.

   _____

   _____

   _____

   _____

2. Suppose the cable is not a regular serial cable but a specialized cable. How might you give the user the pin-outs necessary to order new custom-made cables?

   _____

   _____

   _____

   _____

   _____

So far you have used a multimeter to discover cable specifications. Next, you will use the multimeter to measure the resistances of several resistors.

1. Measure each resistor and record the results in Table 10-6. Note that resistors have colored bands indicating their intended resistance.

10

Table 10-6   Resistor measurements

Resistor	Resistance Reading

CRITICAL THINKING (additional 45 minutes)

An Ethernet network uses a patch cable to connect a PC to a hub or other network device but uses a crossover cable to connect a PC to another PC or to connect a hub to another hub. Answer the following questions:

1. How many pins does an RJ-11 patch cable or crossover cable have?

   _____

2. Research the Internet for the pin-outs of a crossover cable and a patch cable. Draw a diagram of the pin-outs of each cable.

3. Have your instructor give you one patch cable and one crossover cable. Can you tell which cable is which by physically examining them?

   _____

4. Use your multimeter to confirm which cable is the patch cable and which is the crossover cable. Which pins did you examine?

   _____

Review Questions

1. When a multimeter is set to measure resistance, what reading would you expect when the probes are touching?

   _____

2. When a multimeter is set to measure resistance, what reading would you expect when the probes are not touching anything?

   _____

3. Suppose all pins match pin-outs except one at each end. Suppose these non-matching pins have no continuity with any other pin. What is the likely condition of the cable?

_____

_____

_____

4. What do the colors on resistors indicate?

_____

5. When you are measuring resistance, is there enough electricity in the wire to cause you harm?

_____

6. In the last lab, you learned you could connect two computers using a null modem cable. What is a faster way to connect two computers when each computer has a NIC installed? What type of cable would you use?

_____

10

LAB 10.6 CRITICAL THINKING: SABOTAGE AND REPAIR A SYSTEM

Objectives

The goal of this lab is to learn to troubleshoot a system by recovering from a sabotaged system.

Materials Required

This lab will require the following:

➤ A PC (containing no important data) that has been designated for sabotage

➤ Workgroup of 2-4 students

Activity Background

You have learned about several tools and methods that you can use to troubleshoot and repair a failed system or failed hardware devices. This lab gives you the opportunity to use these skills in a simulated troubleshooting situation. Your group will work with another group to first sabotage a system and then repair another failed system.

Estimated completion time: **45 minutes**

ACTIVITY

1. If the hard drive contains important data, back up that data to another media. Back up anything else you would like to save before the system is sabotaged by another group and note it below.

   _____

2. Trade systems with another group and sabotage the other group's system while they sabotage your system. Do one thing that will cause the system to fail to work or give errors after booting. Use any of the problems introduced in Lab 10.3 or introduce a new problem. (Do *not* alter the operating system files.) What did you do to sabotage the other team's system?

   _____

   _____

3. Return to your system and troubleshoot it.

4. Describe the problem as a user would describe it to you if you were working at a Help desk.

   _____

   _____

5. What is your first guess as to the source of the problem?

   _____

6. List the steps you took in the troubleshooting process.

   _____

   _____

   _____

   _____

   _____

   _____

7. What did you do that finally solved the problem and returned the system to good working order?

_____

_____

Review Questions

1. Thinking back on this troubleshooting experience, what would you do differently the next time the same symptoms present themselves?

_____

2. What software utilities did you use or could you have used to solve the problem?

_____

3. What third-party software utility or hardware device might have been useful in solving this problem?

_____

4. In a real-life situation, what might cause this problem to occur? List three possible causes.

_____

_____

_____

10

CHAPTER ELEVEN

MULTIMEDIA DEVICES AND MASS STORAGE

Labs included in this chapter

➤ Lab 11.1 Install a Sound Card

➤ Lab 11.2 Install a PC Video Camera

➤ Lab 11.3 Compare CD and DVD Technologies

➤ Lab 11.4 Install Dual Monitors in Windows XP

➤ Lab 11.5 Research Digital Cameras

➤ Lab 11.6 Explore Windows XP Audio Features

The following grid shows the correlation between the labs in this chapter and the A+ Guides to Hardware and Software.

A+ Guide to Managing and Maintaining Your PC, Fifth Edition	A+ Guide to Hardware, Third Edition	A+ Guide to Software, Third Edition
Lab 11.1 Install a Sound Card	Chapter 9	
Lab 11.2 Install a PC Video Camera	Chapter 9	
Lab 11.3 Compare CD and DVD Technologies	Chapter 9	
Lab 11.4 Install Dual Monitors in Windows XP	Chapter 9	
Lab 11.5 Research Digital Cameras	Chapter 9	
Lab 11.6 Explore Windows XP Audio Features	Chapter 9	

LAB 11.1 INSTALL A SOUND CARD

Objectives

The goal of this lab is to help you install a sound card. After completing this lab, you will be able to:

➤ Physically install a sound card

➤ Install device drivers

➤ Test the card and adjust the volume

Materials Required

This lab will require the following:

➤ Windows 2000 operating system

➤ Windows 2000 installation CD or installation files stored in another location as specified by your instructor

➤ Empty expansion slot

➤ Compatible sound card with speakers or headphones

➤ Sound card device drivers (on an installation floppy disk or CD, or stored in another location as specified by your instructor)

➤ Motherboard documentation if your system uses embedded audio

➤ PC toolkit with ground strap

➤ Internet access (optional)

Activity Background

Two of the most popular multimedia devices are the sound card and the embedded audio device. A sound card enables a computer to receive sound input and to output sound such as when playing a music CD. Alternatively, many newer systems have audio embedded on the motherboard. As an A+ computer technician you will need to know how to install a sound card, either when you are putting together a computer from scratch, repairing a failed device, or upgrading components on an existing system. In this lab, you will install, configure, and test a sound card.

Estimated completion time: **45 minutes**

ACTIVITY

First you must discover whether your system has a sound card, embedded audio device, or perhaps both or neither. Use the skills you have learned to discover and describe what audio configuration your system currently has. Describe the configuration below, and then work through the necessary steps to complete the lab in the following general order:

- Disable any existing audio devices in Windows.

- Remove or disable the hardware device(s).

- Verify that the audio is disabled.

- Physically install the sound card.

- Install the drivers in Windows.

- Verify the function of audio features.

- Return the system to its original state (optional, per instructor's directions).

_____

_____

_____

Follow these steps to uninstall a sound card or embedded audio device in Windows:

1. After you have logged on as an administrator, open the Control Panel.

2. From the Control Panel, double-click the **Add/Remove Hardware** icon to launch the Add/Remove Hardware Wizard. The wizard opens.

3. In the Add/Remove Hardware Wizard dialog box, select the radio button next to **Uninstall/Unplug a device**. Click **Next** to continue.

4. In the Add/Remove Hardware Wizard dialog box, select the radio button next to **Uninstall a device**, as shown in Figure 11-1. Click **Next** to continue.

11

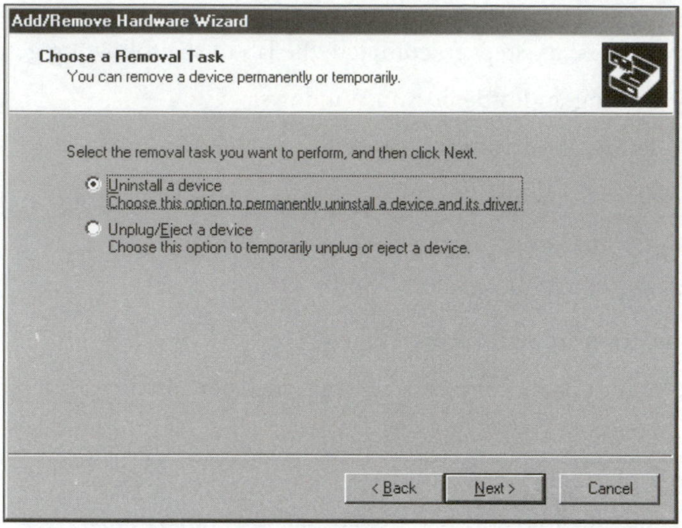

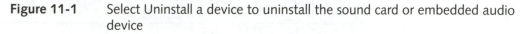

Figure 11-1 Select Uninstall a device to uninstall the sound card or embedded audio device

5. In the Devices list of the Add/Remove Hardware Wizard dialog box, scroll down until you locate your audio device. Click your device to select and highlight it, then click **Next** to continue.

6. In the Add/Remove Hardware Wizard dialog box, select the radio button next to **Yes, I want to uninstall this device**. Figure 11-2 shows this dialog box. Click **Next** to continue.

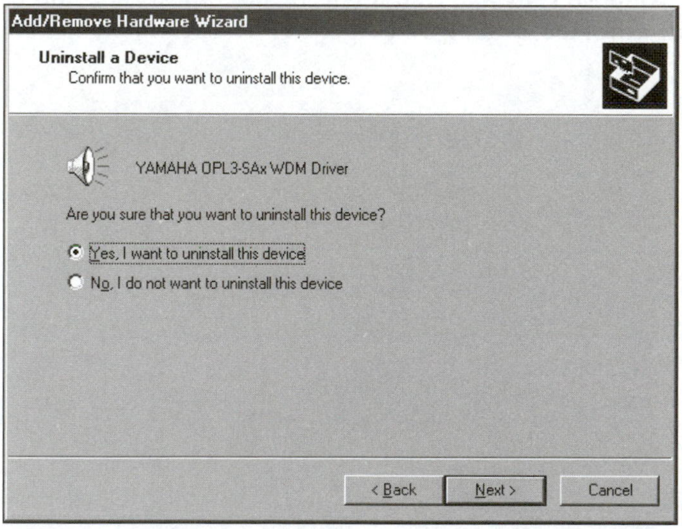

Figure 11-2 Confirm that this device is to be uninstalled

7. When the Add/Remove Hardware Wizard reports that you have successfully uninstalled your audio device, click **Finish** to close the dialog box.

8. Shut down your computer.

Follow these steps to physically remove the sound card:

1. Disconnect all external cables from the case.

2. Remove the case cover and locate the sound card. List any cables connected to the sound card.

_____

_____

3. Disconnect any cables from the sound card and secure them. Remove the sound card and place it in a safe place.

4. Reassemble the system and boot to Windows to verify that audio does not function.

Follow these steps to disable the embedded audio device:

1. Consult the motherboard documentation and learn the means to disable the embedded audio device. Also, take note of any internal audio cables. The means to disable the device is often a jumper setting, but in other cases you may have to disable the device in the CMOS setup utility. If you must disable the device in CMOS, describe the steps that you took in the space provided, then complete steps 2 and 3.

_____

_____

_____

2. Disconnect all external cables. Remove the case cover and locate the means to disable the embedded audio (if applicable). List the steps, then remove and secure any internal audio cables.

_____

_____

3. Reassemble the system and boot to Windows to verify that audio does not function.

Follow these steps to physically install a sound card:

1. Shut down the computer and disconnect all external cables from the case.

2. Remove the case cover.

11

3. Locate an empty expansion slot that you can use for the sound card. On some systems, expansion cards are attached to a riser card, which you might have to remove at this time. If necessary, remove the expansion slot faceplate on the case so that the sound card will fit into the expansion slot.

4. Insert the sound card into the expansion slot on the motherboard (or insert the sound card into the riser card and the riser card into the motherboard). Line up the sound card on the slot and press it straight down, making sure that the tab on the backplate (the metal plate on the rear of the card where sound ports are located) fits into the slot on the case. It normally requires a little effort to seat the card, but do not force it. If the card does not insert with just a little effort, something is preventing the card from seating. Check for obstructions and try again, removing components that are in the way, if necessary.

5. Once the card is installed, secure it with a screw. The screw goes through a hole in the card's backplate, securing the backplate to the case.

6. Attach any cable required to carry an audio signal from other multimedia devices, such as a CD-ROM drive.

7. Replace any components that you removed while installing the sound card, and replace and secure the cover on the case.

8. Reattach all cables from external devices to the appropriate ports. Attach speakers or headphones. (Some speakers receive power from the computer, and others have to be plugged into an external power source such as a wall outlet.)

Next, you will configure the drivers and other software for your sound card. If you have the documentation for your sound card, follow the exact instructions given in the documentation. Otherwise, follow these general steps to install software for most sound cards, keeping in mind that your sound card might require a slightly different procedure.

1. Start the computer, and log on as an administrator. Windows displays a Found New Hardware dialog box, attempts to determine what type of new hardware is present, and displays the result.

2. The Add New Hardware Wizard launches, informing you that it will help you install a driver. Click **Next** to continue.

3. The Add New Hardware Wizard displays a message asking how you want to install the software. Click the **Search for a suitable driver for my device (Recommended)** option button, and click **Next** to continue.

4. The Add New Hardware Wizard displays a message asking where the drivers for the new device are located. See Figure 11-3. Insert the floppy disk or CD containing the drivers and select the appropriate check box to indicate the location of the drivers. (If the CD Autorun program launches when you insert the CD, close the application.) Click **Next** to continue. If your files are not located on removable media, choose **Specify a location**. A dialog box opens prompting

you to type the path or browse to the file location. Use either method you prefer, and when you finish, click **OK** to continue.

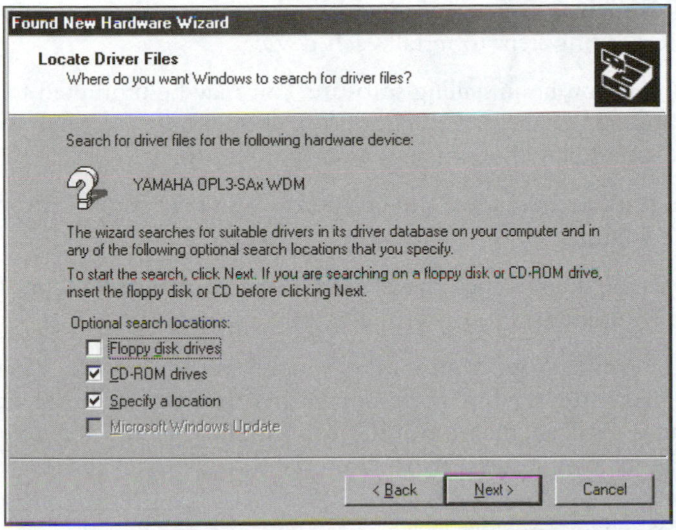

Figure 11-3   Use the appropriate method to direct the New Hardware Wizard to the correct location of the drivers

5. If the Add New Hardware Wizard is able to locate the correct driver, it displays a message identifying the sound card model name, driver location, and driver file name. Click **Next** to continue and then skip to step 7. If the wizard reports that it is unable to find the drivers, proceed to step 6.

6. If the Add New Hardware Wizard reports that it was unable to locate the drivers, click **Back** and repeat step 4, but this time select the **Specify Location** option and then click **Browse**. This opens the Browse for a Folder window. Browse to the location of the setup files, expanding folders as necessary, and look for a folder named Win2000, Win2k, or similar. (If you are not sure which .inf file to choose, consult the readme.txt file. This file should include instructions and last-minute information. Do not be surprised if you are instructed to use Windows NT 4 drivers for some devices!) After you select the correct folder, click the **OK** button to close the Browse for Folder window, and then click **Next** in the Add New Hardware Wizard. If the wizard finds the driver, continue to step 7; otherwise, consult the documentation further for the correct installation procedure.

7. After locating and installing the drivers, the Add New Hardware Wizard displays a message notifying you that the installation of the device is complete. Click **Finish** to close the Add New Hardware Wizard. At some point during the process, you may be required to supply the location of the i386 directory holding Windows installation files.

8. After the sound card is completely installed, Windows may detect additional devices. Sound cards sometimes include embedded features such as MIDI Wave Audio, SB16 Emulation, Game Port, and so on. The Add New Hardware Wizard will launch as necessary to install each of these devices separately. Follow the preceding steps to install each device.

9. When Windows finishes installing software, you may be prompted to reboot. If you are prompted, go ahead and reboot. You should hear the Microsoft sound (the default sound played on startup) after you log on.

Follow these steps to test the sound card and customize Windows sound settings. You will start by adjusting the volume.

1. In Control Panel, double-click the **Sounds and Multimedia** icon. The Sounds and Multimedia Properties dialog box appears.

2. At the bottom of the Sounds tab of the Sounds and Multimedia Properties dialog box, make sure the box corresponding with **Show volume control on the taskbar** is checked, then move the volume slider all the way to high, as shown in Figure 11-4. Click **OK** to close the dialog box. Reboot the system.

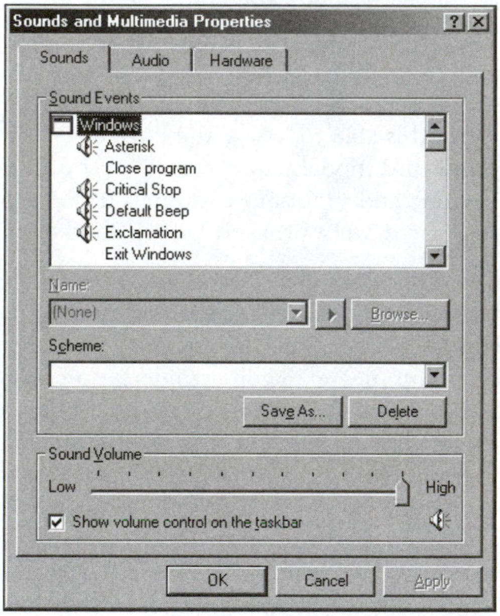

Figure 11-4   Check the settings on the Sounds tab of the Sounds and Multimedia Properties dialog box

3. On the right side of the taskbar on the desktop, you should see the speaker volume setting represented by a speaker icon. Click the speaker icon. A pop-up window opens where you can adjust speaker volume.

4. Drag the volume slider all the way to the top, and then click on the desktop. The pop-up window closes.

5. Double-click the speaker icon. The Play Control dialog box opens. Note that this dialog box gives you more control than the pop-up window you used in step 4. Among other things, it allows you to adjust the volume of various inputs including the master volume, which controls the actual volume of the signal fed to the speakers. List here the various volume controls from left to right and identify two settings (other than volume) that can be changed.

_____

_____

_____

6. Set the master volume slider (the one on the far left) to half volume and close the Volume Control window.

Follow these steps to control which sounds play for certain Windows events:

1. Open the Control Panel, and double-click the **Sounds and Multimedia** icon. The Sounds and Multimedia Properties dialog box opens. Scroll down the Sound Events list box on the Sounds tab, and note that a speaker icon next to an event indicates that a specific sound will play when that event occurs. Complete Table 11-1 by clicking each event listed in the table and noting the sound associated with that event. (The name of the sound file associated with the selected event appears in the Name list box.) Also note that not all Windows events are assigned a sound.

Table 11-1

Event	Sound name
Start Windows	
Empty Recycle Bin	
Critical Stop	

2. In the Sound Events list box, click **Empty Recycle Bin** and then click the **Play** button to the right of the Name list box. The recycle sound plays.

3. Use the Name list arrow to select and play several different sounds until you find one that you like better than the recycle sound. In the Scheme list box, select **Windows Default**. Click **Save As** in the Schemes section. In the **Save Scheme As** dialog box that appears, type **Custom** to change the name of the

11

scheme from Windows Default to Custom, and then click **OK** to close the Save Scheme As dialog box. What sound did you choose?

_____

4. Click **OK** to apply and save the revised Sounds and Multimedia Properties. Next, you will test the new sound by emptying the Recycle Bin.

5. Right-click the **Recycle Bin** on the desktop, and then click **Empty Recycle Bin** in the shortcut menu. Click **Yes** to confirm. Note that if there are no files in the Recycle Bin, this option is unavailable.

6. Using the Sounds applet in Control Panel, change the sound that plays when Windows starts. What sound did you use?

_____

7. Restart Windows and listen to the new sound.

8. After you have verified that the new sound plays, repeat the process and return the sound to the original settings.

9. If you have Internet access, use a search engine and locate a Lion.wav file and play it to hear a lion's roar. What was the Web site where you found the file?

_____

Review Questions

1. What Windows feature walks you through the process of installing drivers for a new device?

_____

2. Other than driver files included with the sound card, what other software might be requested by Windows 2000 when configuring a new sound card?

_____

3. What other devices embedded on the sound card might Windows detect after the sound card installation is finished?

_____

_____

4. How does Windows handle the installation of these additional devices?

_____

_____

5. What Control Panel applet, and which specific tab in its properties dialog box, allows you to test the sound card by playing sounds for Windows events?

_____

6. Besides the output to the speakers on the sound card or embedded audio device interface, what other outputs/inputs are available on the card? What are their uses?

_____

_____

_____

LAB 11.2 INSTALL A PC VIDEO CAMERA

Objectives

The goal of this lab is to help you complete the process of installing and testing a PC camera. After completing this lab, you will be able to:

➤ Install a PC video camera

➤ Use Windows XP Movie Maker to test your PC camera

➤ Use Windows 98 NetMeeting to test your PC camera

Materials Required

This lab will require the following:

➤ Windows XP or Windows 98 operating system

➤ Windows installation CD or installation files stored in another location as specified by your instructor

➤ USB connective PC camera compatible with your system

➤ Spare USB port on the system

➤ Device drivers for the camera

➤ Sound card, speakers, and microphone (optional)

➤ Internet access (optional)

Activity Background

PC cameras are becoming increasingly popular. Using these cameras, you can set up a video conference, record or send video images to your family and friends, and monitor

11

your house over the Internet. You can even detach some PC cameras and use them to take still pictures while away from your system, uploading them to the computer when you return. Most PC cameras install via the USB port, making physical installation a relatively simple process. In this lab, you will install, configure, and test a basic PC camera.

Estimated completion time: **45 minutes**

ACTIVITY

For Windows XP, follow these steps to install a PC camera:

1. Start the computer and, if necessary, log on as an administrator.

2. Locate an unused USB port. Insert the PC camera's cable into the USB port. (Do not force it. If the cable does not insert easily, flip the connector over, and try again; it should insert easily.)

3. Windows detects the new USB device and the Found New Hardware icon appears in the Taskbar Notification area (think System Tray). A balloon tip above the icon informs you that new hardware has been found. Next the balloon tip will identify the hardware as a camera, and then it will notify you that it has identified the particular model of camera. Finally, the balloon tip will notify you that the camera has been successfully installed. Windows XP likely will not give you the opportunity to use the camera manufacturer's device drivers. However, if it is requested, insert the camera installation CD or floppy disk. (If the Autorun program launches, close it.)

Now you will use Windows XP My Computer to collect information about your camera. Complete the following steps and list the information indicated:

1. Open My Computer. List the section title that the camera appears under in the right pane of My Computer.

   _____

2. Right-click the icon for your camera and choose **Properties** from the shortcut menu. The *Cameraname* **Properties** dialog box opens. List the five types of information available in the **Camera Status** section of the **General** tab.

   _____

   _____

   _____

3. Click the **Test Camera** button in the Diagnostics section of the dialog box. A new dialog box appears. Describe below the results reported, then click **OK** to close the dialog box. Click **OK** again to close the *Cameraname* Properties dialog box.

_____

_____

4. Now double-click the camera icon in My Computer. Record what happens and what tasks are available in the Camera Tasks section.

_____

_____

_____

5. Use what you know about Windows and list two ways, other than My Computer or Windows Explorer but within Windows XP, where you can find information about the camera. Briefly describe any differences from My Computer on the amount of information available or the way it is presented for each source.

_____

_____

_____

_____

11

Now you will use a feature new to Windows in Windows XP called **Windows Movie Maker** to put your camera to use. Complete the following steps:

1. From the Start Menu select **All Programs**, then **Accessories**, then click **Windows Movie Maker**. Windows Movie Maker launches. See Figure 11-5.

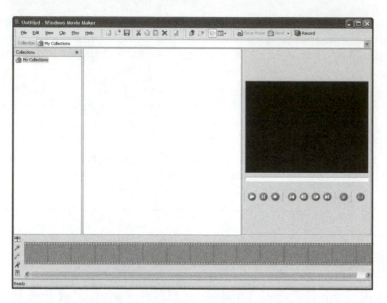

Figure 11-5 Windows Movie Maker

2. On the Windows Movie Maker toolbar, click **Record**. The Record dialog box opens.

3. On the Record dialog box, click the arrow for the **Record:** field drop-down menu and list the choices you have for recording.

_____

_____

4. On the Record dialog box, click the **Change Device** button. The Change Device dialog box opens. What devices are currently selected?

_____

5. In the Change Device dialog box, click the arrow for the **Line:** field drop-down menu and select the microphone on the camera. If your camera does not have a microphone, leave the default setting. Click **OK** to close the dialog box.

6. To record a video clip, click the **Record** button on the Record dialog box. See Figure 11-6. The Record button changes to **Stop** and the **Elapsed** time counter starts ticking. Take several seconds of footage, then click **Stop**. What is

the title of the dialog box that appears? What is the default path in the new
dialog box?

_____

_____

_____

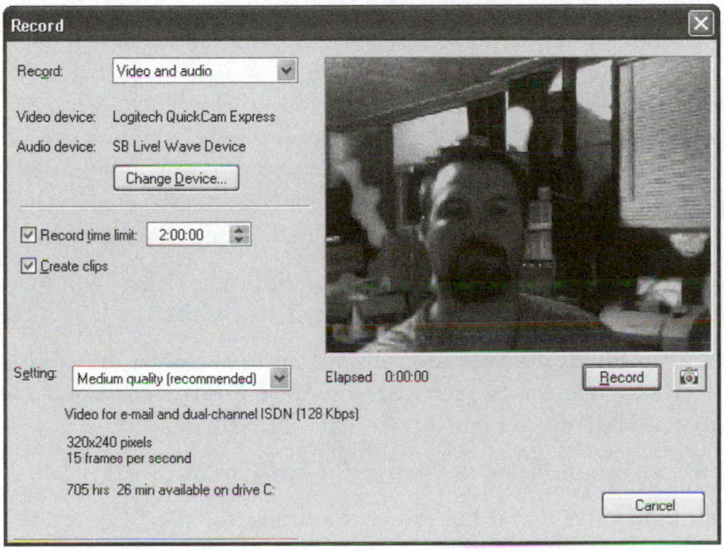

Figure 11-6   Record dialog box for Windows Movie Maker

7. Save your file as a test with the default extension. The Record dialog box
closes and a **Creating Clips** dialog box appears showing the Save progress,
then closes automatically when the clip is saved. Where does your clip appear
in the Windows Movie Maker screen?

_____

_____

8. When you click a clip and highlight it, you can play that clip in the interface on
the right side of your screen. In addition, you can drag and drop a clip to the
Timeline/Storyboard interface at the bottom of Windows Movie Maker to edit
it. Take a few minutes to explore and experiment with Windows Movie Maker,
then record and save a clip describing what features you find interesting about
the capability to record and edit video on your system.

For Windows 98, follow these steps to install a PC camera:

1. Start the computer and log on, if necessary.

2. Insert the PC camera's installation CD or floppy disk. (If the CD Autorun program launches, close it.)

3. Locate an unused USB port. Insert the PC camera's cable into the USB port. (Do not force it. If the cable does not insert easily, flip the connector over and try again; it should insert easily.)

4. Windows detects the new USB device and the Found New Hardware window opens, informing you that a USB device has been detected. A second window opens, informing you that Windows is forming a New Driver Database; when the new database is finished, the second window closes. The Found New Hardware window closes as well. (If Windows does not detect the camera, check the Device Manager or BIOS settings to discover whether the USB controller has problems or has been disabled. If necessary, enable the USB controller in Device Manager and CMOS setup and begin again with step 1.)

5. The Add New Hardware Wizard opens and indicates that it will begin searching for drivers for a USB device. Click **Next** to continue.

6. The Add New Hardware Wizard prompts you to specify a driver or search for the best driver. Click the **Search for the Best Driver for Your Device (Recommended)** option button and click **Next** to continue.

7. Locate the installation files as you learned how to do in Lab 11.1 and click **Next**.

8. The wizard indicates that it has found the driver for the PC camera and displays the driver's location and file name. Click **Next** to continue.

9. The wizard copies all necessary files and displays a message indicating that the installation is complete. Click **Finish** to close the wizard. Many PC cameras have built-in microphones as well as other devices. If this is the case, the wizard may launch again for each device. It is also possible that during any installation, the wizard will prompt you to provide the location of Windows 98 installation files.

Now you will use Windows 98 NetMeeting to test your camera. NetMeeting is video conferencing software included with Windows 98. To perform a full video conference with two or more people, you can use a directory service, an online database that NetMeeting uses to locate participants in a NetMeeting conference. One such directory service is Microsoft Internet Directory. When you install NetMeeting, you are prompted to enter information about yourself and are then given the opportunity to be added to the Microsoft Internet Directory. The following steps tell you to use the Microsoft Internet Directory, although your instructor might ask you to use a different directory service. Follow these steps to install NetMeeting if it is not already installed:

1. Open the Control Panel, open the **Add/Remove Programs** applet, and then click the **Windows Setup** tab. Windows searches for Windows Components.

2. Double-click the **Communications** group in the Components list box. The Communications dialog box opens.

3. Scroll down the Components list box, select the **Microsoft NetMeeting** check box, and then click **OK**. The Communications dialog box closes.

4. Click **OK** to close the Add/Remove Properties dialog box. The Copying Files dialog box appears, indicating that the copying process has begun. If prompted, supply the location of Windows 98 installation files. When the files are copied, the Copying Files dialog box closes. Reboot your PC if prompted to do so.

Now you will launch Windows 98 NetMeeting and configure it. Follow these steps:

1. Click **Start** on the taskbar, point to **Programs**, and then look for Microsoft NetMeeting on one of the submenus. You might find it located under Internet Explorer or under Accessories\Communications.

2. Click **Microsoft NetMeeting**.

3. Microsoft NetMeeting begins configuring your connection. Click **Next** to continue.

4. In the NetMeeting dialog box shown in Figure 11-7, accept **Microsoft Internet Directory** as the server name (unless your instructor gives you different directions) and then click **Next**.

Figure 11-7   By default, installing NetMeeting adds you to the Microsoft
Internet Directory

5. Supply the requested identification information, including your name and e-mail address, and then click **Next** to continue. (Keep in mind that your identification information will be available to other NetMeeting users on the directory server.)

6. What you see on the next screen depends on the version of NetMeeting installed. You might see a screen asking you what category to use for your personal info (personal use for all ages, business use for all ages, or adults–only use). Select a category and click **Next**. For some versions of NetMeeting, the screen will give you the option of selecting a directory server. In this case, the default is Microsoft Internet Directory. Leave the default selected and click **Next**.

7. On the next screen, you are asked to specify your connection speed. Select **Local Area Network** (or other speed as specified by your instructor) and then click **Next** to continue.

8. You are asked to specify your video capturing device. Select your camera from the drop-down menu, if it is not already selected, and then click **Next** to continue.

9. NetMeeting informs you that it will help tune your audio settings. Click **Next** to continue.

10. Set and test your audio settings. When they are satisfactory, click **Next** to continue.

11. When the installation is complete, click **Finish**. NetMeeting launches.

12. Click **Current Call** and then click the **Play** button in the My Video frame. You should be able to see video supplied by your PC camera in the My Video screen. This demonstrates that your video camera was installed correctly.

CRITICAL THINKING (additional 20 minutes)

If others in the lab are connected to NetMeeting and you have access to a sound card, speakers, and microphone, join someone else in a video conference. To make the connection, you can use an IP address of another computer on the LAN, instead of using a directory server. To use Windows 98 to determine the IP address of a workstation, enter **winipcfg** in the Run dialog box and then select the network adapter from the drop-down list. Figure 11-8 shows a full NetMeeting video conference complete with shared whiteboard, chat window, and video.

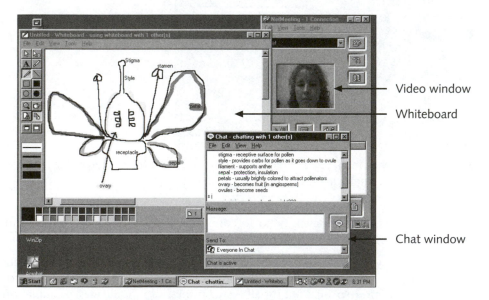

Figure 11-8   NetMeeting provides three windows during a session

Review Questions

1. Typically, via what type of port do PC cameras attach to a system?

   _____

2. What type of audio device may be embedded in a PC camera?

   _____

   _____

3. Do you have to power down the system before connecting a USB camera? Why or why not?

   _____

   _____

4. What feature of Windows XP is designed to create video content?

   _____

   _____

   _____

5. What application can you use to test the video supplied by your PC camera?

   _____

   _____

6. When would using a PC camera be beneficial to you?

   _____

   _____

LAB 11.3 COMPARE CD AND DVD TECHNOLOGIES

Objectives

The goal of this lab is to help you use the Internet to research CD and DVD standards. After completing this lab, you will be able to:

➤ Recognize CD and DVD specifications

Materials Required

This lab will require the following:

➤ Internet access

Activity Background

Many multimedia PCs include CD or DVD drives (and sometimes both). These drives may be of three types: read-only (ROM), write/record (R), or write/record and re-write (RW or RAM). (The last two types can only write and record to specialized disks.) You will research the features and limitations of CD and DVD standards in this lab.

Estimated completion time: **60 minutes**

ACTIVITY

Use the Internet and your favorite search sites such as Google (*www.google.com*) or Yahoo! (*www.yahoo.com*) to answer the following questions on CD standards. Print the source page or pages supporting your answers.

1. What is the maximum storage capacity of a CD?

   _____

2. Briefly, how is information recorded on a CD-ROM disk?

   _____

   _____

3. Are CDs capable of storing data on both sides of the disk?

   _____

4. What type or color of laser is used in a CD drive?

   _____

5. What is a limitation of a CD-R drive that is not an issue with a CD-RW drive?

   _____

   _____

6. What kind of problems might occur if you tried to use an older CD–ROM drive or a CD player to play a CD–R or a CD–RW disk?

_____

_____

7. Define "constant angular velocity" and explain how it applies to CD standards.

_____

_____

8. Define "constant linear velocity" and explain how it applies to CD standards.

_____

_____

9. What term is used to refer to the process of writing data to a disk?

_____

10. Can any CD hold video data? Explain.

_____

11. On a CD disk, is data written in concentric circles or in a continuous spiral track?

_____

12. What are three common standards CD drives use to interface with a system?

_____

13. What does the X factor of a drive indicate? What is the specification of one X?

_____

_____

11

14. Briefly describe how a CD-RW writes data to a disk and how it is able to rewrite data.

_____

_____

_____

_____

_____

15. How much would you pay for a package of CD-R disks? How much for a package of CD-RW disks? How many disks are in a package of each type?

_____

Use the Internet and your favorite search sites to answer the following questions on DVD standards. Print the source page or pages supporting your answers.

1. What is the maximum storage capacity of a DVD disk?

_____

2. What two characteristics give a DVD disk more storage capacity than a CD disk?

_____

_____

_____

3. Describe the difference between DVD-R and DVD-RAM.

_____

_____

_____

_____

4. Besides DVD-R, what other standards are available for burning DVDs?

_____

5. Explain how DVD audio and CD audio differ.

_____

_____

_____

6. How many CDs worth of data can a single DVD hold?

_____

7. How many layers of data can be stored on one side of a DVD?

_____

8. How many data areas are on a single side of a DVD-R?

_____

9. List the versions and maximum capacities of DVD-RAM.

_____

_____

10. Can DVDs be used in CD devices? Explain.

_____

11. Explain the use of the UDF file system and how it applies to a DVD.

_____

_____

_____

_____

_____

Review Questions

1. What factors, other than storage capacity, would you consider when choosing between a DVD drive and a CD drive?

_____

_____

2. What characteristics do DVD and CD drives share?

_____

_____

3. If you wanted to create a disk that would never need to be altered and could
   be used on the maximum number of systems, what type of disk would you use
   and why?

_____

_____

_____

4. Why do you think motion pictures are released on DVDs instead of CDs?

_____

_____

_____

LAB 11.4 INSTALL DUAL MONITORS IN WINDOWS XP

Objectives

The goal of this lab is to help you set up a second monitor on a system. After completing this lab, you will be able to:

➤ Install a display adapter and its drivers

➤ Attach a second monitor

➤ Configure the system to use both monitors at the same time

Materials Required

This lab will require the following:

➤ Windows XP operating system

➤ PC toolkit with ground strap

➤ Second display adapter with drivers

➤ Second monitor

Activity Background

It is often quite handy to have two monitors on a system. For instance, if you have a second monitor, you can have a Web browser maximized on one and a video editing application maximized on the other. This has the effect of making your desktop larger and making it easier to work with multiple applications simultaneously, which is often very useful when developing multimedia presentations. In this lab, you will install and configure a second monitor on a computer.

Estimated completion time: **45 minutes**

ACTIVITY

It is important to verify that the original hardware is working properly before you try to add a second display adapter and monitor. That way, if a problem arises after you install new hardware, you can be pretty sure that something is amiss with the newly added components rather than with the original equipment. It is also important to make sure that the hardware is either on the Windows XP HCL (recommended) or, at the very least, that the device manufacturer offers drivers and specific instructions for use with Windows XP.

Follow these steps to physically install the second display adapter:

1. Check to make sure that the original display adapter uses the PCI or AGP standard, and decide whether it will be the primary or secondary monitor.

2. Install the second adapter card in the PCI slot nearest to the AGP slot (if the original is an AGP adapter) or in the PCI slot immediately next to the original PCI adapter (if the original is a PCI adapter). If you need additional guidance on installing a card, refer to Lab 11.1.

3. Attach the second monitor to the port on the back of the display adapter.

4. Boot your PC and enter CMOS setup. If your setup has the display settings for dual monitors, adjust them so that the primary display adapter is initialized first. If you don't see this setting, then your BIOS does not support, it so you can exit CMOS setup and wait for your system to reboot.

5. In CMOS setup, if you see the settings for dual monitors, for a system with an AGP slot, make sure the AGP adapter is selected as your primary adapter and the PCI adapter as the secondary adapter. For a system that uses two PCI adapters, it does not matter which adapter is the primary one; you can leave the setting as is. For additional guidance on adjusting BIOS settings refer to Lab 5.1. Exit CMOS setup and wait for your system to reboot.

Follow these steps to install device drivers and adjust Windows display settings:

1. When the system reboots, log on as an administrator. Windows XP recognizes the new adapter and displays a Found New Hardware icon in the Notification area of the taskbar (next to the clock). Above the Found New Hardware icon, a balloon tip appears with the notification.

2. At this point, Windows may automatically install the drivers for you (if the drivers were available when XP was published) or launch the Found New Hardware Wizard if the adapter is new enough that XP is not aware of the correct drivers. Complete the steps in the wizard to install the adapter. When installation is complete, reboot. Refer to Lab 11.1 if you need additional information on using the wizard.

Before you use a second monitor, you must activate it. You will activate your second monitor in the following steps:

1. Log on as an administrator, open the Control Panel, and click the **Appearance and Themes** icon. Then click the **Display** icon. The Display Properties dialog box appears.

2. Select the Settings tab on the Display Properties dialog box, as shown in Figure 11-9. The field at the top of the settings tab now displays two monitors. Click the image of the monitor with the number 2 in it, or in the Display list box select the video adapter that you just installed.

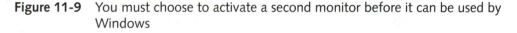

Figure 11-9   You must choose to activate a second monitor before it can be used by Windows

3. Adjust the resolution and color settings to your preference, and then select the **Extend My Windows Desktop Onto This Monitor** check box.

4. Click **Apply** to apply the settings. The second monitor displays the desktop.

Follow these steps to test your dual-monitor configuration:

1. Open Paint, and then drag and drop it to the second monitor. Does your desktop extend to the second monitor as expected?

   _____

2. Open Windows Explorer and maximize it on the original monitor. Can you see your mouse move as expected from one monitor to the next? Does the mouse interact with applications on each monitor?

   _____

3. Close Paint and Windows Explorer and open Device Manager.

Follow these steps to remove the second adapter and return to a single monitor configuration:

1. Open Device Manager, find the second display adapter, and highlight it. (Make sure you are looking at the second adapter and not the first.)

2. Click **Uninstall**. If prompted, verify that you do wish to remove the device, and when asked if you want to restart the computer, click **No**.

3. Shut down the computer. Do not restart the computer at this time.

4. Remove the secondary monitor and adapter card. If necessary, reverse any BIOS changes you made that affect the display initialization sequence, and reboot the system to verify that the adapter card is no longer recognized by the system.

Review Questions

1. Before installing a second monitor, why is it important to know if your existing configuration is working properly?

   _____

2. Why might it be necessary to change the sequence in which the system initializes display adapters?

   _____

   _____

3. In Display Properties, what is one way to select the monitor you wish to adjust?

   _____

4. What would probably happen if the new adapter was on the Windows XP HCL and was in production prior to the release of Windows XP?

   _____

5. Does adjusting the settings of one monitor affect the settings of the other?

_____

6. Why would a user want to install multiple monitors on a system?

_____

_____

7. Which would be cheaper, adding a second 17" monitor to an existing system or buying a 21" monitor in single-monitor mode?

_____

_____

_____

8. How did you arrive at your answer to Question 7?

_____

Lab 11.5 Research Digital Cameras

Objectives

The goal of this lab is to help you research digital cameras and learn how you might integrate them with a multimedia PC. In this lab, you will research:

➤ Camera picture quality and compatibility

➤ Camera storage technology

➤ Methods of transferring images to a PC

Materials Required

This lab will require the following:

➤ Internet access

Activity Background

As digital cameras have become more common and popular, they have also become more refined. Their special features, image quality, methods of file storage, and methods of transferring image data to the PC have improved over earlier models. Also, the prices of digital cameras have decreased significantly. In this lab, you will research digital cameras and learn how they are used with multimedia PCs.

Estimated completion time: **60 minutes**

Activity

Research digital photography on the Internet. Try searching for "digital camera" or "digital photography" on your favorite search engine. Web sites that might be useful include:

➤ *www.cnet.com* by CNET Networks, Inc.

➤ *www.dpreview.com* by Digital Photography Review

➤ *www.shutterline.com* by Shutterline

➤ *www.keyworlds.com/d/digital_photography.htm* by KeyWorlds.com

Answer these questions about general camera topics. Print the Web page or pages supporting your answer.

1. How is image quality measured? Will all digital cameras produce the same image quality?

   _____

   _____

2. What are three storage technologies that digital cameras might use to store images in a camera?

   _____

   _____

   _____

3. Name four technologies a camera might use to transfer images to a PC. What requirements must a PC meet for each?

   _____

   _____

   _____

   _____

11

4. Name and print information about at least two digital cameras that offer features such as changeable lenses, manual focus, aperture settings (f-stops), and shutter-speed settings (exposure).

_____

_____

Answer these questions regarding basic image characteristics.

1. What three file types might a digital camera use to store images?

_____

2. Name three factors that affect the number of images that a camera can store on a single storage device.

_____

_____

_____

3. Do most digital cameras offer the ability to control image quality? Explain.

_____

4. Can you remove an image that you do not like from a camera without transferring the image to a PC? Explain.

_____

5. What are three means of obtaining an actual printed photo of an image taken by a digital camera?

_____

_____

_____

6. Will any digital cameras record images other than still shots?

_____

Answer these questions about how cameras transfer images to a PC.

1. Which means of transfer offers the highest transfer speed and what is that speed?

_____

_____

2. Which means of transfer requires the least specialized hardware on the PC?

_____

3. Which storage technologies allow the direct transfers of images by removing the storage device from the camera and inserting it in the PC?

_____

_____

4. What devices can be added to a PC to allow it to directly read flash memory cards?

_____

_____

_____

_____

5. What means of image transfer does not require you to remove a device from the camera or use cabling to the PC?

_____

6. Does image resolution have any effect on transfer speed? Explain.

_____

_____

_____

_____

Answer these questions about photo-quality printers:

1. What resolution would you recommend for a printer capable of reproducing digital pictures?

_____

11

2. Do you need special paper to get the best quality in photo printing? Explain.

_____

3. Describe one way you could get your pictures from your digital camera to the printer.

_____

_____

_____

Review Questions

1. What are three advantages of a digital camera over a 35mm camera?

_____

_____

_____

2. What are some disadvantages of a digital camera compared to a 35mm camera?

_____

_____

3. What are some features that you would like on a digital camera if you were to buy one? Explain your choices.

_____

_____

_____

4. What could be done to maximize the number of images stored on the camera without modifying the storage device capacity?

_____

_____

_____

5. Typically, would a 3.1 megapixel camera have a superior or inferior picture quality compared to a 4.9 megapixel camera?

_____

6. When purchasing a photo printer, would you consider the cost of purchasing ink refills? Why or why not?

_____

_____

Lab 11.6 Explore Windows XP Audio Features

Objectives

The goal of this lab is to let you experiment with different audio features and capabilities of Windows XP. After completing this lab, you will be able to:

➤ Identify audio media types

➤ Download and install Nullsoft Winamp, a third-party sound software application

➤ Control audio CD playback with Windows Media Player and Nullsoft's Winamp

➤ Customize sounds that Windows plays for events

Materials Required

This lab will require the following:

➤ Windows XP operating system

➤ Windows XP CD or installation files

➤ Internet access

➤ CD-ROM drive and an audio CD

Activity Background

Windows XP provides various features that let the user experience and use audio files in different ways. Various Windows events may be configured to play a certain sound when the event occurs. These features can be used simply to make using Windows more enjoyable to the average user, but to a sight-impaired user they can be vital tools.

Windows XP provides Windows Media Player as a means to experience audio CDs as well as other multimedia types. In this lab you will experiment with Windows audio capabilities and use Nullsoft's Winamp, a third-party sound software application.

11

Estimated completion time: **40 minutes**

ACTIVITY

Follow these steps to adjust the Windows volume level:

1. On the right side of the taskbar, you should see the Windows volume represented by a speaker symbol. Click once on the speaker symbol. This opens the Volume Control pop-up window.

2. Drag the volume slider all the way to the top, and click on the desktop. The Volume Control dialog box closes.

3. Double-click the speaker symbol. This opens the Play Control window. Note that this window lets you adjust the volume of various inputs independent of and including the master volume. The number of volume controls offered here depend on the capabilities of your sound card. List here the various volume controls from left to right, and identify two settings (other than volume sliders) that can be made.

   _____

   _____

   _____

   _____

   _____

4. Set the "master" volume slider (the one on the far left) to half volume and close the Volume Control window.

Follow these steps to customize Windows sound settings:

1. From the Control Panel, double-click the **Sounds, Speech and Audio Devices** icon, then click the **Sounds and Audio Devices Control Panel** icon to open the Sounds and Audio Devices Properties dialog box.

2. On the Sounds tab of the Sounds and Audio Devices Properties dialog box, scroll down the Program Events field, and note that each event with a speaker symbol has a sound assigned that plays when the event occurs, as shown in Figure 11-10. Click **Start Windows** in the Program event-field, and then click the **Play** button between the Sounds field and the Browse button. The Windows XP Startup sound plays. If you do not hear the sound, check your volume levels and make sure that the volume is not muted.

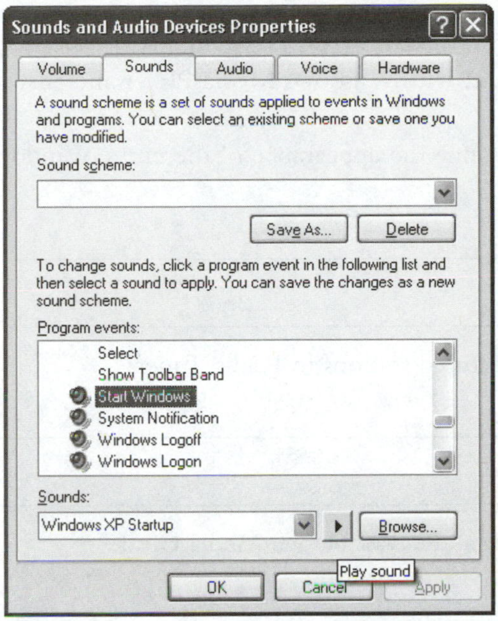

Figure 11-10   A speaker symbol indicates which events will initiate a sound when activated

3. From the drop-down menu of the Sounds field, select and play several different sounds until you find one that you like better than the Microsoft sound. Click **Save As** in the Sound scheme section, type **Custom** in the dialog box that appears, and click **OK** to save the new settings. (You could also apply the Windows Default scheme by selecting it from the Schemes drop-down menu.)

4. Click **OK** to apply and save Sound Properties. Restart Windows and log on to the same account to hear the new sound.

Follow these steps to play an audio CD with Windows Media Player:

1. Insert the audio disk in the CD-ROM drive. An Audio CD dialog box will appear. In the Audio CD dialog box, select **Play Audio CD using Windows Media Player**, then click **OK** to close the dialog box.

2. Windows Media Player should launch and automatically begin playing the CD. Adjust the volume so it is not distracting to others.

3. The right pane of Windows Media Player displays the tracks on the CD. The center section displays different images to accompany the audio output. Experiment with customizing this image by right-clicking this section and selecting something from the shortcut menu. List below three of your favorite selections.

_____

_____

4. Windows Media Player, has the standard set of control features that you would expect with a CD player. On the left of Windows Media Player are a number of other features. Experiment with Windows Media Player and answer the following questions:

■ Which feature would change the appearance of the entire Windows Media Player interface?

_____

_____

■ What are some of the featured stations in Radio Tuner?

_____

_____

■ What types of information are available via Media Guide?

_____

_____

Follow the steps below to install Winamp and use it to play the audio CD. Bear in mind that new versions of software are released often, so these directions might differ slightly, depending on the latest release:

1. In your Web browser, go to the Nullsoft Winamp Web site at *www.winamp.com*. Follow the Download Now! link and download the default version of Winamp. (This file will be named Winamp3_0-full.exe or something similar.) What is the name of the file you found to download?

_____

2. In Windows Explorer find your download location and double-click **winamp3_0-full.exe** to launch Winamp Setup and begin the installation process. The Winamp Setup process is very similar to other installation wizards you have previously completed. Work through the installation using default settings for everything. If you do not wish to receive e-mail from Nullsoft, select the **Stop Bugging Me** check box if it appears on the information screen for Winamp Setup. When prompted, click **Run Winamp** to launch Winamp, which will download additional information in the Winamp browser.

3. Close Winamp and the Winamp browser. Remove the audio CD and then insert the audio CD again. This time, when the Audio CD dialog box opens, select **Play Audio CD using Winamp3**. Winamp will launch again and begin playing your audio CD.

4. Experiment with Winamp to answer these questions:

   ■ Does Winamp have the same basic features as Windows Media Player?

   _____

   ■ What feature does Winamp provide that allows you to customize the sound tone?

   _____

   ■ Name three popular music file types that Winamp supports.

   _____

   ■ Could you set up a playlist that would play all the files on your CD in an order that you chose, instead of first to last? Explain your answer.

   _____

   _____

   _____

Review Questions

1. What icon do you single-click to access the Windows volume control?

   _____

2. What feature of Windows Media Player would allow you to listen to streaming audio content?

   _____

3. What is the default sound played during Windows XP startup?

   _____

   _____

4. Which player provided more features, and which was easier to use? Explain your answers.

   _____

   _____

   _____

   _____

5. How can you lower the volume of CD playback while keeping the Windows event sounds volume the same?

_____

_____

SUPPORTING WINDOWS 9x

Labs included in this chapter

➤ Lab 12.1 Use Windows Keyboard Shortcuts

➤ Lab 12.2 Customize Your Desktop

➤ Lab 12.3 Update Drivers with Device Manager

➤ Lab 12.4 Examine the Windows 9x CD

➤ Lab 12.5 Perform a Custom Windows 98 Installation and Write Documentation

➤ Lab 12.6 Manage Windows File Associations

➤ Lab 12.7 Update Windows

➤ Lab 12.8 Optimize Windows

➤ Lab 12.9 Modify System Configuration Files

➤ Lab 12.10 Save, Modify, and Restore the Registry

➤ Lab 12.11 Critical Thinking: Sabotage and Repair Windows 98

The following grid shows the correlation between the labs in this chapter and the A+ Guides to Hardware and Software.

A+ Guide to Managing and Maintaining Your PC, Fifth Edition	A+ Guide to Hardware, Third Edition	A+ Guide to Software, Third Edition
Lab 12.1 Use Windows Keyboard Shortcuts		Chapter 4
Lab 12.2 Customize Your Desktop		Chapter 4
Lab 12.3 Update Drivers with Device Manager		Chapter 4
Lab 12.4 Examine the Windows 9x CD		Chapter 4
Lab 12.5 Perform a Custom Windows 98 Installation and Write Documentation		Chapter 4
Lab 12.6 Manage Windows File Associations		Chapter 4
Lab 12.7 Update Windows		Chapter 4
Lab 12.8 Optimize Windows		Chapter 4
Lab 12.9 Modify System Configuration Files		Chapter 4
Lab 12.10 Save, Modify, and Restore the Registry		Chapter 4
Lab 12.11 Critical Thinking: Sabotage and Repair Windows 98		Chapter 4

LAB 12.1 USE WINDOWS KEYBOARD SHORTCUTS

Objectives

The goal of this lab is to introduce you to some keyboard shortcuts. After completing this lab, you will be able to use the keyboard to:

➤ Display the Start menu

➤ Switch between open applications

➤ Launch utilities with the Windows logo key

Materials Required

This lab will require the following:

➤ Windows 9x operating system

Activity Background

Certain keys or key combinations (called keyboard shortcuts) allow you to perform repetitive tasks more efficiently. These shortcuts are also useful when the mouse is not working. In this lab, you will learn to use some common keyboard shortcuts.

> Estimated completion time: **30 minutes**

ACTIVITY

The F1 key is the universal keyboard shortcut for launching Help. To learn more, follow these steps:

1. Open **Paint** and then minimize it.

2. Open the **Control Panel** and then minimize it.

3. Click the desktop and then press the **F1** key. Windows Help launches.

4. Close Windows Help. Restore Paint.

5. Press the **F1** key. Because Paint is the active window, Help for Paint launches. Close Help for Paint.

6. Restore the Control Panel and then press the **F1** key. Help for Control Panel launches.

You can activate many shortcuts by pressing the Windows logo key in combination with other keys. An enhanced keyboard has two Windows logo keys, usually located between the Ctrl and Alt keys on either side of the space bar. Try the combinations listed in the next table, and record the result of each key combination in the Result column. (Close each window you open before proceeding to the next key combination.)

Key or Key Combination	Result
1. Windows Logo	
2. Windows Logo + E	
3. Windows Logo + F	
4. Windows Logo + R	
5. Windows Logo + Break	
6. Windows Logo + M	

Suppose for some reason that your mouse is not working and that you have to print a text file. In that case, you would have to use the keyboard to find, select, open, and print the document. To learn more, follow these steps:

1. Boot the computer, wait for the Windows desktop to appear, and then unplug the mouse.

2. Press the **Tab** key a few times until one of the desktop icons is highlighted.

3. Use the arrow keys to highlight **My Computer**.

4. Press **Enter**. My Computer opens.

5. Press the **Tab** key a few times until drive **A:** is highlighted.

6. Use the arrow keys again to select the **C:** drive, and then press **Enter** to open it.

7. Use similar methods to find, select, and open the **Test.txt** file (within the Test folder) that you created in Lab 3.6. You should see the contents of the file displayed in Notepad.

8. Notice on the Notepad window that one letter of each menu item is underlined. For example, in the File menu, the F is underlined. You can select menu options by holding down the Alt key while you press this underlined letter. For example, to open the File menu in Notepad, hold down the **Alt** key and press the **F** key. After the menu is open, you can use the arrow keys to move over the menu and select an option by pressing Enter, or you can type the underlined letter of a menu option. With the **Alt** key pressed down, press the **F** key. The File menu opens.

9. Press the **P** key to select Print. The Print dialog box opens.

10. Verify that the correct printer is selected. (To select a different printer, use the arrow keys.)

11. To send the print job to the printer, use the tab key until the Print button is active and then press **Enter**. (Or you can press Alt and P.)

12. Practice editing text, using the following shortcuts for cutting, copying, and pasting:

   ■ To delete one or more characters, move your cursor to the beginning of the text you want to delete, hold down the **Shift** key, and use the arrow keys to highlight the text. (If you were using a mouse, you could hold down the left mouse button and drag the mouse until the entire block was highlighted.)

12

- With the text highlighted, hold down the **Ctrl** key and press the **X** key, then release both keys. This cuts the highlighted text from its original location and moves it to the clipboard. You can then paste it in another location, if you wish.

- To copy a highlighted block of characters to the clipboard (without removing it from its original location), hold down the **Ctrl** key, press the **C** key, and then release both keys. A copy of the highlighted block of characters is placed on the clipboard. You can then paste it in another location, if you wish.

- To paste text from the clipboard to a new location, move the cursor to the desired location, press and hold the **Ctrl** key, and press the **V** key, and then release both.

CRITICAL THINKING (additional 15 minutes)

Using the keyboard skills you have learned in this lab, perform the following steps without using the mouse and answer the questions:

1. Open Device Manager and view the resources for the mouse. What status does Device Manager report about the mouse?

    _____

2. What IRQ is used by the mouse?

    _____

3. According to Windows Explorer, how much space is available on the hard drive?

    _____

Review Questions

1. What key is universally used to launch Help?

    _____

2. How many Windows logo keys are usually included on an enhanced keyboard?

    _____

3. What shortcut combination can you use to paste a block of text?

    _____

4. What key combination can you use to switch between open applications?

    _____

5. Is it possible to open the Start menu by pressing only one key?

    _____

LAB 12.2 CUSTOMIZE YOUR DESKTOP

Objectives

The goal of this lab is to show you how to personalize your desktop. After completing this lab, you will be able to:

➤ Choose and apply a background for your desktop

➤ Modify Appearance settings to match the dominant color of the desktop background

➤ Rename My Computer

Materials Required

➤ Windows 9x operating system

Activity Background

Windows allows you to customize certain settings on your computer so that the desktop is set up exactly the way you want it. Once you create custom settings on a computer, those settings go into effect each time you log onto that computer. If another user logs onto that same computer, the system configures the desktop according to that user's settings rather than yours. This ensures that each user has access to his or her own customized work environment. As you will see in the following steps, you customize the desktop via the Display Properties dialog box.

Estimated completion time: **30 minutes**

ACTIVITY

Perform the following steps to customize your desktop colors:

1. Boot the computer and take a moment to examine the Windows desktop. Note the color of the desktop itself, as well as any other features on the desktop.

2. Open the Control Panel and double-click the **Display Properties** icon, or right-click the **desktop** and click **Properties**. The Display Properties dialog box opens.

3. Click the **Background** tab, and scroll through the list of backgrounds available to you.

4. Click a background in the list. A preview appears in the monitor graphic at the top of the dialog box, similar to the one shown in Figure 12-1.

12

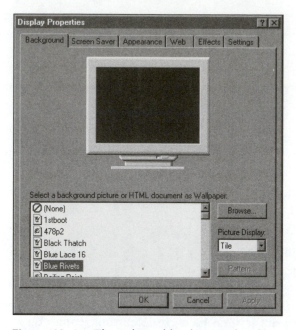

Figure 12-1   The selected background is shown in the monitor graphic in the Display Properties window

5. If you wish, experiment with the Picture Display list arrow, selecting different background options.

6. When you find a background that you like, click **Apply**, and note that the new settings have been applied to your desktop. (The Display Properties dialog box should remain open.) Note that some backgrounds require that Active Desktop be enabled. It's best not to use Active Desktop because it can slow down a system. If you see a message indicating that the background you selected requires Active Desktop, select a new background.

7. At this point, the color behind the text on the desktop might not match your background. You can adjust the color behind the text (which is considered the desktop color) using the Appearance tab.

8. Click the **Appearance** tab, click the **Item** list arrow, and note all the items whose color you could change if you wanted. For instance, you could select Active Title bar if you wanted to change the color of the title bar for the active application.

9. Click **Desktop** in the Item list (if necessary), click the **Color** list arrow, and then click the color you want to use as your desktop color. See Figure 12-2. You see a sample of the color you selected at the top of the dialog box, behind the various sample windows.

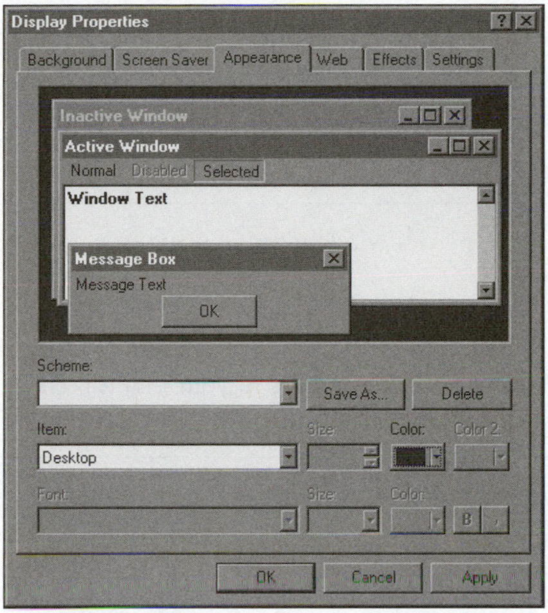

Figure 12-2   On the Appearance tab of the Display Properties window, you can change specific colors

10. Click **Apply**. The new color appears behind all the text on the desktop. (Note that if you had not already selected a background for your desktop, the entire desktop would change to the color you just selected. In this case, because you previously selected a background, the color change only affects the rectangles behind any text on the desktop.)

In addition to modifying desktop colors, you can change the name of My Computer. To learn how, follow these steps:

1. Right-click the **My Computer** icon (located on the Windows desktop) and then click **Rename**. The text below the My Computer icon is highlighted, ready for you to type a new name for the icon.

2. Type a new name for the My Computer icon, and then press **Enter**. You should be aware that this change does not affect the identity of the system for networking purposes. (You will learn more about a computer's name on a network in Chapters 18 and 21.)

3. Change the name back to "My Computer," or remember that any mention of "My Computer" in this book refers to that icon.

Review Questions

1. What are two ways to open the Display Properties window?

_____

_____

2. What tab in the Display Properties window can you use to change the color of specific items in Windows?

_____

3. What button must you click to make changes to your desktop take effect?

_____

4. Describe how to rename My Computer. Does this change the name of your computer for networking purposes?

_____

_____

_____

5. Can different users have different desktop settings on the same computer? How does Windows know which user is currently using the system?

_____

_____

LAB 12.3 UPDATE DRIVERS WITH DEVICE MANAGER

Objectives

The goal of this lab is to explore the functions of Device Manager. After completing this lab, you will be able to:

➤ Select your display adapter in Device Manager
➤ Update the driver for your display adapter from Device Manager

Materials Required

This lab will require the following:

➤ Windows 9x operating system
➤ Windows 9x CD or access to the setup files stored in a different location as designated by your instructor

Activity Background

Device Manager allows you to not only monitor resource use but also update device drivers. If you find a new driver for a particular device, you can use Device Manager to select the device and update the driver. In this lab, you will use Windows 9x Device Manager to update the driver for your display adapter.

> Estimated completion time: **30 minutes**

ACTIVITY

1. Open Device Manager and select your display adapter from the Display Adapters section.

2. Open the Properties window for your display adapter, and then click the **Driver** tab.

3. Click **Driver File Details**. Write the path to the Driver files and then back up these files to a disk or another directory so you can backtrack, if necessary.

4. Return to the Driver tab in Device Manager, and then click **Update Driver**. The Update Driver Wizard starts.

5. In the first wizard dialog box, click **Next**.

6. In the second wizard dialog box, click **Search for...** and then click **Next**.

7. In the next wizard dialog box, select the **Specify a location and CD** check box (if you are using the Windows 9x CD), deselect any other check boxes, and then click **Next**.

8. In the next wizard dialog box, type the location of the Windows CD installation file or use the **Browse** button to select a location designated by your instructor. After you have specified a location, click the **OK** button. Windows searches the location and reports its findings.

9. If the wizard indicates that it has found a file relating to the device you selected in step 1 (that is, the display adapter), click **Next** to continue. If the wizard reports that it cannot find the file, verify that you have correctly located the installation files.

10. After Windows locates the drivers, it copies the driver files. If a file being copied is older than the file the system is currently using, you will be prompted to confirm that you want to use the older file. Usually, newer drivers are better than older drivers. However, you may wish to use an older one if, after having recently updated drivers, you encounter problems. In this case, you may wish to reinstall the old driver that was not causing problems.

11. When the files have been copied, click **Finish** to complete the installation.

12. Restart the computer if prompted to do so.

12

CRITICAL THINKING (additional 30 minutes)

Use Device Manager to identify the display adapter installed. Search the Web site of the device manufacturer for new video drivers for this adapter. If you find drivers newer than the one currently in use, install the updated drivers.

Review Questions

1. Describe the steps required to access Device Manager.

_____

_____

2. How can you access a device's properties in Device Manager?

_____

_____

3. What tab in the Properties window will allow you to update a driver?

_____

4. Besides typing the path, what other option do you have to specify a driver's location?

_____

_____

5. Why might you wish to use an older driver?

_____

_____

LAB 12.4 EXAMINE THE WINDOWS 9X CD

Objectives

The goal of this lab is to familiarize you with the contents of the Windows 9x installation CD. After completing this lab, you will be able to:

➤ Find files on the Windows 9x installation CD

➤ Print a screen shot of some files on the Windows installation CD

Materials Required

This lab will require the following:

➤ Windows 9x operating system

➤ Windows 9x installation CD or access to a copy of the files on the CD at a location designated by your instructor

Activity Background

In this lab, you will explore a Windows installation CD. (You can use the installation CD for Windows 95, 98, or ME—whichever Windows CD you can access.) The CDs for the various versions of Windows differ in several ways, but the process of finding files on the CDs is the same.

Estimated completion time: 30 minutes

ACTIVITY

If you are using a CD, follow these steps and answer the questions:

1. Insert the CD into the CD-ROM drive. What happened after you inserted the CD?

   _____

   _____

2. In the Setup menu, click **Browse This CD**. Windows Explorer launches, showing the root directory of the CD. List the files at the root of the CD.

   _____

   _____

If you are using a copy of the CD files stored at a different location, follow these steps:

1. Start Explorer and browse to the location of the CD files.

2. List the files at the root of the main CD directory.

   _____

   _____

Continue exploring the installation files (whether on the CD or at another location), by following these steps:

1. Open the **winXX** folder, where *XX* is your version of Windows.

12

2. What is the file extension of the majority of files in this folder? What does this file extension stand for?

_____

These compressed files contain all the files used to build Windows on the computer during the installation process. These files are also used when you decide to add another Windows component.

1. How many files in this folder have an .exe file extension? _____

2. How many files in this folder have a .com file extension? _____

Files with .exe and .com extensions are the program files that are used during installation. Some of these files are useful in other situations as well. For instance, the program Scandisk.exe will check file structure, file fragmentation, and the disk surface. Format.com is the program that you use to format a disk. These two files are useful when stored on a troubleshooting floppy disk. To learn more about other files, continue with these steps:

1. Double-click **Setup.txt**. The file opens in Notepad. What is this file's intended use?

_____

2. Print Setup.txt from Notepad. Close Notepad.

3. Another file called **Intl.txt** may also be included in the folder. Examine this file as well. What is this file's intended use?

_____

4. Close any open Notepad windows.

5. Return to the root of the CD in Explorer and then open the **Drivers** folder. List the categories of drivers contained in this folder.

_____

_____

6. Double-click the **Readme.txt** file and then print this file. What URL is mentioned in this file?

_____

7. What does this URL provide?

_____

_____

8. Return to the root of the CD in Windows Explorer and then open the **Tools** folder.

9. Open the **Oldmsdos** folder. Both folders contain utilities that are useful on a troubleshooting floppy disk.

Sometimes it is helpful to create a hardcopy of a list of files on the installation CD. To do that, you paste a copy of the screen into Paint, and then print the Paint file. To learn more, follow these steps:

1. Click **Start** on the taskbar, point to **Programs**, point to **Accessories**, and then click **Paint**.

2. Minimize Paint.

3. Click the Windows Explorer title bar to make it the active window.

4. Hold down the **Alt** key and press the **Print Screen** key, which is usually located to the right of the F12 key. This action copies the image of the active window (Windows Explorer) onto the clipboard. Throughout the rest of this lab manual, this process will be referred to as "taking a screen shot."

5. Restore Paint, click **Edit** on the menu bar, and then click **Paste**. (Note that you can also use the key combination Ctrl + V to paste the image of Windows Explorer from the clipboard into Paint.) You will probably be notified that the image is larger than the bitmap (the white square in the Paint window). See Figure 12-3.

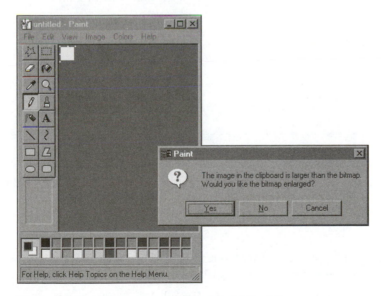

Figure 12-3   When prompted, expand the bitmap

6. Click **Yes** to expand the bitmap.

7. Print the screen shot and then close Paint without saving any changes.

8. Remove the CD from the CD-ROM drive, place it in its protective case, and store it in a safe location (or return it to your instructor).

Review Questions

1. What are files with .exe and .com extensions used for?

   _____

2. List the steps needed to take and print a screen shot.

   _____

   _____

   _____

   _____

3. What type of information is contained in the Readme.txt file?

   _____

4. Name two folders that contain useful utilities for a troubleshooting diskette.

   _____

   _____

5. What key combination is used to paste a screen shot from the clipboard into the Paint program?

   _____

LAB 12.5 PERFORM A CUSTOM WINDOWS 98 INSTALLATION AND WRITE DOCUMENTATION

Objectives

The goal of this lab is to compare the differences between a typical and custom installation of Windows 98. After completing this lab, you will be able to:

➤ Perform a custom installation of Windows 98

➤ Explain the differences between typical and custom installations

➤ Explain when to use each type of installation

➤ Write documentation to install Windows 9x

Materials Required

This lab will require the following:

➤ Windows 98 operating system

➤ Windows 98 CD-ROM or access to the setup files on another location designated by your instructor

Activity Background

In the Case Project at the end of Chapter 4 in the textbook *A+ Guide to Software: Managing, Maintaining, and Troubleshooting*, or in the Hands-on Project at the end of Chapter 12 in the textbook *A+ Guide to Managing and Maintaining Your PC*, you performed a typical installation of Windows 98. In this lab, you will perform a custom installation and note the differences.

Estimated completion time: **60 minutes**

ACTIVITY

This project will erase everything on your hard drive. Do not do it if you have important data on the hard drive.

1. Prepare a hard drive for a clean install of Windows 98 by formatting the hard drive.

2. Copy files from the Windows 98 CD to a folder on the hard drive named C:\WIN98CD.

3. Perform a custom installation of Windows 98 using the clean install method.

4. On another sheet of paper, as you are performing the installation, write user documentation that would guide an individual step-by-step through the process of performing a custom installation of Windows 98. Write the documentation as detailed as you think is necessary for a computer user who has never performed an operating system installation.

5. Record each decision you made and values that you entered during the setup process.

_____

_____

_____

_____

_____

_____

_____

6. Give your user documentation to another student to perform a critique of it. Have the student enter the following information:

Student name: _____

Rate the documentation for:

- Clarity of each step:

_____

- What to do if problems occur:

_____

- How to respond to questions asked by setup:

_____

- Any other helpful comments:

_____

_____

_____

Review Questions

1. Compare your notes on the custom installation you performed in this lab to the typical installation you performed in the Case Project in Chapter 4 of the textbook *A+ Guide to Software: Managing, Maintaining, and Troubleshooting*, or in the Hands-on Project at the end of Chapter 12 in the textbook *A+ Guide to*

Managing and Maintaining Your PC. What are the differences between a typical and custom installation? Be specific.

_____

_____

_____

_____

2. What added control do you have when performing a custom installation compared to a typical installation?

_____

_____

_____

_____

3. When would you recommend a custom installation rather than a typical installation?

_____

_____

_____

12

LAB 12.6 MANAGE WINDOWS FILE ASSOCIATIONS

Objectives

The goal of this lab is to give you some experience managing Windows file associations. After completing this lab, you will be able to:

➤ Associate a default application with a file type

➤ Associate an additional application with a file type

Materials Required

This lab will require the following:

➤ Windows 9x operating system

Activity Background

In Windows, file extensions are associated with specific applications. For example, a file with a .doc file extension is associated with Microsoft Word. This means that when you double-click a file with the .doc file extension in Windows Explorer, the file opens in Word. (If Word is not yet open, it will open automatically and then display the file.) Often, when you install a new application, the installation process will specify which file extensions will be associated with that application.

It is possible to associate multiple applications with one file extension. However, you must specify a default application for that file type—that is, you must indicate which application you want to open automatically when you double-click a file with that file extension.

When you double-click any file in Windows Explorer, Windows will first attempt to find an application associated with it. If Windows fails to locate the associated application, Windows then gives you the opportunity to choose an application with which to open the file.

Keep in mind that file associations are sometimes lost when you remove an application from a system. This can be caused by poorly written uninstall software. It can also happen if you delete the application's files rather than using the application's uninstall option.

In this lab, you will create a new text file from Windows Explorer. You will check to see which application is associated with that file type and then associate a different application with that file type.

Estimated completion time: **30 minutes**

ACTIVITY

In the following steps you will create a new file and then determine which application is associated with it:

1. Right-click the **Start** button and then click **Explore**. In Windows Explorer, open the **My Documents** folder, right-click a blank area in the right pane, click **New** in the shortcut menu, and then click **Text Document**.

2. Name the new file **associ8.txt**.

3. Double-click **associ8.txt**. In what application does the file open?

   _____

4. Close the application.

You can use Windows Explorer to view and change associations between applications and file types. Follow these steps:

1. If necessary, open Windows Explorer, click **Tools** on the menu bar, and then click **Folder Options**.

2. Click the **File Types** tab. Note that the Extension, Content Type (MIME), and the default application associated with a file type (Opens with) are displayed in the **File type details** section.

3. Scroll down the **Registered file types** list box and then click **Text Document**. What application opens this type of file by default?

_____

4. With Text Document highlighted, click **Edit**. The Edit File Type dialog box opens. Here you can modify all the information found on the File Types tab. Modifying the settings here changes how Windows handles interactions with this file type.

5. In the Actions list box, click **open** and then click the **Edit** button. The Editing action for type: Text document dialog box opens. Here you can specify which application to use to perform an action. If you don't know which one you are going to use or where it is located, you can browse for an application to associate with this file type.

6. Next to the **Application used to perform action** field, click the **Browse** button and open the **Program Files\Accessories** directory. Click **Wordpad.exe,** and then click the **Open** button. You return to the Editing action for type dialog box.

7. To associate this application with the selected file type, click the **Application used to perform action** text box, move the cursor after the close quotation mark, press the **space bar** once, and then type **"%1"** including the quotation marks. See Figure 12-4. The "%1" is a temporary holding place used by COMMAND.COM, and tells Windows that Wordpad.exe is to be used to open files of type Text Document. Click **OK**. The Editing action for type dialog box closes and you return to the Edit File Type dialog box.

12

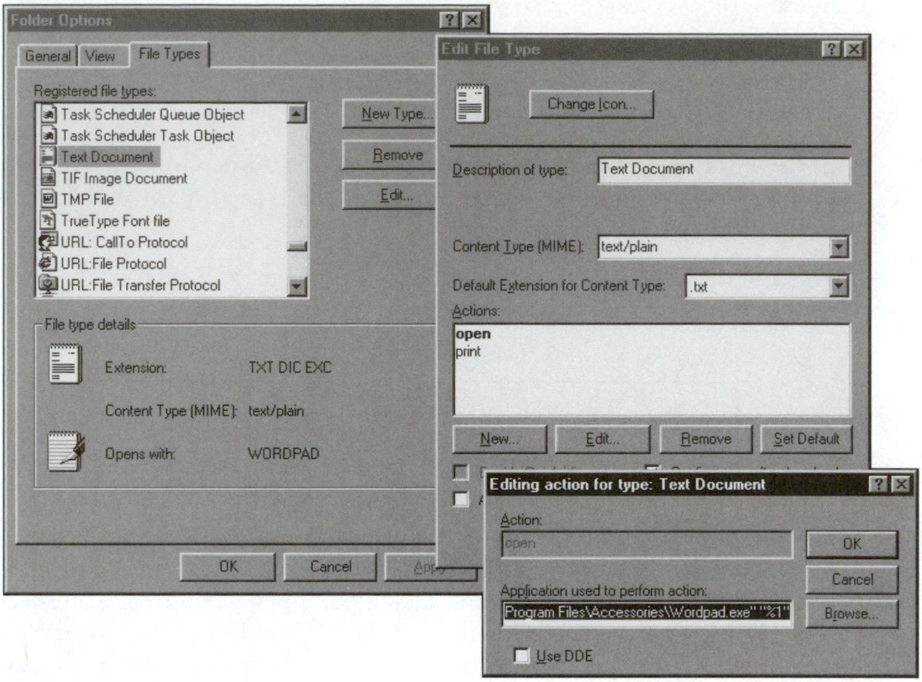

Figure 12-4   Change the application associated with a file type

8. Click **Close**. The Edit File Type dialog box closes and your changes are saved.

9. Click **Close** to exit the Folder Options dialog box.

You have finished changing the application associated with the .txt file extension. Now you can test the new association. Follow these steps:

1. In Windows Explorer, double-click **associ8.txt**. What application opens the file now?

_____

2. Type a sentence in the associ8.txt file, save the change, and close the application window.

To change the file association back to its original setting, follow these steps:

1. In Windows Explorer, click **Tools** on the menu bar and then click **Folder Options**.

2. Click the **File Types** tab, scroll down the Registered file types list box, click **Text Document**, and then click the **Edit** button. The Edit File Type dialog box opens.

3. In the **Actions** list box, click **open** and then click **Edit**. The Editing action for type dialog box opens.

4. Click the **Browse** button, browse to the **Windows** directory, click **notepad.exe**, and then click **Open**. You return to the Editing action for type dialog box. Click **OK** to close the Editing action for type dialog box.

5. Click **Close**. The Edit File Type dialog box closes and your changes are saved.

6. Click **Close** to exit the Folder Options dialog box.

7. In Windows Explorer, double-click **associ8.txt**. What application opens the file now? Close the application that was launched.

You saw earlier that you can double-click a file in Windows Explorer to open the file in the default application. Another way to open a file is to right-click the file and select **Open** from the shortcut menu. If you would like the option of using more than one application to open a particular file type, you can add a new entry to the shortcut menu. Follow these steps to add WordPad to the shortcut menu for text files:

1. Return to Windows Explorer and open the Folder Options dialog box. Select the **File Types** tab. In the Registered File Types field, double-click **Text Document**. The Edit File Type dialog box opens. Click **New**. The New Action dialog box opens.

2. In the New Action dialog box, click the **Action** text box and type **Open with WordPad**.

3. Click the **Browse** button, browse to the **Program Files\Accessories** directory, click **wordpad.exe**, and then click **Open**. You return to the New Action dialog box.

4. Click the **Application used to perform action** text box, position the cursor after the close quotation mark, press the space bar once, and type **"%1"** including the quotation marks.

5. Click **OK**. The Editing action for type dialog box closes. You return to the Edit File Type dialog box.

6. Click **Close**. The Edit File type dialog box closes and your changes are saved.

7. Close the Folder Options dialog box.

To test the new shortcut menu option, do the following:

1. In Windows Explorer, right-click **associ8.txt**, and then click **Open with WordPad**. The document opens in WordPad.

2. To remove the **Open with WordPad** option from the shortcut menu, return to the Edit File Types dialog box. In the Actions list box click **Open in WordPad** and then click the **Remove** button. Click **Yes** to remove this action.

3. Click **Close** to close the Edit File Type dialog box and save your changes. Then close the Folder Options dialog box.

Review Questions

1. What Windows utility is used to manage associations between file types and applications?

_____

2. What tab in the Folder Options window lets you modify file associations?

_____

3. In Windows, what indicates a file's type?

_____

4. Which text editor does Windows normally associate with .txt files?

_____

5. How can you open a file in an application when the file's type is not associated with that application?

_____

6. Why might you wish to add a second file association?

_____

7. Using the Internet, find the definition of MIME and give a brief explanation of its importance.

_____

_____

LAB 12.7 UPDATE WINDOWS

Objectives

The goal of this lab is to show you how to update Windows to keep current with the latest fixes and features. After completing this lab, you will be able to:

➤ Update Windows with the Critical Update Package

➤ Upgrade Internet Explorer to the latest version

Materials Required

➤ Windows 9x operating system

➤ Internet access

 Some educational institutions have polices applied to their Internet firewalls that prevent you from downloading Microsoft updates. If you cannot download the updates from your institution's lab PC, you might have to perform this lab at home.

Activity Background

Microsoft continuously updates many of its products to provide enhancements or repair newly discovered problems. You can take advantage of these improvements by installing these updates on your system. Keep in mind, however, that an update is not the same thing as an upgrade. Operating system updates typically make fairly minor changes to the existing version of Windows, whereas an upgrade installs a new version of Windows. It's important to update your Microsoft products regularly to ensure that they can take advantage of the most recent developments in technology. This is especially important with products such as Internet Explorer, which interact regularly with many computers and other software. Such products will not work correctly without regular updates because they will lack the technology required to interact with more current systems. In this lab, you will update your current version of Windows 9x to its most current state and upgrade Internet Explorer to the most recent version.

Estimated completion time: **45 minutes (not including download time)**

ACTIVITY

Use the following steps to update Windows:

1. Open your browser and go to *windowsupdate.microsoft.com* and click the **Product Updates** link. You may receive a Security Warning asking if you want to install and run "Windows Update Control"; click **Yes** to install it. The browser displays a message indicating that Microsoft is examining your system and customizing the update selection for your system. Next, a list of available updates is displayed, with the Critical Updates Package selected.

2. Scroll through the available updates and notice that they are grouped into categories and include a brief description indicating the purpose of each update.

3. Click the **Download** link. Depending on your update package and how you are connected to the Internet (28.8 modem, DSL, cable modem, and so forth), downloading might take considerable time.

4. When prompted, confirm the update files you selected.

5. Click the **View Instructions** link and make a note of any special instructions not included in this lab.

6. Close the View Instructions window and click the **Start Download** link.

7. Your update may require you to accept an End User Licensing Agreement (EULA). If you are prompted to do so, accept the agreement.

8. A window appears indicating the download progress.

9. When the installation process is complete, you will be prompted to restart your computer. Click **Yes** to restart. When your system is in text mode, a message appears indicating that "setup will update configuration files." Next, you might see a message indicating that the update is complete. Windows will then continue to load to the desktop.

Follow these steps to upgrade to the latest version of Internet Explorer:

1. Open **Internet Explorer**, click **Help**, and then click **About Internet Explorer**. Make a notation of your current version of Internet Explorer.

2. Go to *www.microsoft.com/windows/ie/default.asp* and click the **Download Now** link to download the most current version of Internet Explorer.

3. You see a page describing the most current version of Internet Explorer. Verify that the correct language is selected in the Select a Language list box, and then click **Go**.

4. Directions for downloading and installing the new version of Internet Explorer appear. Read the directions carefully. Note that you can choose to download the file to your hard drive and execute the downloaded file later, or you can install the update from the Microsoft server. To save time, choose to install from the Microsoft Server across the Internet.

5. Click the link for downloading the latest version of Internet Explorer—for example, **Internet Explorer 6 Service Pack 1**—and then follow the installation directions.

6. If at any time during the process you see a warning about receiving files, select the **Always trust content from Microsoft** check box and then continue.

7. Windows asks whether you wish to save to disk or run from the current location. To indicate that you want to install the file from its current location, click **Open**.

8. The installation wizard launches, ready to guide you through the Internet Explorer upgrade. When the End User Licensing Agreement (EULA) appears, click the **Agree** button to continue.

9. Next, click the **Install Now** option button and then click **Next**.

10. You are asked if you want to accept additional files to be downloaded as necessary. Click **Yes** to allow the download of additional files. The download process

begins and you see a window indicating the progress of the download. When the download is complete, the installation process begins.

11. When the installation is complete, click **Finish** to restart the computer.

12. Start Internet Explorer and verify that the new version has been installed.

13. Close Internet Explorer.

CRITICAL THINKING (additional 15 minutes)

1. What is the specific version of Windows 9x you are using?

_____

2. Explain how you got your answer for Question 1.

_____

3. Assign a new name for My Computer on your desktop that includes your version of Windows. List the steps required to perform this task.

_____

_____

Review Questions

1. What types of change are normally associated with an operating system update? What types of change are associated with an operating system upgrade?

_____

_____

2. Why does Microsoft need to examine your system before displaying update files?

_____

3. What is an EULA?

_____

4. What is the most current version of Internet Explorer?

_____

12

5. Did you load your new version of Internet Explorer over the Internet or did you save it to the hard drive and run it from there? Why did you choose this option?

_____

_____

LAB 12.8 OPTIMIZE WINDOWS

Objectives

The goal of this lab is to give you practice using common methods for optimizing Windows performance and security. After completing this lab, you will be able to:

➤ Enable and disable a screen saver with password protection

➤ Defragment a drive

➤ Improve the performance of Internet Explorer

Materials Required

This lab will require the following:

➤ Windows 9x operating system

➤ Internet Explorer version 6 or higher

Activity Background

As a result of normal use, your computer's performance will gradually deteriorate—perhaps not dramatically, but enough that you will eventually notice it. This slowing in performance is caused by a number of factors. For example, as files are copied, moved, and deleted, a drive will become fragmented, a condition in which segments of a file are scattered over the disk, prolonging read and write times.

Another potential problem relates to the fact that Internet Explorer caches (or stores) Web pages each time you visit them. Normally, this feature can speed up browsing if you return to the same pages often and the pages don't change much. (For example, if you go to a site that you have visited previously, half of the site's Web pages might already be stored in the cache; as a result, only half of the Web pages would have to be downloaded over the Internet, thereby increasing the speed with which the pages are displayed.) However, when this cache, called Temporary Internet Files, becomes very large, caching can have the opposite effect and actually increase the time it takes to display Web pages. The reason for this is that your browser searches the cache every time you enter a URL (or click a link) to determine what Web pages it should get from the Internet and what is already in the cache. Searching a very large cache can take more time than simply downloading all Web pages over the Internet.

You can prevent problems like these, which arise as a result of normal use, by optimizing your system, using tools provided by Windows for just that purpose. In this lab, you will have a chance to practice using some of these tools. You will start, however, by using a tool designed to protect your system from mischief—in particular, a special screen saver that activates password protection if you are away from your system for a specified amount of time. This does not completely prevent someone else from accessing your system, but it does make unauthorized access more difficult.

Estimated completion time: **30 minutes**

ACTIVITY

To enable a password-protected screen saver, follow these steps:

1. Right-click the desktop and then click **Properties** in the shortcut menu. (You can also open the Control Panel and then double-click the **Display** icon.) The Display Properties window appears.

2. Click the **Screen Saver** tab.

3. Click the **Screen Saver** list arrow, and then click a screen saver. You see a preview in the monitor at the top of the dialog box.

4. Try out several screen savers and choose one that you like.

5. Click the **Settings** button and customize the appearance of your selected screen saver. Then click **OK** to save the settings.

6. Click the **Preview** button. The screen saver appears on your monitor.

7. Press any key or move the mouse. You return to the Display Properties dialog box.

Now that you have selected a screen saver, you can assign a password to it:

1. Select the **Password protected** check box and then click **Change**. The Change Password dialog box appears, in which you can specify a password.

2. Type the password, retype it to confirm it, and then click **OK**. This password can be, but does not have to be, the same as your Windows login password. You return to the Display Properties dialog box.

3. In the **Wait** field, you can specify how long the system will be inactive before the screen saver appears. Change this setting to **one minute**.

4. Click **Apply** to save your settings, then click **OK** and set aside the mouse and keyboard.

5. Wait one minute. The screen saver appears.

6. Move the mouse. A password dialog box appears.

7. Type your password and then click **OK**. The Windows desktop appears.

8. Reopen the **Display Properties** dialog box and list the required steps to disable the screen saver:

_____

_____

Next, you will practice defragmenting a hard drive. This process can take quite a while, so it is best done when you don't need your computer for a while and can walk away from it. Many people choose to run the utility during the night, when they are not using the computer. The Disk Defragmenter utility will have to start over if interrupted by a screen saver, so you will begin by disabling the screen saver you selected in the preceding steps. To defragment drive C on your system, follow these steps:

1. Because the Disk Defragmenter utility will have to start over if interrupted by a screen saver or other tasks, disable the screen saver.

2. To open Disk Defragmenter, click **Start** on the menu bar, point to **Programs**, point to **Accessories**, point to **System Tools**, and then click **Disk Defragmenter**.

3. Verify that drive C is selected and then click **OK**.

4. Continue using Disk Defragmenter even if you see a message indicating that the drive is only slightly fragmented. (This message tells you that the drive does not really require defragmentation. But to practice using the Disk Defragmenter, you will go ahead and defragment it anyway.)

5. A window appears displaying the progress of defragmentation. Click **Show Details**. A graphical illustration of the defragmentation progress appears.

6. Observe the progress window and answer the following questions while the drive is being defragmented:

   ■ What unit of division does each box represent?

   _____

   ■ What does a green box represent?

   _____

   ■ What does a red box represent?

   _____

   ■ What does a box with a red slash through it represent?

   _____

■ What color represents Free Space?

7. When defragmentation is complete, click **Yes** to exit Disk Defragmenter.

Follow these steps to clear temporary Internet files:

1. Open the **Control Panel**, and then open the **Internet Options** applet.

2. Click the **General** tab, and then, in the Temporary Internet Files section, click **Settings**. The Settings dialog box opens.

3. In the Amount of disk space to use section, you can specify a size for the cache. The best size for your cache will depend on your surfing habits, but for a multi–GB hard drive, it should never exceed 1% of the drive size. Over time, you will want to experiment with this setting until you achieve the best performance for your system.

4. Click **View Files**. The Temporary Internet Files folder opens, and you can see a list of files in the cache.

5. Drag this window to the side but do not close it. The cache might contain many types of files. Examine the cache and list four file types found there.

6. Click **OK**. The Settings dialog box closes and you return to the Internet Properties dialog box.

7. To delete most files in the cache, click **Delete Files**. Click **OK** to confirm deletion.

8. Click the window that displays the Temporary Internet Files contents and press **F5** to refresh the window's display. The list of files is updated to reflect the fact that you just deleted files. Note that all the files have disappeared except for files with names similar to dave@abcnews.go(1).txt. These files are called cookies. Cookies are files that are created by Web servers when you visit a site. They are often used in a good way to help customize content to match your preferences when you revisit a page. However, cookies can also be used to invade your privacy and to secretly send private information from your computer to another computer. Periodically deleting cookies is a good idea if you value your privacy.

9. Click **Delete Cookies** in the Temporary Internet Files section of the Internet Properties dialog box.

10. Again click the window displaying the Temporary Internet Files contents and then press **F5** to refresh. There should be no files visible in your Temporary Internet cache.

12

11. Click **OK** to close the Internet Options dialog box and to close the window displaying the cache.

Review Questions

1. Why should you disable your screen saver before defragmenting a drive?

   _____

2. Why might a drive need defragmenting?

   _____

   _____

3. What Control Panel utility allows you to enable the screen saver?

   _____

4. What is the name of the Internet Explorer cache that contains content from Web sites you have viewed?

   _____

5. What factors might determine the size of your Internet cache?

   _____

   _____

LAB 12.9 MODIFY SYSTEM CONFIGURATION FILES

Objectives

The goal of this lab is to familiarize you with working with Windows configuration files. After completing this lab, you will be able to:

➤ Use the System Configuration Editor to modify configuration files

➤ Edit Msdos.sys

Materials Required

This lab will require the following:

➤ Windows 9x operating system

Activity Background

Windows uses several configuration files when booting. In previous labs, you worked with two of these files, autoexec.bat and config.sys. In this lab you will work with the System Configuration Editor utility to examine and adjust several other configuration files. You will also edit one configuration file, msdos.sys, from the command line.

Estimated completion time: **30 minutes**

ACTIVITY

Follow these steps to edit msdos.sys using the text edit utility, Edit.com:

1. Open a command-prompt window.

2. To remove the hidden, system, and read-only status from the msdos.sys file, enter the command **attrib –h –s –r C:\msdos.sys**, and then press **Enter**.

3. Type **Edit C:\msdos.sys** and press **Enter**. The msdos.sys configuration file opens in the command-prompt window. msdos.sys can be modified to control where Windows files are located and how Windows boots. The Paths section indicates on what drive, and in which directory Windows system files can be found. The Options section controls how Window boots.

4. Notice the remarks (or comment lines), which begin with a semicolon, indicating that extra characters have been added to ensure that msdos.sys is greater than 1024 bytes in size.

5. Locate the line **Boot GUI=1**. You can think of the 1 as meaning yes and the 0 as meaning no. Thus, this line tells the system to load a graphical user interface (also known as a GUI). Change the 1 to a 0, so that it reads: **Boot GUI =0**. (Be sure to type a zero and not a capital letter "O".) What are you instructing the system to do the next time it boots?

   _____

   _____

6. Press and release the **Alt** key. This activates the menu options in the edit utility that you are using from within the command-prompt window.

7. Press the **F** key. This activates the File menu.

8. Press the **S** key. The file is saved.

9. Press and release the **Alt** key again, press **F** to access the File menu, and then press **X** to exit the edit utility.

10. Type **exit** and then press **Enter**. The command-prompt window closes.

12

11. Restart Windows. Describe what happens. Was your prediction from Step 5 accurate?

_____

_____

Now you will make another change to the msdos.sys file and observe the change. Follow these steps:

1. Open a command-prompt window, type **edit msdos.sys**, and press **Enter**.

2. Change the **BootGUI** entry to **=1**.

3. Save your changes, exit, close the command-prompt window and reboot, observing the boot process. What changed?

_____

Now you will make a third change to the msdos.sys file and observe the change. Follow these steps:

1. Open the **msdos.sys** file for editing.

2. Place the cursor under the "D" in the Doublebuffer line and press **Enter**.

3. Press the up arrow to move the cursor to the new blank line and type **Logo=0** . (Again, be sure to type a zero and not a capital letter "O".) What do you think you just instructed the system to do?

_____

4. Save your changes, exit, close the command-prompt window, and reboot, observing the boot process. What changed?

_____

_____

Next, you will practice working with files using the Sysedit utility, which is a Windows utility used to edit system files. You'll start by creating a new user called Test1 on your system. Follow these steps:

1. Restart your PC and log in as **Test1**, entering a password. Windows creates a new user, Test1, making entries in the \Windows\System.ini file and creating a new password file in the Windows folder named Test1.pwl.

2. Log out as **Test1** and then log back in as another authorized user on the computer (using your own name or whatever login you were using on the computer previously).

3. Next, you will use the System Configuration Editor utility to examine the Windows\system.ini file. Click **Start** on the task bar, click **Run**, type **sysedit**, and then click **OK**.

4. The System Configuration Editor utility opens, displaying five files. List these files here:

_____

_____

_____

5. Click the title bar of the window showing the C:\windows\system.ini file bringing it to the front, and scroll down to the Password Lists section. In this section you see an entry for each user account on this computer.

6. Using the Delete or Backspace key, delete the entry for Test1. Do not delete anything other than the entry for Test1.

7. To save the changes to System.ini, with the Windows\system.ini window selected, click **File** on the menu bar and then click **Save**. Your changes are saved.

8. To examine the Win.ini file, which is also opened by Sysedit, click the **Windows\win.ini file** window.

9. Click **Search** on the menu bar and then click **Find**.

10. In the Find dialog box, type **colors** and then click **Next**.

11. The Windows\win.ini file displays the **[colors]** section, with the word *colors* highlighted. After you specify a search item in the Find dialog box, you can use the F3 key to find the next instance of the search text (in this case, *colors*).

12. Press **F3** to jump to the next instance of the word *colors*. Was there another instance of the word *colors*? What message do you see?

_____

_____

13. Exit the System Configuration Editor.

14. Log out and try to log back in as **Test1**.

15. Did you have to enter a password? _____

16. Did Test1 show up in the users list? _____

Review Questions

1. What was the purpose of the Test1 entry in System.ini?

_____

12

2. What utility can you use to modify the msdos.sys file?

_____

3. What is the minimum size of msdos.sys in megabytes?

_____

4. What are the five configuration files you can automatically edit with the System Configuration Editor?

_____

5. Of the five files you listed in Question 4, which two are used by MS-DOS and Windows in real mode?

_____

_____

LAB 12.10 SAVE, MODIFY, AND RESTORE THE REGISTRY

Objectives

The goal of this lab is to learn to save, modify, and restore the Windows 98 registry. After completing this lab, you will be able to:

➤ Modify the registry

➤ Observe the effects of a damaged registry

➤ Restore the registry

Materials Required

This lab will require the following:

➤ Windows 98 operating system

Activity Background

The registry is a database of configuration information stored in two files, system.dat and user.dat. Each time Windows boots it rebuilds the registry from the configuration files and stores it in RAM. When you need to modify the behavior of Windows, you should consider editing the registry as a last resort. Errors in the registry can make your system inoperable, and there is no way for Windows to inform you that you have made a mistake. For this reason, many people are afraid to work with the registry. If you follow the rule of backing up the registry before you make any change, you can feel confident that even if you happen to make a mistake, you can restore the registry to its original condition. In this lab you will back up, change, and restore the registry.

Estimated completion time: **45 minutes**

ACTIVITY

Follow these directions to back up the registry:

1. Click **Start** on the taskbar, click **Run**, type **scanreg**, and then click **OK**.

2. The **Windows Registry Checker** utility opens. (You may see an MS-DOS prompt briefly and a message indicating that the registry has already been backed up. This is because, once a day by default, the registry is backed up the first time Windows successfully starts.)

3. Click **yes** to back up the registry again.

4. When the backup is complete, click **OK** to close the Windows Registry Checker. Windows, by default, stores the last five copies of the registry in the windows\backup folder. The backups are compressed in cabinet files, named rb001.cab or similar.

5. Open **Windows Explorer**, locate the **windows\sysbackup** folder, and determine, by checking the date and time that the file was created, the name of the backup you just created. Record the name, date, and time of this file:

_____

As you know, it's possible to modify many features of Windows by using the appropriate tools included in Windows. But in some cases, the only way to make a modification is to edit the registry. In these steps, you will see examples of one feature that you can modify using a Windows shortcut menu and one that you can modify only through the registry. Follow these steps:

1. Right-click the **My Computer** icon on your desktop. Note that the shortcut menu gives you the option of renaming this icon.

2. Right-click the **Recycle Bin** icon. Note that the shortcut menu does not give you the option of renaming this icon. To rename it, you would have to install and use a special Microsoft utility, called **TweekUI**, which allows you to make some special changes to Windows. Alternatively, you can change the name of the recycle bin through the registry.

3. Click **Start** on the taskbar, click **Run**, type **regedit**, and then click **OK**. The **Registry Editor** opens, displaying the system registry hierarchy in the left pane and any entries for the selected registry item in the right pane.

12

The registry is very large, and searching through it manually (that is, by scrolling down through all the entries) can be tedious even if you have a good idea of where to look. To save time, you can use the Registry Editor's search feature. You will use this feature now to find the section governing the Recycle Bin.

1. To ensure you are searching the entire registry, if necessary, collapse the Registry Keys, click **Edit** on the menu bar, and then click **Find**.

2. Type **Recycle Bin** in the search field. Notice that you can further narrow your search by limiting which items to search. What four ways can you further define your search?

_____

3. Click **Find Next** to begin searching the registry. What is the first instance of Recycle Bin shown in the right pane?

_____

4. Press **F3** to find the next instance. At this point, the right pane of your Registry Editor should display the two items shown in Figure 12-5.

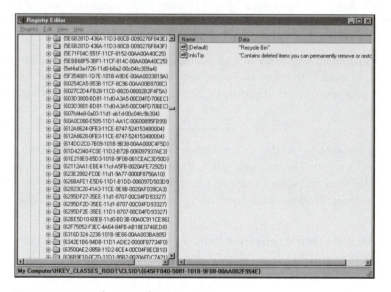

Figure 12-5   The Windows registry

5. Double-click the **Default** entry. The Edit String dialog box opens.

6. In the Value data field, replace "Recycle Bin" with **Trash** and then click **OK**.

7. Notice that "Trash" has replaced "Recycle Bin" in the right pane.

Next, you will edit the Info Tip for the Recycle Bin. (The Info Tip is the pop-up text that appears when your mouse pointer hovers over a Windows item.)

1. Double-click the **Info Tip** entry, type **This used to be named Recycle Bin**, and then click **OK**.

2. Note the change in the right pane. Next, you will close the Registry Editor.

3. Click **Registry** on the menu bar and then click **Exit**. Note that you were not prompted to save your changes to the registry—your changes were saved the instant you made them. This is why editing the registry is so unforgiving. There are no safeguards. You can't undo your work by choosing to exit without saving changes, as you can, for instance, in Microsoft Word.

4. Right-click the desktop and then click **Refresh** in the shortcut menu. Note that the Recycle Bin icon is now named "Trash."

5. Move the mouse pointer over the Trash icon. The new Info Tip appears.

Finally, you need to undo your changes to the Recycle Bin by restoring the previous version of the registry. Follow these steps to use the Registry Checker to restore the previous version:

1. Restart Windows. Hold down the **Ctrl** key during the boot process to activate the Startup Menu.

2. In the Startup Menu, select **Command Prompt Only**. A command prompt appears.

3. Type **scanreg** and then press **Enter**. The Microsoft Registry Checker starts.

4. Press **Enter** to start a registry scan that will check for a corrupted registry. The Microsoft Registry Checker will not usually find errors if the registry has been correctly modified using the Registry Editor. Thus, assuming you performed the steps in this lab correctly, the Microsoft Registry Checker will not find any errors. However, if the Microsoft Registry Checker detects any corruption in the registry, it will offer to repair it.

5. After the scan is complete, select **View Backups** and use your knowledge about the registry to restore the most current saved state.

Review Questions

1. How often does Windows automatically save the registry?

2. Where are registry backups usually stored?

12

3. What type of safeguards does the Registry Editor provide to keep you from making mistakes?

_____

4. What files constitute the registry? As what type of file are they saved during backup?

_____

_____

_____

5. In the previous example, how did you check to make sure that your registry was restored?

_____

_____

LAB 12.11 CRITICAL THINKING: SABOTAGE AND REPAIR WINDOWS 98

Objectives

The goal of this lab is to give you practice troubleshooting Windows 98 by repairing a sabotaged system.

Materials Required

This lab will require the following:

➤ Windows 98 operating system installed on a PC designated for sabotage

➤ Access to the Windows installation CD or the setup files stored in another location

➤ Workgroup of 2–4 students

Activity Background

You have learned about several tools and methods that you can use to recover Windows 98 when it fails. This lab gives you the opportunity to use these skills in a troubleshooting situation. Your group will work with another group to first sabotage a system and then recover the failed system.

Estimated completion time: **60 minutes**

ACTIVITY

1. If the hard drive contains important data, back up that data to another media. Is there anything else you should back up before the system is sabotaged by another group? Note that item here and then back it up.

   _____

2. Trade systems with another group and sabotage the other group's system while they sabotage your system. Do one thing that will cause the system to fail to boot or to generate errors after booting. The following list offers some sabotage suggestions. You can choose one of these options, or do something else. Do *not*, however, alter the hardware.

   - Rename a system file (in the root directory) that is required to boot the system (for example, io.sys or msdos.sys). Alternatively, you could move one of these files to a different directory. Note that you should *not* delete any system files.

   - Using the Registry Editor, delete several important keys (or values) in the registry.

   - Rename important system files in the \Windows directory or move one of these files to another directory.

   - Put a corrupted program file in the folder that will cause the program to automatically launch at startup. Record the name of that folder here:

   _____

   - Use display settings that are not readable, such as black text on a black background.

3. What did you do to sabotage the system?

   _____

   _____

4. Return to your system and troubleshoot it.

5. Describe the problem as a user would describe it to you if you were working at a help desk.

   _____

   _____

6. What is your first guess as to the source of the problem?

_____

7. List the steps you took in the troubleshooting process.

_____

_____

_____

_____

_____

_____

8. What did you do that finally solved the problem and returned the system to good working order?

_____

_____

Review Questions

1. Now that you have been through the previous troubleshooting experience, what would you do differently the next time you encounter the same symptoms?

_____

2. What Windows utilities did you use or could you have used to solve the problem?

_____

3. What third-party software utility might have been useful in solving this problem?

_____

4. In a real-life situation, what might actually cause this problem to happen? List three possible causes.

_____

_____

_____

UNDERSTANDING AND INSTALLING WINDOWS 2000 AND WINDOWS NT

Labs included in this chapter

➤ Lab 13.1 Install or Upgrade to Windows 2000

➤ Lab 13.2 Use Windows Help and Troubleshooters

➤ Lab 13.3 Install and Use Windows 2000 Support Tools

➤ Lab 13.4 Use the Windows 2000 Setup Manager Wizard

➤ Lab 13.5 Manage User Accounts in Windows NT

➤ Lab 13.6 Create Windows NT Setup and Repair Disks

➤ Lab 13.7 Repair Windows NT Workstation

➤ Lab 13.8 Observe and Repair Video Problems

➤ Lab 13.9 Critical Thinking: Sabotage and Repair Windows NT

The following grid shows the correlation between the labs in this chapter and the A+ Guides to Hardware and Software.

A+ Guide to Managing and Maintaining Your PC, Fifth Edition	A+ Guide to Hardware, Third Edition	A+ Guide to Software, Third Edition
Lab 13.1 Install or Upgrade to Windows 2000		Chapter 5
Lab 13.2 Use Windows Help and Troubleshooters		Chapter 5
Lab 13.3 Install and Use Windows 2000 Support Tools		Chapter 5
Lab 13.4 Use the Windows 2000 Setup Manager Wizard		Chapter 5
Lab 13.5 Manage User Accounts in Windows NT		Chapter 5
Lab 13.6 Create Windows NT Setup and Repair Disks		Chapter 5
Lab 13.7 Repair Windows NT Workstation		Chapter 5
Lab 13.8 Observe and Repair Video Problems		Chapter 5
Lab 13.9 Critical Thinking: Sabotage and Repair Windows NT		Chapter 5

Lab 13.1 Install or Upgrade to Windows 2000

Objectives

The goal of this lab is to help you to install, or upgrade to, Windows 2000 Professional. After completing this lab, you will be able to:

➤ Plan an upgrade or installation

➤ Identify the benefits of an upgrade or a new installation

➤ Install or upgrade to Windows 2000 Professional

Materials Required

This lab will require the following:

➤ Windows 98 operating system

➤ Access to drivers or Internet access for downloading drivers

➤ Windows 2000 Professional installation files or installation CD

➤ Key from installation CD

Activity Background

Many people are intimidated at the thought of installing or upgrading an operating system. The process doesn't need to be difficult. In fact, if you carefully plan your installation and are prepared to supply required information and device drivers, your main complaint might be that the process is time-consuming. Even that annoyance can be minimized, using techniques designed to reduce the total installation time. In this lab, you will plan and prepare for an installation or an upgrade to Windows 2000 Professional and then perform the upgrade or installation.

Estimated completion time: **120 minutes**

Activity

Follow these steps to plan and prepare for a Windows 2000 Professional installation on your computer:

1. Obtain a list of devices in the system and detailed system specifications, such as processor speed and drive capacity. If no list currently exists, you can use Device Manager or SANDRA to compile one.

2. Make another list of important applications, and check to see if they are compatible with Windows 2000. If you find any that are not compatible, check to see if any patches or upgrades are available to make them compatible.

3. Check each system specification and device against both the Hardware Compatibility List and the system requirements list for Windows 2000 on the Microsoft Web site (*www.microsoft.com*). Your system will most likely be compatible with Windows 2000. However, in the future, when working on other systems, you might discover significant incompatibilities. In that case, you would have to decide whether upgrading to Windows 2000 was really an option. If you decided to go ahead with the upgrade, you would then have to decide which applications or hardware you needed to upgrade before upgrading the operating system. The Windows 2000 installation CD offers a Check Upgrade Only mode that you can use to check for incompatibility issues in your system before you actually install the OS; however, the information on the Microsoft Web site, which you are using in this step, is often more current and easier to access. Answer the following:

■ Does your system qualify for Windows 2000?

_____

■ If not, what hardware or application does not qualify?

_____

■ Will you install using FAT32 or NTFS? Explain your decision.

_____

_____

4. Download, or otherwise obtain, all necessary drivers, service packs, and application patches from the manufacturer's or the Microsoft Web site for both installed applications and hardware. Record a summary of the components you were required to install to make your system compatible with Windows 2000.

_____

_____

_____

5. Gather any network-specific information in preparation for the installation. If you are connected to a network, answer the following:

■ If you are using a TCP/IP network, how is your IP address configured?

_____

■ For a static IP address, what is the IP address?

_____

13

■ What is the workgroup name or domain name of the network?

_____

■ What is your computer name?

_____

6. Make sure you have the correct CD key for your installation CD. The CD key, which is provided with the Windows 2000 installation CD, usually consists of a set of alphanumeric characters. You must enter the CD key to complete the installation—even if you are installing the operating system from setup files located somewhere other than on the installation CD.

7. Review the information you have collected so far, and then decide whether to do a fresh installation or an upgrade. For instance, if all the important applications on your system are compatible with Windows 2000, an upgrade will probably save time because it leaves compatible applications in working condition. On the other hand, if you know that you will have to install new applications anyway because of incompatibilities, you might choose to perform a fresh installation. In many ways a fresh installation is preferable because it ensures that no misconfigured system settings will be carried over to the new operating system.

■ Will you perform a clean install or an upgrade?

_____

■ Give a brief explanation as to why you chose the option you chose.

_____

_____

_____

8. Back up any critical data files (that is, any work you or others have stored on your computer that you cannot afford to lose during the installation process).

■ If you have critical data files on the PC, where did you back them up to?

_____

You are ready to begin installing Windows 2000 Professional. This lab assumes that you have Windows 98 installed and running. This is not the only situation in which you would install, or even upgrade to, Windows 2000, but it is very common. It is possible to install the operating system using files on the installation CD, on a network drive, or on a local hard disk. To speed up the installation process, consider copying the setup files from the installation CD (or from a network drive) to a local hard disk. This takes extra time initially but is faster overall.

- Are you performing the installation from the Windows 2000 CD, files stored on your hard drive, or a network drive?

The following steps are representative of a typical installation. Your installation process will probably vary in minor ways, depending on the installation options you choose, your system's hardware configuration, and other considerations. The following steps are provided as a general guide to let you know what to expect during the process. Do not become alarmed if your experience differs slightly from the process outlined in these steps. Use your knowledge to solve any problems on your own. Ask your instructor for help if you get stuck. Use the blank lines after the installation steps to record any differences between the steps provided here and your own experience. Also, record any decisions you make during the installation process and any information you enter during the installation process.

1. Before you insert the installation CD or run the setup files from a location on your hard drive or network, use antivirus software to scan the computer's memory and hard drive for viruses. Once the scan is complete, make sure to disable any automatic scans and close the antivirus program before beginning installation.

2. The Setup program starts. This program will guide you through the actual installation. If the Setup program doesn't begin automatically, use the Run command on the Start menu to run WINNT32.exe from the \I386 folder.

   - Did Setup start automatically for you or did you have to use the Run command?

3. Setup informs you that you are running an older version of Windows and asks whether you want to upgrade to Windows 2000. Click **Yes** to continue and follow the instructions in the Setup program. Note that although Setup initially uses the word "upgrade," you will be given the option of doing an upgrade from Windows 98 or a fresh installation of Windows 2000.

4. Accept the EULA (end user license agreement) and click **Next**.

5. When prompted, enter the CD key and click **Next**.

6. Setup examines your system and reports any situations that could cause problems during installation. You are given the opportunity to print the report and exit Setup to correct the problems. Even if some problems are reported, you have done your homework during planning and likely have the solution, so continue the installation.

7. You are given the opportunity to review the Hardware Compatibility List. If you wish to review it again, do so and click **Next** to continue.

8. Specify your file system, either NTFS or FAT32. Windows 98 does not support NTFS, which will be required in a future activity. Instructions will be given on how to convert to NTFS once Windows 2000 is installed. For now, select FAT32 and click **Next**. The system begins to copy files for the installation. Then

13

the text portion of the installation, which provides a DOS interface rather than a Windows GUI, begins. This portion of the installation includes the following:

- Examining hardware
- Deleting old Windows files, if applicable
- Copying Windows 2000 operating system files
- Automatically rebooting your computer

After your computer reboots, the Windows 2000 Setup portion begins. This part of the installation includes the following:

- Verifying the file system
- Checking the file structure
- Converting the file system to NTFS, if applicable
- Automatically rebooting

1. Choose **Windows 2000 Professional** from the startup menu. If you converted your file system to NTFS, you see a message indicating that the conversion was successful.

2. The system installs software for detected devices.

3. When prompted, provide the requested network information. After you have specified how your network is configured, Setup performs some final setup tasks, including the following:

- Configuring the startup menu
- Registering components
- Upgrading programs and system settings
- Saving settings
- Removing temporary files

4. The computer reboots one more time. You are now able to log on as an administrator and install any new applications or devices.

5. Verify that the system is working correctly.

In the following space, record any differences you noted between the preceding installation steps and your own experience. Also record any decisions you made during the installation process and any information you entered during the installation process.

_____

_____

_____

_____

_____

_____

_____

Review Questions

1. List five things you should do before you start the installation process.

   _____

   _____

   _____

   _____

   _____

2. How can you find out if your video card will work with Windows 2000?

   _____

3. What type of installation can save time because it usually retains system settings and leaves applications in working condition?

   _____

   _____

4. What step is critical to ensure that you do not lose important data during installation?

   _____

   _____

5. What step can you take to speed up the actual installation process?

   _____

   _____

13

LAB 13.2 USE WINDOWS HELP AND TROUBLESHOOTERS

Objectives

The goal of this lab is to demonstrate how to use Windows Help tools to find information and how to use Windows Troubleshooters to correct common problems. After completing this lab, you will be able to:

➤ Find information on various topics in Windows Help

➤ Use a Windows Troubleshooter

Materials Required

This lab will require the following:

➤ Windows 2000 Professional operating system

Activity Background

You can use Windows 2000 Help to look up information on various topics related to the operating system. To access Windows 2000 Help, use the Start menu or, with the desktop active, press the F1 key. Help is useful when you need information. If you actually want help solving a problem, you can use the Windows Troubleshooters, which are interactive utilities that walk you through the problem of repairing a misconfigured system. Windows Troubleshooters are often launched automatically when Windows detects a problem. You can also start them manually from within Windows Help.

Estimated completion time: **30 minutes**

ACTIVITY

In the following steps, you will learn to use the main features of Windows 2000 Help. Note that pressing the F1 key starts Help for whatever application happens to be active at that time. To start Windows Help, you need to close or minimize any open applications, thereby making the desktop active. Once the desktop is active, you can press F1 to start Windows Help. To learn more, follow these steps:

1. Log on to your computer as an administrator.

2. Close or minimize any applications that start automatically so that the desktop is active.

3. Press **F1**. (Note that to avoid having to make the desktop active, you could choose to click **Start** on the taskbar and then click **Help**.) Windows 2000 Help launches. As you can see, the Windows Help interface is similar to a Web browser.

- What four tabs are available in Windows Help?

  _____

  _____

- What are the five menu bar items?

  _____

  _____

  _____

4. If no one has used Windows Help on your computer before, the Contents tab will be visible. If Help has been opened previously, the most recently used tab will be visible. Click the Contents tab if it is not already visible.

5. Move the pointer over the Introducing Windows 2000 Professional topic in the left pane, and note that the pointer becomes a hand, as it does in Internet Explorer when you move it over a link. Notice that when you point to the topic, the topic becomes underlined, like a hyperlink.

6. Click **Introducing Windows 2000 Professional** in the left pane. The topic Introducing Windows 2000 Professional expands in the left pane, displaying subtopics. Notice that the right pane has not changed yet.

7. Click **Tips for new users**. Subtopics are displayed in the right pane.

8. Scroll the right pane to get a sense of the information provided there, and then click **locate lost files** in the right pane. The topic expands to show a description of what it contains as well as a link to more information under Overview for locating lost files.

9. Click **Overview for locating lost files**. The right pane displays a list of locations where lost files might be found, along with steps for looking for files in each of these locations. Note that the list begins with the most likely locations for lost files, with less likely possibilities at the bottom of the list. Record the possible locations for lost files:

  _____

  _____

  _____

  _____

  _____

  _____

  _____

13

10. The Windows Help toolbar contains buttons similar to those found in a Web browser, including a Back button (a left-facing arrow) which you can use to display a previous topic. Click the **Back** button in Windows Help. The Tips for new users topic is displayed again in the right pane.

You can also look for topics in Windows Help using the Index and Search tabs, both of which allow you to type in keywords to locate the information you need. These features are useful when you are familiar with Windows Help but don't know where to look for a specific topic in the Contents list. Follow these steps to use the Index and Search features.

1. Click the **Index** tab. If this is the first time the Index has been used, Help will display a small box with a flashlight icon and the message "Preparing index for first use." At the top of the Index tab is a text box where you can type keywords you want to search on. Below the text box is a list of all possible Help topics.

2. Type **los** in the text box.

   ■ As you type, what happens to the list of topics?

   _____

   _____

3. Finish typing "lost files" (without the quotation marks) into the text box. The list of topics below the text box should now include lost files. Highlight the topic **lost files**, if necessary, in the list of topics. Click the **Display** button at the bottom of the pane to display the topic.

   ■ What does Windows prompt you to do?

   _____

4. In the list of topics, click **locating** and then click the **Display** button. The Topics Found dialog box appears, displaying two topics. These topics should look familiar to you.

5. In the Topics Found dialog box, click **Locating lost files** (if necessary to select it), and then click the **Display** button. The Topics Found window closes and information on locating lost files is displayed in the Help window's right pane. How does the information currently displayed compare to the information recorded earlier?

   _____

6. Now click the **Search** tab. Note that the Search tab looks similar to the Index tab except that it does not automatically display topics. Search for Help is an alternative to browsing the Index for a topic. You simply type a topic into the Search box and click the **List Topics** button. Keep search topic strings as short as possible to better focus your search.

7. Type **lost files** in the text box at the top of the tab and then click the **List Topics** button. A list of topics is displayed below the text box. Did the Search tab return more topics than the Index tab or fewer?

_____

8. Click **Tips for new users** and then click the **Display** button. How does the display in the right pane change?

_____

On the Favorites tab, you can record a list of topics that you want to refer to again without having to search for them. Follow these steps:

1. Click the **Favorites** tab.

2. The topic "Tips for new users" is listed at the bottom of the tab, below a blank pane. Click the **Add** button to add this item to your list of favorite topics.

The Windows Help feature enables you to search for information on specific topics related to using Windows. The Troubleshooters provide information on how to fix problems with Windows and its applications. You can access Troubleshooters from within Windows Help. In the following steps you will use a Troubleshooter to troubleshoot non-functioning DOS applications:

1. Click the **Contents** tab in the Help window.

2. In the left pane, locate and click **Troubleshooting and Maintenance**. A list of subtopics appears below "Troubleshooting and Maintenance" in the left pane.

3. In the list of subtopics, click **Windows 2000 troubleshooters**.

4. A table appears in the right pane, with a list and description of Windows troubleshooting tools. In the chart, click **MS-DOS programs**.

5. The Windows Troubleshooter for MS-DOS programs starts in the right pane of Windows Help. The Troubleshooter asks you for details about the problem you are troubleshooting so that it can provide a solution tailored to that problem. For this portion of the activity, assume the following:

   ■ You have only one DOS application that is not working.

   ■ The NTVDM subsystem is working.

   ■ The program works when it is the only program running.

6. To troubleshoot the problem, click the appropriate option buttons for the specified scenario. Use the Next button to advance through the Troubleshooter screens. Notice that the Troubleshooter also provides buttons that you can use to go back to a previous screen and to start over at the beginning of the process. What solution does the Troubleshooter offer for your problem?

_____

_____

13

7. Click the **Start Over** button to troubleshoot a slightly different problem. This time, assume the following:

- No DOS applications work.
- The NTVDM does work.
- The program does not run by itself.
- The program does run in Safe Mode.

Answer the following questions.

- What conclusion does the Troubleshooter reach?

_____

_____

- What two options are offered to temporarily correct the problem?

_____

_____

Review Questions

1. What type of program is Windows Help similar to?

_____

2. What two Help search tabs operate in similar ways? What are the differences between them?

_____

_____

3. What are two ways to launch Windows Help?

_____

_____

4. What tool, accessible from Windows Help, will take you step-by-step through the process of diagnosing and perhaps repairing common problems?

_____

_____

5. Are Troubleshooters ever launched automatically? Explain.

_____

_____

LAB 13.3 INSTALL AND USE WINDOWS 2000 SUPPORT TOOLS

Objectives

The goal of this lab is to help you install and become familiar with Windows 2000 Support Tools. After completing this lab, you will be able to:

➤ Install Support Tools

➤ Access Support Tools

➤ Use Error and Event Message Help to investigate Event Viewer events

➤ Use the Windows 2000 Support Tools Help feature to find out about other tools

➤ Use the Windows 2000 System Information tool to access software information

Materials Required

This lab will require the following:

➤ Windows 2000 Professional operating system

➤ Windows 2000 Professional installation files or installation CD

Activity Background

Windows 2000 provides support tools that you can use to prepare to install Windows 2000, to customize and configure Windows 2000, and to find information on Windows 2000. In this lab, you will install these tools and then practice using some of them.

Estimated completion time: **30 minutes**

ACTIVITY

Follow these steps to install Windows 2000 Support Tools.

1. Log on as an administrator.

2. Open Explorer, navigate to the Support\Tools directory in the Windows 2000 installation files on your hard drive, or click **Browse This CD** on the Windows 2000 setup CD. Then double-click **Setup.exe**. The Setup Wizard launches and welcomes you.

3. Click **Next** to continue.

4. In the User Information window, enter your name and organization in the appropriate fields and click **Next** to continue.

5. In the Select an Installation Type window, select **Typical Installation** and click **Next** to continue.

6. The Begin Installation window appears to let you know that the wizard is ready to begin copying files. Click **Next** to continue.

7. The Installation Progress window appears and displays a progress bar informing you of the progress of the installation. When the installation is complete and the Start menu is set up, the wizard indicates that the installation was successful. Click **Finish** to exit the wizard.

From a student's point of view, one of the most useful support tools is the Error and Event Messages Help tool. This tool gives information on error messages and tells you what steps to take to correct the problems that caused the error messages. Another very useful tool is the Event Viewer, which you will learn more about in Lab 14.2. In Event Viewer, individual events are assigned Event ID numbers. These same Event ID numbers are used in another Windows 2000 Support Tool, the Error and Event Message tool, which allows you to search by Event ID number for further information on the event. The Error and Message tool can explain the situation that caused the error and recommend what to do if the event happens again. To familiarize yourself with the Error and Event Message Help tool, follow these steps:

1. In the Control Panel, double-click the **Administrative Tools** icon. The Administrative Tools window opens.

2. Double-click the **Event Viewer** icon to launch the Event Viewer.

3. In the left pane of Event Viewer, click **System Log** and view the event entries in the right pane.

4. If you see any warning or error events, double-click one of them. Otherwise, double-click an information event. When you double-click any event, the Event Details window opens. Read the information in this window, and record the Event ID number and description.

_____

_____

_____

5. Click **Start** on the taskbar, point to **Programs**, point to **Windows 2000 Support Tools**, and then click **Error and Event Messages**. The Error and Event Messages Help window opens.

6. Click the **Search** tab.

7. Click the **Type in word(s) to search for** field, and then type the Event ID number recorded in Step 4. (Type the number only; do not type the number sign or the words "ID number".) Then click the **List Topics** button. The Select Topic field displays all Help topics that refer to this Event ID number.

8. In the Select Topic field, highlight the item whose title matches the event description recorded in step 4.

9. Click the **Display** button. Information about the highlighted item is displayed in the right pane. Record the explanation of the event and the relevant user action, if that information is provided:

_____

_____

_____

_____

You already know how to use Windows Help to locate information about the operating system. When you need information specifically about the Windows 2000 Support Tools, you can use Tools Help. Follow these steps to find and print information about a particular support tool:

1. Click **Start** on the taskbar, point to **Programs**, point to **Windows 2000 Support Tools**, and then click **Tools Help**. Tools Help opens in a familiar Help window.

2. Now you will use the Search tab to find information about the executable file for the Windows 2000 System Information tool, which provides information on the hardware resources and software environment for your system. The name of this file is msinfo32.exe. Click the **Search** tab (if necessary), type **msinfo32.exe** in the box labeled **Type in the word(s) to search for**, and then click **List Topics**. Topics related to msinfo32.exe are displayed in the Select topic pane.

3. Double-click the topic ranked second. Information on msinfo32.exe is displayed in the right pane.

4. Click **Options** on the Tools Help menu bar and then click **Print**. The Print dialog box opens. If necessary, select a printer and change any settings as necessary.

5. Click **Print** to print the information on msinfo32.exe. Keep the printed information handy so you can refer to it in the next part of this lab.

In the following steps you will actually use the System Information tool (msinfo32.exe). Follow these steps to record information about your system's software environment:

1. Launch System Information, following the directions in the Help information you printed in step 5.

13

2. In the left pane, double-click the **Software Environment** category to display a list of subcategories. Record the subcategories.

_____

_____

_____

_____

_____

3. In the left pane, click **Program Groups**. The program groups for Windows are displayed, showing the software that is installed on the system. What five program groups are always added for each user?

_____

_____

_____

_____

_____

4. In the left pane, click **Startup Programs**. Are the programs listed associated with your Start Menu or are they the programs that launch automatically when you log on to the system? Explain.

_____

_____

Review Questions

1. What directory contains the files necessary to set up Windows 2000 Support Tools?

_____

2. What support tool allows you to search for information based on the Event ID numbers used in Event Viewer?

_____

3. What Windows 2000 Support Tool offers information about all other Support Tools?

_____

4. What is the executable file for the System Information tool?

_____

5. Can you run all of the Support Tools by selecting them from the Start menu?

_____

LAB 13.4 USE THE WINDOWS 2000 SETUP MANAGER WIZARD

Objectives

The goal of this lab is to help you use the Windows Setup Manager Wizard to create an answer file and distribution folder for unattended Windows 2000 installations. After completing this lab, you will be able to:

➤ Install Windows 2000 Setup Manager

➤ Use the Windows 2000 Setup Manager Wizard to create an answer file and distribution folder

Materials Required

This lab will require the following:

➤ Windows 2000 Professional operating system

➤ Windows 2000 installation files or installation CD

➤ WinZip or similar file compression utility

Activity Background

Windows 2000 Professional (and other versions of Windows) allows you to perform an unattended installation. This type of installation can be a time-saver, especially if you have a number of machines on which you want to install Windows 2000. As you know, several pieces of information must be provided during the installation process to correctly configure the operating system. During an unattended installation, this information is supplied by an answer file. In the past, creating an answer file meant typing or editing a text file saved in a specific text format. To speed up the process of setting up an unattended installation and creating an answer file, Windows 2000 offers a support wizard designed to guide you through the process. In this lab, you will install and use this wizard, which is called the Windows 2000 Setup Manager Wizard.

13

Estimated completion time: **30 minutes**

ACTIVITY

Follow these steps to install the Windows 2000 Setup Manager:

1. Open Explorer and select the **C:** drive. Create a new folder named **Deploy**.

2. Using Explorer, navigate to the Support\Tools directory in the Windows 2000 installation files on your hard drive, or on the Windows 2000 setup CD.

3. Double-click **Deploy.cab** and follow directions on screen to copy **contents of Deploy.cab** to the Deploy directory on drive C.

Now that you have installed the Windows 2000 Setup Manager, you can use Windows 2000 Setup Manager Wizard to create an unattended installation answer file. Follow these steps:

1. Verify that the C:\Deploy directory is still open in Windows Explorer, and then double-click **setupmgr.exe**. The Windows 2000 Setup Manager Wizard starts and displays a welcome message.

2. Click **Next** to continue.

3. In the New or Existing Answer File section, select **Create a new answer File** and then click **Next**.

4. In the Product to Install section, select **Windows 2000 Unattended Installation**. What other types of product does this wizard support?

_____

_____

5. Click **Next** to continue.

6. In the Platform Type section, select **Windows 2000 Professional** and then click **Next** to continue.

7. In the User Interaction Level section of the wizard, select **Fully Automated** and then click **Next** to continue.

8. In the License Agreement section, accept the EULA and then click **Next** to continue.

9. In the Customize the Software section, specify the user name and the organization name and then click **Next** to continue.

10. In the Computer Names section, type the computer name and then click **Add**. Note that you could use the answer file you are creating to install Windows 2000 on several computers as long as the computers' hardware configurations are identical.

11. Click **Next** to continue.

12. In the Administrator Password section, specify the Administrator password for this computer, confirm the password, and then click **Next** to continue.

13. In the Display Settings section of the wizard, specify **Preferred Video Settings**. These settings include color, screen area, and refresh rate and will depend on the settings supported by the video cards in the computers on which the unattended installation will be performed.

14. Click **Next** to continue.

15. In the Network Settings section, select the correct Network Type and Settings for your network and then click **Next**.

16. In the Workgroup or Domain section, specify whether the computer is part of a workgroup or domain. If the computer is a part of a domain, specify the Administrator user name and password account.

17. Click **Next** to continue.

18. In the Time Zone section, specify your time zone and then click **Next**.

19. In the Additional Settings section, you could select additional settings that are required for other devices. These settings include telephone information, regional settings such as country and currency, the preferred language for menus and other operating system features, and printers that you might want to install automatically. For this exercise, click the **No, do not edit the additional settings** option button and then click **Next** to continue.

20. In the Distribution Folder section, you can specify whether you want to install the operating system from a CD or to create a distribution folder, typically on a network location. When you use a distribution folder, all necessary source files are copied to that location. For this exercise, however, you will choose to install from a CD. Click the option button indicating installation from a CD and then click **Next** to continue.

21. In the Answer File Name section, specify the name (sysprep.inf) and location for the answer file you are creating (the Sysprep folder at the root level of the drive on which Windows will be installed). Click **Next** to continue.

22. Click **Finish** to exit the wizard and close Windows 2000 Setup Manager. The wizard creates the answer file in the specified location.

CRITICAL THINKING: USING THE ANSWER FILE (additional 120 minutes)

Install Windows 2000 using the answer file you just created and then answer these questions:

➤ Where were the installation files located?

_____

➤ How did you launch the installation process?

_____

_____

➤ How did you tell Setup to use your answer file?

_____

_____

➤ What, if anything, did you have to do while the installation was in progress?

_____

_____

➤ What error messages, if any, did you see? What did you do about them?

_____

_____

_____

Review Questions

1. What type of file does the Windows 2000 Setup Manager Wizard create, and what is this file used for?

_____

_____

2. Before the wizard was developed, how was this type of file created?

_____

_____

3. What other operations does this wizard support?

_____

_____

4. Could you use the Setup Manager Wizard to create a file to assist an unattended installation that automatically creates an account on a Windows domain? Explain.

_____

5. If you choose to create a distribution folder, why won't the Windows 2000 Professional installation CD be necessary during the unattended installation?

_____

_____

LAB 13.5 MANAGE USER ACCOUNTS IN WINDOWS NT

Objectives

The goal of this lab is to give you experience adding and modifying user accounts using User Manager. After completing this lab, you will be able to:

➤ Add users

➤ Reset passwords

➤ Control password policies

➤ Unlock user accounts

Materials Required

➤ Windows NT Workstation

➤ Administrator account and password

Activity Background

Creating user accounts in Windows NT is easy. NT just needs a few things to get a user set: a unique username; user's full name; a description of the user (typically his or her title and department); and a password. Managing users can take quite a bit of administration time. Much of this time is taken up by helping users who have forgotten their passwords or who entered their passwords incorrectly multiple times, causing Windows NT to lock their accounts. In this lab you will practice managing user accounts and passwords using User Manager.

13

Estimated completion time: **30 minutes**

ACTIVITY

Your first task is to start User Manager. Follow these steps:

1. Log on as an administrator.

2. Using Windows Explorer, create a folder named **Users** in the root directory of drive **C**.

3. Click **Start** on the taskbar, point to **Programs**, point to **Administrative Tools (Common)**, and then click **User Manager**. The User Manager window appears, as shown in Figure 13-1. Examine the User Manager window and answer the following questions:

User Manager		
User Policies Options Help		
Username	**Full Name**	**Description**
Administrator		Built-in account for administering the com
Guest		Built-in account for guest access to the co

Groups	**Description**
Administrators	Members can fully administer the computer/domain
Backup Operators	Members can bypass file security to back up files
Guests	Users granted guest access to the computer/domain
Power Users	Members can share directories and printers
Replicator	Supports file replication in a domain
Users	Ordinary users

Figure 13-1   The Windows NT User Manager window

- Based on your knowledge of Windows NT, what two User accounts are included on a Windows NT system by default?

_____

_____

- Does your system contain any personal user accounts? If so, list them here:

_____

_____

- What user groups are included on your Windows NT system?

In User Manager you can add and configure users on a local computer. To learn how, follow these steps:

1. From the User Manager menu, click **User** and then click **New User**. The New User window opens.

2. Type a username—that is, the name that will be used to log on to Windows NT. Keep in mind that each username in your system must be unique. For user names, you can use alphanumeric characters and some symbols (such as "!" and "." but not "\"). Also, note that user names in Windows NT are not case sensitive.

3. Type a full name and description for the account.

4. Enter and confirm a password, then make sure that the **User Must Change Password at Next Logon** check box is selected.

5. Note that User Manager provides other options concerning password setup. Do not select these options now, but record them here:

What other check box could you select?

To add the new user to a user group, do the following:

1. Click the **Groups** button at the bottom of the New User window. The Group Membership window opens.

    What group is the New User a member of by default?

13

How does membership in this group differ from membership in the Administrators group?

_____

_____

_____

2. In the **Not Member of** list box, click **Power Users** and then click **Add**. This makes the New User a member of both Users and Power Users groups.

3. Click **OK**. The Group Membership window closes.

4. Click the **Profiles** button next to the Groups button. The User Environment Profile window opens. Note that, in the User Profiles section, you can configure the profile and logon script location. (You will not do that now, however.)

Now you will set up the user's home directory under the C:\Users directory. With the User Environment Profile window still open, do the following:

1. In the Home Directory section of the User Environment Profile window, click **Local Path** and then type **C:\Users\%username%**. The entry "%username%" tells User Manager to use the account's logon name as the folder name for the user's home directory. The "C:\Users\" part of the entry tells User Manager to place the home directory under C:\Users. (If you wanted to place the Home Directory on a remote system somewhere on the network, you would select **Connect**, specify a drive letter, and then specify a path in the To section.)

2. Click **OK**. The User Environment Profile window closes and you return to the User Properties window.

Note: If you wanted a user to be able to access this computer using a dial-up connection, you would click Dialing and then grant permission and configure this user account for dial-up access using Remote Access Service (RAS). You will not do that at this time, however.

3. Click **OK** to add this user to the system.

4. You have now finished adding a user to the system. Repeat this process to set up accounts for each user in your lab group.

Follow these steps to examine the settings created for new accounts and discover what you can and cannot do with the newly created accounts:

1. Log off as an administrator and log back in using one of your new user accounts.

What did you have to do when you logged on with your user account?

_____

2. Open a command-prompt window. Judging by the command prompt, what folder are you currently working in?

_____

_____

3. Open User Manager and add a new user account called **Test**. Do not adjust group memberships or profiles. When might you not be able to create this account?

_____

4. Log out and then log in as Test.

5. Open a command prompt window. In what folder are you currently working?

_____

6. Open User Manager, add an account called **Test1** without adjusting profiles or group membership, and then attempt to delete the Guest account. Why could you not create an account?

_____

_____

Why could you not delete the Guest account?

_____

_____

13

When attempting to gain unauthorized access to a system, hackers sometimes try to enter multiple combinations of usernames and passwords until they happen to find a combination that works, giving them access to a user account. To prevent this type of unauthorized access, you can configure a system to lock an account after a user makes several unsuccessful attempts to log on to it. Once an account is locked, an administrator must intervene to make the account accessible again. Follow these steps to configure the lockout feature:

1. Log off as Test and log on as an administrator.

2. Open User Manager, click **Policies** on the menu bar, and then click **Accounts**. The Account Policy window opens. The Password restrictions provide four ways to customize a password policy. Record and explain these options here:

_____

_____

_____

_____

3. In the section below the Password Restrictions of the Account Policy window, click **Account Lockout**.

4. Set the Lockout after field to **3 bad logon attempts**.

5. In the Lockout Duration section, select **Forever**. This option tells Windows NT to keep the account locked until the administrator unlocks it.

6. Click **OK** to close the Account Policy dialog box.

To lock and unlock an account, follow these steps:

1. Log off as an administrator and then attempt to log on as Test several times, using an incorrect password. What message appears at the fourth logon attempt?

_____

_____

2. Log on as an administrator and open User Manager.

3. Double-click the **Test** account, clear the **Account Locked-out** check box, and then click **OK**.

4. Log off as an administrator and then log back on as Test. Explain what happens.

_____

Review Questions

1. Besides adding and deleting users, what other tasks can you perform with User Manager? List five.

_____

_____

_____

_____

_____

_____

2. Besides the Administrators group, what other group has permission to add and delete users? What group does not?

_____

_____

_____

3. List the steps required to change the group to which an account belongs.

_____

_____

_____

_____

4. What setting determines the current directory when the command prompt window opens?

_____

_____

5. How would you implement a policy dictating that all passwords be at least eight characters long?

_____

_____

_____

_____

13

LAB 13.6 CREATE WINDOWS NT SETUP AND REPAIR DISKS

Objectives

The goal of this lab is to show you how to create special floppy disks to use when setting up and repairing Windows NT workstations. After completing this lab, you will be able to:

➤ Create Windows NT setup floppy disks

➤ Create a Windows NT Emergency Repair Disk (ERD)

➤ Identify files used on the setup disks and the ERD

Materials Required

This lab will require the following:

➤ Windows NT Workstation

➤ Four blank floppy disks

➤ Access to a copy of Windows NT setup files or installation CD

➤ User account with administrative privileges

Activity Background

Windows NT relies heavily on floppy disks for installation and repair. For example, the setup disks are used to boot the PC if the hard drive becomes corrupted. Another important tool, the Emergency Repair Disk (ERD), is used along with the startup disks to recover from errors. You can make the Emergency Repair Disk while installing Windows NT. If necessary, you can also create one after Windows NT is installed. The Windows NT setup disks can be created on any computer and used on any computer, but the Emergency Repair Disk must be created on the same computer it will be used on. Also, note that the Windows NT setup disks can be created on a computer running an operating system other than Windows NT, as long as you have access to the Windows NT setup files. In this lab, you will learn to create these setup disks and an ERD.

> Estimated completion time: **30 minutes**

ACTIVITY

To create the Windows NT setup disks, you need to open a command-prompt window and switch to the directory containing the Windows NT setup files. Then you need to type the correct command. When creating the disks from a command prompt in real mode, you would use the following command: **winnt /ox**. When creating the setup disks from a command prompt using a 32-bit operating system (such as Windows 9x or Windows NT), you would use this command: **winnt32 /ox**. Because you're working on a Windows NT system, you'll use the latter command. Follow these steps:

1. Log in as an administrator.

2. Open a command-prompt window, and make the directory containing the Windows NT setup files the current directory. (In most cases, you'll find the files for systems with Intel compatible processors in the \i386 directory on the Windows NT installation CD.)

3. At the command prompt, type **winnt32 /ox** and then press **Enter**.

4. The Windows NT 4.00 Upgrade/Installation utility window opens. What does the message say about copying files?

_____

_____

_____

5. Specify the path to the Windows NT setup files (typically the i386 directory on the installation CD), and click **Continue**.

6. The three setup disks are created in reverse order (3, 2, 1). When prompted, label the disk **Setup Disk 3**, insert the disk, and then click **OK**. Setup files are written to each disk. Repeat the procedure for Disks 2 and 1.

7. When the last disk is finished, the utility closes and you return to the command-prompt window. Remove Disk 1.

You are now ready to create the Emergency Repair Disk. Follow these steps:

1. Open a command-prompt window.

2. At the command-prompt, type **Rdisk / S** and then press **Enter**.

3. The Repair Disk Utility opens and begins by notifying you that it is saving the configuration that should only be used to recover a bootable system in case of failure. What options are included in this utility?

_____

_____

4. Label a floppy disk "ERD" and insert it in the drive. Click **Create Repair Disk** to create an Emergency Repair Disk. Windows formats the floppy disk, examines the system's configuration, and creates an ERD that matches the system's current configuration. (Note that each time you change your system's configuration you need to make a new ERD.)

5. Remove the ERD, click **Exit**, and then close the command-prompt window.

Now you can examine the contents of the disks you've created. Use Windows Explorer to display the contents of each disk and answer the following questions:

1. On Setup Disk 1, what files with .exe extensions are included?

_____

_____

13

2. On Setup Disks 2 and 3, what file extensions are used?

_____

_____

3. Name five files that are included on the ERD. What types of information do you think these files contain?

_____

_____

_____

_____

_____

_____

Review Questions

1. What command do you use to create Windows NT setup disks when using DOS?

_____

2. Why might it be convenient to copy the files on the Windows NT installation CD to a hard drive shared over the local network?

_____

_____

_____

3. In what directory are Windows NT setup files for Intel-based computers stored?

_____

4. When should you create a new ERD?

_____

_____

5. Why should you safeguard your ERD?

_____

_____

_____

LAB 13.7 REPAIR WINDOWS NT WORKSTATION

Objectives

The goal of this lab is to help you use setup disks and an ERD to repair a Windows NT installation. After completing this lab, you will be able to:

➤ Generate a Windows NT boot error

➤ Boot with the Windows NT setup disks

➤ Use the ERD to repair Windows NT

Materials Required

This lab will require the following:

➤ Computer designated for sabotage, with Windows NT Workstation installed

➤ The three setup disks for Windows NT that you created in Lab 13.6

➤ Windows NT Workstation installation CD or access to the installation files

➤ A current version of the Emergency Repair Disk created for the PC on which you'll be working

➤ Access to the Internet

Note: Some educational institutions have polices applied to their Internet firewalls that prevent you from downloading Microsoft updates. If you cannot download the updates from your institution's lab PC, you might have to perform this lab at home or skip the part of the lab to update Windows.

Activity Background

Unlike Windows 9x or Windows 2000, Windows NT lacks Safe Mode or a related recovery process. To repair Windows NT, you have only a few options. If Windows NT is damaged to the point that it will not boot, you must boot with the setup disks and then use the ERD to repair Windows NT. By using these disks, you can restore the system to a bootable state. However, they will not restore the software configuration that existed before the problem. To do that, you will need to reinstall software applications, service packs, and so on. In this lab, you will remove system files to make Windows NT unbootable, boot with a startup disk, and then repair the files with the ERD.

13

Estimated completion time: **30 minutes**

ACTIVITY

In the following steps you will sabotage your Windows NT computer so that it will no longer boot. You will do this by removing the Windows NT system files required to boot the system. You will begin by displaying hidden files, because system files are not displayed by default. Follow these steps:

1. Log on as an administrator.

2. Open Windows Explorer, in the left pane highlight the root directory of drive C, click **View** on the menu bar, and then click **Options**. The Options dialog box opens.

3. Click the **View** tab, select the **Show All Files** option button, clear the **Hide file extensions for known file types** check box, and then click the **OK** button. Your changes are applied and the Options window closes. Hidden files are now visible in Windows Explorer.

4. In the right pane, right-click **boot.ini** and then click **Properties**. The Boot.ini Properties dialog box opens.

5. Deselect the **Hidden** and **Read-only** check boxes, so that the files will appear and so that you can make changes to them.

6. Click **OK**. The Boot.ini Properties dialog box closes and you return to Windows Explorer.

7. Right-click **boot.ini** and then click **Open**. Boot.ini opens in Notepad.

8. Delete the line that begins "Default=".

9. Click **File** on the Notepad menu bar and then click **Save**. The boot.ini Default= line specifies where to find system files, so removing this line renders the system unbootable.

10. Windows NT is now damaged. To verify this, attempt to boot your system and record the process. What do you see?

_____

_____

_____

_____

_____

_____

Next, you will boot from the ERD:

1. Insert the ERD and boot the system.

2. Describe what happens:

   _____

   _____

To repair the system, do the following:

1. Insert the Windows NT Workstation installation CD in the CD-ROM drive.

2. Insert setup Disk 1 and reboot the PC.

3. Insert Disk 2 when prompted.

4. At the Windows NT setup menu, press **R** to repair the installation.

5. Setup displays a list of tests that it will perform to find the problem. If you had a very good idea of what was wrong, you could deselect some of these options to save time. With Continue highlighted, press **Enter** to proceed as though you have no idea what the problem is.

6. To allow setup to detect disk controllers, press **Enter**.

7. When prompted, insert disk 3 and press **Enter**.

8. Setup detects your hard disk controller and loads the drivers needed for this controller as well as other drivers needed to access critical devices. Do not be tempted to choose the S option (to skip this step) because Setup needs to load drivers for disk controllers so that it can detect the CD-ROM drive.

9. After Setup detects other drives, press **Enter** to allow Setup to load drivers. If Setup fails to detect a necessary drive, press **S**, follow instructions provided by your instructor to enable your device, and then return to this step in the lab.

10. If Setup notifies you that it has discovered large hard drives, press **Enter** to continue.

11. Setup asks if you have the ERD. What will Setup attempt if you do not have the ERD?

    _____

    _____

12. Press **Enter** to indicate that you have the ERD.

13. Insert the ERD when prompted and press **Enter**.

14. Press **Enter** to let Setup examine the hard drives.

13

15. Setup examines the hard drive and then displays a warning about restoring the registry. What might occur when you restore the registry?

_____

_____

16. Setup displays a list of registry components and system files it can repair and also lists those that appear to be corrupt or missing. To repair Windows NT, Setup will overwrite these selected files with good copies. Because Setup detects no problems with boot.ini, it is not listed as either missing or corrupt. Therefore, no repair options will be automatically selected. Using the up and down arrow keys and the Enter key, select all components except Security and SAM, highlight **Continue**, and then press **Enter**. If you overwrite the SAM (which contains username and account information for all users), only default user accounts will be restored to the system.

17. If you are informed that the files do not match the original files, press **A** to continue replacing all files anyway.

18. When the repair process is finished, remove the ERD and the CD.

19. Press **Enter** to reboot the PC, then log on to Windows NT with your user name and password.

CRITICAL THINKING (additional 30 minutes)

After Windows NT is restored, access the Internet, check for the latest service packs for this workstation, and then install them. What service packs did you install?

_____

_____

Review Questions

1. Recall that the Windows 9x ERD is bootable. Is the Windows NT ERD bootable?

_____

_____

2. In theory, is there any hope of successfully completing the repair process if you do not have an ERD? Explain.

_____

_____

_____

3. In the repair process, what steps must not be skipped so that the CD-ROM drive is detected?

_____

_____

4. What happens to user accounts you created after installing Windows NT if you restore the security and SAM files during the repair process?

_____

5. What should you do immediately after you restore the system to a bootable state?

_____

LAB 13.8 OBSERVE AND REPAIR VIDEO PROBLEMS

Objectives

The goal of this lab is to help you use the Last Known Good Configuration option and VGA Mode Only option to recover from startup problems. After completing this lab, you will be able to:

➤ Install and correct video drivers

➤ Observe the effect of incorrect display drivers

➤ Use the Last Known Good Configuration to recover from an improper driver

➤ Use VGA Only mode

Materials Required

This lab will require the following:

➤ Windows NT Workstation

➤ Incorrect video drivers designated by your instructor

Activity Background

Windows NT provides minimal recovery options. One of the few options at your disposal is the Last Known Good Configuration, which boots the system to the last configuration used to run Windows NT successfully. You can use another option, VGA Only mode, to boot the system with generic display drivers; this is useful in situations when the display is unreadable, allowing you to correct the problem. In this lab, you will install incorrect display drivers, try to recover with the Last Known Good Configuration option, and boot using the VGA Only mode to correct problems with the display drivers.

13

> Estimated completion time: **30 minutes**

ACTIVITY

If you have not reinstalled the correct video adapter after the repair process in the last lab, follow these steps to install the correct adapter:

1. Boot Windows NT and log on as an administrator.

2. Right-click the desktop and then click **Properties**.

3. Click the **Settings** tab and then click **Display Type**.

4. Click **Change**. Select the proper adapter from the lists or click **Have Disk** and browse to the location of the setup files provided by your instructor. If necessary insert the Windows NT Workstation installation CD or point to its location. Also, if necessary, select the correct adapter and then click **OK**.

5. Click **OK** when the drivers have been set up successfully.

6. Click **Close** to exit the Display Type dialog box. You return to the Display Properties dialog box.

7. Click **Apply**. The Display Properties dialog box closes, and you are asked if you want to restart the system.

8. Click **Yes** to restart the system. Windows boots and a message appears indicating that a new display has been adjusted.

9. Click **OK**. The Display Properties dialog box opens, where you can adjust the color and resolution to suit your preference.

10. Click **Test** to test the settings and then click **OK** on the Testing Mode warning message. You see a test bitmap, which is a series of colored and shaded boxes on a green background.

11. The test pattern disappears after five seconds. If you could read the test bitmap display, click **Yes** to keep the settings. Otherwise repeat the test using different display settings until you can read the test bitmap, and then click **Apply** on the Display Properties window. The settings are applied to your desktop.

12. Click **OK** to close Display Properties.

Now that you are sure the correct display adapter is installed, follow these steps to make the display unreadable. (Or follow the directions supplied by your instructor to modify the contents of \Winnt\system32\drivers.):

1. Boot Windows NT and log on as an administrator.

2. Right-click the desktop and then click **Properties** in the shortcut menu. The Display Properties dialog box opens.

3. Select the **Settings** tab and then click **Display Type**. The Display Type dialog box opens.

4. Record your current display adapter and click **Change**. The Change Display dialog box opens.

_____

_____

5. Select the Manufacturer and Display adapter specified by your instructor (drivers that your instructor knows will not work with your display adapter) and then click **OK**.

6. The Third-party Drivers warning appears. Click **Yes** to continue.

7. Next, you need to specify the location of the installation files for this adapter. If necessary insert the Windows NT Workstation installation CD or point to the location of the Windows NT setup files using the Browse button, select the file, and then click **OK**.

8. Click **OK** when the drivers have been installed successfully.

9. Click **Close** to exit the Display Type dialog box. You return to the Display Properties dialog box.

10. Click **Close**. The Display Properties dialog box closes and you are asked if you want to restart the system.

11. Click **Yes** to restart the computer.

Now that you have configured the display improperly, follow these steps to observe the results:

1. Observe the boot process and record the point at which the display became unreadable.

_____

_____

2. Even though the display is unreadable, press **Ctrl+Alt+Del** to access the Logon dialog box. Next, press the **Tab** key four times (five times if you log onto a domain controller) and then press **Enter** twice. This should shut the system down.

To restore video on a failed system, new technicians often try the following steps. As you will see, these steps will not, in fact, solve the problem:

1. Restart the computer.

2. When the Windows NT Start Up menu appears, press the spacebar to invoke the **Last Known Good** option.

13

3. Select **Original Configuration** and then press **Enter**. Did this solve the display problem? Explain why or why not.

_____

_____

4. Again, restart your computer.

Complete the following steps to correct the display problem:

1. Boot the PC and at the Windows NT Start Up menu, highlight **Windows NT Workstation (VGA Only)**, and then press **Enter**.

2. Log in to Windows NT as an administrator.

3. Now that you know how to change display adapters, change your adapter back to the one recorded in step 4, above, where you configured the incorrect adapter.

4. Reboot, and then select **Windows NT Workstation** at the Start Up menu.

5. Verify that you can read the display.

Review Questions

1. Why can you not just start in Safe Mode to troubleshoot a video problem?

_____

2. Suppose your Windows NT display is unreadable and that you need to shut down the system. What keystrokes can you use to shut down the system?

_____

_____

3. For each of the keystrokes that you listed in Question 2, list the corresponding task performed in Windows NT.

_____

_____

_____

_____

4. What key can you press to invoke the Last Known Good Configuration?

_____

5. When changing display properties, what is the advantage of using the Test option before you apply settings?

_____

_____

LAB 13.9 CRITICAL THINKING: SABOTAGE AND REPAIR WINDOWS NT

Objectives

The goal of this lab is to learn to troubleshoot Windows NT by repairing a sabotaged system.

Materials Required

This lab will require the following:

➤ Windows NT Workstation installed on a PC designated for sabotage

➤ Access to the Windows NT installation CD or the Windows NT setup files stored in another location

➤ Workgroup of 2-4 students

Activity Background

You have learned about several tools and methods that you can use to repair Windows NT when it fails. This lab gives you the opportunity to use these skills in a troubleshooting situation. Your group will sabotage another group's system while that group sabotages your system. Then your group will repair its own system.

Estimated completion time: **45 minutes**

ACTIVITY

1. If your system's hard drive contains important data, back up that data to another media. Is there anything else you would like to back up before the system is sabotaged by another group? Note that item here and then back it up.

_____

_____

2. Trade systems with another group and sabotage the other group's system while they sabotage your system. Do one thing that will cause the system to fail to boot or give errors after booting. The following list offers some sabotage suggestions. Do something included in this list, or think of another option. (Do *not* alter the hardware.)

   ■ Find a system file in the root directory that is required to boot the computer, and either rename it or move it to a different directory. (Don't delete the file.)

   ■ Using the Registry Editor, regedit.exe, delete several important keys or values in the registry.

   ■ Locate important system files in the \Winnt directory and either rename them or move them to another directory.

   ■ Put a corrupted program file in the folder that will cause the program to automatically launch at startup. Note the name of that folder:

   _____

   ■ Use display settings that are not readable, such as black text on a black background.

3. What did you do to sabotage the other team's system?

   _____

   _____

   _____

4. Return to your system and troubleshoot it.

5. Describe the problem as a user would describe it to you if you were working at a help desk.

   _____

   _____

   _____

6. What is your first guess as to the source of the problem?

   _____

   _____

7. List the steps you took in the troubleshooting process.

_____

_____

_____

_____

_____

_____

_____

8. How did you finally solve the problem and return the system to good work-ing order?

_____

_____

_____

Review Questions

1. What would you do differently the next time you encountered the same symptoms?

_____

2. What Windows utilities did you use or could you have used to solve the problem?

_____

3. What third-party software utility might have been useful in solving this problem?

_____

4. In a real–life situation, what might cause this problem to happen? List three possible causes.

_____

_____

_____

_____

13

CHAPTER FOURTEEN

SUPPORTING AND TROUBLESHOOTING WINDOWS 2000

Labs included in this chapter

➤ Lab 14.1 Use the Microsoft Management Console

➤ Lab 14.2 Analyze a System with Windows NT/2000/XP Event Viewer

➤ Lab 14.3 Use Task Manager

➤ Lab 14.4 Use Dr. Watson

➤ Lab 14.5 Critical Thinking: Sabotage and Repair Windows 2000

The following grid shows the correlation between the labs in this chapter and the A+ Guides to Hardware and Software.

A+ Guide to Managing and Maintaining Your PC, Fifth Edition	A+ Guide to Hardware, Third Edition	A+ Guide to Software, Third Edition
Lab 14.1 Use the Microsoft Management Console		Chapter 6
Lab 14.2 Analyze a System with Windows NT/2000/XP Event Viewer		Chapter 6
Lab 14.3 Use Task Manager		Chapter 6
Lab 14.4 Use Dr. Watson		Chapter 6
Lab 14.5 Critical Thinking: Sabotage and Repair Windows 2000		Chapter 6

LAB 14.1 USE THE MICROSOFT MANAGEMENT CONSOLE

Objectives

The goal of this lab is to help you add snap-ins and save settings to create a customized console using the Microsoft Management Console (MMC). After completing this lab, you will be able to:

➤ Use the MMC to add snap-ins

➤ Save a customized console

➤ Identify how to launch a console from the Start menu

Materials Required

This lab will require the following:

➤ Windows 2000 Professional operating system

Activity Background

The Microsoft Management Console (MMC) is a standard management tool that you can use to create a customized console by adding administrative tools called snap-ins. You can use snap-ins provided by Microsoft or other vendors. Many of the administrative tools you have already used (such as Device Manager) can be added to a console as a snap-in. The console itself serves as a convenient interface that helps you organize and manage the administrative tools you use most often. In this lab, you will use MMC to create a customized console.

Estimated completion time: **30 minutes**

ACTIVITY

Follow these steps to build a customized console:

1. Log on as an administrator.

2. Click **Start** on the taskbar and then click **Run**. The Run dialog box opens.

3. In the Open text box, type **mmc** and then click **OK**. An MMC window named Console 1 opens. Inside the Console 1 window is another window named Console Root, which is used to display the contents of the console. In the Console 1 menu bar, click **Console** and then click **Add/Remove Snap-in**.

4. The Add/Remove Snap-in window opens. Console 1 is currently empty—that is, it doesn't yet contain any snap-ins. As you can see in the "Snap-ins added to" text box, any new snap-ins will be added to the Console Root folder.

5. Click **Add**. The Add Standalone Snap-in window opens, displaying a list of available snap-ins. Note that this list includes some of the administrative tools you have used so far (such as Device Manager and Event Viewer).

6. Click **Device Manager** and then click **Add**.

7. A Device Manager dialog box opens. Here you need to specify which computer you want this Device Manager snap-in to manage. You want it to manage the computer you are currently working on, so you need to select the Local Computer option. (See Figure 14-1.) Verify that the **Local Computer** option button is selected and then click **Finish**. The Device Manager on the local computer is added to the Add/Remove Snap-in window. The Add Standalone Snap-in window remains open.

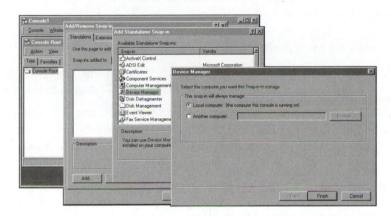

Figure 14-1   Steps to add a new snap-in to a customized console include selecting the computer you want the snap-in to manage

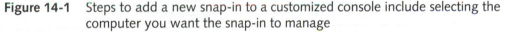

8. Next, you'll add Event Viewer as a snap-in. Click **Event Viewer** in the Standalone Snap-in window and then click **Add**. The Select Computer window opens.

9. Verify that the **Local Computer** option button is selected and then click **Finish**. The Select Computer window closes, and Event Viewer (Local) is added in the Add/Remove Snap-in window. The Add Standalone Snap-in window remains open.

You are finished adding snap-ins for the local computer to your console. Next, you will add another Event Viewer snap-in to be used on a network computer. If your computer is not connected to a network, you can read the following set of steps, but do not attempt to perform them. If your computer is connected to a network, follow these steps:

1. Add another Event Viewer snap-in, and then, in the Select Computer window, click the **Another computer** button. Now you need to specify the name of the computer to which you want this Event Viewer snap-in to apply. You could type the name of the computer, but it's easier to select the computer using the Browse button.

2. Click the **Browse** button. A different Select Computer window opens and begins searching the network for eligible computers. Eventually, it displays a list of eligible computers.

3. In the new Select Computer window, click the name of the computer to which you want to apply this Event Viewer snap-in, and then click **OK**. The second Select Computer dialog box closes, and you return to the first Select Computer dialog box.

4. Click **Finish.** The Select Computer dialog box closes, and a second Event Viewer snap-in is added to the Add/Remove Snap-in window. The new Event Viewer listing is followed by the name of the remote computer in parentheses.

At this point, regardless of whether your computer is connected to a network, the Add Standalone Snap-in window should be active. You are finished adding snap-ins and are ready to return to the Console1 window and save your new, customized console so that you can use it whenever you need it. Perform the following steps:

1. Click **Close** in the Add Standalone Snap-in window. The Add Standalone Snap-in window closes, and you return to the Add/Remove Snap-in window.

2. Click **OK**. The Add/Remove Snap-in window closes, and you return to the Console1 window. The left pane of the Console Root window (within the Console1 window) now contains the following items: Device Manager (local), Event Viewer (local), and Event Viewer (remote computer name).

3. In the Console1 window, click **Console** on the menu bar and then click **Save As**. The Save As window opens with the default location set to C:\Documents and Settings\Administrator\Start Menu\Programs\Administrative Tools. If you save your customized console in this location, Administrative Tools will also be added directly to the Start menu. Instead, choose C:\Documents and Settings\Administrator\Start Menu\Programs for the save location. Be sure to double-click **Programs** so that the file goes inside the Programs folder.

4. Name the console **Custom.msc** and then click **Save**. The Save As dialog box closes.

5. Close the Console1 window.

Follow these steps to open and use your customized console:

1. Click **Start** on the taskbar, point to **Programs**, and then click **Custom**. Your customized console opens in a window named Custom – [Console Root].

2. Maximize the console window, if necessary.

3. In the left pane, click **Device Manager on local computer** and observe the options in the right pane.

4. In the left pane, click the plus sign next to **Event Viewer (Local)**. Subcategories are displayed below Event Viewer (Local). List the subcategories you see:

_____

_____

_____

5. Click **Event Viewer (*remote computer name*)** and observe that the events displayed are events occurring on the remote computer.

6. In the Custom – [Console Root] menu bar, click **Console** and then click **Exit**. A message appears asking if you want to save the current settings.

7. Click **Yes**. The console closes.

8. Launch the customized console from the Start menu again and record the type of information displayed in the right pane when the console opens.

_____

Review Questions

1. What term is used to refer to the specialized tools that you can add to a console using MMC? What are they used for?

_____

2. Suppose you have not yet created a customized MMC. How would you start MMC?

_____

_____

3. How can a customized console be used to manage many computers from a single machine?

_____

_____

4. What information do you see when you open a customized console?

_____

_____

14

5. How do you add a customized console to the Start menu?

_____

_____

LAB 14.2 ANALYZE A SYSTEM WITH WINDOWS NT/2000/XP EVENT VIEWER

Objectives

The goal of this lab is to help you learn to work with Windows NT/2000/XP Event Viewer. After completing this lab, you will be able to use Event Viewer to:

➤ View normal startup events

➤ View failed events

➤ Record event logs

➤ Compare recent events to logged events

Materials Required

This lab will require the following:

➤ Windows 2000 Professional

➤ Network access using the TCP/IP protocol suite

➤ Administrator account and password

Activity Background

Most of the things that happen to your computer while running Windows 2000 are recorded in a log. Windows lets you look at these events with a tool called Event Viewer. Event Viewer is an application included with Windows 2000 that provides information on various operations and tasks (known as events) within Windows. Event Viewer notes the occurrence of various events, lists them chronologically, and gives you the option of saving the list so that you can compare it to a future list. You can use Event Viewer to find out how healthy your system is and to diagnose nonfatal boot-up problems. Fatal boot-up problems don't allow you into Windows far enough to use the Event Viewer. What you learn about Windows 2000 Event Viewer in this lab works the same as it does using Windows NT or Windows XP.

Estimated completion time: **30 minutes**

Activity

Follow these steps to begin using Event Viewer:

1. Boot the system and log on as an administrator.

2. Click **Start** on the taskbar, point to Settings, and click **Control Panel**. The Control Panel opens.

3. Double-click the **Administrative Tools** icon. The Administrative Tools applet opens.

4. Double-click **Event Viewer**. This opens Event Viewer, with the latest events displayed in chronological order from most recent to oldest. See Figure 14-2. The symbols to the left of each event provide important information about the event. For example, the red X indicates a failed event, a lower case i indicates an event that provides information about the system, and an exclamation mark in a triangle indicates a warning, such as a note that a disk is near its capacity. The listing for each event also includes a brief description, along with the time and date the event occurred.

Event Viewer

Type	Date	Time	Source	Category	Event	User
Error	9/20/2002	1:31:16 PM	RemoteAccess	None	20082	N/A
Error	9/20/2002	1:31:16 PM	RemoteAccess	None	20082	N/A
Information	9/20/2002	1:30:40 PM	eventlog	None	6005	N/A
Information	9/20/2002	1:30:40 PM	eventlog	None	6009	N/A
Information	9/20/2002	1:30:42 PM	Ati HotKey Poller	None	105	N/A
Information	9/20/2002	1:28:46 PM	eventlog	None	6006	N/A
Error	9/14/2002	9:54:52 PM	RemoteAccess	None	20082	N/A
Error	9/14/2002	9:54:52 PM	RemoteAccess	None	20082	N/A
Information	9/14/2002	9:54:11 PM	eventlog	None	6005	N/A
Information	9/14/2002	9:54:11 PM	eventlog	None	6009	N/A
Information	9/14/2002	9:54:13 PM	Ati HotKey Poller	None	105	N/A
Information	9/13/2002	5:00:09 PM	eventlog	None	6006	N/A
Warning	9/13/2002	4:35:12 PM	RemoteAccess	None	20169	N/A
Warning	9/13/2002	4:35:12 PM	RemoteAccess	None	20169	N/A
Error	9/13/2002	4:35:12 PM	RemoteAccess	None	20052	N/A
Error	9/13/2002	4:35:12 PM	RemoteAccess	None	20082	N/A
Error	9/13/2002	4:35:12 PM	RemoteAccess	None	20082	N/A

Figure 14-2   The Event Viewer tracks failed events and many successful ones

5. Locate the listings for the four most recent events on your system. For each of those four events, list the source (what triggered the event), the time, and the date:

_____

_____

_____

14

6. Double-click the top (most recent) event. The Event Properties dialog box opens. What additional information does this dialog box provide? Note that you can also see an event's properties by selecting an event and then clicking **Action** on the menu bar. Then select **Properties**.

_____

_____

_____

7. Close the Event Properties box.

You can save the list of events shown in Event Viewer as a special file called a log file. When naming a log file, it's helpful to use the following format: EV*mm-dd-yy*.evt (where *mm*= month, *dd*= day and *yy*= year). For example, you would name a log file saved on January 13, 2004 as EV01-13-04.evt. After you create a log file, you can delete the current list of events from Event Viewer, allowing the utility to begin creating an entirely new list of events. Follow these steps to save the currently displayed events as a log file and then clear the current events:

1. Using Windows Explorer, create a folder called **Logs** in the root directory of drive C.

2. Open Event Viewer (if it is not already open), click somewhere on the Event Viewer window so no one event is selected. Then click **Action** on the menu bar and click **Save Log File As**.

3. Select the **Logs** folder (which you created in step 1), name the file **EV*mm-dd-yy*.evt** (where *mm*= month, *dd*= day and *yy*= year), and then click **Save**. Now you are ready to clear the current list of events from Event Viewer.

4. Click **Action** on the menu bar, and then click **Clear all Events**.

5. When asked if you want to save system log, click **No**. The Event Viewer window no longer displays any events.

6. Close Event Viewer.

Now you will attempt to create an intentional problem by attempting to remove a system file. Recall that Windows 2000 File Protection feature does not allow you to delete or rename a system file. If you attempt to do that, the event is recorded in Event Viewer. To attempt to delete a system file, do the following:

1. Open Windows Explorer and locate the file named **tcpip.sys** in the **\winnt\system32\drivers** folder.

2. Click **tcpip.sys** and press the **Delete** key. The following message is displayed: "Are you sure you want to send "tcpip.sys" to the Recycle Bin?" Click **Yes**. It appears as though tcpip.sys is deleted. Tcpip.sys makes it possible for the computer to communicate over the network. It is a protected system file, so Windows immediately replaces the file. (You will learn more about TCP/IP in later chapters.)

3. Close Windows Explorer and open Event Viewer. Double–click the event labeled **Windows File Protection**. What is the description of the event?

_____

_____

_____

4. What is the Type assigned to this event? _____

5. Close the Event Properties box.

6. Open Windows Explorer. Is tcpip.sys in the \winnt\system32\drivers folder?

_____

You will now create an intentional problem by disconnecting the network cable from your PC and then see how the resulting errors are recorded in Event Viewer. Do the following:

1. Carefully disconnect the network cable from the network port on the back of your PC.

2. Restart the computer and log in as an administrator. Record any messages you receive, if any.

_____

_____

_____

3. Open My Network Places. Are you able to browse the network?

_____

4. Close My Network Places and then open Event Viewer. How many events are displayed?

_____

_____

14

5. List the source, date, and time for any error events (indicated by red X signs) that you see:

_____

_____

_____

_____

_____

_____

6. Click each of the error or warning events and read the details on that event. For each event, write a summary of the information in the Description field. (Within the Event Properties box, click **Close** to exit after you have read the description for each event, or use the arrow buttons on the Event Properties box to scroll through and locate the next error.)

_____

_____

_____

_____

_____

_____

_____

When troubleshooting a system, it's often helpful to compare current events with a list of events that you previously stored in a log file. This can help you spot the point in time when a particular problem occurred. Follow these steps to compare the current list of events to the log you saved earlier:

1. Open another instance of Event Viewer (that is, open a second Event Viewer window without closing the first one).

2. In the new Event Viewer window, click somewhere off the list of events so no one event is selected. Then click **Action** on the menu bar and click **Open Log File**.

3. Open the **Logs** folder, click the log file you created earlier. Under Log Type, select **System** and then click **Open**. If a dialog box appears asking you to confirm opening the file, click **OK**.

4. To position the two instances of Event Viewer on your desktop so you can compare them, right-click a blank spot on the taskbar. A pop-up menu appears, giving you options for how to arrange all the open windows—to cascade the windows or tile them horizontally or vertically. Click **Tile Vertically** to position the two open windows side-by-side. You may notice that the current list of events contains one more successful event than the log of previous events. One of these successful events may in fact be the cause of a failed event. For instance, a service starting and allocating resources that another component was previously using would be listed as a successful event. But the allocation of resources currently in use would in turn cause the component that had been using the resources to fail, thereby resulting in a failed event. Judging by the log file you created earlier, how many events occur in a normal startup?

_____

_____

To restore the network connection and verify that the connection is working properly, follow these steps:

1. Reconnect the network cable to the network port on the back of your computer, restart your computer, and log in. Did you receive any messages after you started Windows 2000 this time?

_____

_____

2. Open Event Viewer and verify that no errors occurred during startup.

3. Open another instance of Event Viewer, open the log you saved earlier (in the Logs folder), and verify that the same events occurred in both cases.

4. Close both Event Viewer windows.

Review Questions

1. Judging by the path to Event Viewer using the Start menu, what type of tool is Event Viewer?

_____

2. Based on what you learned in this lab, what might be your first indication that a problem occurred after startup?

_____

_____

14

3. How can you examine events after you have cleared them from Event Viewer?

_____

_____

4. Explain how to compare a log file with the current set of listed events.

_____

_____

5. Why might you like to keep a log file of events that was made when your computer booted correctly? List the steps to create this log of a successful boot.

_____

_____

_____

_____

_____

CRITICAL THINKING (additional 30 minutes)

Using the Internet for research, find answers to the following questions. Be sure to list the Web site URLs that support your answers.

1. Which version of Windows introduced Windows File Protection? Explain what Windows File Protection does.

_____

2. Does Windows 2000 need DOS to run? Explain your answer.

_____

3. Name two benefits to upgrading to Windows 2000 and explain your answers.

_____

LAB 14.3 USE TASK MANAGER

Objectives

The goal of this lab is to help you use Task Manager to examine your system. After completing this lab, you will be able to:

➤ Identify applications that are currently running

➤ Launch an application

➤ Display general system performance and process information in Task Manager

Materials Required

This lab will require the following:

➤ Windows 2000 Professional operating system

➤ Installed CD drive, installed sound card, and audio CD

Activity Background

Task Manager is a useful tool that allows you to switch between tasks, end tasks, and observe system use and performance. In this lab, you will use Task Manager to manage applications and to observe system performance.

Estimated completion time: **30 minutes**

ACTIVITY

Follow these steps to use Task Manager:

1. Log on as an administrator.

2. Press **Ctrl+Alt+Shift** to open the **Task Manager**, or right-click any unoccupied area on the Windows 2000 taskbar and select **Task Manager** from the menu. The Task Manager window opens. This window consists of tabs providing information about applications, processes, and programs running on the computer, as well as information about system performance.

3. If necessary, click the **Applications** tab. What information is currently listed in the Tasks list?

_____

_____

_____

14

4. Use the Start menu to open Windows Help and then observe the change to the Tasks list in the Applications tab of Task Manager. What change occurred in the Task list?

_____

5. In the Application tab of Task Manager, click the **New Task** button. The Create New Task window opens. This window is almost identical to the one that opens when you use the Run command on the Start menu.

6. In the Open text box, type **command.com** and then click **OK**. A command-prompt window opens. Examine the Application tab in Task Manager and note that \Winnt\System32\command.com now appears in the Task list.

7. Click the command-prompt window. The command-prompt window is now the active window, but notice that the Task Manager window remains on top of all other open windows. This ensures that you can keep track of changes in the system while opening and closing applications.

You can customize Task Manager to suit your preferences. Among other things, you can change the setting that keeps the Task Manager window on top of all other open windows. You can also change the way information is displayed within the Task Manager window. To learn more about changing Task Manager settings, follow these steps:

1. In Task Manager, click **Options** on the menu bar. A menu with a list of options opens. List the available options on the lines below. Note that the check marks indicate which of these options are currently applied. The Always On Top option is currently selected. This is the option that keeps the Task Manager window on top of all other open windows.

2. Click **Always On Top** to remove the check mark and then click the command-prompt window. What happens?

_____

_____

_____

3. Click **Options** on the Task Manager menu bar and then click **Always On Top** to select it again.

4. In the Task Manager menu bar, click **View**. You can use the options on this menu to change the way information is displayed within the Task Manager window. Selected settings are indicated by a dot. List the available settings and the current settings here:

_____

_____

_____

5. Click **Large Icons** to select this setting. Note how this affects the way information is displayed in Task Manager.

6. Return the view to the **Detailed** setting.

Follow these steps to use Task Manager to end a task and observe system usage information:

1. Notice that three types of information are listed at the bottom of the Task Manager window. What three types of information do you see and what are their values?

_____

_____

_____

2. While observing these values, move your mouse around the screen for several seconds and then stop. Which of the three values changed?

_____

3. In the Tasks list, click **Windows 2000 Help** and then click **End Task**.

4. Compare the current processes, CPU time, and memory to the information recorded in step 1. How much memory was Windows 2000 Help using?

_____

Follow these steps to use Task Manager to observe process and performance information.

1. In Task Manager, click the **Processes** tab. This tab lists current processes under Image Name and displays four pieces of information about each process: Process ID (PID), CPU Percent Used By (CPU), a running total of CPU time (CPU Time), and Memory Usage (MEM Usage).

2. Scroll down and examine each process. What process is currently using the highest percentage of CPU resources?

_____

3. Use the Start menu to start Windows 2000 Help.

4. Drag the Windows 2000 Help window to position it as shown in Figure 14-3, so that the left pane is visible on the left side of the Task Manager window.

14

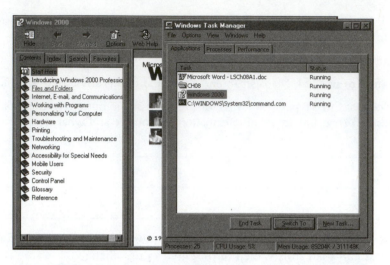

Figure 14-3   Position the Windows 2000 Help window to the left of the
Task Manager window

5. Verify that the Windows 2000 Help window is the active window, then observe the process information in Task Manager as you move the mouse pointer up and down over the topics in the left pane of Windows 2000 Help. Which process or processes begin to use more CPU resources as the mouse moves from topic to topic?

_____

6. In the Processes tab of Task Manager, click **hh.exe** (the Windows 2000 Help program file), and then click **End Process**. What message is displayed?

_____

_____

_____

7. In addition to processes for optional user applications, the Processes tab displays and allows you to end core Windows processes. Thus, this warning serves to inform you of the consequences of ending a potentially essential task. Because Windows 2000 Help is not critical to core Windows functions, it is safe to end this task. Click **Yes** to end.

8. Click the Performance tab and notice that this tab displays CPU usage and memory in bar graphs. This tab also contains a running history graph for both CPU usage and memory. What other four categories of information are displayed on the Performance tab?

_____

_____

9. Insert an audio CD. Configure it to begin playing, if necessary. Observe the CPU and memory usage values, and record them below.

_____

10. Stop the CD from playing and again observe the CPU and memory usage. Compare the usage to the values from step 9. Which value changed the most?

_____

Review Questions

1. Explain one way to launch Task Manager.

_____

_____

_____

2. Which Task Manager tab allows you to switch between applications and end a task?

_____

3. Why could it be dangerous to end a process with Task Manager?

_____

_____

4. How could you tell if the processor recently completed a period of intensive use but is now idle?

_____

_____

5. Did the playback of an audio CD use more system resources than moving the mouse? Explain.

_____

_____

14

Lab 14.4 Use Dr. Watson

Objectives

The goal of this lab is to help you troubleshoot program errors that occur when you are running Windows. After completing this lab you will be able to:

➤ Use Dr. Watson to collect detailed information about the state of your operating system

➤ Use Dr. Watson to troubleshoot program errors

➤ Customize Dr. Watson

Materials Required

➤ Windows 2000 Professional

➤ Access to the Internet

Activity Background

Dr. Watson for Windows is a program error debugger. Dr. Watson is designed to detect problems caused by applications and stop them before the problems affect other applications. The information collected and logged by Dr. Watson can be used by technical support personnel to diagnose a program error for a computer running Windows. If an error occurs, Dr. Watson will start automatically. A text file (Drwatson.log) is created whenever an error is detected and can be delivered to support personnel by various methods.

Estimated completion time: **30 minutes**

Activity

Dr. Watson cannot prevent errors from occurring, but the information recorded in the log file can be used to diagnose the problem. Dr. Watson (drwtsn32.exe) is installed in your system folder when you set up Windows. The default options are set the first time Dr. Watson runs, which can be either when a program error occurs or when you start Dr. Watson yourself.

There are three ways to start Dr. Watson:

➤ Enter the program name (drwtsn32) in the Run dialog box.

➤ Enter the program name (drwtsn32) at a command prompt using a command-prompt window.

➤ Use the Tools menu of the System Information window. (To access the System Information window, click Start, Programs, Accessories, and System Tools.)

In this lab, you will start Dr. Watson using the first method. Do the following:

1. Click **Start** and click **Run**. The Run dialog box opens. Type **drwtsn32** and then click **OK**. The Dr. Watson for Windows dialog box opens and an icon for Dr. Watson is displayed on the taskbar.

2. Click the **Browse** button to the right of the Log File Path. What is the path to the log file?

   _____

3. Using Windows Explorer, look in this folder. Is there a log file there? If so, what is the size of the file in bytes?

   _____

4. Double-click the log file. The file should open using Notepad. A sample log file is showing in Figure 14-4. Scroll through the file looking for dates that information was recorded to the file. What applications caused errors and on what dates did these errors occur?

   _____

   _____

   _____

5. Close the log file.

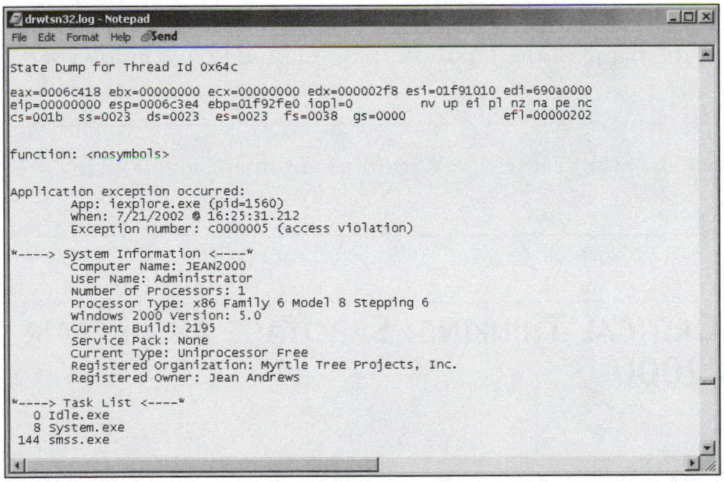

Figure 14-4   A sample Dr. Watson log file

Dr. Watson is available under Windows 98 and Windows NT/2000/XP, but the filename and path to the program file and log file are not the same in each OS. Research the information about these file names and paths, and fill in the following table. You can get your information by searching the hard drives of computers that have these Windows OSs installed, or you can search the Microsoft Web site (*support.microsoft.com*) for the information.

Operating system	Path and filename to the Dr. Watson program	Path and filename to the Dr. Watson log file
Windows 98		
Windows NT		
Windows 2000		
Windows XP		

Review Questions

1. Describe the purpose of the Dr. Watson utility.

   _____

   _____

2. Who might find the information recorded in the Dr. Watson log file or dump file useful?

   _____

3. What is the name of the Dr. Watson log file used by Windows 98?

   _____

4. What is the name of the Dr. Watson log file used by Windows XP?

   _____

5. What type of event causes Dr. Watson to automatically launch?

   _____

Lab 14.5 Critical Thinking: Sabotage and Repair Windows 2000

Objectives

The goal of this lab is to give you practice troubleshooting Windows 2000 by repairing a sabotaged system. After completing this lab, you will be able to:

➤ Troubleshoot and repair a system that is not working correctly

Materials Required

This lab will require the following:

➤ Windows 2000 operating system installed on a PC designated for sabotage

➤ Access to the Windows installation CD or the installation files stored in another location

➤ Workgroup of 2–4 students

Activity Background

You have learned about several tools and methods that you can use to recover Windows 2000 when it fails. This lab gives you the opportunity to use these skills in a troubleshooting situation. Your group will work with another group to first sabotage a system and then repair the failed system.

Estimated completion time: **60 minutes**

ACTIVITY

1. If the hard drive contains important data, back up that data to another media. Is there anything else you should back up before the system is sabotaged by another group? Note that item here and then back it up.

2. Trade systems with another group and sabotage the other group's system while they sabotage your system. Do one thing that will cause the system to fail to boot or give errors after the boot. The following list offers some sabotage suggestions. You can choose one of these options or do something else. Do not, however, alter the hardware.

   - Rename a system file (in the root directory) that is required to boot the system (for example, Ntldr or Ntdetect). Alternatively, you could move one of these files to a different directory. Note that you should not delete any system files.

   - Using the Registry Editor, delete several important keys or values in the registry.

   - Rename important system files in the \Windows directory or move one of these files to another directory.

   - Put a corrupted program file in the folder that will cause the program to automatically launch at startup. Record the name of that folder here:

   - Use display settings that are not readable, such as black text on a black background.

14

3. Because Windows 2000 has features that are designed to prevent sabotage, reboot and make sure the system does indeed have an error.

4. How did you sabotage the system?

_____

_____

5. Retrieve your original system and troubleshoot it.

6. Describe the problem as a user would describe it to you if you were working at a help desk.

_____

_____

7. What is your first guess as to the source of the problem?

_____

8. List the steps you took in the troubleshooting process.

_____

_____

_____

_____

_____

9. How did you finally solve the problem and return the system to good working order?

_____

_____

Review Questions

1. Now that you have been through the previous troubleshooting experience, what would you do differently the next time you encounter the same symptoms?

_____

2. What Windows utilities did you use to solve the problem? What other Windows utilities might you have used?

_____

3. What third-party software utility might have been useful in solving this problem?

_____

4. In a real-life situation, what might actually cause this problem? List three possible causes.

_____

_____

_____

14

INSTALLING AND USING WINDOWS XP

Labs included in this chapter

➤ Lab 15.1 Install Windows XP

➤ Lab 15.2 Allow Two Users to Log on Simultaneously

➤ Lab 15.3 Navigate and Customize Windows XP

➤ Lab 15.4 Manage User Accounts in Windows XP

➤ Lab 15.5 Use Windows Media Player

The following grid shows the correlation between the labs in this chapter and the A+ Guides to Hardware and Software.

A+ Guide to Managing and Maintaining Your PC, Fifth Edition	A+ Guide to Hardware, Third Edition	A+ Guide to Software, Third Edition
Lab 15.1 Install Windows XP		Chapter 7
Lab 15.2 Allow Two Users to Log on Simultaneously		Chapter 7
Lab 15.3 Navigate and Customize Windows XP		Chapter 7
Lab 15.4 Manage User Accounts in Windows XP		Chapter 7
Lab 15.5 Use Windows Media Player		Chapter 7

Lab 15.1 Install Windows XP

Objectives

The goal of this lab is to help you install, or upgrade to, Windows XP Professional. After completing this lab, you will be able to:

➤ Plan an upgrade or installation

➤ Identify the benefits of an upgrade or new installation

➤ Install or upgrade to Windows XP Professional

Materials Required

This lab will require the following:

➤ Windows 98SE operating system

➤ Access to drivers or Internet access for downloading drivers

➤ Windows XP Professional operating system

➤ Key from installation CD

➤ Floppy disks (to store updated device drivers)

Activity Background

Windows XP is designed to be reliable and has a new user interface to give you a more personalized computing experience. The operating system's updated look uses more graphics to simplify the user interface. It has a task-oriented design, which gives you options specifically associated with the task or file you are working on. You can upgrade your computer's operating system to Windows XP Professional from Microsoft Windows 98/98SE, Windows Me, Windows NT Workstation 4.0, Windows 2000, or Windows XP Home Edition. For this activity, you will upgrade from Windows 98SE. The process for installing or upgrading an operating system is not difficult. Careful planning will minimize or eliminate many of the headaches some users have experienced when upgrading to Windows XP.

Estimated completion time: **90 minutes**

Activity

Your lab system will most likely be compatible with Windows XP. However, in the future, when working on other systems, you might discover significant incompatibilities. In that case, you would have to decide whether upgrading to Windows XP Professional is really an option. Many users have experienced significant problems with device drivers when upgrading to Windows XP. For this reason, it is extremely important to do your research and download device drivers that will be compatible with Windows XP Professional before you install the upgrade. You may need to visit the Web sites of the manufacturers of all your devices, such as scanners, printers, modems, keyboards, mouse, camera, and so on, to see if they are compatible with Windows XP Professional. If the manufacturer provides an updated device driver to support Windows XP Professional, you will need to download the files to storage media. Also, when planning an upgrade, it is helpful to record information collected in a table, such as Table 15-1. Follow these steps to create a plan and prepare for a Windows XP Professional upgrade on your computer:

1. Use Device Manager or SANDRA to compile the information in the first row of Table 15-1.

Table 15-1   Things to do and information to collect when planning a Windows upgrade

Things to do	Further information
Does the PC meet the minimum or recommended hardware requirement?	CPU: _____ RAM: _____ Hard drive size: _____ Free space on the hard drive: _____
Have you checked all your applications to verify that they qualify for Windows XP or need patches to qualify?	Applications that need to be upgraded: _____ _____ _____
Have you checked the Microsoft Web site to verify that all your hardware qualifies?	Hardware that needs to be upgraded: _____ _____ _____
Have you decided how you will join a network?	Workgroup name: _____ Domain name: _____ Computer name: _____
Do you have the product key available?	Product key: _____
Have you backed up critical data?	Location of backup files: _____
Verify that your hard drive is ready.	Size of the hard drive partition: _____ Free space on the partition: _____ File system you plan to use: _____

2. Compare your information to the requirements for Windows XP listed in Table 15-2.

   ■ Does your system meet the minimum requirements?

   _____

   ■ Does your system meet the recommended requirements?

   _____

15

Table 15-2 Minimum and recommended requirements for Windows XP Professional

Component or device	Minimum requirement	Recommended requirement
One or two CPUs	Pentium II 233 MHz or better	Pentium II 300 MHz or better
RAM	64 MB	128 MB up to 4 GB
Hard drive partition	2 GB	2 GB or more
Free space on the hard drive partition	640 MB (bare bones)	2 GB or more
CD-ROM drive	12x	12x or faster
Accessories	Keyboard and mouse or other pointing device	Keyboard and mouse or other pointing device

3. Make a list of important applications on your system and verify if they are compatible with Windows XP Professional. If you find any applications that are not compatible, check to see if any patches or upgrades are available to make them compatible. List in Table 15-1 any applications that do not qualify or that need patches to qualify. List below any software upgrades or patches you downloaded to prepare your applications for Windows XP:

_____

_____

_____

4. Install any application upgrades or patches that you have downloaded.

5. Check each hardware device against both the Hardware Compatibility List and the System Requirements list for Windows XP Professional on the Microsoft Web site (*www.microsoft.com*). List in Table 15-1 any hardware devices that need updated drivers.

6. Download, or otherwise obtain, all necessary drivers from the manufacturers' or the Microsoft Web site for your hardware. List any drivers you were required to install to make your hardware compatible with Windows XP Professional:

_____

_____

_____

7. Gather any network-specific information in preparation for the installation. If you are connected to a network, answer the following:

   ■ If you are using a TCP/IP network, how is your IP address configured?

_____

■ For a static IP address, what is the IP address?

_____

■ What is the workgroup name or domain name of the network?

_____

■ What is your computer name?

_____

Record the workgroup or domain name and the computer name in Table 15-1.

8. Based on the information you have collected in Table 15-1, answer the following:

   ■ Does your system qualify for Windows XP Professional?

   _____

   ■ If not, what hardware or application does not qualify?

   _____

9. Make sure you have the correct CD key for your installation CD and record it in Table 15-1. The CD key, which is provided with the Windows XP Professional installation CD, usually consists of a set of alphanumeric characters. You enter the CD key to complete the installation even if you are installing the operating system from setup files located somewhere other than on the installation CD.

10. Review the information you've collected so far, and then decide whether to do a fresh installation or an upgrade. For instance, if all the important applications on your system are compatible with Windows XP Professional, an upgrade will probably save time because it leaves compatible applications in working condition. On the other hand, if you know that you will have to install new applications because of incompatibilities, you might choose to perform a fresh installation. In many ways, a fresh installation is preferable because it ensures that no misconfigured system settings will be carried over to the new operating system.

11. Back up critical data files (that is, any work you or others have stored on your computer that you cannot afford to lose during the installation process).

12. If you have critical files on the PC, to what location did you back them up? Record that information in Table 15-1.

15

13. The hard drive partition that is to be the active partition for Windows XP must be at least 2 GB in size and have at least 2 GB free. Record the size of the hard drive partition and the amount of free space on that partition in Table 15-1. Answer these questions:

    ■ What Windows utility (utilities) or command(s) did you use to determine the size of the active partition?

    _____

    ■ What Windows utility (utilities) or command(s) did you use to determine how much free space is on that partition?

    _____

    _____

14. When installing Windows XP, you have a choice of using either the FAT or NTFS file system. For this installation, use the FAT file system already installed. Record that in Table 15-1.

You are ready to begin installing Windows XP Professional. This lab assumes that you have Windows 98SE installed and running. This is not the only situation in which you would install or upgrade to Windows XP Professional, but it is very common. It is possible to install Windows XP using setup files stored on the installation CD, on a network drive, or on a local hard disk.

The following steps are representative of a typical upgrade. Your installation process will probably vary in minor ways depending on the installation options you choose, your system's hardware configurations, and other considerations. The following steps are provided as a guide to let you know what to expect during the process. Do not become alarmed if your experience differs slightly from the process outlined in these steps. Use your knowledge to solve any problems on your own. Ask your instructor for help if you get stuck. Use the blank lines after the installation steps to record any differences between the steps provided here and your own experience. Also, record any decisions you make during the installation process and any information you enter during the installation process.

1. Before you insert the installation CD or run the installation files from a location on your hard drive or network, use antivirus software to scan the computer's memory and hard drive for viruses. Once the scan is complete, make sure to disable any automatic scans and close the antivirus program before beginning installation.

2. Insert the Windows XP Professional CD. The Setup program starts. This program will guide you through the actual installation. If the Setup program doesn't begin automatically, use the Run command on the Start menu to browse for the Setup.exe file to begin the installation.

3. The Welcome to Microsoft Windows XP window appears with three options. What options do you see?

_____

_____

_____

4. Click **Install Windows XP**. The setup program begins collecting information. The Welcome to Windows Setup window opens with the Installation Type: Upgrade (Recommended) in the text box. Click **Next**.

5. Accept the EULA (End user license agreement) and click **Next**.

6. When prompted, enter the CD key and click **Next**.

7. The Windows Setup Upgrade Report window opens. If necessary, select the option, **Show me hardware issues and a limited set of software issues (Recommended),** and click **Next**.

8. The Windows Setup Get Update Setup Files window opens. Because we can check for updates at a later time and we are focusing on upgrading for now, select **No, skip this step and continue installing Windows**, and click **Next**.

9. Windows is now preparing the installation of Windows XP Professional by analyzing your computer. The setup will be complete in approximately 60 minutes. Read the informational screens as they appear. You can gain a lot of insight into Windows XP through this mini tutorial. Your computer will reboot several times during the installation and setup process.

10. When the installation is complete and Windows XP has rebooted for the last time, you will see the Welcome to Microsoft Windows screen. Click **Next** to continue.

11. At the "Ready to Register with Microsoft" screen, click **No, not at this time**, and then click **Next**.

12. You are now ready to enter your user information. You can type the name of each person who will use this computer. Windows will create a separate user account for each person so you can personalize the way you want Windows to organize and display information, protect your files and computer settings, and customize the desktop. The user names you enter will appear at the Welcome screen in alphabetical order. When you start Windows, you will simply click on your name in the Welcome screen to begin working in Windows XP Professional. For now, enter only your first name and click **Next**.

13. You will receive a Thank You message. Click **Finish** to continue.

15

14. You can also set a password for all Windows XP accounts. Enter a password to be used for all of the listed accounts. If you want to change the passwords later, go to the User Accounts applet in Control Panel.

15. To begin using Windows XP, click your user name and enter your password. A Welcome screen appears. Wait while Windows XP loads your personal settings. The first time you start Windows XP, the Start menu is displayed until you click something else. Thereafter, you will open the Start menu by clicking the Start button at the left end of the taskbar.

16. Remove the installation CD from the drive and return it to the instructor.

Review Questions

1. Was the Windows XP upgrade a success? If so, what did you find to be most challenging about the upgrade process?

_____

_____

2. Describe the Windows XP desktop.

_____

_____

3. By default, which icon appears on the Windows XP desktop?

_____

_____

4. At first glance, what is your impression of the user interface?

_____

_____

5. How does Windows XP offer to help you learn about the exciting new features in Windows XP?

_____

_____

LAB 15.2 ALLOW TWO USERS TO LOG ON SIMULTANEOUSLY

Objectives

The goal of this lab is to help you understand Windows XP support for multiple logons. After completing this lab, you will be able to:

➤ Create a user account

➤ Log on as two different users simultaneously

➤ Customize desktop settings for both users

➤ Switch between two user accounts that are both logged on to the system

Materials Required

This lab will require the following:

➤ Windows XP Professional operating system (If you are using Windows XP Home Edition, some of the instructions in this lab might work differently.)

➤ User account with administrative privileges

Activity Background

Windows XP includes a new feature that allows more than one user to be logged on to the same computer at the same time, each with his or her own preferences set and programs open. This is useful when more than one person needs to use the same computer. In this lab, you will create a new user account, log onto that account, open a program, change desktop settings, switch back to your own account, and observe the effects of switching between the two user accounts.

Estimated completion time: **30 minutes**

15

ACTIVITY

Follow these steps to create a new user account and open an application using the new account:

1. Log on to your computer under your user account, which should have administrative privileges.

2. In the Start menu, right-click **My Computer**, and choose **Manage** from the shortcut menu.

3. The Computer Management console opens. Click the **plus sign (+)** next to Local Users and Groups to expand it.

4. Under Local Users and Groups, right-click the **Users** folder and choose **New User** from the shortcut menu. The New User dialog box opens.

5. In the New User dialog box, enter a user name, full name, description, and password for your new user. Clear the **User must change password at next logon** check box, and then select the **User cannot change password** and **Password never expires** check boxes. (The remaining check box disables the account, which you do not need to do at this time.) Record the user name, full name, and password here.

_____

_____

6. Click the **Create** button to create the new user account, and then click **Close** to close the New User dialog box.

7. Double-click the **Users** folder so that the list of users on your computer appears in the right-hand pane of the Computer Management console, and verify that the new user is listed.

8. Open Microsoft Word, WordPad, or some other application.

Follow these steps to switch between users and make changes as the new user:

1. In the Start menu, click the **Log Off** icon and then answer these questions:

   ■ What options does the Log Off Windows dialog box provide?

   _____

   ■ Hold your mouse pointer over the **Switch User** icon. If balloon text is enabled on your system, some balloon text appears. If the balloon text appears, write down the keyboard shortcut for switching users.

   _____

2. Click the **Switch User** icon. The login screen appears, just as it does when you first turn the computer on and log on to your account. The new user you just created should be listed. Click the icon for that user's name and enter the password for the user when prompted.

3. Now that you are logged on as the new user, right-click an empty area of the desktop, and then click **Properties**. The **Display Properties** window opens. Click the **Desktop** tab and change the desktop background for this user. Next, open an application other than the one you opened earlier. For instance, you might open Microsoft Excel.

4. Choose **Log Off** from the Start menu again and click **Switch User** to display the logon screen.

   ■ What information is listed under your user name and under the new user's name?

   _____

   _____

5. Switch back to your user name, and then switch back to the new user again.

   ■ Does the desktop background change for each user? Do the users' programs remain open?

   _____

6. While logged on as the new user, choose **Turn Off Computer** from the Start Menu and then click the **Turn Off** button.

   ■ What message do you receive?

   _____

   _____

7. Click **No** in the dialog box that appeared when you tried to turn off the computer. You return to the new user's desktop.

8. Now you are ready to log off. To do that, click **Log Off** in the Start menu again. Then, in the Log Off Windows dialog box, click **Log Off** instead of **Switch User**. The logon window reappears.

   ■ What information appears under your user name now? What information appears under the new user's name?

   _____

   _____

Review Questions

1. How do you think the process of switching between users would have been different if you did not assign the user a password? How would it have been different if you had required the user to change the password at the next logon?

   _____

   _____

2. When multiple users are logged on to the same computer, does the logon screen show which programs each user has open? Why do you think this is so?

   _____

   _____

15

3. What are three advantages to multiple logons?

_____

_____

_____

4. List the steps required to render the new user's account inactive without deleting it. After the account has been rendered inactive, would the user still be listed on the logon screen? Explain.

_____

_____

_____

_____

5. In what situation might it be appropriate to disable a user account?

_____

_____

_____

LAB 15.3 NAVIGATE AND CUSTOMIZE WINDOWS XP

Objectives

The goal of this lab is to help you become comfortable navigating and customizing the Windows XP user interface. After completing this lab, you will be able to:

➤ Customize the taskbar

➤ Work with a program shortcut

➤ Customize the Start menu

➤ Clean up the Windows XP desktop

➤ Locate essential system information

Materials Required

This lab will require the following:

➤ Windows XP Professional operating system

Activity Background

Becoming proficient at navigating a new operating system can be unnerving. Windows XP is the newest version of Windows. Upgrading from Windows 98SE to Windows XP Professional is a giant step to take, especially once you look at the differences in the user interface. From the redesigned Start menu to the new task links in folder windows, just about everything looks a bit different in Windows XP, and locating previously used utilities might prove a challenge. In this lab you will explore how Windows XP handles some of your routine tasks.

> Estimated completion time: **30 minutes**

ACTIVITY

To customize the taskbar, follow these steps:

1. Place the mouse pointer over an empty part of the taskbar. Press and hold the left mouse button and drag the taskbar to the right side of the screen.

   ■ Were you able to move the taskbar? If not, what do you think the problem might be?

   _____

2. Right-click an empty area of the taskbar. Deselect **Lock the Taskbar** by clicking it. Now try to move the taskbar to the right side of the screen. Return the taskbar to its default position.

   ■ Were you able to move the taskbar?

   _____

You can create shortcuts and place them on the desktop to provide quick access to programs. You can also rename and delete a shortcut on your desktop. To create, rename, and delete a desktop shortcut, follow these steps:

1. Click **Start** and place the mouse pointer over **All Programs** and then **Accessories**.

2. Right-click **Calculator**. In the menu that opens, choose **Send To**, and then select **Desktop (create shortcut)**. Windows adds the shortcut to your desktop. (You might need to minimize any open windows to see it.)

3. Right-click the shortcut. In the menu that opens, click **Rename**.

4. Type a new name for the shortcut, and press **Enter**.

5. To delete a shortcut icon from the desktop, right-click it, and choose **Delete** from the menu that appears. In the Confirm File Delete dialog box, click **Yes** to delete the shortcut. The shortcut is deleted from the desktop.

15

The Start menu has been significantly redesigned in Windows XP to provide the user with easy access to programs. When it first opens, it looks something like Figure 15-1. When you install most programs, they are added automatically to the Start menu. If a program is not added during installation, you can add it yourself. Windows XP enables you to "pin" a program to your Start menu.

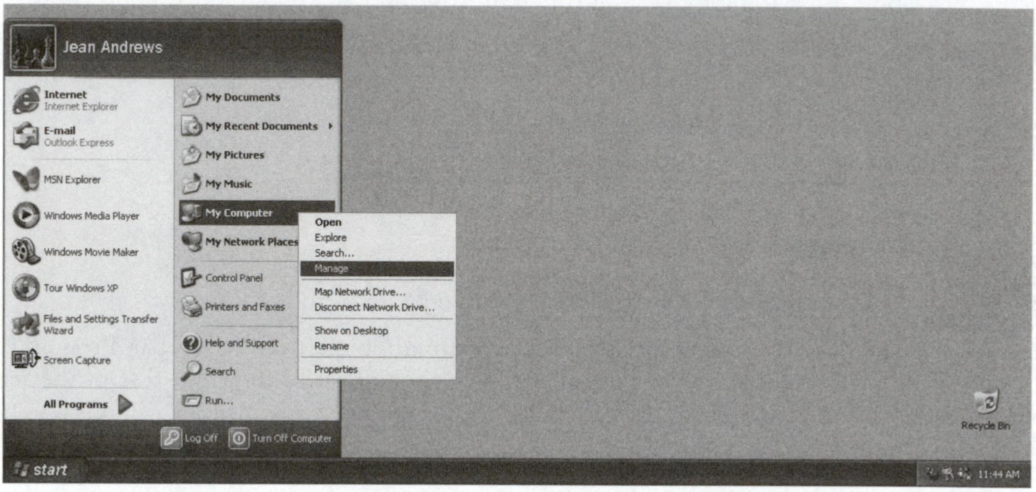

Figure 15-1   The Windows XP desktop and Start menu

To customize the Start menu, follow these steps:

1. First you will need to navigate your folder structure to locate a program to pin to the Start menu. Because performing a backup is an essential task in maintaining your PC, you will pin the backup utility to the Start menu. Click **Start** and place the pointer over **All Programs**, then **Accessories**, and then **System Tools**. Right-click **Backup**.

2. Choose **Pin to Start Menu** from the menu that appears. The program is added to your Start menu.

   ■ Write the steps you would take to unpin the Backup program from the Start menu.

   _____

   _____

   _____

   If you are accustomed to the Windows 98SE Start menu style, which is now called Classic menu, you might find the changes to the Start menu take some getting used to. It is recommended that you give the new Start menu a try because it was designed to increase efficiency. If you are unable to adjust, you have the option of changing to the Classic version.

To revert to the Classic version Start menu, follow these steps:

1. Right-click the **Start** button and select **Properties** from the menu that appears.

2. Click the **Classic Start menu** button and click **Apply**. Click **OK**.

3. Which Start menu version do you prefer, and why?

_____

_____

The Desktop Cleanup Wizard helps you clean up your desktop by moving rarely used shortcuts to a desktop folder called Unused Desktop Shortcuts. The Unused Desktop Shortcuts folder is a temporary holding area for shortcuts you are not using. You can restore shortcuts from this folder or delete the entire folder. In this exercise, you will use the Desktop Cleanup Wizard to clean up your desktop, and you will then delete some desktop shortcuts.

To use the Desktop Cleanup Wizard to remove rarely used shortcuts, follow these steps:

1. Right-click any open area of the desktop, point to **Arrange Icons By** on the shortcut menu, and then click **Run Desktop Cleanup Wizard**. The first page of the Desktop Cleanup Wizard appears.

2. Click **Next** to open the Shortcuts dialog box. A list of Shortcuts to Clean Up is displayed along with the Date Last Used.

3. To leave a shortcut on your desktop, clear its check box. Only those shortcuts with a check mark in the box will be moved to the Unused Desktop Shortcuts folder. Select a shortcut from your list and then click **Next**.

4. You will see a confirmation message indicating which shortcuts will be moved. Click **Finish**.

5. Click **Yes to All**. You will be returned to the Windows desktop. You should see a new folder called Unused Desktop Shortcuts.

6. Next you will move the entire folder to the Recycle Bin. Before you do, take notice of the Recycle Bin icon. Now drag the new folder to the Recycle Bin.

   ■ Did the appearance of the Recycle Bin icon change? If so, explain the change.

_____

_____

15

You may have noticed by now that there are quite a few changes to the way you view and navigate Windows XP compared to Windows 98SE. In the next exercise, you will locate essential system information using My Computer and Control Panel. Remember, however, with the new interface, it may not be so easy to locate some of these items.

To locate essential system information using My Computer and Control panel, follow these steps:

1. Click the **Start** menu and then click **My Computer**.

   - How does the way Windows XP displays the information in My Computer differ from that of Windows 98?

   _____

   _____

   - What happens when you click the drive C icon?

   _____

   _____

2. Double-click the **drive C** icon.

   - Describe how Windows XP displays information about your hard drive.

   _____

   _____

   - What happens when you click **Show the contents of this drive**?

   _____

   _____

3. Click the **Back** button on the Standard buttons bar (which is the bar below the menu bar). Close the My Computer window.

4. Click **Start**, and then click **Control Panel**.

   - What categories of information are displayed in the Control Panel?

   _____

   _____

   _____

■ List the steps you would take to view information or make changes to your mouse settings.

_____

_____

_____

_____

5. Close the Control Panel and return to the Windows XP desktop.

Review Questions

1. What steps must you take to locate the Device Manager?

_____

_____

_____

2. Using the Help and Support feature in Windows XP, locate information on installing new or updated printer drivers. How did you find the information?

_____

_____

_____

3. What Windows XP utility can you use to transfer user files and preferences from one computer to another?

_____

4. Why does Windows XP allow you to change to a Classic Start menu?

_____

_____

5. What Windows XP tool can be used to remove unused shortcuts from the desktop?

_____

15

LAB 15.4 MANAGE USER ACCOUNTS IN WINDOWS XP

Objectives

The goal of this lab is to give you experience adding and modifying user accounts using Computer Management. After completing this lab, you will be able to:

➤ Add users

➤ Reset passwords

➤ Control password policies

Materials Required

➤ Windows XP Professional

➤ Administrator account and password

Activity Background

Creating user accounts in Windows XP is easy. XP needs just a few things to get a user set: a unique username; the user's full name; a description of the user (typically title and department); and a password. Managing users can take quite a bit of administrative time. Much of this time is taken up by helping users who have forgotten their passwords or who entered their passwords incorrectly multiple times, causing Windows XP to lock their accounts. In this lab, you will practice managing user accounts and passwords using Computer Management.

Estimated completion time: **30 minutes**

ACTIVITY

Your first task is to start Computer Management. Follow these steps:

1. Log on as an administrator.

2. Click **Start** on the taskbar, click **Control Panel**, and then click **Performance and Maintenance**.

3. Click **Administrative Tools** and double-click **Computer Management**. The Computer Management window appears, similar to that shown in Figure 15-2. (Another way to get to the Computer Management window is to right-click My Computer and select Manage from the shortcut menu.)

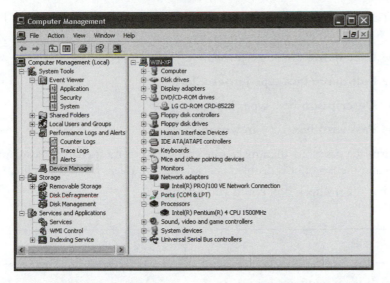

Figure 15-2   The Computer Management console

4. Click the **plus sign (+)** next to **Local Users and Groups** to expand the category. Examine the Computer Management window and answer the following questions:

■ Based on your knowledge of Windows XP, what two user accounts are included on a Windows XP system by default?

_____

_____

■ Does your system contain any personal user accounts? If so, list them here:

_____

_____

■ What user groups are included on your Windows XP system?

_____

_____

In Computer Management you can add and configure users on a local computer. To learn how, follow these steps:

1. From the left pane of the Local Users and Groups, click the **Users** folder to display a list of current user names.

15

2. Right-click **Users** and select **New User** from the shortcut window. The New User window opens.

3. In the **User name** box, type **James**.

4. In the **Full name** box, type **James Clark**.

5. In the **Description** box, type **Supervisor**.

6. In the **Password** box, type **newuser**.

7. Confirm the password, then make sure that the User must change password at next logon and the Account is disabled check boxes are cleared, and then click **Create**.

   ■ What other check box could you select?

   _____

   _____

8. Close all open windows.

When Windows XP creates a new user, that user is automatically added to the Limited group, which means the account cannot create, delete, or change other accounts; make system-wide changes; or install software. To give the account administrative privileges, do the following:

1. Open the Control Panel and double-click the **User Account** applet. The User Account window opens listing all accounts.

2. Click **Change an Account** and select the account for James Clark. The User Accounts window changes so that you can change the account.

   ■ What are the five things you can do to an account on this window?

   _____

   _____

   _____

   _____

   _____

3. Select **Change the account type**.

4. On the next window, select **Computer administrator** and click **Change Account Type**. Click **Back** on the menu bar to return to the opening window.

5. Log off your computer and log on as James Clark. List the steps you did to accomplish that.

_____

_____

_____

Review Questions

1. Besides adding and deleting users, what other tasks can you perform with Computer Management for Local Users and Groups?

_____

2. List the five types of Windows XP user groups created when Windows XP is first installed and what each group can do.

_____

_____

_____

_____

_____

_____

_____

3. List the steps required to change the group to which an account belongs.

_____

_____

_____

_____

15

4. List the steps to delete a user account.

_____

_____

_____

5. Why is it a good idea to have the user change his or her password the first time the user logs on?

_____

LAB 15.5 USE WINDOWS MEDIA PLAYER

Objectives

The goal of this lab is to give you experience managing Audio and Video using Windows Media Player. After completing this lab, you will be able to:

➤ Launch Windows Media Player

➤ Change Windows Media Player options

➤ Create and use a Music Playlist

Materials Required

➤ Windows XP Professional

➤ Internet access

➤ Music CD that is not copyrighted

Activity Background

Many people enjoy playing music or videos on their computers. Windows Media Player gives you the possibility of having an entertainment center on your desktop. Windows XP Professional comes with Windows Media Player 8, which you can use to play, copy, and catalog audio and video files from your computer, CDs, DVDs, or the Internet. You can display Media Player in one of two modes: **full mode** or **skin mode**. By default, Media Player will open in skin mode.

Estimated completion time: **30 minutes**

ACTIVITY

To launch Windows Media Player, follow these steps:

1. If necessary, log on to Windows XP.

2. On the Start menu, point to **All Programs**, and then click **Windows Media Player**. The Windows Media Player opens. A sample playlist will probably open and start playing the first selection. The display area shows the default visualization.

3. On the taskbar, click **Now Playing**, if necessary, to display the current playlist. To play a song, double click a song in the list.

Visualizations are shapes and colors that appear on the Windows Media Player window to enhance the audio while songs are playing. You can change the visualization options. Do the following:

1. Click the **Select visualization or album art button** (round button with * on it labeled in Figure 15-3), and then click **Spikes** on the drop-down list.

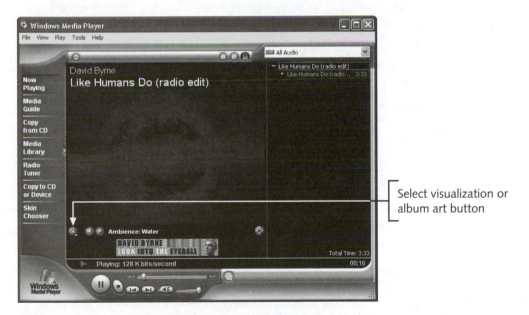

Select visualization or album art button

Figure 15-3   Windows Media Player window

2. Click the **Next visualization** button to move to the next Spikes options, **Spikes: Amoeba**.

3. Use the Select visualization or album art button and the Next visualization button to view other available options. List five of these options here:

_____

_____

_____

_____

_____

Using Windows Media Player, you can browse the Internet for songs. Do the following:

1. On the taskbar, click **Media Guide**. If you are connected to the Internet, the Windows Media Web site opens.

2. Browse through the Web site to see what it has to offer.

3. On the taskbar, click **Radio Tuner**. The Radio Tuner opens with a list of featured stations displayed.

4. In the **Featured Stations** list, click through the radio stations until you find one that has a Play button.

5. Click the **Play** button to hear the station. The radio station's Web site opens in a new window in the background.

6. Describe how the Web site is set up so that you can choose what music you want to hear:

_____

_____

_____

7. Click **Close** to close the Windows Media Player window and then close the window displaying the radio station's Web site.

Those who have used Media Player and taken advantage of downloading files to their hard disk soon find out that they have accumulated hundreds of songs. Just as important as managing data files on your hard drives, you should also practice good file management of the music files you accumulate. Windows XP helps solve the problem of scrolling through endless lists of files searching for the next song you want to hear by creating playlists. A playlist is a list of digital media files, such as songs, video clips, and links to radio stations. You can create a playlist as a collection, which will allow you to play, copy, or burn it to a CD.

To create a Music Playlist and add a song to it, follow these steps:

1. Open the Windows Media Player window.

2. Click **Media Library**, and then click **New Playlist** in the upper-left part of the window. The New Playlist dialog box appears.

3. Type **MyBestSongs**, which will be a subgroup under MyPlaylists. Click **OK**. MyBestSongs is now listed under My Playlists. If you click MyBestSongs, no songs are listed.

Now you will copy two songs from a CD to your hard drive and then add one of these songs to your playlist, MyBestSongs. Do the following:

1. Insert a music CD that is not copyright protected in the CD-ROM drive; the music CD might start playing. Click **Copy from CD**. A list of songs on the CD is displayed in the right pane. All songs on the CD are selected for copying. Clear the check boxes next to all except two songs.

2. Click **Copy Music** to copy the two selected songs to your hard drive.

3. A dialog box is displayed informing you that, if the CD is copy protected, you cannot proceed. Click **OK**.

4. The two selected songs are copied to your My Music folder and are also listed under Media Library. When the copying is complete, click **Media Library**. The two songs are listed in the right pane.

5. Drag one of the songs to the **MyBestSongs** playlist under My Playlists. Your musical selection will appear in your custom playlist. Play the selection.

6. Stop the current selection from playing and close Windows Media Player.

There is a simple way to listen to songs you have put into your My Music folder. Do the following:

1. Click **Start**, then **My Music**.

2. Locate the song in the folder or its subfolder and double-click the song.

   - What application launches to play the song?

Review Questions

1. Describe how visualizations are used by Windows Media Player.

2. Using Windows Media Player, is it possible to copy music files to a CD? If so, explain how you would accomplish that task.

15

_____

_____

3. When you first open Windows Media Player, it appears in a default mode (Windows style). How many other available modes are there? Explain how you change the mode in Media Player.

_____

_____

_____

4. Explain how you switch from skin mode to full mode and back again.

_____

_____

_____

16
SUPPORTING AND
TROUBLESHOOTING WINDOWS XP

Labs included in this chapter

➤ Lab 16.1 Set Disk Quotas

➤ Lab 16.2 Use Encryption

➤ Lab 16.3 Restore the System State

➤ Lab 16.4 Install Recovery Console as an Option on the Boot Loader Menu

➤ Lab 16.5 Use Recovery Console to Copy Files

➤ Lab 16.6 Monitor the Memory Counter

➤ Lab 16.7 Critical Thinking: Sabotage and Repair Windows XP

The following grid shows the correlation between the labs in this chapter and the A+ Guides to Hardware and Software.

A+ Guide to Managing and Maintaining Your PC, Fifth Edition	A+ Guide to Hardware, Third Edition	A+ Guide to Software, Third Edition
Lab 16.1 Set Disk Quotas		Chapter 8
Lab 16.2 Use Encryption		Chapter 8
Lab 16.3 Restore the System State		Chapter 8
Lab 16.4 Install Recovery Console as an Option on the Boot Loader Menu		Chapter 8
Lab 16.5 Use Recovery Console to Copy Files		Chapter 8
Lab 16.6 Monitor the Memory Counter		Chapter 8
Lab 16.7 Critical Thinking: Sabotage and Repair Windows XP		Chapter 8

LAB 16.1 SET DISK QUOTAS

Objectives

The goal of this lab is to teach you how to set and monitor disk quotas. After completing this lab, you will be able to:

➤ Convert a logical drive from FAT to NTFS

➤ Set disk quotas for new users

➤ Monitor quota logs

➤ Identify when quotas have been exceeded

Materials Required

This lab will require the following:

➤ Windows XP Professional operating system

➤ An NTFS partition that might be the partition where Windows XP is installed

Activity Background

When a system is used by more than one account or when server storage space is limited, it is often desirable to set storage limits for each user. No one account should monopolize storage space by filling up the server and preventing other users from storing data. Note, however, that you can impose disk quotas only on drives formatted with NTFS. In this lab, you will use disk quotas to limit user storage space.

Estimated completion time: **30 minutes**

ACTIVITY

In the following steps you will set very small disk quotas for all users. That way you can later easily exceed the disk quota limit and observe the results. Do the following to verify that you are using an NTFS file system:

1. Log on as an administrator.

2. Using Windows Explorer, right-click drive **C** (or another logical drive designated by your instructor) and select **Properties** from the shortcut menu. The Local Disk (C) Properties window appears. On the **General** tab, verify that the drive is using the NTFS file system.

If you currently have the FAT32 file system and need to convert to NTFS, use the following steps, and then begin again with step 1. If you already have NTFS, skip the next three steps.

1. Open a command-prompt window.

2. In the command-prompt window, type: **convert C: /fs:ntfs**. (If necessary, substitute the drive letter for another logical drive in the command line as specified by your instructor.)

3. After the command executes, reboot your computer for the conversion to NTFS to complete.

To enable disk quotas, do the following:

1. In the Disk Properties window, click the **Quota** tab.

2. Select the **Enable quota management** check box. This option allows you to set and change quotas.

3. Select the **Deny disk space to users exceeding quota limit** check box. This option prevents a user from using more disk space after using up his or her quota.

4. Verify that the **Limit disk space to** option button is selected, and that **1** appears in the text box to the right. Then select **MB** in the drop-down list. This sets the disk quota to 1 MB of storage space.

5. Click the **Set warning level to** text box, type **500**, and then verify that **KB** is displayed in the text box to the right. This ensures that users will receive warnings once they have used 500 KB of disk space.

6. Select **Log event when a user exceeds their quota limit**. This ensures that a record will be made when a user exceeds the quota limit.

7. Select **Log event when a user exceeds their warning level**. This ensures that a record will be made when a user reaches his or her warning limit. (You will be able to view the records from the Disk Properties window.)

8. Click **OK** to apply the new settings and close the Disk Properties window.

Follow these steps to exceed the quota limits you have just set:

1. Using what you learned in Lab 15.2, create a new restricted user called **Quota Test**.

2. Create a directory called **Quota** in the root of the NTFS drive.

3. Log out as an administrator, and log in as **Quota Test**.

4. Open the **Windows** or **WINNT** folder in Explorer and click **Show Files**. One at a time, copy (*do not cut*) all .gif and .bmp files in the Windows or WINNT folder and paste them into the Quota folder.

   ■ What happens when you exceed the warning level and then the storage quota? Record what happens.

   _____

   _____

5. Log out as the Quota Test user.

16

Because of the options you checked when you created the disk quota, logs were created when you exceeded the warning level and the storage quota. To view these quota logs, follow these steps:

1. Log in as an administrator.

2. Open the NTFS Disk Properties window, click the **Quota** tab, and then click the **Quota Entries** button. The Quota Entries window opens, displaying the quota log of quota entries for certain events.

   ▪ What types of information are displayed for each entry?

   _____

   _____

3. Double-click an entry for Quota Test. The Quota Settings window for that user opens. Note that in this window you can raise or lower the user's disk quotas.

4. Check the Quota Settings for each entry, and record any entry for which you were unable to adjust settings.

   _____

   _____

Review Questions

1. How would you set up disk quotas on a drive formatted with FAT32?

   _____

   _____

2. Why might you wish to impose disk quotas?

   _____

   _____

3. What option must be checked to specify a warning level?

   _____

   _____

4. What options must be selected to prevent a user from exceeding his or her quota?

_____

_____

5. Explain how to monitor and change disk quotas.

_____

_____

LAB 16.2 USE ENCRYPTION

Objectives

The goal of this lab is to help you work with encryption and observe the effects of trying to use an encrypted file without permission. After completing this lab, you will be able to:

➤ Encrypt a directory

➤ Save files to the encrypted directory

➤ Access the encrypted files as a different user

Materials Required

This lab will require the following:

➤ Windows XP Professional operating system

➤ An NTFS partition that might be the partition where Windows XP is installed

➤ Blank floppy disk

Activity Background

Despite your best efforts, unauthorized users might sometimes gain access to sensitive files. To protect these files from such a security breach, you can use file encryption, which prevents unauthorized users from actually being able to view files, even if they do manage to gain access to them. You can encrypt individual files or entire directories. As with disk quotas, you can use file encryption only on NTFS drives. The FAT file systems do not support file encryption. In this lab, you will create and encrypt an entire directory and then create a test file in that encrypted directory.

16

Estimated completion time: **30 minutes**

ACTIVITY

Follow these steps to create an encrypted directory and a test file within that directory:

1. Log on as an administrator.

2. Create a directory in the NTFS root called **Encrypt**.

3. Right-click the **Encrypt** folder, and then click **Properties**. The Folder Properties dialog box opens.

4. Click the **Advanced** button to open the Advanced Attributes window.

5. In the Advanced Attributes window, select the **Encrypt contents to secure data** option to choose to encrypt the contents of the Encrypt folder.

6. Click **OK** to apply the settings and close the Advanced Attributes window. You return to the Encrypt Properties window.

7. Click **OK** to apply encryption.

8. Double-click the **Encrypt** folder to open it.

9. Select the **Encrypt** folder, point to **File** on the menu bar, point to **New**, and click **Text Document**. Double-click the **New Text Document** and type **This file is encrypted**. Close the file, saving it as **Secure.txt**.

Follow these steps to see the effects of encrypting a file in Windows:

1. Double-click **Secure.txt** in the Encrypt folder and record what happens.

_____

2. Log out as an administrator, and log back in as a different user.

3. Double-click **Secure.txt** in the Encrypt folder and record the results.

_____

_____

4. Copy **Secure.txt** to the **Quota** folder and record the results.

_____

5. Log out and then log back in as an administrator.

6. Copy **Secure.txt** to the **Quota** folder and record the results.

_____

7. Insert a blank, formatted floppy disk and copy **Secure.txt** to drive A and record the results.

8. Log out and then log back in as the previous user.

9. Double-click **Secure.txt** in the **Quota** folder and record the results.

_____

10. Double-click **Secure.txt** in drive A and record the results.

_____

_____

11. Right-click the **Secure.txt** file located on drive A, and then click **Properties** in the shortcut menu. The file's Properties window opens. Is there an **Advanced** button?

_____

12. Right-click the **Secure.txt** file located in the Quota directory, and then click **Properties** in the shortcut menu. The file's Properties window opens.

13. Click the **Advanced** button, clear the **Encrypt contents to secure data** check box, and then click **OK**. Record the results.

_____

_____

Review Questions

1. Which file system must be used to enable encryption?

_____

2. How would you encrypt a single file?

_____

3. What happens when an unauthorized user tries to open an encrypted file?

_____

_____

16

4. What happens when an unauthorized user tries to unencrypt a file?

_____

_____

5. What happens to an encrypted file that is removed from a NTFS partition?

_____

_____

_____

LAB 16.3 RESTORE THE SYSTEM STATE

Objectives

The goal of this lab is to help you restore the system state on a Windows XP computer. After completing this lab, you will be able to:

➤ Create a restore point using System Restore

➤ Change system settings

➤ Restore the system state using the restore point you created

Materials Required

This lab will require the following:

➤ Windows XP Professional operating system

Activity Background

The System Restore tool in Windows XP enables you to restore the system to the time a snapshot, called a restore point, was taken of the system state. The settings recorded in a restore point include system settings and configurations and files necessary for a successful boot. When the system state is restored to a restore point, user data on the hard drive is not affected, but software and hardware might be affected. Restore points are useful if, for example, something goes wrong with a software or hardware installation. In this lab, you will create a restore point, make changes to system settings, and then use the restore point to restore the system state.

Estimated completion time: **30 minutes**

ACTIVITY

To use the System Restore tool to create a restore point, follow these steps:

1. On the Start menu, point to **All Programs**, point to **Accessories**, point to **System Tools**, and then click **System Restore**.

2. The System Restore window appears, giving you two choices: Restore my computer to an earlier time and Create a restore point. The first option restores your computer to an existing restore point. Read the information on the left side of the window and answer these questions:

   ■ Can changes made by System Restore be undone? What type of data does System Restore leave unaffected?

   _____

   ■ What is the term for the restore points that the system creates automatically?

   _____

   ■ As you've read, it's helpful to create a restore point before you install software or hardware. In what other situations might you want to create a restore point?

   _____

   _____

3. Click the **Create a restore point** button and click the **Next** button.

4. In the next window, type a description of the restore point. The description should be something that makes it easy to identify the restore point at a later time, such as, Restore [*today's date*].

5. Click the **Create** button.

6. A message appears indicating that the restore point was created. The date, time, and name of the restore point are also shown. Click the **Close** button.

Next, you'll make two changes to the system: uninstalling a Windows component and changing display settings. First, you will uninstall the MSN (Microsoft Network) Explorer component. (If this is currently not installed, then ask your instructor which Windows component you should uninstall instead.)

1. From the Control Panel, double-click the **Add or Remove Programs** icon.

2. The Add or Remove Programs window appears. To see a list of Windows components, click the **Add/Remove Windows Components** icon.

16

3. The Add or Remove Programs window remains open, and the Windows Components Wizard launches. In the list box in the middle of the screen, components that are checked are currently installed. Scroll down until you see the **MSN Explorer** component, and then click the check box next to its name.

4. A message appears asking whether you want to uninstall this component. Click **Yes** to continue.

5. The message disappears, and the MSN Explorer check box is cleared. Click **Next** to continue.

6. A progress window indicates the component the system is currently uninstalling. When the process is complete, a message appears indicating that you have completed the Windows Components Wizard. Click **Finish**.

7. Click **Close** in the Add or Remove Programs window.

Next, you will change some display settings:

1. From the Control Panel, switch to Classic View, and then double-click the **Display** icon.

2. The Display Properties window appears. Click the **Desktop** tab.

3. In the Background list, click a background, and then click the **OK** button.

4. The Display Properties window closes. Close the Control Panel window. Notice that the background has changed to the one you selected.

Follow these steps to use the restore point you created to restore the system state:

1. Open the System Restore tool as specified earlier in this lab.

2. Click the **Restore my computer to an earlier time** option button and click **Next**.

3. A window appears showing a calendar of the current month, with the current date highlighted and all dates on which restore points were made shown in bold. Answer these questions:

   ■ How many restore points were created in the current month?

   _____

   ■ Click each bold date and list the reasons why the restore points were made.

   _____

   _____

   _____

4. Click the current date. In the list on the right, click the name of the restore point you created earlier in the lab, and then click **Next**.

5. A confirmation screen appears. Click **Next** to continue.

   ■ Describe what happens when you click the Next button.

   _____

   _____

   _____

6. After the system restarts, click your login name to return to the Windows XP desktop. A message appears indicating that the restoration is complete. Click **OK**.

   ■ Did the display settings change back to their original settings?

   _____

7. Access the Windows Components Wizard as you did earlier in this lab.

   ■ Is MSN Explorer installed?

   _____

Review Questions

1. List three situations in which you might want to create a restore point.

   _____

   _____

2. What types of restore point are created by the system and what types are created by the user?

   _____

   _____

3. How often does the system automatically create restore points?

   _____

   _____

4. Can more than one restore point be made on a specific date?

   _____

16

5. Which of your changes was reversed when you used the restore point to restore the system state and which change was not reversed? Explain why you think this happened.

_____

_____

_____

Lab 16.4 Install Recovery Console as an Option on the Boot Loader Menu

Objectives

The goal of this lab is to help you install the Recovery Console as a startup option. After completing this lab, you will be able to:

➤ Install the Recovery Console

➤ Open the Recovery Console from the Boot Loader Menu

Materials Required

This lab will require the following:

➤ Windows XP Professional operating system

➤ Windows XP Professional installation CD or installation files at another location accessible by a drive letter, as specified by your instructor.

Activity Background

The Recovery Console tool in Windows XP allows you to start the computer when other startup and recovery options, such as System Restore, safe mode, and the ASR (Automated System Recovery) process, do not work. In the Recovery Console, you can use a limited group of DOS-like commands to format a hard drive, copy files from a floppy disk or CD to the hard drive, start and stop certain system processes, and perform other administrative tasks and troubleshooting tasks. If the Recovery Console is not installed on your computer, you will have to run it from the Windows XP installation CD. This lab shows you how to install the Recovery Console on your Windows XP computer so that it appears as an option when the computer starts up.

Estimated completion time: **30 minutes**

ACTIVITY

Follow these steps to install the Recovery Console as a startup option:

1. Insert the Windows XP installation CD into your CD-ROM drive. If the Autorun feature launches, close it. If your instructor has given you an alternate location for the installation files, what is the drive letter required to access them?

   _____

2. Click the **Start** button on the taskbar, and then click **Run**. The Run dialog box opens.

3. Type **cmd** and then click **OK**. A command window opens.

4. To switch to your CD–ROM drive (or other drive holding the installation files), type the drive letter followed by a colon and then press **Enter**.

5. You will now execute the Windows XP setup program stored on this drive. The path to the program might vary depending on the release of Windows XP you are using. Here are three possibilities. Try each one until you locate and execute the program:

   - Type **\i386\winnt32.exe /cmdcons** and then press **Enter**.
   - Type **\english\winxp\pro\i386\winnt32.exe /cmdcons** and press **Enter**.
   - Type **\english\winxp\home\i386\winnt32.exe /cmdcons** and press **Enter**.
   - Which command launched the setup program?

   _____

6. A message appears asking if you want to install the Recovery Console. Click **Yes** to continue.

7. The Windows Setup window opens and shows that Setup is checking for updates. When the update check completes, a progress indicator appears. When the installation is complete, a message appears indicating that the Recovery Console was successfully installed. Click **OK** to continue.

8. Restart your computer.

16

9. When the Boot Loader menu appears, select **Microsoft Recovery Console** and press **Enter**. What do you see when the Recovery Console launches?

_____

_____

_____

_____

10. Type **1** (to choose to log on to your Windows installation) and then press **Enter**.

11. When prompted, type the administrator password for your computer and press **Enter**.

12. Type **help** and then press **Enter** to see a list of commands available in the Recovery Console.

13. Type **Exit** to close the Recovery Console and restart the computer.

Review Questions

1. What is the advantage of being able to access the Recovery Console from your hard drive instead of from the CD drive?

_____

_____

2. What is another way to exit the Recovery Console without logging on to your Windows installation?

_____

3. In the Recovery Console, what command deletes a directory? What command can you use to list services that are running?

_____

4. Name at least two tasks that you think you might not be able to complete from within the Recovery Console.

_____

_____

_____

5. Why is an administrator password needed for access to the Recovery Console?

_____

6. Why should you use the Recovery Console only after other tools have failed?

_____

_____

LAB 16.5 USE RECOVERY CONSOLE TO COPY FILES

Objectives

The goal of this lab is to help you learn how to copy files using the Recovery Console. After completing this lab, you will be able to:

➤ Copy files from a floppy disk to your hard drive using the Recovery Console

Materials Required

This lab will require the following:

➤ Windows XP operating system

➤ Floppy disk

Activity Background

The Windows XP Recovery Console is useful when you need to restore system files after they have been corrupted (perhaps by a virus) or accidentally deleted from the hard drive. In this lab, you will use the Recovery Console (which you installed in Lab 16.4) to restore a system file, System.ini, from a floppy disk. (Windows XP does not need this file to boot; it is included in Windows XP to allow for backward compatibility with older Windows software.)

16

Estimated completion time: **30 minutes**

ACTIVITY

Follow these steps to copy the file System.ini to a floppy disk and then copy it from the floppy to the hard drive using the Recovery Console:

1. Insert the floppy disk in the floppy drive.

2. Using Windows Explorer, locate the file **System.ini** (which is usually found in the C:\Windows folder).

3. Copy the file **System.ini** to the floppy disk and then eject the floppy disk from the drive.

4. Locate **System.ini** on your hard drive again and rename it as **System.old**. When prompted, click **Yes** to confirm that you want to rename the file.

5. Restart the computer again, this time choosing the **Recovery Console**.

6. Insert the floppy disk in the floppy disk drive. In the Recovery Console, log on using the Administrator password and type this command: **copy a:\ system.ini c:\windows\system.ini**. This command will copy System.ini from the floppy disk to its original location (C:\Windows).

7. Press **Enter**. What message does Recovery Console display?

_____

8. If C:\Windows is not the active directory, change to that directory and then use the **dir** command to view the contents of the directory. Verify that System.ini was copied to this directory. You might have to use the spacebar to scroll down.

9. Exit the Recovery Console and restart the computer.

Review Questions

1. You could have used the Recovery Console to rename the System.old file instead of copying the original version from the floppy disk. What command would you have used to perform this task?

_____

_____

2. Assume you moved the System file to the My Documents folder. What command would you use in the Recovery Console to move it back to the C:\Windows folder?

_____

_____

3. When might it be useful to be able to copy files from a CD to the hard drive using the Recovery Console?

_____

_____

4. Why does Windows XP include the System.ini file?

_____

_____

5. When might you want to use Recovery Console to copy files from the hard drive to a floppy disk?

_____

_____

LAB 16.6 MONITOR THE MEMORY COUNTER

Objectives

The goal of this lab is to help you monitor the memory counter to investigate a possible memory shortage. After completing this lab, you will be able to:

➤ Add memory counters to System Monitor

➤ Defragment your hard drive

➤ Analyze memory usage during defragmentation

Materials Required

This lab will require the following:

➤ Windows XP Professional operating system

Activity Background

In Windows XP, you can use the System Monitor utility to observe system performance. You can add counters to Windows XP to collect data about the system. In this activity, you will add and monitor counters that measure available memory, memory paging, and the read and write times for disk access. These counters can help you determine how much of the total system resources a particular process (such as defragmenting the hard drive) is using.

Estimated completion time: **30 minutes**

16

ACTIVITY

Follow these steps to add counters to System Monitor:

1. Click **Start** on the taskbar, point to **All Programs**, point to **Administrative Tools**, and then click **Performance**. (If Administrative Tools does not appear on your All Programs menu, you need to add it. To do this, right-click the **Start menu**, click **Properties**, click the **Start menu tab** on the Properties window, click **Customize**, click the **Advanced tab** in the Customize window, scroll down to **System Administrative tools**, click **Display** on the All Programs menu, and

then click **OK** in both windows. After adding Administrative Tools to the All Programs menu, begin again with Step 1.)

2. The Performance console opens. Make sure that System Monitor is selected in the left pane. In the right pane, right-click in the blank area, and then click **Add Counters** in the shortcut menu.

3. The Add Counters window opens. In the Performance object drop-down list, click the **Memory** object. Scroll down the **Select counters from list** scroll box, click the **Available Bytes** counter, and then click the **Add** button. This adds the selected counter (Available Bytes) to the Performance console.

4. Click the **Explain** button and record the explanation of the selected counter (Available Bytes):

_____

_____

5. Repeat step 3 to add the **Pages/sec** counter for the Memory object, the **Processor Time** counter for the Processor object, and the **Disk Read Time** and **Disk Write Time** counters for the Physical Disk object. Record the explanations of each of these counters:

_____

_____

_____

_____

6. Click the **Close** button in the Add Counters window. You return to the Performance Console, where the counters you added are listed in the right pane. Look in the Color column and make sure each counter is monitored using a different color. (If you find any of the colors difficult to read, you can change them. To change the color of the line indicating a particular counter, left-click the counter once to select it, then right-click it, select **Properties** from the shortcut menu, click a color in the Color drop-down list on the Properties window, and then click **OK**.)

Follow these steps to monitor the counters for two different applications:

1. With the Performance window still open, open the **Notepad** application. Wait a few seconds, and then close it again.

2. In the Performance window, click the **Freeze Display** button (a red circle with a white x) and then click the highlight button (a lightbulb). Use the up and down arrows to move between counters in the list below the performance display.

- How did the display change when you highlighted a particular counter?

_____

_____

- Which resources did Notepad use primarily? What other resources did it use?

_____

_____

3. Click **Start** on the taskbar, point to **All Programs**, point to **Administrative Tools**, and then click **Computer Management**.

4. The Computer Management console opens. Under Storage in the left pane, click **Disk Defragmenter**, and then click **Analyze** in the right pane. What message appears when the analysis is complete?

_____

_____

5. Click **Close** to close the message window.

6. Close the Computer Management console and return to the Performance window. Click the **Freeze Display** button and the highlight button as you did for Notepad. Which resources did Disk Defragmenter use primarily? Which other resources did it use?

_____

_____

Review Questions

1. Did Notepad and Disk Defragmenter use the same resources? Why do you think this is?

_____

_____

2. How do you think the performance display might have changed if both applications had been open at once?

_____

_____

16

3. What are some other counters that could be useful for monitoring system performance?

_____

_____

4. What system resources that you were monitoring might have been used if you had actually proceeded to defragment your hard drive?

_____

_____

5. If you were considering whether to upgrade your system's memory or processor, which counters would you choose to monitor and why? How would you decide whether you needed to make the upgrade or not?

_____

_____

_____

_____

LAB 16.7 CRITICAL THINKING: SABOTAGE AND REPAIR WINDOWS XP

Objectives

The goal of this lab is to learn to troubleshoot Windows XP by repairing a sabotaged system.

Materials Required

This lab will require the following:

➤ Windows XP Professional on a PC designated for a sabotage

➤ Access to the Windows XP Professional Installation CD or the Windows XP Professional setup files stored in another location

➤ Workgroup of 2–4 students

Activity Background

You have learned about several tools and methods that you can use to recover Windows XP when it fails. This lab gives you the opportunity to use these skills in a troubleshooting situation. Your group will sabotage another group's system, while that group sabotages your system. Then your group will repair its own system.

> **Estimated completion time: 45 minutes**

ACTIVITY

1. If your system's hard drive contains important data, back up that data to another media. Is there anything else you would like to back up before the system is sabotaged by another group? Note that item here and then back it up.

   _____

2. Trade systems with another group and sabotage the other group's system while they sabotage your system. Do one thing that will cause the system to fail to boot, give errors after the boot, or prevent a device or application from working. The following list offers some sabotage suggestions. Windows XP has several features that are designed to prevent sabotage, so you might find it a little challenging to actually prevent it from booting by deleting or renaming system files. Do something included in this list, or think of another option. (Do _not_ alter the hardware.)

   - Find a system file in the root directory that is required to boot the computer, and either rename it or move it to a different directory. (Don't delete the file.)
   - Using the Registry Editor, regedit.exe, delete several important keys or values in the registry.
   - Locate important system files in the \Windows directory, and either rename them or move them to another directory.
   - Put a corrupted program file in the folder that will cause the program to automatically launch at startup. Note the name of that program file and folder here:

   _____

   - Use display settings that are not readable, such as black text on a black background.
   - Disable a critical device driver.

3. Reboot the system and verify that a problem exists.

4. How did you sabotage the other team's system?

   _____

   _____

16

5. Return to your system and troubleshoot it.

6. Describe the problem as a user would describe it to you if you were working at a Help desk.

_____

_____

7. What is your first guess as to the source of the problem?

_____

8. List the steps you took in the troubleshooting process.

_____

_____

_____

_____

_____

_____

9. How did you finally solve the problem and return the system to good working order?

_____

_____

Review Questions

1. What would you do differently the next time you encountered the same symptoms?

_____

2. What Windows utilities did you use or could you have used to solve the problem?

_____

3. In a real-life situation, what might cause this problem to happen? List three possible causes.

_____

_____

_____

4. If you were the PC support technician responsible for this computer in an office environment, what could you do to prevent this problem from happening in the future or limit its impact on users if it did happen?

_____

16

CHAPTER SEVENTEEN

COMMUNICATING OVER PHONE LINES

Labs included in this chapter

➤ Lab 17.1 Simulate Serial Port Communication

➤ Lab 17.2 Install and Test a Modem

➤ Lab 17.3 Use AT Commands to Control a Modem

➤ Lab 17.4 Simulate Modem Problems

➤ Lab 17.5 Critical Thinking: Use Two Modems to Create a Multilink Connection

---

The following grid shows the correlation between the labs in this chapter and the A+ Guides to Hardware and Software.

A+ Guide to Managing and Maintaining Your PC, Fifth Edition	A+ Guide to Hardware, Third Edition	A+ Guide to Software, Third Edition
Lab 17.1 Simulate Serial Port Communication	Chapter 10	
Lab 17.2 Install and Test a Modem	Chapter 10	
Lab 17.3 Use AT Commands to Control a Modem	Chapter 10	
Lab 17.4 Simulate Modem Problems	Chapter 10	
Lab 17.5 Critical Thinking: Use Two Modems to Create a Multilink Connection	Chapter 10	

LAB 17.1 SIMULATE SERIAL PORT COMMUNICATION

Objectives

The goal of this lab is to illustrate serial communication using a game. After completing this lab, you will be able to:

➤ Identify pin arrangements

➤ Explain which pins are used for handshake and data transfer

Materials Required

This lab will require the following:

➤ Eight pieces of string, each approximately four feet long

➤ Workgroup of eight students

Activity Background

RS-232 standards specify cabling and communication methods for the PC. Among other things, they specify the sequence of signals that must travel across a serial cable in order to complete a handshake and transmit data between devices. In this lab, to keep things simple, you will simulate a handshake and data transfer on a null modem cable. You and your fellow students will play the part of the serial ports, using pieces of string for the cable.

Estimated completion time: **30 minutes**

ACTIVITY

Follow these steps to simulate a cable connection between two devices:

1. Position eight students in two rows facing each other, with four on each side. Designate the students on one side as Students A through D. Designate the students on the other side as Students E through H. Students E and A should be facing each other, as should Students B and F, and so on down the line. The two groups of students make up Computer ABCD and Computer EFGH.

2. Stretch seven strings between the eight students as shown in Figure 17-1. Student A's left hand and Student E's right hand are Pin 1 on their respective serial ports. The numbers should proceed down the line until Pin 8 is Student D's right hand and Student H's left hand. Table 17-1 describes the null modem cable communication you are simulating. Notice that Pins 1 and 9 are not used in a null modem cable communication and are therefore omitted from this simulation.

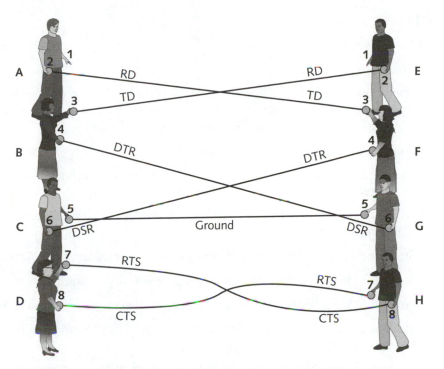

Figure 17-1   Simulating null modem cable communication

Table 17-1   Pin connections for a 9-pin null modem cable

Pin number on one connection	Pin number of the other connector	How the wire connecting the two pins is used
1	1	Not used
2 (RD)	3 (TD)	Data sent by one computer is received by the other
3 (TD)	2 (RD)	Data received by one computer is sent by the other
4 (DTR)	6 (DSR)	One end says to the other end, "I'm able to talk"
5 (Ground)	5 (Ground)	Both ends are grounded
6 (DSR)	4 (DTR)	One end hears the other end say, "I'm able to talk"
7 (RTS)	8 (CTS)	One end says to the other, "I'm ready to talk"
8 (CTS)	7 (RTS)	One end hears the other say, "I'm ready to talk"
9	9	Not used

Here are the meanings of the acronyms in the table:

RD – Receive data

TD – Transmit data

DTR – Data terminal ready

DSR – Data set ready

CTS – Clear to send

RTS – Request to send

Follow these steps to perform the handshake and then to send and receive data. Suppose that Computer EFGH has initiated communication to Computer ABCD, and that Computer ABCD is ready to receive data from Computer EFGH.

1. Student G raises his left hand indicating that he is able to talk (DSR high).

2. Student B raises his hand on the other end of the same string to indicate that he has received Student G's communication.

3. Student C raises his right hand, indicating he understands that Computer EFGH is able to talk (DTR high).

4. Student F raises his left hand indicating he has received the communication.

5. Student H raises his right hand indicating he is ready to talk (RTS high).

6. Student D raises his hand indicating he has received the communication.

7. Student D raises his left hand indicating he is ready to receive data from Computer EFGH.

8. Student H raises his hand indicating he has received the communication.

   Computer ABCD has just indicated that it is able and ready to have a conversation. (As you'll recall, DTR indicates that Computer ABCD is open to having a conversation, and RTS tells Computer EFGH to go ahead and start talking.) Computer EFGH is now ready to start talking to Computer ABCD.

9. Student F repeatedly raises and lowers his hand—which represents the TD (TXD) pin—to indicate that data is being sent. (Each raise of the hand represents one bit transmitted.)

10. Student A sees this signal and repeatedly raises and lowers his right hand—which represents the RD (RXD) pin—to indicate the reception of each bit.

    Now suppose that computer EFGH has been transmitting for a while and Computer ABCD has noticed that its buffer is getting full. (That is, it has to process what Computer EFGH has said.) This ability of the receiving computer to stop transmission so it can catch up is called flow control.

11. Student D lowers his left hand (RTS) to indicate that Computer ABCD is processing and doesn't want to hear any more right now.

12. Student H quits receiving CTS high and lowers his hand to indicate he has received the communication.

13. Other students keep their hands raised, indicating that the conversation is still not yet over.

14. Student F quits sending data and keeps his hand down.

    At this point, computer EFGH has quit talking, but has not yet finished sending all the data. After a pause, computer ABCD finishes processing and the buffer is empty. Computer ABCD is now ready to listen again.

15. Student D raises his hand, raising RTS high.

16. Student H raises his hand, indicating CTS high. In response, Student F starts sending data again until all data is sent.

17. Students H and G lower their hands indicating that Computer EFGH has nothing more to say and wants to end the conversation.

18. All students then lower their hands in response to Students H and G. The conversation is ended.

    Now that you have seen how Computer EFGH sends data to Computer ABCD, answer the following questions regarding communication from Computer ABCD to Computer EFGH.

    ■ Which hands should be raised to indicate that Computer EFGH is able to communicate with Computer ABCD?

    _____

    ■ Which hands should be raised to indicate that Computer EFGH is ready to receive data?

    _____

    ■ Which hands should be raised to indicate data flowing from Computer ABCD to Computer EFGH?

    _____

    ■ Which hands should be lowered when Computer EFGH's buffers are full?

    _____

    ■ Which hands should be lowered when the communication is finished?

    _____

19. Now raise and lower your hands to simulate communication from Computer ABCD to Computer EFGH.

17

Review Questions

1. Pins 1 and 9 are not used for communication via a null modem cable. How are they used by a modem?

   _____

   _____

2. What is indicated by a signal raised on Pin 8?

   _____

3. Pin 4 on one end of the cable is connected to Pin _____ on the other end of the cable.

4. Data passes from Pin _____ on one end of the cable to Pin _____ on the other end of the cable.

5. What is the sole purpose of Pin 5's participation in the network communication?

   _____

Lab 17.2 Install and Test a Modem

Objectives

The goal of this lab is to help you install and test a modem. After completing this lab, you will be able to:

➤ Physically install a modem

➤ Test the modem using Modem Properties

Materials Required

This lab will require the following:

➤ Windows 98 operating system

➤ Windows 98 installation CD or installation files stored in another location

➤ Modem with drivers

➤ PC toolkit with ground strap

➤ Windows 2000/XP operating system and installation files (optional activity)

Activity Background

Most users dial in to their ISP using a modem and Plain Old Telephone Service (POTS). Such dial-up connections can be unreliable, for several reasons. So as an A+ technician, you need to be prepared to install modems and troubleshoot modem connections. In this lab, you will install a modem and then run some simple diagnostics to test the modem.

Estimated completion time: **30 minutes**

ACTIVITY

Follow these steps to install a modem:

1. Remove all cables from the case and remove the case cover.

2. Locate the expansion slot that you will use to install the modem and then remove the slot's cover.

3. Install and secure the modem card.

4. Replace the case cover and reattach all cables, including the telephone cable, to the Line–In port on the back of the modem card.

5. Boot the computer and log on, if necessary. The Found New Hardware Wizard launches and informs you that it is ready to search for drivers. Click **Next** to continue.

6. The wizard asks how you want to locate the drivers. Select the **Search for the Best Driver for Your Device (Recommended)** option button and click **Next** to continue.

7. The wizard asks you to specify a location for the drivers. Insert the floppy disk or CD containing the drivers and select the appropriate check box to indicate the location of the drivers. (If the CD Autorun program launches when you insert the CD, close the application.) Note that you can temporarily disable Autorun by holding down the Shift key while you insert the CD.

8. The wizard reports the device name and location of the driver. Click **Next** to continue.

9. The wizard informs you that the installation was successful. Click **Finish** to close the Found New Hardware Wizard.

10. Additional Found New Hardware Wizards might launch for any devices embedded in the modem, such as voice or fax devices. Complete the wizards for these devices. Be prepared to provide any Windows 98 installation files as necessary.

Follow these steps to verify that your modem is working properly:

1. Check that your modem is displayed in Device Manager. Device Manager should report no problems with the modem. If necessary, review Chapter 2, Lab 2.1 for a reminder of how to use Device Manager.

17

2. Open the Control Panel, double-click the **Modems** icon to open the Modems Properties dialog box, and then select the **Diagnostics** tab. What type of port information does the Diagnostics tab provide?

_____

3. Select the modem you just installed, and note the port it is associated with. Record that information here.

_____

4. Click the **More Info** button.

5. The More Info dialog box opens. The system uses its modem diagnostic tool to test the modem and then displays the test results. Take and print a screen shot of this dialog box and then click **OK** to close the More Info dialog box. Answer these questions:

   ■ When you open the More Info dialog box, what type of commands are used to test the modem?

   _____

   ■ List two commands and the purpose of each command.

   _____

   _____

6. Click **OK** to close the Modems Properties dialog box.

Leave the modem installed for use in upcoming labs in this chapter.

CRITICAL THINKING (additional 30 minutes)

Install a modem in a Windows 2000 or Windows XP system. When you start up the system, the Found New Hardware Wizard launches to install the modem drivers. Verify that the modem is working using Device Manager. In Device Manager, right-click the modem and select **Properties** from the shortcut menu. The modem's Properties box opens. Click the **Diagnostics** tab and then click the **Query Modem** button. What are the results of this query?

_____

_____

_____

_____

Review Questions

1. Were any devices embedded in your modem? How could you tell?

   _____

   _____

2. What are two system resources that a modem requires?

   _____

3. What is the format of the diagnostic commands shown in your screen shots?

   _____

4. In what situation might you use the modem diagnostic tool?

   _____

LAB 17.3 USE AT COMMANDS TO CONTROL A MODEM

Objectives

The goal of this lab is to help you use AT commands to initiate and receive calls. After completing this lab, you will be able to:

➤ Install HyperTerminal

➤ Use several modem commands to control a HyperTerminal session, dial a number, receive a call, and test your modem

Materials Required

This lab will require the following:

➤ Windows 98 or Windows 2000/XP operating system

➤ Windows installation CD or installation files in another location

➤ Access to a phone line that can send and receive calls

➤ The line's telephone number

➤ A lab partner to whom you can make modem calls

Note that you might not have access to a phone line in a classroom lab environment. In this case, this lab might have to be completed at home.

17

Activity Background

The AT command set is a set of commands that can be used to control a modem. When the modem receives commands, each command line is prefaced with AT for ATtention. A modem stays in command mode any time it is not connected to another modem. When a modem is in command mode and bits and bytes are sent to it from a PC, the modem interprets the bytes as commands to be followed, rather than as data to be sent over a phone line. It leaves command mode when it either receives an incoming call or dials out, and returns to command mode when a call is completed or a special escape sequence is sent to it by its computer. A modem responds to a command with OK or gives the results after performing the command. AT commands allow you to control virtually every aspect of modem behavior and are useful in troubleshooting modem hardware and connections. Table 17-2 lists a few of the core AT commands that most modems understand.

Table 17-2 AT commands for Hayes-compatible modems

Command	Description	Some values and their meanings
AT	Gets the modem's attention	AT (Modem should respond with OK)
*70	Disable call waiting	ATDT*70,4045551212
+++	Escape sequence: tells the modem to return to command mode. You should pause at least 1 second before you sequence. After you end it, wait another second before you send another command. Don't begin this command with AT.	+++ (Follow each + with a short pause; use this when trying to unlock a hung modem; don't begin the command with AT)
On	Go Online: tells the modem to return to online data mode. This is the reverse command for the escape sequence above.	ATO0 Return online ATO1 Return online and retrain (perform training or handshaking again with the remote system)
A/	Repeat last command: repeat last command performed by the modem. Don't begin the command with AT, but do follow it with Enter. Useful when redialing a busy number.	
In	Identification: instructs the modem to return to product identification information	ATI0 Return the product code ATI3 Return the modem ROM version
Zn	Reset: instructs the modem to reset and restore the configuration to that defined at power on	ATZ0 Reset and return to user profile 0 ATZ1 Reset and return to user profile 1

Table 17-2   AT commands for Hayes-compatible modems (continued)

Command	Description	Some values and their meanings
&F	Factory default: instructs the modem to reload the factory default profile. In most cases, use this command to reset the modem rather than using the Z command	AT&F (This method is preferred to ATZ when trying to solve a modem problem)
A	Answer the phone: instructs the modem to answer the phone, transmit the answer tone, and wait for a carrier from the remote modem	
D*n*	Dial: tells the modem to dial a number. Several parameters can be added to this command. A few are listed on the right.	ATD5551212 Dial the given number ATDD Causes the dialing to pause ATDP Use pulse dialing ATDT Use tone dialing ATDW Wait for dial tone ATD& Wait for the credit card dialing tone before continuing with the remaining dial string
H*n*	Hang up: tells the modem to hang up	ATH0 Hang up ATH1 Hang up and enter command mode
M*n*	Speaker control: instructs the modem as to how it is to use the speaker	ATM0 Speaker always off ATM1 Speaker on until carrier detect ATM2 Speaker always on
L*n*	Loudness: sets the loudness of the modem's speaker	ATL1 Low ATL2 Medium ATL3 High
X*n*	Response: tells the modem how it is to respond to a dial tone and busy signal	ATX0 Blind dialing; the modem does not need to hear the dial tone and will not hear a busy signal. ATX4 Modem must first hear the dial tone and responds to a busy signal (This is the default value.)

17

You can type a command from a communications software window to be executed immediately or enter a command from a dialog box for the modem configuration to be executed later when the modem makes a call. HyperTerminal is an excellent utility you can use to make a quick and easy phone call from a Windows PC. HyperTerminal is installed by default under Windows 2000/XP but is not automatically installed by Windows 98. By using HyperTerminal, you can test a newly installed modem with AT commands. In this lab, you will use AT commands to make and receive calls and to adjust modem settings.

Estimated completion time: **45 minutes**

ACTIVITY

For Windows 98, follow these steps to install HyperTerminal:

1. Open the Control Panel, double-click the **Add/Remove Programs** icon, and then click the **Windows Setup** tab.

2. In the Components list box, double-click the **Communications** group. The Communications dialog box opens.

3. Select the **HyperTerminal** check box and then click **OK**. The Communications dialog box closes and you return to the Add/Remove Programs Properties dialog box.

4. Click **OK** to close the Add/Remove Programs dialog box. Supply Windows 98 installation files as necessary.

For Windows 98 andWindow 2000/XP, follow these steps to use AT commands in HyperTerminal:

1. Click **Start** on the taskbar, point to **Programs** (for Windows XP, **All Programs**), point to **Accessories**, point to **Communications**, and then click **HyperTerminal**. This opens the HyperTerminal folder.

2. For Windows 98, double-click **Hypertrm.exe**. HyperTerminal starts, with the Connection Description dialog box displayed.

3. In the Connection Description dialog box, type **Test 1** in the Name field and then click **OK**. The Connect To dialog box opens.

4. Select your modem from the drop-down list and then click **Cancel** to close the Connect To dialog box. The Connect To dialog box closes, and the main HyperTerminal window is active.

5. Click in the blank field in HyperTerminal to position the cursor there.

At this point, if you start typing AT commands, the commands will be executed but you might not actually be able to see the commands as you type them in the HyperTerminal window. To make it possible to see the AT commands as you type them (if displaying commands has not already been enabled), you must begin with the AT echo command, ATE1. To practice using this command, follow these steps:

1. Type **ATE1** and press **Enter**. The modem's response (OK) appears under the cursor. Note that you couldn't see the command, ATE1, as you typed it. But from now on you should be able to see commands as you type.

2. Type **ATE0** and press **Enter**. (Be sure to type a zero and not the letter "o.") The command ATE0 appears on the screen as you type. OK appears below ATE0 after you press Enter.

3. Type **AT** and press **Enter**. The AT command issued by itself should always return an OK response, and, in fact, OK does appear on the screen. But this time the command you typed is not displayed on the screen. Which command caused the text not to appear as you typed (i.e., caused the text not to "echo")?

_____

4. Execute the ATE1 command to again echo the commands as you type.

Now that you know how to make commands appear as you type, you are ready to test your modem using HyperTerminal. Follow these steps:

1. To verify that a working phone line is connected to the modem, type **ATD** followed by your computer's telephone number (for example, ATD5551212) and then press **Enter**. You should hear the modem dial. What message does HyperTerminal return?

_____

2. Type **ATL3**, press **Enter**, and then use the ATD command to dial your computer's number again.

   ■ What difference do you notice from the first time you dialed the number?

   _____

   _____

   ■ What do you think the L in the ATL command stands for?

   _____

3. HyperTerminal can also be controlled using commands on its menu bar. Click **Call** on the HyperTerminal menu bar and then click **Wait for a Call**.

4. Give your lab partner your computer's number and have him or her dial and connect to your computer. What messages does HyperTerminal display on your computer?

   _____

   _____

   _____

5. Click the button that shows the phone handset hanging up on the phone cradle (shown in Figure 17-2 for Windows 98). Your modem disconnects.

17

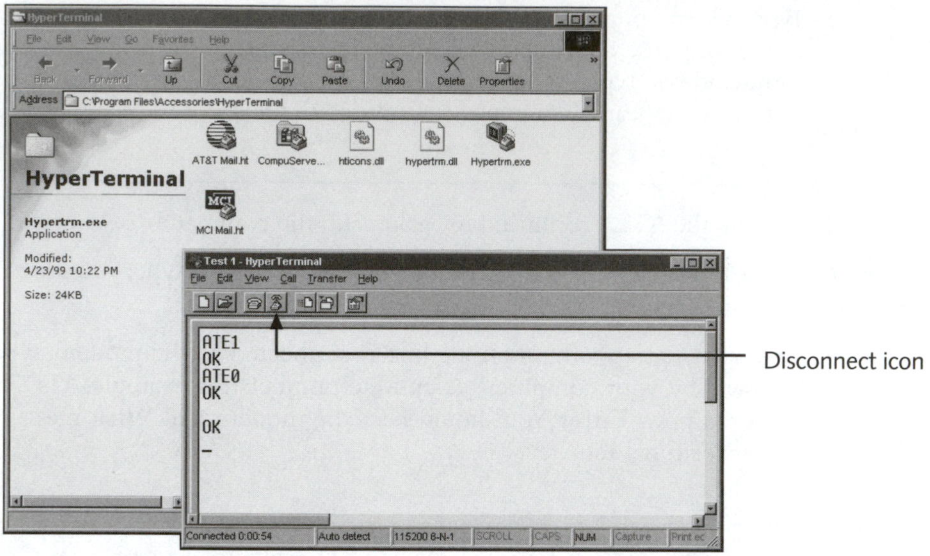

Figure 17-2   HyperTerminal window

6. Type **AT&T1** and press **Enter**. HyperTerminal runs a local analog loop to make sure the modem is working correctly. Record the results below.

_____

_____

_____

_____

7. To end the test, type **AT&T0** and press **Enter**. (Ending the test might take a few moments.)

8. Click the disconnection button on the toolbar.

9. If you begin testing a working modem with AT commands and the modem begins to experience problems, you can use the AT&F command to reset the modem to factory settings. Type **AT&F** and press **Enter**. The modem's default settings are restored.

10. To close HyperTerminal, click **File** and then click **Exit**. When asked if you wish to disconnect, click **Yes**. When asked if you wish to save the session, click **No**.

Review Questions

1. What Windows application is commonly used for working with AT commands?

_____

2. What command turns on the text echo so that you can see what you are typing?

_____

3. What command dials a number?

_____

4. What command returns the modem to its default settings?

_____

5. What method, other than an AT command, can be used to receive an incoming call?

_____

_____

6. Look in Table 17-2 for additional AT commands. What are some other AT commands not used in this lab that you would find useful in debugging a modem?

_____

_____

_____

LAB 17.4 SIMULATE MODEM PROBLEMS

Objectives

The goal of this lab is to help you simulate, diagnose, and remedy common modem problems. After completing this lab, you will be able to:

➤ Diagnose problems with a modem

➤ Remedy problems with a modem

Materials Required

This lab will require the following:

➤ Windows 98 or Windows 2000/XP operating system

➤ Modem installed in a PC and connected to a phone line

➤ PC toolkit with ground strap

➤ Modem installation drivers

17

> ➤ Windows installation CD or installation files

> ➤ Standard phone

> ➤ Lab partner with whom you can swap PCs

Activity Background

Dial-up connections are notoriously unreliable. One of the challenges of troubleshooting such connections is determining whether a dial-up failure is related to a problem with the modem itself or to a problem with the phone line. In this lab, you will diagnose and remedy common modem problems. Mastering these skills will make it easier for you to determine when the modem itself is the source of trouble in a dial-up connection.

Estimated completion time: **90 minutes**

ACTIVITY

1. To verify that your modem is working, start HyperTerminal, dial any reliable phone number, and listen for the sound of the modem dialing and attempting to connect. (The actual connection is not necessary at this point.) Disconnect the call and close HyperTerminal.

2. Sabotage your modem by introducing one of the problems listed below:
   - If your modem has jumpers or DIP switches, record the original settings and then change the settings.
   - In BIOS or Device Manager, disable the modem's COM port.
   - Loosen the modem card in the expansion slot so that it does not make good contact.
   - Unplug the phone cord from the wall.
   - Change the port the phone line connects to on the back of the modem.
   - Uninstall the modem in Device Manager.
   - Change or disable the IRQ for the modem.
   - Using Device Manager, disable the modem in the current hardware configuration.

3. Swap PCs with your partner and then troubleshoot and repair your partner's PC.

4. Answer these questions:
   - What is the initial symptom of a problem as a user would describe it?

   _____

   _____

■ How did you discover the source of the problem?

_____

_____

_____

_____

■ What did you do to resolve the problem?

_____

_____

_____

_____

5. Introduce another problem from the list in step 2 and swap again. Continue this process until you have introduced and remedied all of the problems listed in step 2.

Review Questions

1. What was the easiest problem to diagnose and why?

_____

_____

2. Which problems would not be apparent in Device Manager but would result in no dial tone when dialing?

_____

_____

3. Did all of the problems listed in step 2 actually prevent the modem from working? Which (if any) did not prevent the modem from working?

_____

17

4. Which problem prevented the modem from being displayed in Modems Properties?

_____

_____

_____

5. What was the simplest way to determine if there definitely was a dial tone?

_____

_____

6. Suppose a user says, "I can't dial out using my modem." List the first three things you would check, in the order you would check them.

_____

_____

_____

Lab 17.5 Critical Thinking: Use Two Modems to Create a Multilink Connection

Objectives

The goal of this lab is to help you set up a Dial-Up Networking connection involving two modems to increase connection performance. After completing this lab, you will be able to:

➤ Install a second modem

➤ Create a Dial-Up Networking connection

➤ Configure a Dial-Up Networking connection for multilink

➤ Download a file to compare single modem and multilink connection performance

Materials Required

This lab will require the following:

➤ Windows 98 operating system

➤ Two modems and any necessary drivers

- ➤ Two phone lines and phone jacks
- ➤ ISP that allows multilink connections
- ➤ User name and password for your ISP connection, as provided by your instructor
- ➤ Dial-up phone number for your ISP, as provided by your instructor

Note that if you don't have a second modem and phone line and an ISP that supports multilink connections, you can still do most of this lab to create and test a single-link connection.

Activity Background

A broadband connection is the best option when you need to transfer lots of data at high speeds. But if you don't have access to a broadband connection, you can make do by using two phone lines and two modems to create a multilink connection. (Note that not all ISPs support multilink connections, and those that do will charge extra for the service.) Assuming both modems connect at the same speed, a multilink connection can roughly double your usual dial-up connection speed. In this lab, you will configure a multilink connection and compare its performance to a single modem connection. You will start by creating a dial-up connection for the modem you installed in Lab 17.2. You will then install a second modem and combine the two modems in a multilink connection.

Estimated completion time: **90 minutes**

ACTIVITY

Follow these steps to create a Dial-Up Networking connection using the modem you installed in Lab 17.2:

1. In Windows Explorer, click the **Dial–Up Networking** icon to view Dial-Up Networking icons in the left pane of Explorer.

2. Double-click the **Make New Connection** icon to open the Make New Connection dialog box.

3. Type in the name for the connection you are about to create, select the modem to use in the drop-down menu if it is not already selected, and then click **Next** to continue.

4. The Make New Connection dialog box opens. Here you need to specify the number your computer will dial to complete the dial-up connection. Enter your ISP's area code and phone number (as provided by your instructor), and select the country code from the drop-down menu. Click **Next** to continue.

5. The Make New Connection dialog box informs you that the connection was created successfully. Click **Finish** to close the Make New Connection dialog box. Your new connection appears in the Dial-Up Networking window.

17

Follow these steps to configure and test your connection:

1. Double-click your connection in the Dial-Up Networking window.

2. The Connect To dialog box opens, showing the connection name. Enter the User Name and Password supplied by your instructor, and then click **Dial Properties** to open the Dialing Properties dialog box.

3. Select the **I am Dialing From:** text box and replace its contents with **LAB**.

4. Click **Area Code Rules** to open the Area Code Rules dialog box, select the **Always Dial the Area Code (10-digit dialing)** check box, and then click **OK**. The Area Code Rules dialog box closes.

   Note that creating multiple dial-up connections is a useful technique on a portable computer. You can configure a separate connection for each location where you intend to travel, with separate dialing rules for each connection. For example, suppose you live in Kentucky and have a dial-up connection to a local ISP. You could create one dial-up connection for your home office that does not require an area code (because the ISP is local). You could also create a connection for dialing into your ISP from a hotel in Boston. This connection might include dialing 9 for an outside line as well as dialing your ISP's area code. You could create yet another connection for dialing into your ISP from a private home in Orlando where you have the local phone number for your ISP's point of presence (POP) in Orlando.

5. Adjust the appropriate settings in the "When Dialing From Here:" section as necessary to reach an outside line or to disable call waiting. What other options can you adjust in the Dialing Properties dialog box?

   _____

   _____

   _____

6. Click **OK** to close the Dialing Properties dialog box.

7. In the Connect To dialog box, notice that the Dialing From: field has changed to "Lab."

8. Select the **Save Password** check box so that you won't have to enter your password each time you connect.

9. Click **Connect** to dial.

10. The Connecting To dialog box appears and displays messages indicating what task is currently being performed ("Dialing…" and "Verifying User Name and Password…," and so forth). When the connection is completed, a connection symbol appears in the system tray, as shown in Figure 17-3.

Connection icon

Figure 17-3   A connection icon appears in the system tray when the connection is completed

11. Double-click the connection symbol in the system tray. The Connected To dialog box opens. Record your connection speed and any other information provided in this dialog box.

_____

_____

_____

Now that you have established a dial-up connection, you can use it to download the driver required by your second modem (which you will install in this lab).

12. Open your Web browser and navigate to the Web site for the manufacturer of your second modem.

13. Download the latest driver for this modem. As the file is being downloaded, take and print a screen shot of the download progress indicator.

Now that you have created a Dial-Up connection and tested it using a single modem, you will create a multilink connection. Do the following:

1. Install a second modem using the driver you just downloaded.

2. Create a Dial-Up connection for the second modem and test it by dialing up your ISP and completing the connection.

Next, you need to adjust the connection properties of your first Dial-Up connection to allow a multilink connection. Follow these steps:

1. Right-click the connection's icon in the Dial-Up Networking window and then click **Properties** in the shortcut menu. The connection's Properties window opens.

2. Click the **Multilink** tab.

3. Select the **Use Additional Devices** check box, and then click **Add**.

4. Select the second modem from the list of available devices, and then click **OK**.

Now you are ready to use the multilink connection.

1. Following the directions given above, use the multilink connection to dial up your ISP.

17

2. Compare the speed of this connection to that of a single connection by down-loading the same driver file as you did in step 13, taking and printing a screen shot of the download progress. What are the differences in the connection speed and process?

_____

_____

_____

_____

3. Uninstall the second modem and reconfigure the original modem connection.

Answer the following questions about using an ISP for a multilink connection:

1. What is one other ISP that allows multilink connections?

_____

2. What are the costs associated with multilink connections using this ISP?

_____

_____

Review Questions

1. What Windows feature allows you to configure and save connection information?

_____

2. List the steps required to adjust the number of digits required to dial a local phone number.

_____

_____

3. How does a multilink connection improve performance?

_____

_____

_____

4. What are the requirements for a multilink connection?

_____

_____

5. What is the advantage of creating several Dial-Up connections for a single modem?

_____

_____

17

18

PCs ON A NETWORK

Labs included in this chapter

➤ Lab 18.1 Install and Test an Ethernet NIC

➤ Lab 18.2 Inspect Cables

➤ Lab 18.3 Compare Options for a Home LAN

➤ Lab 18.4 Troubleshoot with TCP/IP Utilities

➤ Lab 18.5 Practice Solving Network Connectivity Problems

➤ Lab 18.6 Share Resources on a Network

➤ Lab 18.7 Use NetBUI Instead of TCP/IP

➤ Lab 18.8 Use a Parallel Port for Direct Cable Connection

➤ Lab 18.9 Configure and Use Dial-Up Server

The following grid shows the correlation between the labs in this chapter and the A+ Guides to Hardware and Software.

A+ Guide to Managing and Maintaining Your PC, Fifth Edition	A+ Guide to Hardware, Third Edition	A+ Guide to Software, Third Edition
Lab 18.1 Install and Test an Ethernet NIC	Chapter 11	
Lab 18.2 Inspect Cables	Chapter 11	
Lab 18.3 Compare Options for a Home LAN	Chapter 11	
Lab 18.4 Troubleshoot with TCP/IP Utilities	Chapter 11	
Lab 18.5 Practice Solving Network Connectivity Problems	Chapter 11	
Lab 18.6 Share Resources on a Network		Chapter 11
Lab 18.7 Use NetBEUI Instead of TCP/IP		Chapter 11
Lab 18.8 Use a Parallel Port for Direct Cable Connection		Chapter 11
Lab 18.9 Configure and Use Dial-Up Server		Chapter 11

Lab 18.1 Install and Test an Ethernet NIC

Objectives

The goal of this lab is to install and configure an Ethernet network interface card (NIC). After completing this lab, you will be able to:

➤ Remove a NIC (and network protocols, if necessary)

➤ Install a NIC (and network protocol, if necessary)

➤ Perform a loopback test

Materials Required

This lab will require the following:

➤ Windows 98 operating system with no modem or dial-up networking installed or Windows 2000/XP operating system

➤ NIC and drivers

➤ Windows installation CD or installation files stored in another location

➤ PC toolkit with ground strap

➤ Crossover cable

➤ Workgroup partner

Activity Background

A computer connects to a wired network through a network interface card (NIC). In this lab, you will install a NIC, configure necessary network settings, and verify that the NIC is functioning properly. Working with a partner, you will create a simple network of two PCs. By default, Windows 98 does not install network protocols needed to support a network, but Windows 2000/XP has these components installed. This fact makes installing a NIC under Windows 2000/XP much simpler than under Windows 98.

Estimated completion time: **30 minutes**

Activity

For Windows 98, if your computer does not already have a NIC installed, skip to the next section. Otherwise, follow these steps on your Windows 98 computer to remove the computer's networking components:

1. Right-click the **Network Neighborhood** icon and select **Properties** in the shortcut menu. The Network dialog box opens.

2. If necessary, click the **Configuration** tab, click **Client for Microsoft Networks**, and then click **Properties**. The Client for Microsoft Networks Properties dialog box opens.

3. In the General section, make sure that the **Log on to Windows NT domain** check box is not selected. Click **OK** to close the Client for Microsoft Networks Properties dialog box. Then close the Network Properties dialog box and reboot when prompted.

4. After the computer has rebooted, open the Network dialog box again by right-clicking the **Network Neighborhood** icon and selecting **Properties**. On the Configuration tab of the Network Properties dialog box, click your NIC (indicated by an adapter symbol) and then click **Remove**. The NIC and any protocol associated with it are uninstalled; Client for Microsoft Networks is also uninstalled.

5. Click **OK** to close the Network dialog box. You might see a message indicating that the network is incomplete.

6. Click **Yes** to continue. You are prompted to restart your computer.

7. Click **No**.

8. Shut down your computer, but do not reboot.

9. Remove your computer's NIC, or, if your instructor directs you to do so, remove the network cable but leave the NIC in place.

For Windows 98, follow these steps to install and configure your NIC:

1. If your NIC is not installed, physically install it as you would other expansion cards. If you need a refresher on the process, review Lab 5.4 or Lab 11.1.

2. Boot the system. The Add New Hardware Wizard detects the NIC and begins the driver installation process. Complete the Add New Hardware Wizard as in previous labs. Reboot when prompted.

3. The Network Neighborhood icon reappears on the desktop. Right-click the **Network Neighborhood** icon and then click **Properties**. The Network dialog box opens.

4. Select the **Configuration** tab and examine the Network Components displayed on the tab. List the installed components.

_____

_____

_____

_____

_____

18

5. Verify that your NIC appears in the list and that TCP/IP is installed and bound to the NIC, as indicated by an item in the list that includes TCP/IP with an arrow that points to the name of your NIC. Select this item and then click **Properties**. The TCP/IP dialog box opens.

6. On the IP Address tab of the TCP/IP dialog box, click the **Specify an IP Address** option button.

7. Next you will configure the network connection. For the configuration, you and your partner will need an IP address, a computer name, and a workgroup name, which are all listed in the following table. Write your name and your partner's name in the table.

Your names:		
IP address:	192.168.1.1	192.168.1.2
Computer name:	Lab 1	Lab 2
Workgroup name:	NIC Lab	NIC Lab

8. In the IP Address field of the TCP/IP Properties dialog box, type **192.168.1.1** or **192.168.1.2**. (Your lab partner should use one and you the other.) In the Subnet Mask field, enter **255.255.255.0**. (Both you and your partner should do this.) Note that it is possible for a server (called a DHCP server) to assign these two necessary values (which enable TCP/IP communication), but in this lab, you'll assume no such server is available.

9. Click **OK** to close the TCP/IP dialog box.

10. To identify each computer on the network, click the **Identification** tab in the Network dialog box. Record the computer name displayed in the Computer Name field. Replace this name with either the name **Lab 1** or the name **Lab 2**. (Again, your partner should use one of these names while you use the other.) In the Workgroup field, type **NIC Lab**. Although it's not necessary, you can type a description for your computer if you want. When you are browsing the network, this description will appear in the computer's Properties dialog box (under the Comment Heading). This description can help users determine what resources might be available on the computer. What description, if any, did you enter?

_____

11. Click **OK** to close the Network window and save your settings. Supply the Windows 98 CD or the location of the installation files if prompted. If you receive a message indicating that a file being copied is older than the current file, click **Yes** to keep the current file. (This is usually the best practice, unless you suspect that the newer file has been the source of any existing problem.)

12. Click **Yes** when prompted to restart the computer.

For Windows 2000/XP, follow these steps to install and configure your NIC:

1. Physically install your NIC as you would other expansion cards. If you need a refresher on the process, review Lab 5.4 or Lab 11.1.

2. Boot the system. The Found New Hardware Wizard detects the NIC and begins the driver installation process. In some cases, Windows XP will not give you the opportunity to use non-Microsoft drivers. If given the opportunity, click **Have Disk** and provide the manufacturer's drivers for the NIC. Reboot if prompted to do so.

 If you want to force Windows XP to use manufacturer's drivers, run the setup program on the CD or floppy disk that comes bundled with the NIC *before* you physically install the NIC. Then, after you boot with the new card installed, Windows will find the already-installed manufacturer drivers and use those drivers.

Now you will give the computer an IP address, a computer name, and a workgroup name as listed in the table in step 7.

First you will assign an IP address to the computer.

1. Right-click **My Network Places** and select **Properties** from the shortcut menu. The Network Connections window appears.

2. Right-click **Local Area Connection** and select **Properties** from the shortcut menu. The Local Area Connection Properties dialog box appears.

3. In the list of connection items, select **Internet Protocol (TCP/IP)** and click **Properties**. The Internet Protocol (TCP/IP) Properties dialog box appears. Select **Use the following IP address** and enter your IP address (192.168.1.1 or 192.168.1.2) and subnet mask (255.255.255.0). Click **OK** twice to close both Properties boxes and then close the Network Connections window.

Now you will assign a computer name and workgroup name to your computer.

1. Right-click **My Computer** and select **Properties** from the shortcut menu. The System Properties window appears.

2. For Windows XP, click the **Computer Name** tab, then click the **Change** button. The Computer Name Changes dialog box appears (see Figure 18-1). For Windows 2000, click the **Network Identification** tab, and then click the **Properties** button. The Identification Changes window appears.

3. Enter the Computer name (**Lab 1** in the example shown in Figure 18-1). Each computer name must be unique within a workgroup or domain.

4. Select **Workgroup** and enter the name of the workgroup (**NIC LAB** in this example).

5. Click **OK** to exit the Windows XP Computer Name Changes dialog box or the Windows 2000 Identification Changes window, and click **OK** to exit the System Properties window. You will be asked to reboot the computer for changes to take effect.

6. Reboot your computer.

18

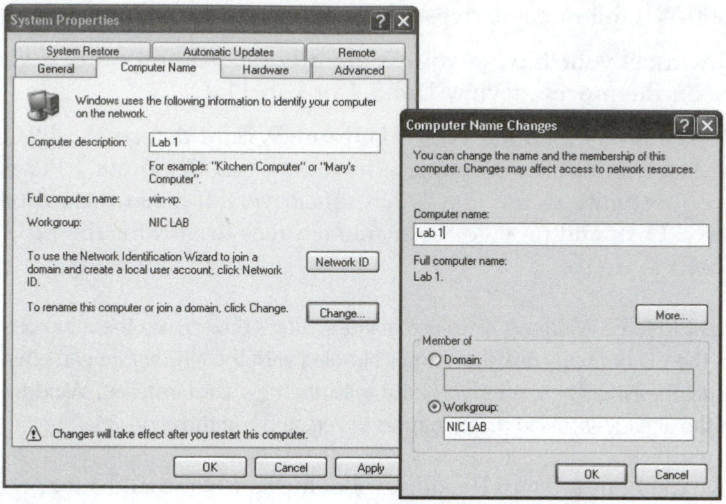

Figure 18-1 Windows XP uses the Computer Name Changes dialog box to assign a host name to a computer on a network

Using Windows 98 or Windows 2000/XP, follow these steps to test your NIC:

1. Open a command-prompt window.

2. Type **ping 127.0.0.1** and press **Enter**. Ping is a TCP/IP utility used to test whether an address is reachable and able to respond. Any 127.x.x.x address is a loopback address. Essentially, a loopback address is a stand-in for your computer's own address. When you use a loopback address in a ping test, the Ping utility sends packets to your local computer's NIC, thereby allowing you to verify that your computer's NIC has a functioning TCP/IP connection. If your computer is connected to a printer, take a screen shot of the results and print the screen shot of the loopback ping command.

3. Examine the results of the loopback test and answer these questions:

   ■ How many bytes were sent in each packet?

   _____

   ■ How many packets were sent with one ping command?

   _____

   ■ How many responses were received from one ping command?

   _____

   ■ Were any packets lost?

   _____

For Windows 98, use the configuration utility Winipcfg to verify your IP configuration. Do the following to check your NIC's configuration:

1. At the command prompt, type **winipcfg** and press **Enter**.

2. Select your NIC from the drop-down list and examine your IP configuration. Answer the following:

■ Is the configuration the same information that you originally configured?

_____

■ What is the MAC address of your NIC?

_____

For Windows 2000/XP, use the configuration utility Ipconfig to verify your IP configuration. Do the following to check your NIC's configuration:

1. At the command prompt, type **ipconfig /all |more** and press **Enter**. An IP configuration report is displayed one screen at a time. If necessary, press **Enter** to see each new line. Answer the following:

■ Is the configuration the same information that you originally configured?

_____

■ What is the physical address (MAC address) of your NIC?

_____

For Windows 98 or Windows 2000/XP, another way to test an NIC is to use its assigned IP address in a ping test.

1. Use the ping command with the IP address you assigned to your computer. The results should be similar or identical to the loopback test results, except for the address listed in the ping results.

2. Now ping your partner's IP address. Describe what happened to the request.

_____

_____

_____

You will now connect the two PCs using the crossover cable. Then you will test your network.

1. Close the command-prompt window and shut down both computers.

2. Connect one end of the crossover cable to the NIC on your partner's computer and the other end to the NIC on your computer.

3. Reboot the computers and open a command-prompt window.

4. Ping your partner's IP address. If your computer is connected to a printer, take and print a screen shot of the results. How do these results differ from your earlier attempt to ping your partner's IP address?

_____

_____

18

Review Questions

1. What window is used to configure network adapters and protocols?

   _____

2. What two name fields are used to identify a computer on a workgroup?

   _____

   _____

3. Other than the IP address, what other information is required for TCP/IP communication?

   _____

4. What are two ways to use the ping utility to test the local computer's NIC?

   _____

   _____

5. What conclusion should you draw from a loopback test that reports dropped packets or an unreachable host?

   _____

   _____

Lab 18.2 Inspect Cables

Objectives

The goal of this lab is to help you visually inspect and use a multimeter to test a set of cables. After completing this lab, you will be able to:

➤ Identify two CAT-5 wiring systems

➤ Test cables with a multimeter

➤ Draw pin-outs for cable connectors

➤ Determine if a cable is a patch cable (also known as a straight-through cable) or a crossover cable

➤ Visually inspect cables and connectors

Materials Required

This lab will require the following:

➤ A variety of cables including a patch cable and a crossover cable

➤ Multimeter

➤ Internet access

Activity Background

Once you narrow down a problem to physical connectivity, you must inspect the connections to verify that they are not loose. If you eliminate that possibility, then you can assume that the cable is the problem. In this lab, you will physically inspect the cables and the connector and then test the cable for continuity and pin-out using the multimeter.

Estimated completion time: **45 minutes**

ACTIVITY

1. Consult the information at *www.atcomservices.com/highlights/cat5notes.htm* or search the Internet for information about a patch cable diagram, a crossover cable diagram, and a CAT-5 wiring diagram. List the two standards of CAT-5 wiring schemes. What Web site did you use?

   _____

   _____

   _____

2. Print a wiring diagram for a patch cable wired to each scheme and for a crossover cable using each scheme.

Follow these steps to visually inspect cables:

1. Examine the length of the cable for obvious damage. The damage could be in the form of a cut or abrasion in the outer sleeve with further damage to the twisted pairs inside. A completely cut strand is an obvious problem, but the proper conductor inside the cable might be broken even if the insulator is intact. Any visible copper is an indication that you need a new cable.

2. Inspect the RJ-45 connectors. Particularly look for exposed twisted pairs between the clear plastic connector and the cable sleeve. This is an indication that the cable was assembled improperly or that excessive force was used when pulling on the cable. The cable sleeve should be crimped inside the RJ-45 connector. It is sometimes possible to identify a nonconforming wiring scheme by noting the color of the insulation through the clear connector, but the cable should be checked with a multimeter to verify the condition.

3. Next, verify that the retaining clip on the connector is present. Often when an assembled cable is pulled, this clip will snag on carpet or other cables and break off. This results in a connector that is likely to become loose or fall out of the jack. Worse still, this connection may be intermittent. Some cables have hooded guards to prevent the clip from snagging when pulled. These guards themselves can cause problems when seating the connector in the jack if the guard has slid too far toward the end of the cable.

4. Test your cables using a multimeter and complete Table 18-1.

18

Table 18-1

	Pin #	End A		End B		Questions about the cable
		Insulator color	Pin tied to pin at End B	Insulator color	Pin tied to pin at End A	Is the cable good or bad?
Cable 1	1					
	2					Wired with what scheme?
	3					
	4					
	5					Is the cable a crossover or a patch cable?
	6					
	7					
	8					
	Pin #	Insulator color	Pin tied to pin at End B	Insulator color	Pin tied to pin at End A	Is the cable good or bad?
Cable 2	1					
	2					Wired with what scheme?
	3					
	4					
	5					Is the cable a crossover or a patch cable?
	6					
	7					
	8					
	Pin #	Insulator color	Pin tied to pin at End B	Insulator color	Pin tied to pin at End A	Is the cable good or bad?
Cable 3	1					
	2					Wired with what scheme?
	3					
	4					
	5					Is the cable a crossover or a patch cable?
	6					
	7					
	8					

Review Questions

1. If you can see a copper conductor in a cable, what should you do with the cable?

_____

_____

2. What type of connector is used with CAT-5 cable?

_____

3. Based on your research, what cabling scheme is more common?

_____

4. On a patch cable, pin 3 on one end connects to pin _____ on the opposite end of the cable.

5. On a crossover cable, pin 2 on one end connects to pin _____ on the other end of the cable.

LAB 18.3 COMPARE OPTIONS FOR A HOME LAN

Objectives

The goal of this lab is to help you research the costs and capabilities of both a wired and a wireless home LAN. After completing this lab, you will be able to:

➤ Research wired and wireless Ethernet

➤ Research 802.11 standards

➤ Identify the strengths and weaknesses of each option

Materials Required

This lab will require the following:

➤ Internet access

Activity Background

As the price of equipment and computers fall, installing a home LAN has become increasingly popular. In this lab, you will research wired and wireless Ethernet and determine which option is best in certain situations.

Estimated completion time: **30 minutes**

ACTIVITY

Use your favorite search site to investigate and answer the following questions regarding wireless LAN standards.

1. List the 802.x standards used to specify wireless networks.

_____

_____

18

2. What industry name is associated with 802.11b?

   _____

3. What is the simplest form of a wireless network? What devices are needed to create this type of network and what mode does this type of network use?

   _____

   _____

   _____

4. What device connects wireless users to a wired network?

   _____

5. What standard speeds are supported by 802.11x?

   _____

   _____

   _____

6. What kind of encryption is used with 802.11b?

   _____

   _____

7. Give four examples of devices (besides PCs) that will probably eventually run on wireless LANs.

   _____

   _____

   _____

   _____

8. What does the acronym Wi-Fi stand for?

   _____

9. What is the approximate maximum range for 802.11b technology?

   _____

10. What inherent feature of 802.11b, seen as a significant problem by businesses, might affect your decision to not use Wi-Fi at home as well?

_____

_____

11. In the context of how they physically interface with a computer, what are the three basic types of wireless adapter?

_____

_____

_____

12. What mode requires a wireless access point?

_____

13. How many 802.11b devices can be used at one time with a single access point?

_____

14. What radio band and speed does 802.11a use?

_____

_____

15. Which standard offers a faster transfer rate, 802.11a or 802.11b? List their transfer rates.

_____

_____

16. List components and prices required to connect four PCs in ad hoc mode. List the device and extra expense necessary to connect the same four PCs to a cable modem.

_____

_____

_____

_____

18

Use the Internet to research and answer these questions on an Ethernet home LAN:

1. What is the maximum cable length for a 100BaseT Ethernet LAN?

   _____

2. Must you use a hub to connect three PCs? Two PCs? Explain.

   _____

   _____

   _____

3. What type of cabling is typically used for 100BaseT?

   _____

4. Are special tools required when working with CAT-5 cabling to create patch or crossover cables?

   _____

5. What feature included with Windows 98 or Windows XP allows more than one computer to share a connection to the Internet?

   _____

6. What type of cable connector is used for fast Ethernet?

   _____

7. What standard supports a speed of 100 Mbps using two sets of CAT-3 cable?

   _____

8. What is the name for a cable that connects a computer to a hub?

   _____

9. Suppose you have a LAN consisting of a 100BaseT hub, two computers with 10BaseT NICs, and a computer with a 10/100BaseT NIC. At what speed would this LAN operate? Why?

   _____

   _____

10. Given a budget of $200 to connect five computers, would you choose 100BaseT or 10BaseT? Explain your choice.

_____

_____

_____

11. What is the name for a cable that connects a hub to a hub?

_____

12. In theory, if File X is transferred in 4.5 seconds on a fast Ethernet LAN, how long would the same file transfer take on a 10BaseT LAN?

_____

13. Give three examples of ways to physically interface a NIC to a computer.

_____

_____

_____

14. What device might you use to connect two or more PCs to a single cable modem?

_____

15. List the components, including cables, required to connect four PCs. Include the price of each component. List the changes and additional devices required to connect all four PCs to a cable modem and provide a hardware firewall.

_____

_____

_____

_____

_____

18

Review Questions

1. Based on your research, does wireless or 100BaseT offer the best performance for the money?

   _____

   _____

2. Would wireless or 100BaseT be easier to configure in a home? Why?

   _____

   _____

3. What factors dictate the transmission range of 802.11x?

   _____

   _____

   _____

4. What determines the speed of a LAN that consists of both 10Mbps and 100Mbps devices?

   _____

   _____

5. Would a wired or wireless LAN offer better security?

   _____

6. Could you combine a wireless and wired LAN in the same home? Why would you?

   _____

   _____

   _____

LAB 18.4 TROUBLESHOOT WITH TCP/IP UTILITIES

Objectives

The goal of this lab is to help you use Windows 2000/XP TCP/IP utilities to troubleshoot connectivity problems. After completing this lab, you will be able to:

➤ Use IPConfig

➤ Use the Ping utility

➤ Use Tracert

➤ Identify the point at which your packets will no longer travel

Materials Required

This lab will require the following:

➤ Windows 2000/XP operating system

➤ DHCP server

➤ Internet access

Activity Background

Perhaps nothing frustrates users more than a suddenly unavailable network connection. As a PC technician, you might be asked to restore such a connection. In some cases, in fact, you may have to deal with multiple failed connections at one time. When troubleshooting network connections, it helps to know if many users in one area of a network are having the same connection problem. That information can help you narrow down the source of the problem. Once you have an idea of what machine is causing the problem, you can use a few TCP/IP utilities to prove your theory without actually physically checking the system. In this lab, you will learn to use TCP/IP utilities to isolate connection problems.

Estimated completion time: **30 minutes**

ACTIVITY

Follow these steps to display IP settings in Windows 2000/XP:

1. Right-click **My Network Places** and select **Properties** from the shortcut menu. For Windows 2000, the Network and Dialup Connections window opens, and for Windows XP, the Network Connections window opens.

2. In the window, right-click **Local Area Connection** and select **Properties** from the shortcut menu. The Local Area Connection Properties dialog box opens.

18

3. Click **Internet Protocol (TCP/IP)** and then click **Properties**. The Internet Protocol (TCP/IP) dialog box opens. In the Internet Protocol (TCP/IP) dialog box, notice the different options. What two ways can you set up the IP configuration?

_____

_____

4. Verify that **Obtain an IP address automatically** is selected.

5. Click **OK** to close the Internet Protocol (TCP/IP) dialog box, and then click **Close** to exit the Local Area Connection Properties dialog box. Close the Network and Dialup Connections window (for Windows 2000) or the Network Connections window (for Windows XP).

Follow these steps to adjust the command prompt so that you can view more information at a time:

1. Open a command-prompt window.

2. Right-click the title bar of the command-prompt window and select **Properties** from the shortcut menu. The MS-DOS Prompt Properties dialog box opens.

3. In the Screen Buffer size section of the Layout tab, specify **150** for width and **300** for height. This will allow you to scroll in the command-prompt window and view the last 300 lines of 150 characters. If you wish, you can adjust the Window Size section, but it is generally best to wait to adjust each command-prompt window after it opens. This ensures that you do not make the window too large for your monitor's display settings. Click **OK** to save the settings.

4. The Apply Properties to Shortcut dialog box appears. To specify that you wish to apply the properties every time you open a command-prompt window, select **Modify the shortcut that started this window** and then click **OK**.

Follow these steps to learn how to display IP information from the command line:

1. Open a command-prompt window.

2. Type **IPConfig** and press **Enter**. Displayed are three types of information. List them below.

_____

_____

_____

3. To get more information about your IP settings, type **IPConfig /all** and press **Enter**. Take a screen shot of these results, print the screen shot, and answer these questions.

■ What is the purpose of DHCP?

_____

_____

■ What is the address of the DHCP server?

_____

4. Because your system is using DHCP to obtain an IP address, type **IPConfig /renew** and press **Enter**. The command-prompt window again displays IP information.

5. Again, type **IPConfig /all** and press **Enter**. Compare the current lease information to the information in the screen shot. What information changed?

_____

_____

6. Next, type **IPConfig /release** and press **Enter**. What message is displayed? What implications do you predict this will have on connectivity?

_____

_____

7. Using your screen shot as a reference, attempt to ping the DHCP server and the DNS server. What are the results?

_____

_____

8. Type **IPConfig** and press **Enter**. Note that your adapter has no IP address and no subnet mask. These two parameters are necessary to communicate using TCP/IP.

9. To re-obtain an IP address lease, type **IPConfig /renew** and press **Enter**. New IP information, which may be the same address as before, is assigned.

10. Find your new lease information. List the command you used to obtain this information. Also list the lease information itself.

_____

_____

_____

18

11. For Windows XP, you can use the Network Connections window to release and renew the IP address. Right-click **My Network Places** and select **Properties** from the shortcut menu. The Network Connections window appears. Select the network connection you want to repair and click **Repair this connection**. Note that you can also right-click the network connection you want to repair and select Repair from the shortcut menu.

If you are connected to the Internet, follow these steps to determine what route your packets take to reach an Internet address:

1. Open a command-prompt window.

2. Type **Tracert** followed by a single space, followed by a domain name on the Internet that you seldom use, and then press **Enter**. (Use a domain name you don't regularly access, because any recently accessed addresses might be cached on your system.)

3. The domain name is resolved by the DNS server and an associated IP address is listed, indicating that you can reach at least one DNS server. This tells you that your packets are traveling at least that far. Next, each hop (or router your packet passed through) is listed with the time in milliseconds the packet took to reach its destination. How many hops will Tracert list? How many hops did the packet take to reach the domain you specified?

_____

4. Now use the Tracert command with an illegal name such as *www.mydomain.c*. What are the results of this command?

_____

When troubleshooting connectivity problems, always consider the number of users experiencing the problem. If many users have similar difficulties, it is unlikely the problem lies with any one user's computer. Thus, you can probably eliminate the need to run extensive local tests on each computer. Instead, you can examine a device that all the computers commonly use.

As a general rule, when troubleshooting, you should start by examining devices close to the computer that is experiencing problems and then move further away. The following steps show you how to apply this principle, by first examining the local computer, and then moving outward to other devices on the network.

1. Verify that the computer is physically connected (that is, that both ends of the cable are connected).

2. Verify that the NIC is installed and that TCP/IP is bound to the NIC.

3. Perform a loopback test to verify that the NIC is functioning properly.

4. Check the IP settings with the following command: **IPCONFIG /ALL**. Verify that an IP address is assigned.

5. Ping other computers on the local network. If you get no response, begin by examining a hub or punch-down panel (a panel where cables convene before connecting to a hub).

6. If you can ping other computers on the local network, then ping the default gateway, which is the first stop for transmissions being sent to addresses that are not on the local network.

7. Continue troubleshooting connections, beginning with nearby devices and working outward until you discover an IP address that returns no response. That will be the source of the trouble.

8. If the device is under your supervision, take the necessary steps to repair it. If the device is out of your control, contact the appropriate administrator.

Review Questions

1. Name four additional pieces of information that the IPCONFIG command with the /ALL switch provides that the IPCONFIG command alone does not.

   _____

   _____

   _____

   _____

2. What type of server resolves a domain name to an IP address?

   _____

3. Using Windows 2000/XP, what command discards the IP address?

   _____

4. What command would you use to determine whether you are able to reach another computer on the local network? Would this command work if the default gateway were down?

   _____

   _____

18

5. If many users suddenly encountered connection problems, would you suspect problems with their local computers or problems with other devices on the network? Explain.

_____

_____

_____

Lab 18.5 Practice Solving Network Connectivity Problems

Objectives

The goal of this lab is to troubleshoot and remedy common network connectivity problems. After completing this lab, you will be able to:

➤ Diagnose and solve connectivity problems

➤ Document the process

Materials Required

This lab will require the following:

➤ Windows 98 or Windows 2000/XP operating system connected to a network and to the Internet

➤ Windows 98 or Windows 2000/XP installation CD or installation files stored in another location

➤ PC toolkit with ground strap

➤ Workgroup partner

Activity Background

To a casual user, Internet and network connections can be confusing. When users experience a connectivity problem, they usually have no idea how to remedy the situation. In this lab, you will introduce and solve common connectivity problems.

Estimated completion time: **30 minutes**

Activity

1. Verify that your network is working correctly by browsing the network and connecting to a Web site.

2. Do one of the following:

- Change your PC's IP address
- Change your PC's subnet mask
- Remove your PC's network cable
- Remove TCP/IP from your PC
- Remove your PC's adapter in the Network dialog box
- Unseat or remove your PC's NIC, but leave it installed in the Network window
- Disable your PC's NIC in the Device Manager
- Release your PC's IP address (if DHCP is enabled)

3. Swap PCs with your partner and troubleshoot your partner's PC.

4. On a separate sheet of paper, answer these questions about the problem you solved:

- What is the initial symptom of the problem as user might describe it?

  _____

  _____

- What steps did you take to discover the source of the problem?

  _____

  _____

  _____

  _____

- What steps did you take to resolve the problem?

  _____

  _____

  _____

  _____

18

5. Repeat steps 1–4 until you and your partner have each used all the options listed in step 2. Be sure to answer the questions in step 4 for each troubleshooting scenario.

Review Questions

1. What problem could you resolve by issuing only one command? What was the command you used?

_____

2. Which problem (or problems) forced you to reboot the computer after repairing it?

_____

_____

_____

3. What two pieces of information are necessary for TCP/IP communication on the local network?

_____

4. When using Windows 98, what problem (or problems) caused the Network Neighborhood icon to disappear?

_____

_____

5. What TCP/IP utility was the most useful, in your opinion, for troubleshooting these problems? Why?

_____

_____

6. What situation would not necessarily cause a communication problem if a network protocol other than TCP/IP (such as NetBEUI) were installed on this and other computers on the network?

_____

LAB 18.6 SHARE RESOURCES ON A NETWORK

Objectives

The goal of this lab is to demonstrate the process of sharing resources and using these shared resources on a remote computer on the network. After completing this lab, you will be able to:

➤ Share resources

➤ Control access to shared resources

➤ Connect to shared resources

Materials Required

This lab will require the following:

➤ Two or more Windows 98 or Windows 2000/XP computers on a network

➤ Windows 98 or Windows 2000/XP installation CD or installation files stored in another location

➤ Workgroup of 2–4 students

Activity Background

The primary reason to network computers is to make it possible to share files, printers, Internet connections, and other resources. To share resources in a Windows workgroup, you need to make sure each computer has two Windows components installed: Client for Microsoft Networks and File and Print Sharing. Those components are installed by default in Windows 2000/XP, and Client for Microsoft Networks is installed by default in Windows 98. In this lab, you will install them on a Windows 98 computer (if they are not already installed or have been uninstalled). Then you will share resources and connect to these shared resources. Instructions are written for Windows 98, although they work about the same for Windows 2000/XP if you substitute My Network Places for Network Neighborhood in the instructions. Other differences between Windows 98 and Windows 2000/XP are noted.

Estimated completion time: **30 minutes**

18

ACTIVITY

To share resources on a Windows peer-to-peer network, computers must belong to the same workgroup. Do the following to verify that all computers in your group belong to the same Windows workgroup:

1. To determine the name of the workgroup, right-click **Network Neighborhood**, click **Properties** in the shortcut menu, and then click the **Identification** tab. For Windows 2000/XP, right-click **My Computer**, click **Properties** in the

shortcut menu, and then for Windows 2000, click the **Network Identification** tab. For Windows XP, click the **Computer Name** tab.

What is the workgroup name for this computer?

2. Change the workgroup name, if necessary, so that all the computers in your group belong to the same workgroup. If you are asked to reboot the PC, wait to do that until after you have installed the components in the next group of steps.

For each Windows 98 computer, follow these steps to check to see if Client for Microsoft Networks and File and Print Sharing are installed on your computer, and, if necessary, install these components:

1. Right-click the **Network Neighborhood** icon on the desktop and then click **Properties** in the shortcut menu. The Network dialog box opens.

2. If Client for Microsoft Networks is not listed as an installed component, you need to install it. To do that, click **Add**. The Add Network Component Type dialog box opens.

3. Click **Client**, and then click **Add**. The Select Network Client dialog box opens.

4. In the left pane of the Select Network Client dialog box, click **Microsoft**, and then click **Client for Microsoft Networks** in the right pane. Click **OK** to continue. The Add Network Component Type dialog box and the Select Network Client dialog box close. You return to the Network dialog box.

5. If File and Printer Sharing for Microsoft networks is not listed as an installed component in the Network dialog box, you need to install it. To do that, click **Add**. The Add Network Component Type dialog box opens again.

6. Click **Service**, and then click **Add**. The Select Network Service dialog box opens.

7. Select **File and printer sharing for Microsoft Networks** and click **OK**. Insert the Windows installation CD or point to the location of the installation files as instructed in the dialog box that appears. When the service is installed, you return to the Network dialog box.

8. To enable File and Print Sharing, click **File and Print Sharing** in the Network dialog box. The File and Print Sharing dialog box opens.

9. Select the **I want to be able to give others access to my files** check box and the **I want to be able to allow others to print to my printers** check box. Selecting these two options makes it possible for other computers on the network to access this computer's files and printers. Click **OK** to close the File and Print Sharing dialog box. You return to the Network dialog box.

10. Click **OK** to close the Network dialog box and save your new settings. The Systems Settings Change dialog box appears and notifies you that before the settings will take effect, the system must be restarted. Click **Yes** to reboot.

Now that you have enabled file and printer sharing, you are ready to set up folders or printers on your PC to be shared by others on the network. Follow these steps to share folders and control access to their contents:

1. Using Windows Explorer, create three folders at the root of drive C. Name the folders **Read**, **Full**, and **Depends**. Create a text file called **readtest.txt** in the Read folder, a text file called **fulltest.txt** in the Full folder, and a text file called **deptest.txt** in the Depends folder. Type a short sentence in each text file, save your changes, and close the files. Click the **Shared As** option button.

2. In the right pane of Windows Explorer, right-click the **Read** folder and then click **Sharing** in the shortcut menu. The Read Properties dialog box opens, with the Sharing tab selected.

3. In the Access Type section, select **Read-Only**. This setting gives users on the network read-only access to all the files in the Read folder.

4. In the Password section, click the **Read-Only Password** text box and then type **read**. Click **OK**. The Password Confirmation dialog box opens.

5. In the Password Confirmation dialog box, re-enter **read** in the Read Only Password text box and then click **OK**. Both the Confirm Password dialog box and the Read Properties dialog box close.

6. Repeat steps 2–5 for the other two folders you just created, selecting the access types associated with their names. For the Full folder, use "full" as the Full Access Type Password. For the Depends folder, supply both Read-Only and Full Access Type passwords. Use the password associated with the access type.

So far you have: verified that all computers that will share resources are in the same workgroup; installed Windows components to share resources; and set up the folders that will be shared. You are now ready to use shared resources over the network. Follow these steps to access the shared folders:

1. In Windows Explorer, click the **Network Neighborhood** icon. The right pane of Windows Explorer displays a list of computers on the network.

2. In the right pane of Windows Explorer, double-click your partner's computer icon to display the shared resources available on that computer.

3. In the right pane of Windows Explorer, double-click the **Read** folder. The Enter Network Password dialog box opens. Here you need to enter the password for this folder.

4. Type **Read** and click **OK**. The contents of the Read folder are displayed in Windows Explorer.

18

5. Double-click **readtest.txt**. The file opens in Notepad. Attempt to save the file, and record your results below.

_____

_____

6. Now attempt to save the file in the My Documents folder on your computer. Record the results below. Why did your results in step 5 differ from your results here?

_____

_____

_____

7. Close Notepad, click the **Network Neighborhood** icon in the left pane of Windows Explorer, and double-click the icon for your partner's computer in the right pane.

8. Double-click the **Full** folder in the right pane and, when prompted, enter the password and click **OK**. The contents of the Full folder are displayed in Explorer.

9. Double-click **fulltest.txt**. The file opens in Notepad. Attempt to save the file, and record your results below.

_____

_____

10. Attempt to save the file in the My Documents folder on your computer, and record the results below. Did you note any difference between the results of step 9 and step 10? If so, explain the difference.

_____

11. Close Notepad, return to the desktop, and open your **My Documents** folder.

12. Rename the file fulltest.txt using a new name of your choice. Attempt to copy, or drag and drop, this file into the Full folder on your partner's PC. Were you successful? Why or why not?

_____

You have just seen how you can use Network Neighborhood to access shared folders on the network. You can make these shared folders appear to be a local drive on your PC, thereby making it more convenient to access these folders. When a shared folder on the network is made to appear to be a local drive on your PC, the folder is called a network drive. Follow these steps to map a network drive and configure it to connect at logon:

1. In the left pane of Windows Explorer, click the **Network Neighborhood** icon. A list of computers on your network appears in the right pane.

2. Double-click the icon for your partner's computer. A list of shared resources appears.

3. Right-click the **Full** folder and then click **Map Network Drive** in the shortcut menu. The Map Network Drive dialog box opens.

4. In the Map Network Drive dialog box, click the **Drive** drop-down menu and then select the drive letter you wish to assign to this folder.

5. In the Map Network Drive dialog box, select the **Reconnect at Logon** check box and then click **OK**.

6. When prompted, enter the correct password and click **OK**. The drive is connected and a window opens displaying the contents of the Full folder. The title of the window includes the drive letter you assigned.

7. Check Windows Explorer and verify that the drive letter is now listed under My Computer.

8. Log off and then log back on to test that the drive reconnects. What did you have to do to reconnect when you logged back on?

_____

_____

ALTERNATE ACTIVITY

To map a drive using a Windows 2000/XP computer, open Windows Explorer, right-click the **My Network Places** icon, and then click **Map Network Drive** in the shortcut menu. The Map Network Drive dialog box opens. Click **Browse** and locate the folder on the network that you want to map to the network drive. Then begin with step 3.

Review Questions

1. What is the main advantage of connecting computers into networks?

_____

_____

2. What term refers to the process of allowing others to use resources on your computer?

_____

18

3. What two Windows network components must be installed before you can grant others access to resources on your computer and use their resources?

_____

4. How can you provide full access to some of your files while giving read-only access to other files shared on the network?

_____

_____

5. Explain how to allow some people to make changes to files in shared folders while only allowing others to view and read the contents of the same folder.

_____

_____

_____

_____

Lab 18.7 Use NetBEUI Instead of TCP/IP

Objectives

Most networks use the TCP/IP network protocol suite. The goal of this lab is to demonstrate how to replace TCP/IP with NetBEUI. After completing this lab, you will be able to:

➤ Install NetBEUI

➤ Remove TCP/IP

➤ Observe the results of using NetBEUI

Materials Required

This lab will require the following:

➤ Windows 2000/XP operating system

➤ NIC configured to use only TCP/IP

➤ IP information or a DHCP server on the network

➤ Internet access

➤ Windows 2000/XP Professional installation CD or installation files stored in another location

➤ Network workgroup consisting of two computers

➤ Workgroup of 2–4 students

Activity Background

TCP/IP is probably the network protocol with which you are most familiar, but it is not the only network protocol, nor is it the best for all situations. NetBEUI (NetBIOS Enhanced User Interface) was originally developed by IBM to make it possible to use NetBIOS names as official network addresses. NetBEUI is faster than TCP/IP and much easier to configure. Its main disadvantage is that it is nonroutable (that is, it is only able to communicate with computers on its network). In this lab you will configure one computer in your workgroup to use NetBEUI and then observe the effect of this change on both computers in the workgroup. Then you will use NetBEUI as the only network protocol in your workgroup.

Estimated completion time: **30 minutes**

ACTIVITY

First you need to determine what the network looks like before you install NetBEUI and remove TCP/IP. Follow these steps:

1. On one of the two computers in the workgroup, open **My Network Places**. For Windows 2000, double-click **Computers Near Me**. For Windows XP, click **View workgroup computers**. A list of computers on your network appears. Take and print a screen shot of this list. To do that, press the **Alt+ PrintScreen** keys, which copies the window into the clipboard. Open Windows Paint. Click **Edit**, **Paste**. Then click **File**, **Print** to print the window. Close Windows Paint without saving your work.

2. Repeat step 1 for the other computer on your network.

Now you are ready to follow these steps to install NetBEUI as the network protocol on one of the computers in your workgroup:

1. Right-click the **My Network Places** icon and click **Properties** in the shortcut menu. The Network and Dial-Up Connections window opens.

2. Right-click the **Local Area Connection** icon and select **Properties** in the shortcut menu. The Local Area Connection Properties dialog box opens.

3. In the Local Area Connection Properties dialog box, click **Install**. The Select Network Component Type dialog box opens.

18

4. Click **Protocol** and then click **Add**. The Select Network Protocol dialog box opens.

5. Click **NetBEUI Protocol** and then click **OK**. The Select Network Protocol and Select Network Component Type dialog boxes close.

Your next job is to uninstall TCP/IP on the computer on which you installed NetBEUI. You'll begin by recording the TCP/IP configuration information for that computer. Then you will uninstall TCP/IP. (You'll need configuration information when you reinstall TCP/IP at the end of this lab.) Follow these steps:

1. Right-click **My Network Places** and select **Properties** from the shortcut menu. The Network and Dial-Up Connections window opens.

2. Right-click the **Local Area Connection** icon and select **Properties** from the shortcut menu. The Local Area Connection Properties window opens.

3. Select **Internet Protocol (TCP/IP)** from the list of components and click **Properties**. The TCP/IP Properties window opens.

4. Record all the configuration information available in this window:

_____

_____

_____

_____

5. Click **Cancel** to close the TCP/IP Properties window.

6. In the Local Area Connection Properties dialog box, click **Internet Protocol (TCP/IP)** and then click **Uninstall**. A message appears informing you that you are about to remove the protocol from all connections.

7. Click **Yes** to continue. The Internet Protocol (TCP/IP) is removed from the Local Area Connection Properties dialog box.

8. The Local Network dialog box opens and informs you that you must restart the computer before the changes can take effect.

9. Click **Yes** to restart the computer.

Follow these steps to observe the effects of using NetBEUI:

1. Go to the computer that you did not alter (that is, to the computer that is still running TCP/IP).

2. If it is not already open, open the **My Network Places** window and double-click **Computers Near Me**. If Computers Near Me was already open, then press **F5** to refresh the display. (For Windows XP, click **View workgroup computers**.) Answer these questions:

■ What computers are displayed?

_____

_____

_____

_____

■ Compare the current screen to the screen shot you created earlier. What computers are missing?

_____

_____

_____

_____

■ Why are they missing?

_____

_____

3. Go to the computer on which you installed NetBEUI.

4. Open **My Network Places**, and then open **Computers Near Me** or **View workgroup computers**. Answer the following questions:

■ What computers are displayed?

_____

_____

_____

_____

18

■ Compare the current screen to the screen shot you created earlier. What computers are missing?

_____

_____

_____

_____

■ Why are they missing?

_____

_____

5. Press **F5** to refresh the list of computers on the network. Did any new ones appear? Why or why not?

_____

_____

_____

_____

6. On the computer on which you installed NetBEUI, attempt to connect to the Internet and then answer these questions:

■ What message did you receive?

_____

_____

_____

■ Why do you think you were unable to connect to the Internet?

_____

_____

Next, you will use some network utilities to test your network connections. You will start by running a loopback ping test. This test uses the IP address 127.0.0.1 with the Ping command to test the local computer. Follow these steps:

1. On the computer that's running TCP/IP (the one you didn't change), open a command-prompt window, type **Ping 127.0.0.1**, and then press **Enter**. Record the results of the loopback test:

   _____

   _____

   _____

2. Another TCP/IP utility that you can use to test the network configuration and connectivity is Ipconfig. Type **Ipconfig /all** and then press **Enter**. Record the results of the command:

   _____

   _____

   _____

3. On the computer on which you installed NetBEUI, open a command-prompt window and then repeat steps 1 and 2. Record the results below. Why did you receive the results you did?

   _____

   _____

   _____

   _____

Follow these steps to re-install TCP/IP:

1. On the computer on which you installed NetBEUI, right-click the **My Network Places** icon and select **Properties** from the shortcut menu. The Network and Dialup Connections window opens.

2. Right-click the **Local Area Connection** icon and select **Properties** from the shortcut menu. The Local Area Connection Properties dialog box opens.

3. Click **Install**. The Select Network Component Type dialog box opens.

4. Click **Protocol** and then click **Add**. The Select Network Protocol dialog box opens.

18

5. Click **TCP/IP Protocol** and then click **OK**. The Select Network Protocol and Select Network Component Type dialog boxes close.

6. The Local Network dialog box opens and informs you that you must restart the computer before the changes can take effect. Click **Yes** to restart the computer.

You've finished re-installing TCP/IP. Now you need to reconfigure the necessary TCP/IP settings. Follow these steps:

1. Right-click the **My Network Places** icon and select **Properties** from the shortcut menu. The Windows 2000 Network and Dial-Up Connections window or the Windows XP Network Connections window opens.

2. Right-click the **Local Area Connection** icon and select **Properties** from the shortcut menu. The Local Area Connection Properties dialog box opens.

3. In the Local Area Connection Properties dialog box, click **Internet Protocol (TCP/IP)**, and then click **Properties**. The Internet Protocol (TCP/IP) Properties dialog box opens.

4. In the Internet Protocol (TCP/IP) Properties dialog box, reconfigure the settings you recorded in step 3 at the beginning of this lab.

5. Click **OK** to close the Internet Protocol (TCP/IP) Properties dialog box.

6. Click **OK** to close the Local Area Connection Properties dialog box and save your settings.

7. Test your settings by connecting to another computer or the Internet.

ADDITIONAL ACTIVITY (additional 20 minutes)

1. Install NetBEUI and remove TCP/IP on one more computer in your workgroup so that NetBEUI is the only network protocol installed on two computers.

2. Using NetBEUI, transfer files from one computer to the other.

3. Install TCP/IP and configure it and then remove NetBEUI as an installed networking protocol.

Review Questions

1. Is it possible to have more than one network protocol installed on the same network? Explain how you arrived at your answer.

_____

_____

_____

2. If you had to access the Internet from your computer, which protocol would you use?

_____

3. What features of NetBEUI make it appealing for a small network that does not need Internet access?

_____

_____

4. Of the two covered in this lab, which network protocol is better suited for troubleshooting problems? Why?

_____

_____

5. What type of computer name is used on a NetBEUI network?

_____

LAB 18.8 USE A PARALLEL PORT FOR DIRECT CABLE CONNECTION

Objectives

The goal of this lab is to help you use the Direct Cable Connection feature of Windows 98 to connect two computers with a parallel port. After completing this lab, you will be able to:

➤ Install Direct Cable Connection

➤ Link two computers with a parallel cable

➤ Transfer files

Materials Required

This lab will require the following:

➤ Windows 98 operating system

➤ Standard parallel cable with a DB 25-pin connection at both ends (or you can substitute a parallel printer cable with a 36-pin Centronics to DB 25-pin converter)

➤ Two computers that are not connected to the network

➤ Windows 98 installation CD or installation files stored in another location

➤ Workgroup of 2–4 students

18

Activity Background

Included with Windows 98, the Direct Cable Connection feature allows you to connect two computers without the benefit of a conventional network. Although slow in comparison to the typical LAN, this feature does allow you to transfer files using a serial null-modem or parallel cable. The only other requirement is that the computers share a common communications protocol. NetBEUI is ideal for this type of connection because it is easy to configure and is faster than other protocols. In this lab, you will connect two computers using the Direct Cable Connection feature.

Estimated completion time: **30 minutes**

ACTIVITY

First, you need to install the Direct Cable Connection feature on both computers. Follow these steps:

1. Click **Start** on the taskbar, point to **Settings**, click **Control Panel**, and then double-click **Add/Remove Programs**.

2. Click the **Windows Setup** tab.

3. Select **Communications** and then click **Details**. Select the **Direct Cable Connection** check box (if it is not already selected).

To use the Direct Cable Connection, work with at least one partner to follow these steps:

1. Shut down both computers, connect the parallel cable to each computer, and reboot both computers.

2. Decide which computer will be the "host" and which will be the "guest." The guest computer will have access to files on the host computer.

3. On both computers, click **Start**, point to **Programs**, point to **Accessories**, point to **Communications**, and then click **Direct Cable Connection**. The Direct Cable Connection dialog box opens.

4. On the host computer, select **Host** in the Direct Cable Connection dialog box. On the guest computer, select **Guest** on the Direct Cable Connection dialog box. On both computers, click **Next**. If this is the first time that Direct Cable Connection has been used, the Configuring Ports dialog box will open and close, at which point you should continue with step 5. If Direct Cable Connection has been run before, click **Change** in the Direct Cable Connection dialog box and then continue with step 5.

5. The Direct Cable Connection dialog box presents a list of possible ports to use for the cable. In the "Select the port you want to use" list, select **Parallel cable on LPT1** and then click **Next** to continue.

6. On the host computer (not the guest computer), the Direct Cable Connection dialog box explains that it will have access to shared files and lists the steps required to share a folder. Summarize these steps below:

_____

_____

_____

_____

7. On the host computer, click **Next** to continue. On the guest computer, wait until the host computer completes steps 8 and 9 and your partner gives you the go-ahead, and then skip to step 10.

8. On the host computer select the **Use Password Protection** check box and then click **Set Password**. The Direct Cable Connection Password dialog box opens.

9. Type **dcclab** in the Password text box and in the Confirm Password text box and then click **OK**. The Direct Cable Connection Password dialog box closes.

10. On the host computer, click **Finish**. The Direct Cable Connection dialog box displays "Status: Waiting to connect via parallel cable on LPT1." At this time, the host team should signal the guest team to proceed. The guest team should then click **Finish**. The Direct Cable Connection dialog box appears on the guest computer.

11. On the guest computer, enter the password when prompted. Click **OK** to establish the connection.

12. On the guest computer, test the connection by browsing to the host in Network Neighborhood and transferring files from a shared folder.

Review Questions

1. What two kinds of cable could you use to implement a Direct Cable Connection?

_____

_____

2. In a Direct Cable Connection, is it possible to share printers but not files? Is it possible to share files but not printers? Explain.

_____

_____

18

3. Would it make sense to use Direct Cable Connection to connect two computers that already have access to an existing network? Explain your answer.

_____

_____

_____

4. Why might you use Direct Cable Connection to connect two computers, even if one of the computers has access to a network?

_____

_____

_____

5. When using Direct Cable Connection to connect to computers through a printer cable, what must you use in addition to the printer cable? Why?

_____

_____

6. Of the two types of cable that can be used for Direct Cable Connection, which provides better transfer speeds?

_____

LAB 18.9 CONFIGURE AND USE DIAL-UP SERVER

Objectives

The goal of this lab is to give you practice using Dial-Up Server to allow dial-in access to a computer. After completing this lab, you will be able to:

➤ Install Dial-Up Server

➤ Configure Dial-Up Server

➤ Configure a Dial-Up Networking connection

Materials Required

This lab will require the following:

➤ Two Windows 98 computers

➤ Modem and telephone line for each computer

➤ Dial-Up Networking installed on both computers

➤ File and Print Sharing and Client for Microsoft Networks installed on both computers and at least one shared folder on the host computer

➤ Windows 98 installation CD or installation files stored in another location

➤ Workgroup of 2–4 students

Activity Background

You can set up your Windows computer to receive dial-in connections from other computers. You might wish to do this if you travel and want to be able to transfer files to and from your home computer while away. In Windows 95, you must install the Microsoft Plus utility; in Windows 98, you need to install the Dial-Up server component; and Windows NT requires the Remote Access Service (RAS). Windows 2000 and Windows XP have the ability to allow incoming calls by default. In this lab you will set up and use Dial-Up Server in Windows 98.

Estimated completion time: **45 minutes**

ACTIVITY

Follow these steps to install Dial-Up Server:

1. Open the **Control Panel**, double-click the **Add/Remove Programs** icon, and then click the **Windows Setup** tab.

2. In the Components list box, double-click the **Communications** group. The Communications dialog box opens.

3. Select the **Dial-Up Server** check box and then click **OK**. The Communications dialog box closes and you return to the Add/Remove Programs dialog box.

4. Click **OK** to close the Add/Remove Programs dialog box. Supply Windows 98 installation files as necessary.

Follow these steps to configure Dial-Up Server:

1. In Windows Explorer or My Computer, open **Dial-Up Networking**.

2. In Dial-Up Networking, click **Connections** on the menu bar, then click **Dial-Up Server**. The Dial-Up Server dialog box opens.

3. In the Dial-Up Server dialog box, select the **Allow caller access** option button.

4. In the Dial-Up Server dialog box click **Change Password**. The Dial-Up Server Password dialog box opens.

18

5. In the Dial-Up Server Password dialog box, leave the Old password text box blank. In the New password and Confirm new password text boxes type **test**. Click **OK** to close the Dial-Up Server Password dialog box.

6. In the Dial-Up Server dialog box, click **Server Type**. The Server Type dialog box opens.

7. In the Server Type dialog box, click the **Type of Dial-Up server** list arrow and then select **PPP: Internet**, **Windows NT Server**, **Windows 98**.

8. In the Advanced options section of the Server Type dialog box, make sure that the **Enable software compression** and the **Require encrypted password** check boxes are selected, then click **OK** to close the Server Type dialog box.

9. In the Dial-Up Server dialog box, click **OK**. The Dial-Up Server dialog box closes, and a Dial-Up Server symbol appears in the system tray.

10. Double-click the **Dial-Up Server** symbol in the system tray. The Dial-Up Server dialog box opens. Verify that the status of the Dial-Up Server is "Monitoring" (indicating that the system is ready to accept an incoming call). Close the Dial-Up Server dialog box and move to the second computer.

Follow these steps to set up a Dial-Up Networking connection to connect to your Dial-Up Server computer:

1. In Windows Explorer, double-click the **Dial-Up Networking** icon. The Dial-Up Networking window opens.

2. Double-click the **Make New Connection** icon. The Make New Connection dialog box opens.

3. Type **DISLAB** for the name of the connection, select the correct modem if necessary, and then click **Next** to continue.

4. The Made New Connection dialog box opens. Next, specify the number your computer will dial to complete the dial-up connection to the Dial-Up Server. Enter the Dial-Up Server computer's area code and phone number (as provided by your instructor), and select the country code from the drop-down menu. Click **Next** to continue.

5. The Make New Connection dialog box informs you that the connection icon was created successfully. Click **Finish** to close the Make New Connection dialog box. Your new connection appears in the Dial-Up Networking window.

Follow these steps to connect to the Dial-Up Server:

1. Following directions in Lab 18.7, install NetBEUI as the network protocol on both computers. When you are finished installing NetBEUI, you should see it associated with the dial-up adapter in Network Neighborhood.

2. Following directions in Lab 18.6, verify that both computers belong to the same workgroup.

3. To make the connection, double-click the connection icon in the Dial-Up Networking window.

4. The Connect To dialog box opens, showing the connection name. Enter **test** as the password and then click **Connect** to dial up the server.

5. Once the connection is made, verify that you are able to transfer files and then disconnect.

CRITICAL THINKING (additional 15 minutes)

Change the workgroup identity on one of the computers so that the two computers no longer belong to the same workgroup. Attempt to connect and transfer files. At what point did the process fail?

_____

_____

Review Questions

1. What Windows 98 component allows a computer to receive an incoming call?

_____

2. What dialog box includes the Identification tab, which allows you to make changes to the computer's network identity? How do you access that dialog box?

_____

3. Suppose the Dial-Up Server status for your computer is "monitoring." What is Dial-Up Server doing?

_____

_____

_____

4. How does each computer disconnect from a Dial-Up Server session?

_____

_____

_____

_____

_____

18

PCs on the Internet

19

Labs included in this chapter

➤ Lab 19.1 Install Software to Delete Cookies

➤ Lab 19.2 Use FTP to Download a Browser

➤ Lab 19.3 Download and Install Internet Explorer and Install Netscape

➤ Lab 19.4 Set Up NetMeeting

➤ Lab 19.5 Configure a Browser So It Doesn't Download Images

The following grid shows the correlation between the labs in this chapter and the A+ Guides to Hardware and Software.

A+ Guide to Managing and Maintaining Your PC, Fifth Edition	A+ Guide to Hardware, Third Edition	A+ Guide to Software, Third Edition
Lab 19.1 Install Software to Delete Cookies		Chapter 12
Lab 19.2 Use FTP to Download a Browser		Chapter 12
Lab 19.3 Download and Install Internet Explorer and Install Netscape		Chapter 12
Lab 19.4 Set Up NetMeeting		Chapter 12
Lab 19.5 Configure a Browser So It Doesn't Download Images		Chapter 12

LAB 19.1 INSTALL SOFTWARE TO DELETE COOKIES

Objectives

The goal of this lab is to help you install software that will delete cookies each time you boot your computer. After completing this lab, you will be able to:

➤ Locate, download, and install the software

➤ Delete cookies using the software you downloaded

Materials Required

This lab will require the following:

➤ Internet access

➤ Windows 9x or higher

Activity Background

When you visit certain Web sites, cookies are placed on your system to collect information about you, including what Web sites you visit. Besides being an annoyance, cookies can also be a security risk, passing on information that you don't want to make accessible to others. For example, this information could be passed on to companies who might then sell it to someone else or use it for advertising purposes. Several utilities on the market will clean cookies from your computer. One of those is Webroot's Window Washer, which is available for trial download. In this lab, you will install Window Washer and use it to delete cookies.

Estimated completion time: **45 minutes**

ACTIVITY

Follow these steps to download Webroot's Window Washer software. As you are aware, Web sites change often so your steps might differ slightly from these.

1. Go to *www.webroot.com*.

2. Click the **Trial Downloads** link.

3. Scroll down until you see "Window Washer" and then click **Primary Download Site**. (If this download site does not work, you might have to use one of the alternate links listed below it.)

4. The File Download dialog box appears, indicating that you have chosen to download the installation file for Window Washer. Click the **Run this program from its current location** option button and click **OK**.

5. A dialog box appears indicating the progress of the installation. Select the **Close this dialog box when download completes** check box and wait for the download to finish. Depending on the speed of your connection, this could take a few minutes. While you are waiting, look on the Webroot site for information about the Window Washer and record a short description of what it does:

_____

_____

_____

_____

6. When the download is finished, a Security Warning dialog box appears. Click **Yes** to verify that you want to install and run the trial version of Window Washer.

7. The Window Washer Setup dialog box appears. Click **Yes** to continue.

8. The Window Washer installation program launches. In the first dialog box, click **I Agree** to accept the license agreement.

9. The Installation Options dialog box opens. By default, the **Install to:** location is C:\Program Files\Washer, and the options for adding an icon to the desktop and a link to the Start menu are selected. If you wanted to find another location, you would click the Browse button. For this installation, click **Install** to accept the defaults and continue.

10. A message appears asking if, during a wash, you want Window Washer to delete data stored by a browser to be used when auto completing data forms. Click **Yes**.

11. A message appears in the same dialog box informing you that the installation is complete. Deselect the **Run Window Washer Now** checkbox and the **View Release Notes** checkbox and then click **Exit**.

Follow these steps to use Window Washer to delete cookies:

1. Open Internet Explorer and browse the Web for a couple of minutes, visiting a variety of sites such as news sites and commercial sites. Click a few links and ads on those sites. Close Internet Explorer.

2. Open **Windows Explorer**, and then open the **Cookies** folder, which is usually located under C:\Windows. The cookies are stored as text files.

   ■ How many cookies are listed?

_____

19

- What sites appear to have stored cookies on your computer?

  _____

  _____

  _____

3. On the Start menu, point to **Programs**, point to **Window Washer**, and then click **Window Washer**. A dialog box appears showing what information Window Washer is loading. When it finishes loading the required system information, Window Washer opens.

4. At the top of the Window Washer window you see a message indicating that this installation of Windows has never been washed. Click the **Standard Wash Items** button in the Washer Settings pane on the left (if this view is not already active), locate Internet Explorer on the list of Standard Wash items in the right pane, and then click the **Options** button. The Internet Explorer Wash Items dialog box opens. What other items are checked by default?

  _____

  _____

  _____

5. Click **OK** to close the Internet Explorer Wash Items dialog box.

6. Click **Wash Now** in the Washer Controls pane to begin washing your system. Window Washer minimizes itself, and the icon in the system tray moves while the washer is working. Window Washer re-maximizes itself when the wash is complete. How has the message at the top of the window changed?

  _____

  _____

7. Open the Cookies folder again to verify that the cookies are gone.

If you still see cookies in the Cookies folder after you run Window Washer, you might need to click Change Wash Directories in the Standard Wash Items list and then click **Redetect** to have Window Washer locate the folders containing the files you want to delete. You might also need to verify that you checked all the options indicating which files you want to delete before running Window Washer again.

Review Questions

1. What other items can Window Washer clean besides cookies?

   _____

   _____

2. List some reasons why you might not want cookies on your system and why you might want to clear Internet Explorer form data, as well as your document history.

   _____

   _____

   _____

3. What information did the Webroot site provide about how Window Washer works?

   _____

   _____

4. Can you specify your own wash items—that is, items that are not already listed in Window Washer? Explain.

   _____

   _____

5. How might cookies be useful?

   _____

   _____

LAB 19.2 USE FTP TO DOWNLOAD A BROWSER

Objectives

The goal of this lab is to help you use FTP from the command prompt to download a browser. After completing this lab, you will be able to:

➤ Use common FTP commands from a command prompt

➤ Download a browser via FTP

19

Materials Required

This lab will require the following:

➤ Internet access

Activity Background

FTP (File Transfer Protocol) provides a quick and easy way to transfer files over the Internet without first converting them to ASCII text. One situation in which you might use FTP is when transmitting files that are too large to be sent as e-mail attachments. For this lab, imagine that your Web browser has been rendered inoperable, either by a virus or because you accidentally deleted some vital files. Suppose, however, that you can still connect to the Internet. How can you get your browser back? If you are using a network, it might be possible for you to go to another computer on the network, use that computer's browser to download a new browser, and then transfer the downloaded browser file to your computer. Another option is to reinstall Windows on your computer, a process that will install the Microsoft Internet Explorer browser. However, if none of these options are available or are practical, you can use FTP to download a browser. If you have no user-friendly GUI FTP software installed on your computer, you can use FTP from the command prompt. In this lab, you will use FTP commands from the command prompt to locate and download the latest version of Netscape.

Estimated completion time: **45 minutes**

ACTIVITY

Follow these steps to connect to the Netscape FTP site from a command prompt and download the latest version of the Netscape browser:

1. When you download the browser, you will want to store the file in a location on your hard drive that will be easy to find. In Windows Explorer, create a folder on your C: drive called **Downloads**.

2. Open a command prompt window.

3. When the command prompt window opens, the C:\Windows directory will probably be the active directory. When you use FTP, the files you download will be stored in whatever directory was active when you began the session. To change to the Downloads directory, type **cd c:\downloads** and press **Enter**.

4. Once the Downloads directory is active, type **ftp** and press **Enter**. How did the command prompt change?

5. To enter the Netscape FTP site, type **open ftp.netscape.com** and press **Enter**.

6. A message appears indicating that you are connected to the Netscape site and that the server is ready, followed by a User prompt. Many sites, including this one, allow limited access to the site via an anonymous login. Type **anonymous** at the user prompt and press **Enter**.

7. A message appears indicating that your guest logon is OK and requesting your complete e-mail address as a password. Type your e-mail address and press **Enter**. What message do you receive?

---

8. You now have access to certain files on the Netscape FTP site. Browse to the location of the latest version of the Netscape browser. Use the **dir** command to list the contents of the various directories and the **cd** command to change directories as necessary. At the time of this writing, Netscape 6.2.1 was located in the following path: ftp.netscape.com/pub/netscape6/english/6.2.1/ windows/win32/N6Setup.exe. The names and locations of downloadable files can change as versions and site structure change, so you might find the file stored in a different directory. The exact name of the file might be different as well, depending on what the most current version of the browser is. If the location or name of the latest version of the browser setup file differs from the one mentioned earlier in this step, record the correct information here:

---

9. Once you have located the file, type **bin** and press **Enter**. This sets the download mode to specify that you want the file downloaded as a binary (not ASCII) file.

10. To download the file, enter this command (substituting the correct file name if you noted a different one in Step 8): **get N6Setup.exe**. Remember that FTP commands are case sensitive.

11. Press **Enter**. What messages appear?

19

12. Return to Windows Explorer, click **View** on the menu bar, click **Refresh**, then open the **Downloads** folder and verify that the file downloaded successfully.

13. To verify that the browser setup program you downloaded works, double-click the file you downloaded. The setup program opens.

14. Close the setup program, as you will not actually be installing the browser until the next lab.

15. Return to the command prompt window, type **bye** and then press **Enter** to close the FTP session.

Review Questions

1. List all the FTP commands you used in this lab, with a short description of each.

_____

_____

_____

_____

_____

_____

2. In what mode did you download the browser setup file? Why do you think this was necessary?

_____

_____

_____

_____

3. For what other operating systems and in what other languages was Netscape available for download?

_____

_____

4. If you were using FTP to upload a text file that was too large to send as an e-mail attachment, which mode (ASCII or binary) would you choose to upload it and why?

_____

_____

5. Imagine that you are downloading FileABC.txt from the FTP site of CompanyXYZ.com. The file is located in the /pub/documentation/ folder of that site. Your FTP client defaults to binary mode for download. List in order all the commands you would use to open the FTP connection, download the file, and close the connection.

_____

_____

_____

_____

_____

LAB 19.3 DOWNLOAD AND INSTALL INTERNET EXPLORER AND INSTALL NETSCAPE

Objectives

The goal of this lab is to help you download and install the latest versions of Internet Explorer and Netscape. After completing this lab, you will be able to:

➤ Download the latest version of a browser from a company's Web site

➤ Install two downloaded browsers

Materials Required

This lab will require the following:

➤ Internet access

Activity Background

Companies that make Web browsers periodically offer new versions of their products that incorporate new features or fix known bugs. In this lab, you will install the Netscape browser that you downloaded in the previous lab, and you will also download and install an update for Microsoft Internet Explorer. Sometimes it can be helpful to have more than one browser on your machine, so that you can become familiar with, use the features of, and test software with each.

19

Estimated completion time: **30 minutes**

ACTIVITY

Follow these directions to download an update for Internet Explorer. As always, remember that Web sites change often, so your steps might differ slightly from these.

1. Go to *www.microsoft.com*, and locate the link to download the latest version of Internet Explorer. At the time of this writing, the link for downloading the latest version was found at:

   www.microsoft.com/windows/ie/downloads/critical/ie6sp1/default.asp.

   If you find the link for the latest version at a different location, record that location here.

   _____

2. Select **English** and click **Go**. Click the link to begin downloading.

3. The File Download dialog box opens. Click the **Save this program to disk** option button and then click **OK**.

4. The Save As dialog box appears. Locate the C:\Downloads folder you created in the previous lab and click **Save** to save the Internet Explorer setup file (which is called ie6setup.exe or something similar) to that folder.

5. The File Download dialog box closes, and you see a dialog box indicating the progress of the download. Select the **Close this dialog box when download completes** check box. You will know that the download is finished when the File Download dialog box closes. If you did not select this option, the progress indicator and the messages in the File Download dialog box would change to indicate when the download was finished.

Follow these steps to install Netscape (which you downloaded in Lab 19.2):

1. Open Windows Explorer, open the C:\Downloads folder, and double-click the setup file for Netscape.

2. Setup launches, showing the Welcome screen. Click **Next**.

3. The License Agreement screen appears. Click **Accept** to accept the license agreement.

4. The Setup Type screen appears. In this screen, you can choose Recommended, Full, or Custom Setup. For this installation, you will use the **Recommended** setup. Under what circumstances would you choose the Full installation option? The Custom installation?

   _____

   _____

   _____

5. Verify that the **Recommended** option button is selected, and then click **Next**.

6. A dialog box appears asking if you want to create the destination directory. Click **Yes** to continue.

7. The next screen gives you a chance to choose the Quick Launch option, which makes it possible to start Netscape faster by storing parts of the program in memory. Answer the questions below:

   ■ What type of user is this option designed for?

   _____

   ■ If a computer were configured for more than one user, why might you not want to select this option?

   _____

   _____

8. Verify that the **Use Quick Launch for faster startup times** check box is *not* selected, and then click **Next**.

9. The Download Options screen appears. What is one reason you might want to save the installer files rather than allowing the system to delete them from the temporary directory after installation?

   _____

   _____

10. Select the **Save installer files locally** check box, and then click **Next**.

11. The Start Install screen appears with a summary of options you selected. Scroll through the list to verify your choices, and then click **Install** to begin the installation. Use the space below to list the windows that appear on your screen as the installation progresses.

    _____

    _____

    _____

    _____

19

12. When the installation is complete, an Activation dialog box opens. Click the **I don't currently have a Netscape screen name** option button and then click **Activate**.

13. Fill in screen name, password, and Zip code fields; select a country and a language; uncheck the boxes next to the promotional offers if desired; and click **Activate**. (If the screen name you requested is not available, you will be given the chance to try another one.)

14. The Activation dialog box shows a message informing you of successful registration and lists your user name and the features you are configured to use. Click **OK** to close the window.

15. During installation, a window opened behind the Activation dialog box, showing the contents of the Netscape directory. In that window, double-click the **Netscape** icon to launch the browser.

16. A message appears, asking if you want to make Netscape your default browser. Click **No**. The Netscape browser opens.

Follow these directions to install the version of Internet Explorer you downloaded:

1. Close all Netscape windows.

2. Locate and double-click the **Internet Explorer** setup file in Windows Explorer in your C:\Downloads directory.

3. The Internet Explorer setup program opens, showing the license agreement screen. Click the **I accept the agreement** option button and then click **Next**.

4. In the next screen, you can choose a typical or custom installation. Verify that the **Install now** option is selected in order to proceed with a typical installation, and click **Next**.

5. A status screen appears, in which the progress of downloading and installing components is shown. This may take several minutes. When the status screen closes and a message appears prompting you to restart your computer, click **Finish** to restart your computer and complete the installation.

Review Questions

1. Which installation took longer, Internet Explorer or Netscape?

_____

2. Which installation required you to restart your computer? What message was displayed when you restarted?

_____

_____

3. Which installation offered more options for customization during the recommended/typical installation process?

_____

_____

4. List any other differences you noticed between the installation of Netscape and the installation of Internet Explorer.

_____

_____

_____

_____

5. List any differences you found between the procedures given in this lab and the actual steps required to download and install the most current versions of the two browsers.

_____

_____

_____

_____

LAB 19.4 SET UP NETMEETING

Objectives

The goal of this lab is to help you set up and use NetMeeting. After completing this lab, you will be able to:

➤ Install the NetMeeting component

➤ Configure NetMeeting

Materials Required

This lab will require the following:

➤ Windows 98 operating system

➤ Windows 98 installation CD or installation files stored in another location

19

➤ Computer with PC camera installed

➤ Sound card, speakers, and microphone (optional)

Note: You can substitute Windows 2000 or Windows XP for Windows 98 in this lab.

Activity Background

NetMeeting is video conferencing software included with Windows 98 and Windows 2000/XP. One way to find others on a network or the Internet in order to join a conference is to use a directory service, an online database that NetMeeting uses to locate participants in a NetMeeting conference. One such directory service is Microsoft Internet Directory. When you install NetMeeting, you are asked to enter information about yourself, and are then given the opportunity to be added to the Microsoft Internet Directory. The following steps ask you to use the Microsoft Internet Directory, although your instructor might tell you to use a different directory service. You can also use an IP address to locate someone for a conference, or, for others on a local network, you can use a computer name on the network. In this lab, you will install and configure NetMeeting. Instructions given in this lab are for Windows 98, but Windows 2000/XP works about the same way.

Estimated completion time: **45 minutes**

ACTIVITY

Follow these steps to install NetMeeting (if it is not already installed.)

1. Open the Control Panel, open the **Add/Remove Programs** applet and then click the **Windows Setup** tab. Windows searches for Windows Components.

2. Double-click the **Communications** group in the **Components** list box. The Communications dialog box opens.

3. Scroll down the Components list box, select the **Microsoft NetMeeting** checkbox, and then click **OK**. The Communications dialog box closes.

4. Click **OK** to close the Add/Remove Properties dialog box. The Copying Files dialog box appears, indicating that the copying process has begun. If prompted, supply the location of the Windows 98 installation files. When the files are copied, the Copying Files dialog box closes. Reboot your PC if prompted to do so. (Note that for Windows 2000/XP, to install NetMeeting, in Windows Help, locate the topic **Using NetMeeeting**, and follow the directions given under this topic.)

Now you will launch NetMeeting and configure it. Follow these steps:

1. Click **Start** on the taskbar, point to **Programs**, and then look for NetMeeting on one of the submenus. You might find it located under Internet Tools, or under **Accessories** | **Communications**.

2. Click **NetMeeting**.

3. Microsoft NetMeeting begins configuring your connection. Click **Next** to continue.

4. In the next NetMeeting dialog box, supply the requested identification information, including your name and e-mail address, and then click **Next** to continue. (Keep in mind that your identification information will be available to other NetMeeting users on the directory server.)

5. What you see on the next screen depends on the version of NetMeeting installed. You might see a screen asking you what category to use for your personal info (personal use for all ages, business use for all ages or adults-only use). Select the category and click **Next**. For some versions of NetMeeting, the screen will give you the option of selecting a directory server. In this case, the default is Microsoft Internet Directory. Leave the default selected and click **Next**.

6. You are asked to specify your connection speed. Select **Local Area Network** (or other speed as specified by your instructor) and then click **Next** to continue.

7. You are asked for permission to place a shortcut to NetMeeting on the desktop and the Quick Launch bar. Deselect both and click **Next**.

8. You are asked to specify your video capturing device. Select your camera from the drop-down menu, if it is not already selected, and then click **Next** to continue.

9. NetMeeting informs you that it will help tune your audio settings. Click **Next** to continue.

10. Set and test your audio settings. When they are satisfactory, click **Next** to continue.

11. When the installation is complete, click **Finish**. NetMeeting launches.

12. Click **Place Call** and then click the **Start Video** button in the My Video frame. You should be able to see video supplied by your PC camera in the My Video screen.

CRITICAL THINKING (additional 20 minutes)

If others in the lab are connected to NetMeeting and you have access to a sound card, speakers, and microphone, join someone else in a video conference. If you don't have access to a directory server, you can make a connection with NetMeeting using IP addresses instead of a directory service. To find out your IP address:

1. Click **Start**, click **Run** type **Winipcfg** in the Run dialog box and then press **Enter**. (For Windows 2000/XP, to find out your IP address, at a command prompt, enter the **Ipconfig/all** command.)

2. Select your NIC from the list of installed adapters on the resulting IP Configuration window.

3. Exchange IP addresses with others in the lab and make the NetMeeting call to another computer in the lab using that computer's IP address.

19

Figure 19-1 shows a full NetMeeting video conference complete with shared whiteboard, chat window and video.

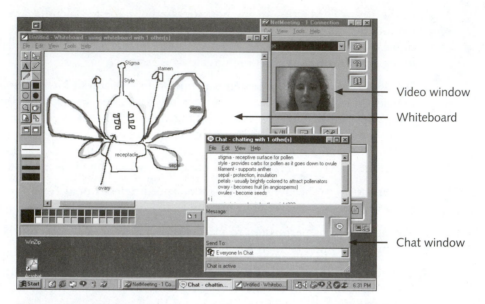

Video window

Whiteboard

Chat window

Figure 19-1 NetMeeting provides three windows during a session

Review Questions

1. What security risks are associated with NetMeeting?

   _____

   _____

2. Why might it be difficult to use NetMeeting over a 56.6K modem connection?

   _____

   _____

3. List at least two scenarios in which you might use NetMeeting.

   _____

   _____

4. What advantages does NetMeeting have over other methods of network communication, such as e-mail or instant messaging? Disadvantages?

_____

_____

_____

5. List all the hardware that would be required for a complete video conference with NetMeeting.

_____

_____

_____

_____

LAB 19.5 CONFIGURE A BROWSER SO IT DOESN'T DOWNLOAD IMAGES

Objectives

The goal of this lab is to help you set up your browser so that it does not download images. After completing this lab, you will be able to:

➤ Configure Netscape so that it does not download images

➤ Configure Internet Explorer so that it does not download images

Materials Required

This lab will require the following:

➤ Netscape and Internet Explorer installed on the same computer (as specified in Lab 19.3)

Activity Background

Slow browser performance can be caused by a variety of factors, such as a full cache, temporary files directory, or history file. It can also be caused by the content of the Web page you are viewing. One way to improve browser performance is to set up your browser so that it downloads only text and not images. In this lab, you will explore Netscape and Internet Explorer (which you installed in Lab 19.3) and find the options that allow you to select text-only downloads.

19

Estimated completion time: **30 minutes**

ACTIVITY

Follow these steps to configure Netscape and Internet Explorer so they don't download images:

1. Open Netscape and browse the Web for a couple of minutes, recording the URLs of the sites you visit. (You'll need these URLs later in this lab.)

   _____

   _____

   _____

   _____

2. Explore the menus on the menu bar, and then locate and click the command that allows you to change your preferences for Netscape. Use the space below to record the name of the menu on which you found the relevant command.

   _____

3. In the list box on the left side of the Preferences window you can select categories and subcategories of preferences that you want to configure. Clicking on the arrow to the left of a category expands that category so that you can see its subcategories, and clicking the name of a category or subcategory displays associated settings to the right of the list box. Explore the categories and subcategories until you find the setting that allows you to configure Netscape so that it does not download images. Record the location of that option here:

   _____

4. When you have located and displayed the image options, click the **Do not load any images** option button and then click **OK** to close the Preferences window.

5. Return to the Netscape browser window and click **Reload** on the View menu. How does the current Web page change?

   _____

6. Revisit the Web sites you recorded in Step 1. Do you notice any differences in how the pages display or in how the browser performs? Why do you think this is, based on the content of the Web pages?

   _____

_____

_____

_____

7. Follow the same basic steps to configure Internet Explorer so that it doesn't download images. Using the space provided below, record the same information and answer the same questions for Internet Explorer as you did for Netscape, noting any differences in locations, names of menus, and the process in general. HINT: You will have to *deselect* a checkbox to configure Internet Explorer not to download images.

_____

_____

_____

_____

_____

_____

_____

_____

_____

Review Questions

1. Which browser was easier to configure? Explain your answer.

_____

_____

_____

19

2. For both browsers, was the option for not downloading images located where you expected it to be? If not, where would you have expected to find it?

_____

_____

3. Did you notice any other similar options in either browser that might also improve browser performance? If so, list them.

_____

_____

4. Did you notice any difference in how the two browsers performed before you blocked downloading images? After you blocked downloading images? Explain your answer.

_____

_____

_____

_____

5. Under what circumstances might you want to block image downloads?

_____

_____

_____

20

NOTEBOOKS AND PDAS

Labs included in this chapter

➤ Lab 20.1 Examine Notebook Documentation

➤ Lab 20.2 Compare Notebooks and Desktops

➤ Lab 20.3 Replace a Notebook Hard Drive

➤ Lab 20.4 Research Software Available for PDAs

➤ Lab 20.5 Battery Calibration and Power Management

The following grid shows the correlation between the labs in this chapter and the A+ Guides to Hardware and Software.

A+ Guide to Managing and Maintaining Your PC, Fifth Edition	A+ Guide to Hardware, Third Edition	A+ Guide to Software, Third Edition
Lab 20.1 Examine Notebook Documentation	Chapter 12	
Lab 20.2 Compare Notebooks and Desktops	Chapter 12	
Lab 20.3 Replace a Notebook Hard Drive	Chapter 12	
Lab 20.4 Research Software Available for PDAs	Chapter 12	
Lab 20.6 Battery Calibration and Power Management	Chapter 3	Chapter 13

LAB 20.1 EXAMINE NOTEBOOK DOCUMENTATION

Objectives

The goal of this lab is to help you acquire documentation for a notebook from a manufacturer's Web site and become familiar with it. After completing this lab, you will be able to:

➤ Locate documentation for specific notebook computer models

➤ Download the documentation

➤ Use a notebook's documentation to find critical information

Materials Required

This lab will require the following:

➤ Internet access

Activity Background

Notebooks are designed for portability, compactness, and energy conservation, and their designs are often highly proprietary. Therefore, establishing general procedures for supporting notebooks is more difficult than for desktop computers. Often it is necessary to consult the documentation for a particular notebook computer to get information on technical specification and support procedures. In this lab, you will locate and download documentation for two different notebook computers and then use that documentation to answer questions about each model.

> Estimated completion time: **30 minutes**

ACTIVITY

Follow these steps to locate and download documentation:

1. Choose two notebook manufacturers listed in Table 20-1, go to their Web sites, and select one model from each to research. List your two choices here.

_____

_____

Table 20-1   Notebook manufacturers

Manufacturer	Web site
Acer America	*global.acer.com*
ARM Computer	*www.armcomputer.com*
Compaq Computer	*www.hp.com*
Dell Computer	*www.dell.com*
Gateway	*www.gateway.com*
Hewlett-Packard	*www.hp.com*
IBM	*www.ibm.com*
Micron PC	*www.buympc.com*
PC Notebook	*www.pcnotebook.com*
Sony	*www.sonystyle.com/vaio*
Toshiba America	*www.csd.toshiba.com*
WinBook	*www.winbook.com*

2. On the support section of each Web site, search for documentation on each of the models you chose and follow the directions to download it. Were you able to find documentation for both models? If not, list the models for which you were unable to find documentation. Try other models until you have located documentation for two.

   _____

   _____

3. Using the documentation you located, answer the following questions for your first model. If you can't answer a question because the information is not included in the documentation, write "information unavailable."

   - What type of processor does the notebook use and how much RAM is installed?

     _____

   - What operating system does the notebook support?

     _____

   - Could you download or save the documentation locally, or did you have to view it on the company's Web site?

     _____

20

- Does the notebook offer quick-launch keys for commonly used applications? If so, can you customize them? How? If they are not customizable, what buttons are offered, and which applications do they launch?

  _____

  _____

  _____

- List the functions assigned to keys F1 through F4.

  _____

  _____

  _____

  _____

- Does the notebook have a sleep or hibernation mode? If so, how do you activate it? How does activating this mode differ from shutting down the computer?

  _____

  _____

  _____

- What other types of download are offered besides the manual?

  _____

  _____

- What type of optical storage (CD, CD-RW, DVD, and so forth) does the notebook offer?

  _____

- What type of networking (modem, NIC, infrared port, wireless LAN port, and so forth) comes built-in?

  _____

  _____

4. Using the documentation you located, answer the following questions for your second model. If you can't answer a question because the information is not included in the documentation, write "information unavailable."

- What type of processor does the notebook use and how much RAM is installed?

_____

- What operating system does the notebook support?

_____

- Could you download or save the documentation locally, or did you have to view it on the company's Web site?

_____

- Does the notebook offer quick-launch keys for commonly used applications? If so, can you customize them? How? If they are not customizable, what buttons are offered, and which applications do they launch?

_____

_____

_____

- List the functions assigned to keys F1 through F4.

_____

_____

_____

- Does the notebook have a sleep or hibernation mode? If so, how do you activate it? How does activating this mode differ from shutting down the computer?

_____

_____

_____

- What other types of download are offered besides the manual?

_____

_____

20

- What type of optical storage (CD, CD-RW, DVD, and so forth) does the notebook offer?

  _____

- What type of networking (modem, NIC, infrared port, wireless LAN port, and so forth) comes built–in?

  _____

  _____

Alternate Activity

If you have access to a notebook computer, do the following:

1. Go to the manufacturer's Web site for your notebook computer and download the user manual, if available. List other downloads that are available:

   _____

   _____

   _____

2. From the list of available downloads, choose a device driver or system update for your notebook. Download and install it using instructions on the site. List the driver or update and the steps you took to install it on your notebook.

   _____

   _____

   _____

   _____

   _____

Review Questions

1. On a manufacturer's Web site, where do you usually find support and documentation information?

   _____

   _____

2. For which model was it easiest to find documentation? Which manufacturer site did you feel was most user friendly and, in general, offered the best support?

_____

_____

3. Besides the questions you researched in the lab, what other type of information is available in the manuals you reviewed?

_____

_____

4. If you were to purchase one of the notebooks you researched, which one would you choose? Explain your answer.

_____

_____

LAB 20.2 COMPARE NOTEBOOKS AND DESKTOPS

Objectives

The goal of this lab is to help you compare the specifications and costs of notebook and desktop computers. After completing this lab, you will be able to:

➤ Compile a list of specifications for a computer according to its purpose

➤ Locate a desktop computer and a notebook computer with similar specifications

➤ Compare the price of a desktop computer to a similar notebook computer and decide which you would purchase

Materials Required

This lab will require the following:

➤ Internet access

Activity Background

When you shop for and purchase a computer, your decisions are generally driven by questions such as, What will the computer be used for? What features are required to accomplish your goals, and what features would be nice to have but are not essential? What features are you willing to compromise on to gain others?

20

One of the most basic of these decisions is whether to choose a notebook computer or a desktop. Unlike desktops, notebooks are portable; however, to make notebooks portable, manufacturers often choose to sacrifice performance or other features. In addition, you'll usually pay more for a notebook than for a desktop computer with comparable features. In this lab, you will compile a list of requirements for a computer, locate a notebook and desktop computer with those features, and compare the two.

Estimated completion time: **30 minutes**

ACTIVITY

1. Determine your requirements by answering the following questions:

   ■ For what will the computer mainly be used? (Possible uses include office applications, graphics and multimedia, gaming, and software development.)

   _____

   ■ Based on the purpose listed, what features are required? Include in your list the desired amount of memory and hard drive space. (Some features you might consider include wireless support, display/screen type, software packages supported, PC card support, and external device support.)

   _____

   _____

   _____

   _____

   ■ List any additional features that you would like but do not require.

   _____

   _____

   _____

   _____

2. Use computer manufacturer Web sites (such as the ones listed in Table 20-1) or comparison Web sites (such as *www.cnet.com* or *www.pricewatch.com*) to find one notebook and one desktop that fulfill as many of your requirements as possible and that are as similar to each other as possible. Summarize your findings by completing Table 20-2. Print the Web pages supporting this information.

Table 20-2   Desktop and notebook computer specifications

Features	Desktop computer	Notebook computer
Manufacturer and model		
Processor type and frequency		
Memory installed		
Hard drive space		
Operating system		
Drive 1		
Drive 2		
Drive 3		
External ports		
Preinstalled applications		
Cost		

3. Based on your research and the requirements you listed in step 1, would you choose to purchase a desktop computer or a laptop? Explain your answer.

_____

_____

_____

Review Questions

1. Which computer was more expensive, the desktop or the laptop? What was the price difference?

_____

_____

2. About what features, if any, were you unable to find information?

_____

_____

3. What features, if any, were missing from the desktop and from the laptop? How did this influence your purchasing decision?

_____

_____

20

4. Did you find that you changed your requirements or expectations based on the products available? Explain your answer.

_____

_____

_____

5. Was it easier to find a comparable desktop and laptop from the same manufacturer or from a different manufacturer? Why do you think this is the case?

_____

_____

_____

LAB 20.3 REPLACE A NOTEBOOK HARD DRIVE

Objectives

The goal of this lab is to describe the process of replacing a hard drive in a notebook computer. After completing this lab, you will be able to:

➤ Locate the hard drive in a notebook computer

➤ Remove the hard drive from a notebook computer

➤ Replace the hard drive in a notebook computer

Materials Required

This lab will require the following:

➤ Notebook computer or Internet access

➤ PC toolkit with ground strap

➤ Additional, smaller screwdrivers, if necessary

Activity Background

Hard disk drives are by nature delicate devices. Dropping one, even if only a few inches, can cause permanent damage to the read/write heads, the platter surfaces, or both. Notebook systems are, of course, often moved and commonly subjected to forces that most 3.5-inch hard drives will never encounter. Although drives intended for use in notebook systems are designed to be resistant to movement and shock, they are still more likely to fail than any other notebook component. In this lab you will remove a hard drive from a notebook computer and then reinstall the same hard drive. If you do not have access to a notebook, perform the alternate activity at the end of this lab.

Hard drives designed for notebook computers tend to be 75 percent to 100 percent more expensive than the standard 3.5-inch drives of comparable capacity for desktop computers. Also, the majority of newer notebooks support most 2.5-inch drives designed for notebooks, but sometimes a notebook computer requires a proprietary hard drive. For these reasons, it is particularly important to research your replacement options carefully. Read the documentation that came with your notebook to determine what drives the notebook supports. If this information is not available in the documentation, search the manufacturer's Web site. For the purpose of this lab, you will remove the existing drive and then reinstall the same drive. The specific steps required for your notebook might be slightly different from the procedures given, so, again, it's important to study the documentation before you begin.

Estimated completion time: **30 minutes**

ACTIVITY

1. What is the manufacturer and model of your notebook computer?

   _____

2. Based on the notebook's documentation or information on the manufacturer's Web site, what type hard drive can be used to replace the existing hard drive? Be as specific as the documentation or the Web site is.

   _____

   _____

3. Search the Internet for a replacement hard drive that meets the requirements for your notebook. Print the Web page showing the specifications for the drive and its cost. How much space does the hard drive have?

   _____

4. Look for specific directions (in the documentation or on the Web site) for removing and replacing your notebook's hard drive. If you find any, summarize those directions here. (If you are using the Web site as your source of information, print any relevant Web pages.)

   _____

   _____

   _____

   _____

20

Follow these general steps to remove the hard drive from a notebook computer. Note that these directions might not list every single step necessary for your particular model. Refer to specific directions in the documentation or the company's Web site, as necessary.

1. Remove the main battery or batteries and, if necessary, unplug the computer from the AC adapter. Close the screen and turn the computer so that the bottom is facing up.

2. Locate and remove the access panel or component enclosing the drive bay. In many notebooks, the hard drive is located beneath a floppy drive or other removable device. For example, see Figure 20-1.

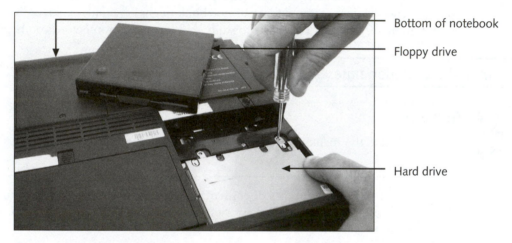

Bottom of notebook

Floppy drive

Hard drive

Figure 20-1   First remove the floppy drive to reveal the hard drive cavity

3. Once you have gained access to the drive, determine how it is secured within the system. The device is commonly attached to a frame or "cradle" with small screws. The cradle is in turn often attached directly to the system chassis. This cradle helps locate and support the drive inside the drive bay. Remove the screws securing the cradle.

4. In most notebooks, data cables do not connect the hard drive to the motherboard as in desktop computers. Instead, a hard drive connects to the notebook's motherboard by way of an edge connector, similar to those found on expansion cards in desktop computers. This type of direct connection has two advantages. First, it improves reliability because it reduces the total number of connection points; fewer connection points mean fewer connections that could shake loose as the notebook is moved around in daily use. The second advantage of a direct connection is that the lack of data cables reduces the overall size and weight of the notebook. To remove the cradle/drive assembly, slide the cradle away from the connector. Slide the assembly back until all pins are clear of the connector. Once the pins are clear, lift the assembly straight up out of the drive bay.

5. Note the orientation of the drive in the cradle so that, when you reinstall the drive, you will be able to mount the drive in the same direction. Remove the screws securing the drive in the cradle, and then remove the drive.

Follow these general steps to reinstall the hard drive in the notebook computer. Note that these directions might not list every single step necessary for your particular model. Refer to specific directions in the documentation or the company's Web site, as necessary.

1. If necessary, configure the jumper settings to indicate master or slave. Place the drive in the cradle so that the pins are correctly oriented and then secure it with screws.

2. Set the drive–cradle assembly straight down into the drive bay. Gently slide the assembly to the connector and verify that the pins are correctly aligned with the connector. Slide the assembly until the drive is fully seated in the connector. The cradle should now align with the holes in the chassis. If the holes do not align, you should remove the assembly, loosen the drive retaining screws, and adjust the position of the drive in the cradle. You should repeat this process until the drive is fully seated, so that there is no room for the drive to move once the cradle is secured. Once the assembly is seated, secure it with screws.

3. Replace any drives or access covers that you removed to get at the hard drive.

4. Reinstall any batteries and reconnect to AC power, if necessary. As with any other hard drive, a notebook drive must be correctly recognized by BIOS, and then partitioned and formatted before it can be used. This process is not necessary in this lab because you have not installed a new hard drive.

Alternate Activity

If you do not have access to a notebook computer:

1. Using the documentation for one of the notebooks you selected in Lab 20.1 as your source, what are the exact requirements for a replacement hard drive for this notebook? Be as specific as the documentation is.

   _____

   _____

2. Search the Internet for information on replacement hard drives, and print the Web page showing the correct specifications for a replacement hard drive. What is the cost of the drive? How much space does the drive have?

   _____

3. Locate the steps for replacing the hard drive. To find this information, use the manuals that you downloaded in Lab 20.1, the manufacturers' Web sites, and other Internet resources (such as the Web sites of manufacturers of replacement notebook hard drives).

20

4. How do the steps you found differ from the steps provided in this lab? Note the differences here:

_____

_____

_____

_____

_____

_____

_____

Review Questions

1. Why should you thoroughly research hard drives when replacing one in a notebook computer?

_____

_____

2. Why is cabling commonly not included in notebook systems?

_____

3. How was the installation procedure for your computer different from the one listed in this lab?

_____

_____

_____

4. Suppose you need to install a hard drive in a notebook that does not include an access panel for the hard drive. Where should you look for the hard drive inside the notebook?

_____

_____

_____

5. What do you have to do in CMOS setup before a new hard drive can be used?

_____

_____

LAB 20.4 RESEARCH SOFTWARE AVAILABLE FOR PDAS

Objectives

The goal of this lab is to help you research and compare PDAs. After completing this lab, you will be able to:

➤ Locate and compare information on available PDAs

Materials Required

This lab will require the following:

➤ Internet access

Activity Background

One common problem with PDAs (personal digital assistants) is finding compatible software (in addition to the software that comes preinstalled on the PDA). There are two basic OS choices for a PDA: Windows Mobile and Palm OS. Earlier handheld OSs by Microsoft are PocketPC and Windows CE. Before you can install additional software, you must verify that the software is compatible both with the PDA's operating system and with the specific PDA model. Some basic models do not allow you to add any software. You also must make sure that the software is compatible with the desktop PC that you want to synchronize with the PDA. Finally, some business organizations will not allow certain PDAs to synchronize with the business network. You will learn more about these issues in this lab, as you research software availability for two different PDA models.

Estimated completion time: **30 minutes**

ACTIVITY

1. Using the manufacturer sites listed in the Tables 20-3 and 20-4, select one Palm OS PDA and one Windows Mobile PDA. Record the name and model number of your choices here:

_____

_____

20

Table 20-3 Manufacturers of Palm OS PDAs

Manufacturer	Web site
HandEra	*www.handera.com*
Handspring	*www.handspring.com*
IBM	*www.ibm.com*
Palm	*www.palm.com*
Sony	*www.sonystyle.com*

Table 20-4 Manufacturers of Windows Mobile and Pocket PC PDAs

Manufacturer	Web site
Casio	*www.casio.com*
Compaq	*www.hp.com*
Hewlett-Packard	*www.hp.com*
Toshiba	*www.toshiba.com*

2. On the manufacturers' Web sites, search for technical specifications and lists of installed software for the first model you selected. Then answer the following questions for this model. Download and search user manuals if necessary.

■ What version of the operating system is installed?

_____

■ What software comes installed on the PDA?

_____

_____

_____

_____

■ Can you install other software? If so, list some available programs.

_____

_____

_____

_____

_____

■ Will the applications on the PDA synchronize with common office applications on a desktop PC or notebook? List the applications on the PDA and the applications on the desktop PC or notebook with which they can synchronize.

_____

_____

_____

_____

_____

_____

■ Does the PDA support upgrades to the OS? Why would you want to have this ability?

_____

_____

■ What add-on devices are available for the PDA, such as recharger cradles, cameras, and so forth?

_____

_____

_____

3. Answer the following questions for the second model PDA:

■ What version of the operating system is installed?

_____

■ What software comes installed on the PDA?

_____

_____

_____

_____

20

■ Can you install other software? If so, list some available programs.

_____

_____

_____

_____

_____

_____

■ Will the applications on the PDA synchronize with common office applications on a desktop PC or notebook? List the applications on the PDA and the applications on the desktop PC or notebook with which they can synchronize.

_____

_____

_____

_____

_____

_____

■ Does the PDA support upgrades to the OS? Why would you want to have this ability?

_____

_____

■ What add-on devices are available for the PDA, such as recharger cradles, cameras, and so forth?

_____

_____

_____

Alternate Activity

If you have access to a PDA, perform the research suggested in this lab for your particular model. Try to locate, download, and install a trial version of an add-on software program for your PDA. Record the necessary steps and the name of the program you installed.

_____

_____

_____

_____

_____

_____

_____

_____

Review Questions

1. Was add-on software available for both of the PDA models you researched?

_____

2. How easy was it to find the information you needed? List the Web sites you visited, ranking them from most user friendly to least user friendly.

_____

_____

_____

3. Which PDA OS appears to support the most PDA applications? Explain your answer.

_____

_____

_____

20

4. Are more software options, or fewer software options, available for the higher priced PDAs? Explain your answer.

_____

_____

_____

_____

5. Would you consider purchasing either of the PDAs you researched in this lab? Why or why not?

_____

_____

_____

_____

6. List three questions you should carefully research about software availability before selecting a PDA.

_____

_____

_____

LAB 20.5 BATTERY CALIBRATION AND POWER MANAGEMENT

Objectives

The goal of this lab is to demonstrate the effect battery calibration has on power management features of a laptop PC. After completing this lab, you will be able to:

➤ Explain the calibration process

➤ Discuss how a battery might drift from calibration

➤ Explain how battery calibration affects some power management features

Materials Required

This lab will require the following:

➤ Windows desktop computer

➤ Windows laptop computer

➤ Internet access

Activity Background

Many factors affect the battery life of a laptop PC. There are two common types of laptop battery: NiMH, or nickel metalhydride, and LiION, or lithium ion. Lithium batteries are the more expensive and longer-lasting type and are more common. A fully charged lithium battery in good condition can provide about 2½ to 3 hours of normal use. By contrast, a healthy, fully charged NiMH battery can provide 1½ to 2 + hours of normal use.

As you might expect, though, "normal use" is a rather subjective term. The actual way you use your laptop can greatly affect battery life. For instance, editing text in a word processor doesn't require much power compared to playing a DVD. The word processor uses only a little processor time and occasionally reads or writes to the hard drive. Playing a DVD is processor intensive and requires powering the laser in the drive, thus requiring even more power than the word processor.

What the laptop does when you stop using it for a time also affects battery life. For instance, if you do not use the laptop for 10 minutes, the laptop might automatically go into hibernation to conserve power. In addition to the many power management features on desktop systems, laptops also employ a few additional features to extend battery life during inactivity and protect data when the battery charge becomes low. Some of these features depend on the laptop being able to accurately judge how much life is left in the battery. If the battery is accurately calibrated, the laptop can make better power-management decisions. In this lab, you will explore how power management and battery life are related.

Estimated completion time: **30 minutes**

ACTIVITY

1. Examine your desktop computer's CMOS setup utility and the Power Management applet in Control Panel. Usually a computer's BIOS offers a greater range of options for defining a power management profile than offered by Windows. Complete Table 20-5 to compare the power-management options offered in BIOS and in Windows.

20

Table 20-5   Comparing power-management options in BIOS and Windows

Power management options and settings	Found in BIOS	Found in Windows

Although many times the two power management systems might work in conjunction, to avoid possible conflict, Microsoft recommends using the BIOS power management as the preferred method if the BIOS power management conforms to ACPI standards. These standards have been set by a group of manufacturers including Microsoft, Intel, and Compaq.

In addition to the BIOS features you just explored, laptops often have additional features or settings that allow the computer to shut down or suspend activity if the battery is about to run out of power. But how does the computer know when power is about to run out? In many batteries, an EPROM (Electronically Programmable Read-Only Memory) is included in the battery assembly to inform the computer about the remaining battery life. The following steps explain the basic procedure for calibrating a battery's EPROM. For specific steps for your laptop, see your laptop's documentation or search the laptop manufacturer's Web site.

1. Verify that your laptop has a fully charged battery that is attached to AC power.

2. Enter the CMOS setup utility and select the Power Management section.

3. In the Power Management section, disable the Power Savings option(s) so that the computer will not attempt to save power during the calibration process.

4. In the Power Management section, disable any Suspend on Low Battery options to prevent interference with calibration.

5. In the Power Management section, select the Battery Calibration option. A warning message appears, indicating that the calibration should be carried out only with a fully charged battery and prompting you to confirm that you wish to continue.

6. Remove the AC power and then immediately press **Y** or **Enter** to continue. A message appears, indicating the estimated remaining battery life. In a real-life situation, when you actually needed to calibrate your laptop's battery, this information would likely be incorrect.

7. Wait for the battery to drain. It may take much more than an hour to drain the battery.

8. The manufacturer may specify that the battery should be left to cool for a period of time after the battery is drained and the laptop switches off. When appropriate, reattach AC power, boot up, and enter CMOS setup.

9. Enter the Power Management section and select **Battery Reset**. This tells the EPROM that the battery is at (or very near) zero charge and takes you back to the Power Management section of CMOS.

10. Reapply your preferred power management settings and save and exit CMOS setup. The battery is now calibrated so that the related power management and suspend features will work properly.

If you have access to a laptop and the permission of your instructor, do the following to calibrate the battery:

1. Locate documentation (in the user manual or on the Web) that explains how to calibrate the battery. Note below how these steps differ from the ones listed previously.

_____

_____

_____

_____

2. Follow the specific steps for your laptop to calibrate the battery. (Do *not* attempt the procedure unless you have the specific steps for your laptop because you might do damage to the laptop or the battery.)

Note that some factors can also prevent power management from functioning as intended. For instance, word processing programs often include an auto-save feature that continually saves changes to a document at specific intervals. This feature is intended to safeguard against lost work but tends to interfere with hard disk power-down settings. Many screen savers cause similar effects and can also prevent a computer from entering or exiting standby or suspend modes.

Review Questions

1. What types of activity do you think might decrease the battery life of a fully charged battery more quickly than reading a document or spreadsheet? Give three examples.

_____

_____

_____

20

2. In your opinion, is aggressive power management more important on a desktop computer or a laptop computer? Explain why.

_____

_____

_____

3. Should BIOS power management always be used in conjunction with Windows Power Management? Why or why not?

_____

_____

4. What types of program might prevent a hard drive power-down setting from saving power as intended? Why?

_____

_____

_____

_____

5. What are two possible consequences of an improperly calibrated battery? Explain.

_____

_____

_____

_____

21
SUPPORTING PRINTERS

Labs included in this chapter

➤ Lab 21.1 Install and Share a Printer

➤ Lab 21.2 Install a Network Printer

➤ Lab 21.3 Update Printer Drivers

➤ Lab 21.4 Printer Maintenance and Troubleshooting

➤ Lab 21.5 Critical Thinking: Sabotage and Repair a Network Printer

---

The following grid shows the correlation between the labs in this chapter and the A+ Guides to Hardware and Software.

A+ Guide to Managing and Maintaining Your PC, Fifth Edition	A+ Guide to Hardware, Third Edition	A+ Guide to Software, Third Edition
Lab 21.1 Install and Share a Printer	Chapter 13	Chapter 13
Lab 21.2 Install a Network Printer		Chapter 13
Lab 21.3 Update Printer Drivers	Chapter 13	Chapter 13
Lab 21.4 Printer Maintenance and Troubleshooting	Chapter 13	
Lab 21.5 Critical Thinking: Sabotage and Repair a Network Printer	Chapter 13	Chapter 13

Lab 21.1 Install and Share a Printer

Objectives

The goal of this lab is to help you install and share a printer. After completing this lab, you will be able to:

➤ Install a local printer on a computer

➤ Share that printer with other users on the network

➤ Using another computer on the network, install and use the shared network printer

Materials Required

This lab will require the following:

➤ A printer and its printer drivers

➤ Two or more Windows 9x or Windows 2000/XP computers connected to a network

➤ Windows installation CD or installation files stored in another location

➤ Workgroup of 3–4 students

Activity Background

A printer can be connected to and dedicated to one particular PC (in which case it is called a local printer), or it can be shared with other PCs on the network (in which case it is called a network printer). For a printer to be shared using a Windows operating system, it must be physically connected to and installed on one computer and then shared with others in the same Windows workgroup. The computer that has the printer physically connected to it must have the Microsoft File and Printer Sharing component installed, and the computer on the network that will use this remote printer must have the Client for Microsoft Networks component installed. In most cases, it is easier to install both components on all computers involved. In this lab, you will install and share a printer in a workgroup and then use the shared printer on the network.

Estimated completion time: **45 minutes**

Activity

You must first install Client for Microsoft Networks and File and Printer Sharing (if they are not already installed). Both of these components are installed on Windows 2000/XP computers by default. Client for Microsoft Networks is installed in Windows 98 by default. To install them on Windows 9x computers (if necessary), use these steps:

1. In the Control Panel, double-click the **Network** applet.

2. The Network dialog box opens. Click **Add**.

3. The Select Network Component Type dialog box opens. In the list box, click **Client** to select it and then click **Add**.

4. The Select Network dialog box opens. Click **Microsoft** on the left and **Client for Microsoft Networks** on the right. Click **OK** and then insert the Windows 98 installation CD. Reboot the PC when prompted.

5. Return to the Network dialog box. Repeat steps 2 and 3, this time selecting **Service** instead of Client.

6. The Select Network Service dialog box opens. Click **File and printer sharing for Microsoft Networks** and then click **OK**. Click **OK** to close the Network dialog box and then insert the Windows 98 installation CD. Reboot the PC when prompted.

7. Return to the Network dialog box and then click **File and Print Sharing**.

8. The File and Print Sharing dialog box opens. Select the **I want to be able to give others access to my files** checkbox and the **I want to be able to allow others to print to my printer(s)** checkbox and then click **OK**. (You will not be practicing file sharing in this lab, but as a general rule you will usually set up files and print sharing at the same time.)

Next, you need to verify that all the computers that need to use the printer are in the same workgroup. Follow these steps:

1. Ask your instructor for the name of the workgroup you are to use for this lab and record the name here:

   _____

2. For Windows 98, right-click the **Network Neighborhood** icon on the desktop and select **Properties** from the shortcut menu. The network's Properties window appears. Click the **Identification** tab. (For Windows 2000/XP, right-click **My Computer** and select **Properties** from the shortcut menu. In the System Properties window for Windows 2000, click the **Network Identification** tab and then click the **Properties** button. The Identification Changes window appears.) For Windows XP, click the **Computer Name** tab and then click **Change**.

3. To what workgroup does this computer belong?

   _____

4. If necessary, change the workgroup assignment to match the one noted in Step 1.

You are now ready to install and share the printer. On a Windows 2000/XP computer that will be physically connected to the printer, follow these steps. Note that the steps for Windows 98 differ slightly, but you can use these steps as a guide.

1. With the computer off, connect the printer cable to the parallel port or USB port on your computer, turn on the printer, and then boot up the computer.

21

2. If the Add Printer Wizard opens, click **Next** and then skip to step 4.

3. If the wizard does not open for Windows 2000, click **Start** on the taskbar, point to **Settings**, and then click **Printers**. For Windows XP, click **Start** and then click **Printers and Faxes**. The Printers window opens. Double-click **Add Printer**. The Add Printer Wizard opens. Click **Next**.

4. Click **Local printer**, select the **Automatically detect and install my Plug and Play printer** checkbox, and click **Next**.

5. A list of ports is displayed. Select **Use the following port**, select **LPT1** and then click **Next**.

6. A list of manufacturers and printer models is displayed. Select first the manufacturer and then the model from the list. If your printer is not listed and you have the correct printer driver on disk or CD, click **Have Disk**. Keep in mind that drivers designed for one Windows operating system might not work for a later version of Windows, so you need to make sure you have the correct drivers for your computer's version of Windows. (You can download printer driver files from the printer manufacturer's Web site.) If you select a manufacturer and model from the Windows list, a dialog box might appear to allow you to specify the location of the Windows setup files. In that case, insert the Windows setup CD or select another location for the files.

7. The next screen in the Add Printer Wizard asks for a name for the printer. This name will later appear in the list of available printers. Windows provides a default name. Accept the default name or enter your own, and then click **Next** to continue.

8. Click **Share as** to indicate that this printer will be shared with others on a network, and select the operating system that other computers on the network will be using. By selecting the operating system here, you ensure that your computer can communicate with the remote computers when they request access to the printer. Click **Next** to continue.

9. Select **Yes** to print the test page, and then click **Next**.

10. Windows displays the printer settings you selected. Click **Finish** to complete the installation.

Once the printer is installed, you need to make it possible for other computers in the network to access it. Follow these directions to share the printer with other computers in the workgroup:

1. On the computer that has the printer installed locally, for Windows 2000, click **Start** on the taskbar, point to **Settings**, and click **Printers**. For Windows XP, click **Start** and then click **Printers and Faxes**.

2. The Printers window opens, showing the printer you just installed. Right-click the printer and select **Sharing** in the shortcut menu.

3. The Properties window for the printer opens with the Sharing tab selected. Click the **Shared as** option button, type a share name for the printer, and then click **OK**.

4. For Windows 2000/XP computers, click **Additional Drivers**, select the operating systems used by the remote computers and then click **OK**. Windows can then provide the remote computers with the necessary driver files when they first attempt to connect to the shared printer. (Windows 98 does not provide this service.)

The printer is now listed in the Network Neighborhood window (or, for Windows 2000/XP, in the My Network Places window) on all the other computers on the network. However, before the printer can be used by a remote computer, printer drivers must be installed on that computer.

There are two approaches to installing a shared network printer on a remote PC. You can perform the installation using the printer drivers installed on the host PC, or you can perform the installation using the drivers on CD (either the Windows CD or printer manufacturer's CD). If you need to install the printer on several remote PCs, it is faster to use the drivers installed on the host PC. The disadvantage of using this method is that you must share the C:\Windows folder on the host PC, an action that is considered a security risk. For this reason, as soon as the printer is installed on all the remote PCs, you should unshare the C:\Windows folder on the host PC to protect that critical folder.

Follow these steps to install the shared printer on the other PCs:

1. On the computer that has the printer connected locally, share the **C:\Windows** folder so that the drivers in this folder will be available to the other computers. To do this, right-click the **C:\Windows** folder in Explorer, click **Properties** in the shortcut menu, click the **Sharing** tab, and select the option **Shared as** to share the folder. Do not require a password to access the folder. Click **OK**.

2. On the remote PCs, open My Network Places or Network Neighborhood and find the printer. Right-click the printer and click **Install** (for Windows 98) or **Connect** (for Windows 2000/XP) on the shortcut menu.

3. Enter a name for the printer and print a test page to complete the installation.

4. After all remote computers have installed the printer, remove the shared option on the C:\Windows folder of the local computer to protect this important folder. To do this, right-click the folder in Explorer, click **Properties**, click the **Sharing** tab, and select **Not Shared**. Click **OK**.

Review Questions

1. What two Windows components must be installed before you can share a printer in a workgroup?

_____

_____

21

2. What would happen if the C:\Windows folder on the host PC were not shared when you tried to install the printer on the remote PCs? How could you have installed the printer on a remote computer if you did not have access to the C:\Windows folder on the host computer?

_____

_____

3. Name an advantage of installing file sharing at the same time you install printer sharing.

_____

_____

4. Suppose you want to stop others on the network from using a shared printer, but you still want the printer to be available to the computer on which it is locally installed. What is the easiest way to accomplish this?

_____

_____

Lab 21.2 Install a Network Printer

In Lab 21.1, you installed a printer as a local printer and as a network printer. This lab gives you further practice in installing local and network printers, showing you an alternate way to install a network printer.

Objectives

The goal of this lab is to give you practice installing a local printer on a computer, sharing it, and then installing it on a remote computer on the network. After completing this lab, you will be able to:

➤ Install a local printer

➤ Install a network printer

➤ Test the printer across the network

Materials Required

This lab will require the following:

➤ Windows 98, Windows 2000, or Windows XP operating system

➤ Printer, printer cable, and printer driver files

➤ Functioning network

➤ Workgroup of 2–4 students

Activity Background

A local printer is one that is connected to a PC by way of a serial, parallel infrared, or USB connection. A local printer is not usually available to the network for general printing jobs, but in some cases it may be useful to allow other computers to print from your local printer. (For example, suppose you have an expensive photo-quality printer installed locally on your computer. You might sometimes want to let users who need to print photos access your printer through the network.) In this lab you will install a local printer and a network printer. Instructions in this lab are written for Windows 98 but work the same for Windows 2000 or Windows XP if you substitute My Network Places for Network Neighborhood.

> Estimated completion time: **30 minutes**

ACTIVITY

The following steps describe the default method for installing a printer in Windows. However, printer manufacturers often provide specialized steps for installing their devices. In that case, you should follow the steps prescribed by the manufacturer of your printer rather than the steps provided here.

1. With the computer off, attach the printer cable to the computer and the printer. Attach the power cable to the printer and then plug it in. Turn on the printer and then the computer. After the computer starts up, insert the installation disk if you have one.

2. Click **Start** on the taskbar, point to **Settings**, and then click **Printers**. The Printers window opens, displaying any installed printers as well as the Add Printers icon.

3. Double-click the **Add Printers** icon to open the Add Printer wizard.

4. In the Add Printer wizard, click **Next** to begin the installation process.

5. What two options do you see in the Add Printer Wizard?

_____

6. In the Add Printer Wizard, select the **Local Printer** option and then click **Next** to continue.

7. In the right pane of the Add Printers Wizard, select the manufacturer of your printer. A list of printers for that manufacturer is displayed in the left pane. Scroll down the list in the left pane to locate your printer.

21

8. If you can locate your printer, click it in the left pane of the Add Printer Wizard, click **Next**, and then skip to step 11. If you cannot locate your printer in the list, click **Have Disk**. The Install From Disk dialog box opens.

9. In the Install From Disk dialog box, click **Browse**. Then locate and select the installation file for your operating system. This file will have an .inf file extension and most likely will be found in a folder that is named according to your operating system (such as \Win98\install.inf or \Windows98\oem.inf or something similar). Click **OK** to tell the wizard to use the selected file.

10. Click **OK** in the Install From Disk dialog box to close it. The Add Printer Wizard identifies your printer. Click **Next** to continue.

11. The Add Printer Wizard asks you to select the port you will use for the printer. In the Available Ports list box, select **LPT1: Printer Port**. This indicates that your printer is attached to the parallel port. Click **Next** to continue.

12. In the Printer name text box type a name for the printer (replacing the model name, which appears by default).

13. You are asked if you want this printer to be your Windows default printer. Click **Yes** and then click **Next**. When asked if you would like to print a test page, click **No** and then click **Finish**. The necessary files are copied to your computer, and in some cases (if the printer has fax capabilities, for instance) a new wizard launches. If this occurs, complete the wizard or follow instructions supplied by your instructor. When the installation process is complete, an icon for the newly installed printer appears in the Printers window.

Follow these steps to test the printer:

1. In the Printers window, right-click the icon for your printer and select **Properties** from the shortcut menu. The printer's Properties dialog box opens.

2. Click the **General** tab and then click **Print Test Page**. A test print job is sent to the printer, and a dialog box opens asking you whether the page printed correctly.

3. Verify that your test page printed correctly (without any gibberish), then click **OK** to close the dialog box.

4. Open Windows Explorer and arrange it so that you can still see your printer's icon in the Printer's window. Using Windows Explorer, locate a .txt file or .bat file and drag the file onto the printer's icon. What happens?

_____

_____

Now that you have tested your printer, share your printer (using Lab 21.1 as a guide). After you have shared your printer, go to the other computer and follow these steps to install a network printer:

1. Open the Printers window and launch the **Add Printer Wizard** as you did previously.

2. Click **Next**.

3. Select **Network Printer** and click **Next** to continue.

4. Click **Browse** to locate the printer that you will install. The Browse for Printer dialog box opens.

5. The Browse for Printer dialog box displays the network in a similar way to Windows Explorer. Locate your printer by expanding the computer on which you installed and shared it. When you have found the correct printer, click it (to select it) and then click **OK** to close the Browse for Printer dialog box.

6. In the Add Printer Wizard, verify that the path displayed is correct and click **Next** to continue.

7. In the Add Printer Wizard, as before, select the manufacturer and model or **Have Disk**, as appropriate for your particular printer.

8. Complete the Add Printer Wizard.

9. Test your printer.

Review Questions

1. A printer is connected to the parallel port on computer A but is shared on the network. Computer B installs the shared computer and connects to it. Computer A considers it a _____ printer and computer B considers it a _____ printer.

2. If a manufacturer's prescribed method for installing its printer differs from the default Windows method, which method should you use?

   _____

3. When installing a local printer that is attached through a parallel cable, what port should you specify?

   _____

21

4. Is it possible for a single printer to be both a local and a network printer? Why or why not?

_____

_____

_____

5. Explain how to print a document without opening it.

_____

_____

LAB 21.3 UPDATE PRINTER DRIVERS

Objectives

The goal of this lab is to give you experience upgrading printer drivers. After completing this lab, you will be able to:

➤ Identify driver information

➤ Locate new drivers

➤ Install new drivers

➤ Test the printer drivers for functionality

Materials Required

➤ Windows 9x, Windows 2000, or Windows XP

➤ Windows installation CD or installation files stored at another location

➤ Administrator account and password, if applicable

➤ File compression tool (optional)

➤ Internet access

➤ Local printer

Activity Background

Printer manufacturers often release new drivers for their existing printers to fix problems with earlier drivers, add new functions, support new applications, and accommodate new operating system features. A PC support technician needs to know how to update printer drivers as they become available. The process of updating printer drivers is similar to that for other devices. You must gather information about the device and the currently installed drivers, download the new drivers, and install them. Like other devices, after the drivers are installed, you should test the printer to be certain it is functioning correctly before turning it over to the end user. Unlike many other devices, it is easy to verify that a printer is working correctly. You will also find that the process of updating printer drivers is similar across various Windows platforms and printer manufacturers. This lab gives you general instructions for updating printer drivers. Modify these instructions to fit your particular situation and printer.

Estimated completion time: **30 minutes**

ACTIVITY

The first step to updating printer drivers is to gather information about your current printer and drivers. Research and list the following information:

1. How is your printer generally used (for example, text, photographs, or graphics)?

   _____

2. What operating system are you using?

   _____

3. Who is the printer manufacturer?

   _____

4. What is the model of the printer?

   _____

5. What is the printer interface (parallel, USB, other)?

   _____

6. Printers typically have many setup options that deal with print quality and paper handling. Right-click the printer and select **Properties** from the shortcut menu. Note any important settings, because it is likely that you will need to reapply them after the driver is updated.

   _____

   _____

   _____

When using Windows 9x, follow these instructions to view driver details:

1. Open Device Manager.

2. In Device Manager, locate your printer and click to highlight it.

21

3. With the device selected, click **Properties** to display the device information. If you see a dialog box with only a General tab, close the dialog box and in Device Manager, click the plus sign + next to the printer to expand the heading and then select the appropriate printer from the displayed printer list. Then click **Properties**. A dialog box with both General and Driver tabs should appear.

4. Select the **Driver** tab and then click the **Driver File Details** button to display the Driver File Details dialog box as shown in Figure 21-1. List all drivers listed in the dialog box under "Driver files."

_____

_____

_____

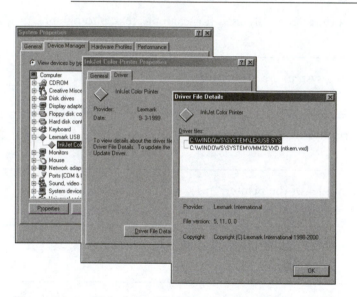

Figure 21-1   Windows 98 driver file details for a local printer

In addition to the previous information, list all driver information shown in the dialog box that will later help you identify the current driver. Include the Provider, File Version, and Copyright information. This will give you a starting point in locating new drivers for your printer.

_____

_____

_____

When using Windows 2000/XP, follow these instructions to identify the printer driver:

1. Open the Printers window.

2. Right-click the **printer** icon and select **Properties** from the shortcut menu. The printer properties dialog box appears.

3. Click the **Advanced** tab (see Figure 21-2). Note that tabs might differ from one printer to another.

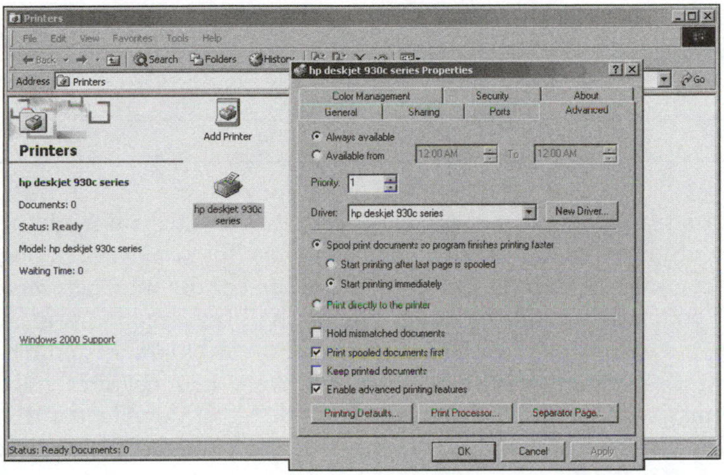

Figure 21-2   Use the printer Properties dialog box to identify the printer driver

4. What is the name of the driver listed under Driver?

Follow these general directions to locate any available driver updates:

1. Go to the printer manufacturer's Web site and locate the driver download section. Use the following table to help you locate the Web site. What is the URL of the driver download page?

21

Printer manufacturer	Web site
Brother	www.brother.com
Canon	usa.canon.com
Hewlett-Packard	www.hp.com
IBM	www.ibm.com
Lexmark	www.lexmark.com
Okidata	www.okidata.com
SATO	www.satoamerica.com
Seiko Epson	www.epson.com
Tally	www.tally.com
Xerox	www.xerox.com

2. When you search for the correct driver on the Web site, you might be presented with more than one driver that will work for your printer, operating system, or application. In most cases, you should select the most recent version that matches your printer and operating system. There are exceptions to this. For instance, if a driver is listed as BETA, it is still in development and has been released for evaluation. Usually, but not always, the manufacturer will have most of the kinks worked out. To be on the safe side, don't download a BETA release driver. List all drivers, with brief descriptions, for your particular printer and operating system.

3. What is the driver that you have selected to download?

4. Identify and list any special installation instructions the manufacturer recommends.

5. Create a folder on your hard drive named C:\Download and then create a subfolder named by the manufacturer, for example, C:\Download\Lexmark. What is your folder name?

6. Download the driver you intend to install to that folder.

With any device, it is best to follow the manufacturer's recommended method of installation rather than the Windows approach. A good manufacturer will have tested the driver as well as the installation process. The exception is when you have several printers installed on a system and you think that one set of drivers might overwrite files needed by another printer. In this case, use Windows to update the drivers. Do the following to install the new driver using the manufacturer's installation process:

1. As a document or digital picture, print an example of the main use of the printer. This printout verifies that your printer is working before you make any changes and will be used for comparison later to verify that the new drivers are working.

2. Using Windows Explorer, double-click the file you downloaded. If it is a compressed file, it will self-extract files or use file compression software on your PC to extract the files. If an installation wizard automatically launches, exit it.

3. Were any files extracted? List them here:

_____

4. Locate any ReadMe text files for late-breaking information about installation.

5. Double-click the setup or install program. Document the process you used to install the new drivers.

_____

_____

_____

Do the following to test the printer and new drivers:

1. Open the Printers window.

2. Right-click the printer and select **Properties** from the shortcut menu. Click the **Print Test Page** button and verify that the test page is legible.

3. Apply the correct printer settings that you recorded.

4. Reprint the typical document or photograph and compare it to the one printed prior to the driver update. List any differences that you see.

_____

Review Questions

1. List four reasons why you might want to update a printer's drivers.

_____

_____

21

2. List four things you should know before you start searching the Web for updated drivers.

_____

_____

_____

_____

3. What does a driver being in BETA release indicate about that driver?

_____

4. List the steps to print a Windows test page.

_____

_____

LAB 21.4 PRINTER MAINTENANCE AND TROUBLESHOOTING

Objectives

The goal of this lab is to give you experience supporting printers. After completing this lab, you will be able to:

➤ Use the Web to help with printer maintenance

➤ Correct common printer problems

Materials Required

➤ Internet access

➤ Printer

Activity Background

Printers require more maintenance than most peripherals. Paper gets jammed, the ink cartridge or toner runs out, and the image or document quality is degraded by dust and misalignment. Most manufacturers and many models have specific instructions for maintaining ink and toner cartridges that apply exclusively to that printer. You must rely on the printer manufacturer for instructions when maintaining a particular printer. In this lab, you will investigate maintenance and troubleshooting instructions for several types of printer.

Estimated completion time: **30 minutes**

ACTIVITY

Use the Internet to research how to solve the following problems. The printer is a high-end laser printer by Hewlett-Packard (*www.hp.com*), the LaserJet 8100. Answer these questions about routine maintenance for this printer:

1. Everything needed for routine maintenance of the LaserJet 8100 can be purchased in a printer maintenance kit. List the printer components included in this kit:

   _____

   _____

   _____

2. On the HP Web site, find the instructions for using the kit to perform the routine maintenance. What should you wear while you do the maintenance?

   _____

3. How many pages can be printed before maintenance should be performed?

The next printer is an inkjet printer, the HP Deskjet 930c. Answer these questions:

1. Your computer displays the message to replace the ink cartridge. You replace the cartridge, but the message is still displayed. Also, you notice the Resume light on the printer is blinking. Search the HP Web site and locate the troubleshooting steps to solve the problem.

2. What is the first thing HP suggests you do when you see these errors?

   _____

3. The second thing HP suggests is that you clean the cartridge contacts. List the steps:

   _____

   _____

   _____

   _____

4. If the problem does not disappear, HP suggests you reclean the cartridge contacts, this time using a cotton swab dipped in _____ .

Now you will investigate how to perform routine maintenance or troubleshoot problems on your local printer. Do the following:

1. List the following information to identify your local printer:
   - Printer manufacturer: _____
   - Printer model: _____
   - Printer interface (parallel, USB, other): _____

21

2. Search the manufacturer's Web site for troubleshooting and maintenance procedures and answer the following questions:

- What types of problem can you find addressed for your printer?

_____

_____

_____

- Does the manufacturer offer a printer maintenance kit? If so, what components are included and how much does the kit cost?

_____

_____

_____

- What maintenance tips for your printer can you find on the Web site?

_____

_____

Review Questions

1. When a printer is not working correctly, what are two ways the problem can be communicated to the user?

_____

_____

2. What is the purpose of a printer maintenance kit?

_____

3. How often should you perform printer maintenance using a printer maintenance kit purchased from the printer manufacturer?

_____

4. After replacing an ink cartridge in an inkjet printer, an error message is displayed. What is the first thing you should do?

_____

LAB 21.5 CRITICAL THINKING: SABOTAGE AND REPAIR A NETWORK PRINTER

Objectives

The goal of this lab is to learn to troubleshoot problems with a network printer.

Materials Required

This lab will require the following:

➤ Two or more computers connected to a network, one with a local printer attached

➤ Access to the Windows installation CD or installation files stored in another location

➤ Workgroup of 2–4 students

Activity Background

Problems with a network printer are common, and a PC support technician is often called on to solve them. This lab will give you practice solving these types of problem.

Estimated completion time: 45 minutes

ACTIVITY

1. Using the steps provided in Lab 21.1, verify that each computer in a work-group is able to print to a network printer, locally installed on one of the computers in the workgroup.

2. Trade systems with another group and sabotage the other group's system while they sabotage your system. Do one or more things that will prevent one or more computers in the workgroup from using the network printer. The following list has some sabotage suggestions. Do something in this list, or think of another option.

   ■ On the host computer, remove the sharing option for the printer

   ■ Uninstall the printer on a remote computer

   ■ Pause printing on one or more computers

   ■ Turn the printer off or offline

   ■ Disconnect the printer cable from the host computer

   ■ Remove paper from the printer

   ■ Introduce an error in the printer configuration on the host computer or a remote computer

3. What did you do to sabotage the other team's system?

   _____

   _____

   _____

4. Return to your system and troubleshoot it.

21

5. Describe the problem as a user would describe it if you were at a help desk.

6. What is your first guess as to the source of the problem?

7. List the steps you took in the troubleshooting process.

8. How did you solve the problem and return the printing system to working order?

Review Questions

1. What would you do differently the next time you encounter the same symptoms?

2. What are three easy things you could ask a user to check that do not require experience with Windows?

3. What might cause this problem to happen? List three possible causes.

22

ALL ABOUT SCSI

Labs included in this chapter

➤ Lab 22.1 Compare SCSI to Competing Technologies

➤ Lab 22.2 Compare SCSI Standards

➤ Lab 22.3 Install a Host Adapter and Hard Drive

➤ Lab 22.4 Install an External Drive

➤ Lab 22.5 Critical Thinking: Plan a SCSI System

The following grid shows the correlation between the labs in this chapter and the A+ Guides to Hardware and Software.

A+ Guide to Managing and Maintaining Your PC, Fifth Edition	A+ Guide to Hardware, Third Edition	A+ Guide to Software, Third Edition
Lab 22.1 Compare SCSI to Competing Technologies	Chapter 14	
Lab 22.2 Compare SCSI Standards	Chapter 14	
Lab 22.3 Install a Host Adapter and Hard Drive	Chapter 14	
Lab 22.4 Install an External Drive	Chapter 14	
Lab 22.5 Critical Thinking: Plan a SCSI System	Chapter 14	

LAB 22.1 COMPARE SCSI TO COMPETING TECHNOLOGIES

Objectives

The goal of this lab is to compare the price of a SCSI system to a similar system without SCSI. After completing this lab, you will be able to:

➤ Recognize the cost of SCSI components

➤ Explain how SCSI components can improve performance

Materials Required

This lab will require the following:

➤ Internet access

Activity Background

SCSI components, in general, cost significantly more than non-SCSI components but offer similar basic functionality. At one time SCSI performance and capabilities far exceeded those of other devices. Due to the emergence of new technologies and the refinement of other technologies, this is not necessarily true today. In this lab you will compare the cost and performance of SCSI components to similar non-SCSI components.

> Estimated completion time: **30 minutes**

ACTIVITY

1. Most motherboards come with embedded EIDE controllers. Generally speaking, they do not come with embedded SCSI controllers or FireWire ports. Use *www.pricewatch.com* and various manufacturers' Web sites to compare controllers for each technology. For each technology, select one mid-priced device and record the information for that device in the table.

	SCSI host adapter	EIDE adapter	FireWire adapter
Model and manufacturer			
Cost			
Number of devices supported			

2. Use *www.pricewatch.com* to compare hard drives that use SCSI, IDE, and FireWire. Decide on a drive capacity to use for your comparisons (for example 50 GB). Try to use drives that are within approximately 5 GB of each other. Also, when comparing drives, try to compare drives with similar rotation speed. For each technology, pick one mid-priced drive, and complete the following tables. For EIDE, use the most common speed, 7200 rpm. Use manufacturer Web sites for any information not available on *www.pricewatch.com*:

	SCSI Drive	EIDE Drive	FireWire Drive
Model and manufacturer			
Capacity (GB)			
Cost			
Rotation speed (rpm)		7200 rpm	
Avg. access time (ms)			
Max. transfer speed (ms)			

3. Use Pricewatch.com and manufacturer Web sites to compare CD-RW drives. Pick one mid-price drive for each technology and complete the following table:

	SCSI CD-RW	EIDE CD-RW	FireWire CD-RW
Model and manufacturer			
Cost			
Read speed			
Write speed			
Rewrite speed			
Avg. access time (ms)			
Max. transfer speed (ms)			

Review Questions

1. What advantages does SCSI hold over EIDE?

2. What advantage over EIDE do SCSI and FireWire share?

22

3. What are two advantages EIDE has over SCSI?

_____

_____

4. What technology is appropriate for an office PC that would need only one
   hard drive and would be used mainly for word processing? Explain your answer.

_____

_____

_____

5. What technology is appropriate for a video editing workstation requiring 200 GB
   of disk space, a high-speed CD-RW drive, and a DVD drive? Assume that
   the workstation would play video files directly from the hard drives. Explain
   your answer.

_____

_____

_____

LAB 22.2 COMPARE SCSI STANDARDS

Objectives

The goal of this lab is to familiarize you with the various SCSI standards. After completing this lab, you will be able to:

> Identify key specifications of various SCSI standards

Materials Required

This lab will require the following:

> Internet access

Activity Background

SCSI standards are a clear illustration of the principle that every improvement to a particular technology complicates the official standard for that technology. For example, the
SCSI-1 standards (introduced in 1986) were relatively straightforward because they were
established before refinements to SCSI technology had been introduced. However, SCSI-2
(introduced in 1994) was more complicated, reflecting various improvements to SCSI technology. At this stage, you shouldn't expect to be an expert on everything related to SCSI

technology. For that, you'll need to investigate one of the many books devoted to the topic. In this lab you will concentrate instead on the basic differences in SCSI specifications.

Estimated completion time: **30 minutes**

ACTIVITY

1. Use the textbook *A+ Guide to Hardware* or the textbook *A+ Guide to Managing and Maintaining Your PC* and the Web site *www.pcguide.com* to complete the following tables:

SCSI-1

Date introduced	ANSI standard	Bus width	Max # of devices	Max transfer rate

SCSI-2

Version	Date introduced	ANSI standard	Bus width	Max # of devices	Max transfer rate
Fast					
Wide					
Fast/Wide					

SCSI-3

Version	Date published	ANSI standard	Bus width	Max # of devices	Max transfer rate	Cable length	
						Single ended	Differ-ential
Fast							
Wide							
Fast/Wide							

Use the textbook *A+ Guide to Hardware* or the textbook *A+ Guide to Managing and Maintaining Your PC* and the Web site *www.pcguide.com* to answer the following questions:

1. What organization actually researches and develops SCSI standards?

_____

2. What signaling specification is used with Ultra 160 SCSI?

_____

3. What does the symbol in Figure 22-1 mean?

_____

22

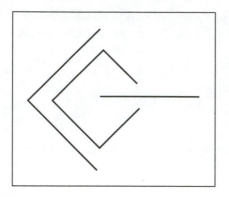

Figure 22-1

4. What is the most popular name for the latest SCSI standard that is officially known as SCSI-3 Parallel Interface 4 or SPI-4?

_____

Review Questions

1. What does SCSI stand for?

_____

2. Can SCSI devices built to differing standards be used on the same bus? Explain.

_____

3. Define the term "active termination."

_____

4. What are four organizations that govern SCSI standards?

_____

5. What SCSI standard has a maximum transfer rate of 80 MBps?

_____

LAB 22.3 INSTALL A HOST ADAPTER AND HARD DRIVE

Objectives

The goal of this lab is to familiarize you with the process of installing SCSI devices. After completing this lab, you will be able to:

➤ Install and configure a SCSI host adapter

➤ Install and configure a SCSI hard drive

Materials Required

➤ Windows 9x or Windows 2000/XP operating system

➤ SCSI host adapter and documentation

➤ Drivers, cables, and terminators

➤ SCSI hard drive and documentation

➤ PC toolkit with ground strap

➤ Workgroup of 2-4 students

Activity Background

A basic SCSI subsystem consists of one or more SCSI devices attached to a SCSI host adapter. The device can be attached either internally or outside the computer case. Recall that if you have more than one SCSI device on a SCSI subsystem, the devices are daisy-chained together, with a terminator at each end of the chain. In this lab, you will learn how to set up a basic SCSI subsystem.

Estimated completion time: **45 minutes**

ACTIVITY

Follow these steps to install a SCSI host adapter and hard drive:

1. Remove the case cover and determine which expansion slot will be used for the host adapter.

2. Consult the host adapter documentation and then configure the host adapter to SCSI ID 7. Enable any onboard termination.

3. Install the host adapter in the expansion slot and secure it with a screw.

4. Consult the hard drive documentation and set the jumper on the drive to assign the hard drive as SCSI ID 6.

5. Physically install the SCSI hard drive in the case. If you think you might want to add a second SCSI drive later, place the drive in a bay that is next to a vacant bay.

6. Attach one terminator to one end of the cable.

7. Attach the cable to the host adapter using the connector closest to the terminator.

8. Attach the SCSI data cable to the hard drive.

9. Attach the terminator to the connector that is closest to the hard drive. Note that the terminator should not be placed between the drive and host adapter (even if that's where the closest connector happens to be located).

10. Attach a power cable to the hard drive.

11. Use rubber bands or cable ties to secure the ends of the SCSI data cable so that it does not fall into other components.

22

12. Boot the PC and follow the manufacturer's instructions to install drivers for the SCSI host adapter.

13. When the installation process is complete, reboot the PC.

14. Observe the boot process and notice that before Windows loads, the SCSI host adapter initializes, scans the bus, and reports devices found.

15. Partition and format the hard drive using the same methods that you would use to partition and format an EIDE hard drive.

16. Verify that Windows recognizes the drive and that you can read from and write to it.

17. If asked to do so by your instructor, remove the SCSI components.

Review Questions

1. What SCSI ID should be assigned to the host adapter?

_____

2. Why didn't you need to use the CMOS setup to identify the hard drive?

_____

3. In what situation would you need to adjust the CMOS setup to use the newly installed hard drive?

_____

4. Where should terminators not be placed? Why?

_____

5. According to the documentation, how many devices will the host adapter support?

_____

LAB 22.4 INSTALL AN EXTERNAL DRIVE

Objectives

The goal of this lab is to give you experience configuring an external SCSI drive. After completing this lab, you will be able to:

➤ Identify the advantages of an external drive

➤ Install the drive in the external chassis

➤ Connect the drive to the system

Materials Required

This lab will require the following:

➤ Windows 9x or Windows 2000/XP operating system

➤ External chassis and drive with documentation

➤ Drivers, if necessary

➤ External cable and terminator

➤ PC toolkit with ground strap

➤ Workgroup of 2-4 students

Activity Background

Suppose you need to add a drive to your SCSI-equipped PC, but have no free drive bays in the case. One option is to upgrade the case, which involves disassembling and reassembling the PC, plus the cost of the case and drive. The simpler, and often cheaper, option is to install an external SCSI drive. This is usually accomplished by installing an internal SCSI component in an external chassis, including its own power supply (eliminating the need for the PC's power supply to power the device). In addition to the external chassis and SCSI drive, you will also need an external SCSI cable and a terminator. The cost of these components is about the same or less than a new case and eliminates the need to rebuild the system. Another advantage of using an external drive is that it can be moved to any compatible SCSI system with little effort. In this lab you will assemble, configure and install an external SCSI drive.

Before you begin, note that the external chassis design varies from one manufacturer to the next. Review the documentation for your external chassis, and look for any steps not included here. Be sure to perform those additional steps when assembling your external SCSI drive.

Note that in a real-world situation, you would first have to decide which SCSI standard to follow. Then you would have to decide which components and adapters (if any) you needed. Then you would have to purchase the components. This lab assumes that your instructor has selected compatible standards for each component and that you have the necessary devices on hand.

Estimated completion time: **45 minutes**

ACTIVITY

To install the internal drive in the external chassis, follow these steps (as well as any additional steps specified in your documentation):

1. Determine what SCSI IDs are available on the bus, and, if necessary, disable termination on the host adapter so you can use the external connector.

22

2. Consult the drive documentation, and then set the jumper on the new drive to assign the SCSI ID.

3. Open the external chassis and examine the cabling. Decide which cable to attach first and whether to secure the drive in the chassis or attach the cabling first. It is usually best to connect the data cable, followed by the power cable, before securing the drive in the chassis.

4. Install and secure the drive in the chassis.

5. Close and secure the external chassis.

6. Attach the SCSI cable to the chassis.

7. Attach the terminator to the chassis.

   Note that many SCSI devices now have internal termination available. This feature is usually activated and deactivated by a jumper setting. In general, using an actual terminator is considered more reliable than internal termination.

8. Attach the power cable to the chassis and to a power source.

Follow these steps to set up the drive and verify that it is functioning:

1. Switch on power to the external drive assembly.

2. Boot the PC and observe the boot process. Did the host adapter detect the new drive?

   _____

3. As necessary, partition and format the new hard drive or follow the manufacturer's instructions to install drivers for the drive.

4. When the drive is fully configured, verify that you can read from and write to the drive.

5. If instructed, remove and disassemble the external assembly.

Review Questions

1. What are some advantages of using an external SCSI drive?

   _____

   _____

2. What should you do before you purchase SCSI components?

   _____

   _____

3. Did you find it easier to connect cabling before securing the drive in the chassis or after securing the drive?

   _____

4. Is it preferable to use internal or external termination?

_____

5. Does the process of partitioning a SCSI hard drive differ from partitioning an IDE hard drive? Why or why not?

_____

_____

LAB 22.5 CRITICAL THINKING: PLAN A SCSI SYSTEM

Objectives

The goal of this lab is to use your knowledge to plan a SCSI-based system. After completing this lab, you will be able to:

➤ Identify and select the best components to meet your performance requirements

➤ Plan the configuration of the system

➤ Estimate the cost of the system

Materials Required

This lab will require the following:

➤ Internet access

Activity Background

Often a customer will give a technician a set of performance requirements and explain that she wants to upgrade her PC to meet those requirements. The technician has to design a configuration to meet the requirements and estimate the cost of the upgrade. You'll practice that in this lab.

Estimated completion time: **45 minutes**

ACTIVITY

1. Review the following information about the customer's existing system:
   - Windows 2000 Professional
   - Pentium 4 1.8 GHz with 256 MB Rambus RAM
   - Mini ATX motherboard with AGP, 3 PCI slots, no embedded SCSI adapter
   - Standard 3.5-inch floppy and internal EIDE Zip drive
   - Internal 40 GB EIDE hard drive, DVD-ROM drive, CD-RW drive

22

- Mid-tower case with 350 Watt power supply, three 5-inch drive bays, and three 3.5-inch drive bays
- AGP video adapter, PCI MPEG card, and PCI Ethernet NIC
- USB mouse and Microsoft keyboard

2. Review this list summarizing the customer's upgrade requirements:
   - Two identical 50 GB SCSI hard drives
   - Transfer rate of at least 40 Mbps
   - Compatibility with a SCSI 10-disk array that will eventually be installed in a server room that is 20 feet away

3. Design an upgrade configuration compatible with the customer's existing system. Explain your configuration on a piece of paper. You may, if necessary, remove one (but only one) component of the existing system. In your design notes, report the physical and logical configuration, including termination and ID assignments. Also include an estimated cost of parts. Use the textbook *A+ Guide to Hardware* or the textbook *A+ Guide to Managing and Maintaining Your PC* and the Internet for research. Print documentation that supports your final configuration.

Review Questions

1. How did you determine on which SCSI standard to base your upgrade?

   _____

   _____

2. Did you decide to remove any existing components? Why or why not?

   _____

   _____

3. How did you determine if your host adapter was compatible with Windows 2000?

   _____

   _____

4. How many IRQs would the SCSI system use with a total of one host adapter and three SCSI devices?

   _____

5. How many devices will your selected host adapter support?

   _____

23

PURCHASING AND UPGRADING A PC

The following grid shows the correlation between the labs in this chapter and the A+ Guides to Hardware and Software.

A+ Guide to Managing and Maintaining Your PC, Fifth Edition	A+ Guide to Hardware, Third Edition	A+ Guide to Software, Third Edition
Lab 23.1 Choose a System	Chapter 15	
Lab 23.2 Determine System Requirements	Chapter 15	
Lab 23.3 Compare What You Need with What You Can Afford	Chapter 15	
Lab 23.4 Check System Compatibility	Chapter 15	
Lab 23.5 Evaluate an Upgrade	Chapter 15	
Lab 23.6 Determine Hardware Compatibility with Windows XP		Chapter 1
Lab 23.7 Compare Windows Versions Using the Microsoft Web Site		Chapter 1
Lab 23.8 Explore the Macintosh World		Chapter 1
Lab 23.9 Examine a Macintosh		Chapter 13
Lab 23.10 Download and Install Shareware on a Mac		Chapter 13
Lab 23.11 Investigate Linux		Chapter 1
Lab 23.12 Explore the GNOME Environment in Linux		Chapter 13
Lab 23.13 Use the vi Editor in Linux		Chapter 13
Lab 23.14 Use Linux Commands		Chapter 13

Lab 23.1 Choose a System

Objectives

The goal of this lab is to help you determine what system you might purchase or build to meet your needs and desires. After completing this lab, you will be able to:

➤ List applications you want to run on your system

➤ Determine the type of system required for several types of application

Materials Required

This lab will require the following:

➤ Workgroup of 2–4 students

Activity Background

The goal of this chapter is to help you learn how to plan and build a new system from scratch. The first four labs in this chapter explore the various stages of creating a new system, and each lab builds on the one before it.

One of the first steps in planning and constructing your own PC is deciding what you're going to use it for and what applications you will be running on it. After you make these decisions, you can decide what components are required to meet your needs. In this lab, you will describe and discuss the kind of system you would build for particular uses. Most of the labs in this chapter will require research, but in this case, all you need to do is discuss issues with your workgroup partners.

Estimated completion time: **20 minutes**

Activity

In the following steps, you will plan four different systems. Each member of the workgroup should work separately, with each member planning four systems. Follow these steps:

1. Plan a system that will be used for gaming and Web surfing. Complete the following:

    ■ Applications that you are likely to install:

    _____

    _____

    ■ Hardware needed:

    _____

    _____

- Most important hardware component(s) needed for gaming and Web surfing:

  _____

2. Plan a system that will be used for programming. Complete the following:
   - Applications that you are likely to install:

     _____

     _____

   - Hardware needed:

     _____

     _____

   - Most important hardware component(s) needed for programming:

     _____

3. Plan a system that will be used for office applications. Complete the following:
   - Applications that you are likely to install:

     _____

     _____

   - Hardware needed:

     _____

     _____

   - Most important hardware component(s) needed for office applications:

     _____

4. Plan a system that will be used for a company file server. Complete the following:
   - Applications that you are likely to install:

     _____

     _____

   - Hardware needed:

     _____

     _____

   - Most important hardware component(s) needed for a company file server:

     _____

5. For each type of system, discuss the differences in the systems planned by each member of your group. List the major differences here:

_____

_____

_____

_____

6. As a group, agree on a set of specifications for each system. How do the specifications agreed on by your group differ from your original specifications?

_____

_____

_____

_____

7. Assign one type of system to each member of the group. List the assignments for each group member. In Lab 23.2 and Lab 23.3, each member of the group will continue planning the type of system assigned here:

_____

_____

_____

_____

Review Questions

1. What type of system was assigned to you?

_____

2. What resources will you need to produce a detailed design for this system?

_____

_____

3. Did you find the process of discussing the different types of systems helpful? Why or why not?

_____

_____

4. On which type of system was there the most disagreement on requirements?

_____

_____

5. If you had a budget crunch, where would you sacrifice on your system? Justify your reasoning.

_____

_____

LAB 23.2 DETERMINE SYSTEM REQUIREMENTS

Objectives

The goal of this lab is to help you determine the specific requirements for the system you plan to build. After completing this lab, you will be able to:

➤ List minimum software and hardware components required for a particular type of system

Materials Required

This lab will require the following:

➤ Internet access

➤ Workgroup of 2–4 students (different people than in Lab 23.1)

Activity Background

In the previous lab, you were assigned a type of system to build and you made some preliminary plans for it. In this lab, you will make more specific decisions regarding the required software and hardware components. For now, we will ignore budget constraints and address those issues in Lab 23.3.

Estimated completion time: **30 minutes**

ACTIVITY

1. Working from the preliminary requirements you formed in Lab 23.1, use the Internet to research system requirements for your assigned type of system. Complete the following list of requirements:

   ■ CPU speed _____

   ■ Memory _____

   ■ Hard drive size _____

- Case _____
- Motherboard _____
- Monitor size and resolution _____
- Type of printer _____
- Expansion cards _____

  _____

  _____

  _____

  _____

- Other peripheral hardware (such as keyboard, mouse, PC camera, speakers, etc.)

  _____

  _____

  _____

  _____

- Drives needed (for example, hard drives, CD or DVD, tape backup, Zip, or floppy)

  _____

  _____

  _____

  _____

- Operating system

  _____

- Applications

  _____

  _____

  _____

  _____

■ Any other requirements

_____

_____

_____

_____

2. Use the Internet or your local computer store to learn more about each component. List the description and cost of each component. If you are doing your research on the Internet, print the Web page describing each component. (The Web page you print should include the component's price.) If you are conducting your research at a computer store, take careful notes, and be sure to note a price for each component. At this point, you are interested in evaluating your options for each component, so collect information on more than one possibility. For example, for a motherboard, gather information for two or three different motherboards that all satisfy your system requirements. Although you need to list the price for each component, do not be concerned about total cost at this point in your research. The following Internet resources might be helpful in your search, although you can use others as well:

■ *www.cnet.com*

■ *www.tomshardware.com*

■ *www.motherboards.com*

■ *www.pricewatch.com*

■ *www.dirtcheapdrives.com*

3. After you have finished gathering system requirements, find another student from another group who planned the same type of system you did. Compare your plans and note the differences.

_____

_____

_____

_____

Review Questions

1. What sites did you use for your research besides the previously listed ones?

_____

_____

2. Did you add any components to your list or remove any from it after researching the type of system you want to build? Explain.

   _____

   _____

   _____

3. What processor manufacturer, model, and speed did you select? Why? How
   much would the same speed processor from another manufacturer cost?

   _____

   _____

4. What amount of memory and hard drive size do you plan to use? How did
   you make your choices?

   _____

   _____

   _____

5. What components did you decide to use in your system other than the ones
   listed in the lab? What purpose will they serve in the new system?

   _____

   _____

   _____

6. List any differences between your plans and the other student's plans for the
   same type of system.

   _____

   _____

   _____

   _____

23

Lab 23.3 Compare What You Need with What You Can Afford

Objectives

The goal of this lab is to help you determine the cost of building your own PC. After completing this lab, you will be able to:

➤ Research and compare component prices

➤ Determine how to build a system within your budget

Materials Required

This lab will require the following:

➤ Internet access

➤ Workgroup of 2–4 students

Activity Background

When planning a system, it is important to consider the cost of the components that you want to include. You might not be able to afford everything that you'd like to have in the system, or you might have to buy less expensive versions of some components to get what you want in another area. In this lab, you will develop several versions of a budget for the system you want to build. You will begin without a budget—that is, by figuring out what your dream system would cost. Then you will prioritize your list of components, and determine ways to reduce the system's total cost.

Estimated completion time: **30 minutes**

Activity

1. Use the information regarding specific hardware components that you compiled in Lab 23.2 to complete Table 23-1. List the price of each component in your dream system in Table 23-1. (Note that you might not use all of the rows in the table.) At the bottom of the table, list the total cost for your dream system.

Table 23-1   Dream system

Component	Manufacturer and model	Cost
Processor		
Memory		
Hard drive		
Case		
Motherboard		
Monitor		
Printer		
Expansion card 1		
Expansion card 2		
Expansion card 3		
Expansion card 4		
Keyboard		
Mouse		
Speakers		
CD or DVD drive		
Tape drive		
Zip drive		
Floppy drive		
Other drive		
Operating system		
Application 1		
Application 2		
Application 3		
Application 4		
Other		
Other		
Other		
Total cost of the system		

2. Review your list of components in Table 23-1 and prioritize them. In Table 23-2, list the components in order of importance. In the Notes column of Table 23-2, make notes regarding how much you need each component and whether you can use a lower-cost version or eliminate it altogether. Indicate which (if any) components you are most willing to sacrifice to be able to afford a better component in another area of the system.

Table 23-2   Priority of system components

Component	Notes

3. Pare down your list to the absolute minimum for the type of system you are building: the lowest amount of memory and hard drive space, the cheapest monitor, and so on. In Table 23-3, list the lowest prices available for each component, and calculate the total cost of your bare-bones system.

Table 23-3   Bare-bones system

Component	Manufacturer and model	Cost
Processor		
Memory		
Hard drive		
Case		
Motherboard		
Monitor		
Printer		
Expansion card 1		
Expansion card 2		
Expansion card 3		
Expansion card 4		
Keyboard		
Mouse		
Speakers		
CD or DVD drive		
Tape drive		
Zip drive		
Floppy drive		
Other drive		
Operating system		
Application 1		
Application 2		
Application 3		
Application 4		
Other		
Other		
Other		
Total cost of the system		

4. In Table 23-4, list the components of a system that is a reasonable compromise between the dream system and the bare-bones system. This midrange system is the one you will work with in the next lab.

23

Table 23-4 Midrange system

Component	Manufacturer and model	Cost
Processor		
Memory		
Hard drive		
Case		
Motherboard		
Monitor		
Printer		
Expansion card 1		
Expansion card 2		
Expansion card 3		
Expansion card 4		
Keyboard		
Mouse		
Speakers		
CD or DVD drive		
Tape drive		
Zip drive		
Floppy drive		
Other drive		
Operating system		
Application 1		
Application 2		
Application 3		
Application 4		
Other		
Other		
Other		
Total cost of the system		

5. Compare your results from steps 1–4 with the results of another student who is planning the same type of system. Compare cost estimates and note differences in the components you both planned to include. Note how you arrived at your calculation.

_____

_____

_____

_____

6. Repeat step 5 with at least one student who is planning a different type of system.

_____

_____

_____

_____

Review Questions

1. What was the cost difference between your dream system and the bare-bones version?

_____

2. On which components were you willing to compromise and why?

_____

_____

3. On which components were you *not* willing to compromise and why?

_____

_____

4. How would the performance of your midrange system compare to the dream system? How would the performance of the midrange system compare to the bare-bones system? How would the performance of the dream system compare to the bare-bones system?

_____

_____

_____

Lab 23.4 Check System Compatibility

Objectives

The goal of this lab is to help you verify that the components in a proposed system are compatible. After completing this lab, you will be able to:

> ➤ Find incompatibilities between components in a proposed system
> ➤ Suggest an alternative system of approximately the same price

Materials Required

This lab will require the following:

> ➤ Internet access
> ➤ Workgroup of 2–4 students

Activity Background

No matter how much time you spend planning and building a PC, the system won't work correctly unless the system components are compatible. You will save yourself a lot of trouble by attempting to discover incompatibilities before you begin to build a system. In this lab you will figure out which components in your proposed system are incompatible and suggest compatible components so that the cost of building the system remains approximately the same.

Estimated completion time: **40 minutes**

Activity

1. Alter your plan for your midrange system (from Lab 23.3) by introducing component incompatibilities. Write this altered version on a separate piece of paper or develop a new plan that incorporates incompatible components. Incompatibilities are suggested below, but you can introduce a problem not listed here:

   - A processor not supported by the motherboard
   - Not enough space in your case for all of your drives (hard drive, CD-ROM, Zip drive)
   - Power supply not powerful enough
   - Too much RAM for your motherboard
   - An incompatible mix of SCSI and IDE devices
   - A type of memory not supported on the motherboard
   - Five parallel ATA IDE devices on a system
   - A video card that uses the wrong kind of AGP slot for the motherboard
   - Expansion cards included with a motherboard that already has built-in logic

2. Calculate and record the total cost of the components in the system:

_____

3. Trade revised PC plans with another student in your group. Ask the other student to find the incompatible components in your plan and suggest replacement components while keeping the price about the same. Do the same with the plan you receive, recording the incompatibilities you find, the original cost of the system, replacement components, and the final cost of the altered system.

_____

_____

_____

_____

_____

4. With the group, discuss the incompatibilities found in the plans and how you fixed them. Make note of incompatibilities that were introduced but not found.

_____

_____

_____

Review Questions

1. Did you, or the other students in your group, introduce incompatibilities not suggested in step 1? If so, list them here:

_____

_____

_____

2. Were all the incompatibilities introduced in the plans discovered? If not, which ones were not, and why might these have been more difficult to find?

_____

_____

_____

3. List the incompatibility problems you located in the other student's plan and explain how you solved them.

_____

_____

_____

_____

4. Did the students in your group have different ways of solving the same incompatibility problems? Explain.

_____

_____

_____

_____

5. For the plan that you reviewed and revised, what was the difference in the original cost and the cost after you incorporated your solutions?

_____

_____

LAB 23.5 EVALUATE AN UPGRADE

Objectives

The goal of this lab is to help you determine the ease and cost of upgrading a PC. After completing this lab, you will be able to:

➤ Determine whether a system needs to be upgraded

➤ Explain why a system needs to be upgraded

➤ List components necessary to upgrade a system

Materials Required

This lab will require the following:

➤ Lab computer

➤ Documentation for computer components, if available

➤ Internet access

Activity Background

An important factor to consider when purchasing or building a PC is how easy it will be to upgrade the system. You might upgrade an existing system rather than replacing it with a new system. Factors that affect the ease of upgrading include the processors supported by the motherboard, the size of the case, and the number and type of ports and expansion slots on the motherboard. In this lab, you will examine a system to determine whether you can make upgrades to it and then evaluate how practical the upgrades are.

Estimated completion time: **45 minutes**

Activity

Follow these steps to determine whether your system can be upgraded:

1. In Table 23-5, list the components currently installed on your system. Useful sources of information include Device Manager, the Control Panel, and the Properties windows for various drives and devices.

Table 23-5   Current system components

Device	Description
Motherboard (make and model)	
BIOS type	
Memory (type and size)	
Hard drive (type and size)	
Other drives installed (floppy, Zip, CD-ROM, etc.)	
Monitor (type and size)	
Printer	
Sound card	
Modem (or other Internet connection)	
NIC	
Other devices	
Operating system (including version number)	
Applications (including version number)	

2. Using the Internet and available documentation, select three components to upgrade. Determine the following for each component and record the information:

   Component 1:_____

23

- Replacement component:

  _____

  _____

- Cost of the upgrade:

  _____

- Are there other components that must also be upgraded for this upgrade to work? If so, what are they?

  _____

  _____

Component 2:_____

- Replacement component:

  _____

  _____

- Cost of the upgrade:

  _____

- Are there other components that must also be upgraded for this upgrade to work? If so, what are they?

  _____

  _____

Component 3:_____

- Replacement component:

  _____

  _____

- Cost of the upgrade:

  _____

- Are there other components that must also be upgraded for this upgrade to work? If so, what are they?

  _____

  _____

3. Print a Web page showing the specifications and cost of each new component. What is the total cost of the upgrades?

_____

4. Suppose you had to sell the system in its current state (without the upgrades). What would be a reasonable price?

_____

5. When upgrading an existing system, the cost of the upgrade should not exceed half the value of the existing system. Will your proposed upgrade exceed that limit?

_____

6. Using *www.cnet.com* (or another Web site where you can compare systems), locate a notebook computer with specifications similar to your lab PC. Compare the cost of upgrading the memory, the processor, and the CD-ROM drive on each. (Substitute another component if your computer does not have a CD-ROM drive.) In Table 23-6, compare the cost of upgrading your lab PC to that of a similar upgrade for a notebook computer.

Table 23-6   PC upgrade versus notebook upgrade

Component	Cost of upgrading on PC	Cost of upgrading on notebook
Processor		
Memory		
CD-ROM drive		

Review Questions

1. What components did you choose to upgrade and why?

_____

_____

_____

2. Which would be cheapest to upgrade, your lab PC or a comparable notebook? Explain your answer.

_____

_____

_____

3. What other resources, besides the ones you used in the lab, do you think might be helpful in planning an upgrade?

_____

_____

4. Among the components you selected, which upgrade was the most expensive?

_____

_____

5. If you were actually performing these upgrades, is there any component or any system that you would *not* choose to upgrade? Explain your answer.

_____

_____

_____

6. Which component is the most popular to upgrade? The easiest? The hardest?

_____

_____

_____

LAB 23.6 DETERMINE HARDWARE COMPATIBILITY WITH WINDOWS XP

Objectives

The goal of this lab is to help you determine if your hardware is compatible with Windows XP. After completing this lab, you will be able to:

➤ Use Windows to identify system components

➤ Find and use the Microsoft Hardware Compatibility List (HCL)

Materials Required

This lab will require the following:

➤ Windows 9x or Windows 2000 operating system

➤ Internet access

Activity Background

You can't assume your operating system will support your hardware. This is especially true of older devices, because software developers focus on supporting the most capable and popular devices. You can verify that Microsoft operating systems support your hardware by checking Microsoft's Hardware Compatibility List (HCL). The HCL, found at *www.microsoft.com/whdc/hcl/default.mspx*, includes devices whose drivers were written by Microsoft, or devices whose drivers have been tested and approved by Microsoft. In this lab you will use Device Manager to inventory devices in a system. Then you will check the HCL to see if the system's devices are supported by Windows XP.

Estimated completion time: **30 minutes**

ACTIVITY

To use Device Manager to inventory your system, follow these steps:

1. Open the **Control Panel** and then double-click the **System** icon.

2. For Windows 9x, select the **Device Manager** tab. (For Windows 2000, select the **Hardware** tab and then click the **Device Manager** button.) The Device Manager window opens.

3. In Device Manager, devices are arranged by category. To see what kind of video adapter is installed on your system, click the + plus sign sign to the left of "Display Adapters."

4. Select your video adapter and click the **Properties** button. Information about the model and manufacturer appears. Record the information.

_____

_____

5. Use Device Manager to find similar information for your network adapter, modem card, or sound card, and record that information here.

_____

_____

Now that you have a list of devices installed on your system, check the HCL to see if these devices are supported by Windows XP. Web sites change often, so the following steps might have to be adjusted to accommodate changes. If you have difficulty following the steps due to Web site changes, see your instructor for help. Otherwise, follow these steps:

1. Open your browser and go to *www.microsoft.com/whdc/hcl/default.mspx*. Click the link **Windows XP: See Windows Catalog**.

2. Click the **Hardware** tab. On the left side of the screen, under **Hardware**, point to **Cameras and Video**, and then click **Video Cards**. Using the information about your video adapter learned from Device Manager, find you video card by scrolling the list or using the search box in the upper-left corner of the screen. If you don't find your adapter, try using a more general description of the adapter. For example, you might type "Intel 82810E". If that doesn't return a result, try typing "Intel".

3. Confirm that you have found your device by verifying that the correct manufacturer and model are listed.

4. Look to the right for an XP logo or a compatible symbol under the XP column. Either one indicates that the device is compatible with XP.

5. Add a note to your list of devices indicating whether the device is compatible with Windows XP.

6. Check the other devices in your list, and note whether they are compatible with Windows XP.

Review Questions

1. Explain how to compile a list of devices installed on your system.

2. How are devices grouped in Device Manager?

3. What does "HCL" stand for?

4. If a device is not listed in the HCL, what are your options when installing Windows XP? List at least two possibilities.

5. Does the hardware in your system qualify for Windows XP? If it doesn't qualify, explain why.

LAB 23.7 COMPARE WINDOWS VERSIONS USING THE MICROSOFT WEB SITE

Objectives

The goal of this lab is to search the Microsoft Web site to compare different Windows versions. After completing this lab, you will be able to:

➤ Look up information on the Microsoft Web site (*www.microsoft.com*)

➤ Use Microsoft's search feature to find information on versions of Windows

➤ Determine which version of Windows is compatible with the most types of hardware

Materials Required

This lab will require the following:

➤ Internet access

Activity Background

The Microsoft Web site is an excellent source of information on Microsoft products. In this lab you will explore the site to see what kind of information is available. Then you will focus on information about the Windows product line.

> Estimated completion time: **30 minutes**

ACTIVITY

1. Open your browser and go to *www.microsoft.com*.

2. What Product Families are listed?

_____

_____

3. Click **More Support** on the lower-right side of the screen. What is the URL for this link that is now showing in your browser address box?

_____

4. Click **Search the Knowledge Base**. The "Search the Knowledge Base" page appears. The Microsoft Knowledge Base is information (grouped into articles) about products or errors. The first step is selecting a Microsoft product. Use the following directions, remembering that specific directions on using the Web site

23

cannot be given here, as the site sometimes changes. If you have difficulty following the steps due to Web site changes, see your instructor for help. Otherwise, follow these steps:

5. Choose to search on **Windows 98** by selecting it from the **Select a Microsoft Product** drop-down list.

6. The Knowledge Base page asks you what you would like to search for. In the **Search for** text box, type **FAT32.**

7. Next, you must specify some search options. If necessary, select **All of the words entered** from the drop-down menu.

8. Leave all other options as they appear by default. Click **Go**.

9. List the titles of the first three articles that appear as a result of your search.

_____

_____

_____

10. Look at any of the articles. When you are finished examining the articles, return to the Microsoft home page at *www.microsoft.com*.

11. Click the **Windows** link (under Product Families). What versions of Windows are listed in the upper-left corner of the page?

_____

_____

_____

12. Click **Previous Versions**. What Previous Versions of Windows do you see?

_____

_____

13. Click **Windows 95,** then click **Get the latest info.**

14. Using the search box on this page, locate the **Windows 95 Installation Requirements (Q138349)** article.

15. Print the page information on the system requirements for Windows 95 by clicking the **Print** button on the browser toolbar (or clicking **File** on the menu bar and then clicking **Print**.) Verify that the correct printer is selected and then click **OK** or **Print** (depending on which version of Windows you are using).

16. Search for and print the system requirements for Windows XP.

Review Questions

1. What information is available in the HCL?

_____

_____

2. What are the minimum system requirements for Windows XP?

_____

_____

3. Name two Product Families offered by Microsoft (besides Windows). For what are these Product Families used?

_____

_____

4. Based on your knowledge of Windows, what do you think is the most recent Windows OS that Microsoft now describes as a "previous version"?

_____

Lab 23.8 Explore the Macintosh World

Objectives

The goal of this lab is to familiarize you with the Macintosh operating systems and the hardware they support. After completing this lab, you will be able to:

➤ Describe the various Apple operating systems, hardware, and applications

➤ Research Apple technology on the Apple Web site (*www.apple.com*)

Materials Required

This lab will require the following:

➤ Internet access

Activity Background

The Macintosh operating systems are designed to be used only on Macintosh (or Mac) computers; they cannot be used on PCs. Many developers (including Apple, the company that created the Macintosh computer) have developed Macintosh applications. The Apple Web site (*www.apple.com*) is the best source of information about the Macintosh products. In this lab, you will investigate Macintosh operating systems, hardware, and applications. Now that you've had practice exploring Web sites in Lab 23.7, you should be able to find information on the Apple Web site. To encourage you to explore the Web site on your own, this lab provides less direction than the preceding labs about which links to use.

Estimated completion time: **30 minutes**

ACTIVITY

1. Open your browser and go to *www.apple.com.* Explore the site on your own and return to the main page. Use the links on the site to answer the following questions.

2. What version of the Mac operating system comes preinstalled on the iMac?

   _____

   _____

3. What is the cost of upgrading your operating system from OS 9 to OS X?

   _____

4. Comparing the iMac, eMac, and Power Mac available for sale on this Apple Web site, what are the speeds or frequencies of the processors used in each computer?

   _____

   _____

5. How much does the 20-inch iMac cost?

   _____

   _____

6. What software comes bundled with the eMac?

   _____

   _____

   _____

7. What is an iBook?

   _____

   _____

8. How much does the most expensive iBook cost?

   _____

9. What features are included with the least expensive iBook?

_____

_____

10. Describe the features of the Apple Pro Mouse.

_____

_____

11. What is the function of an AirPort Extreme Base Station?

_____

12. What Apple computer can use the AirPort Extreme card?

_____

13. What is the purpose of QuickTime software?

_____

_____

14. Describe what the AppleWorks software does.

_____

_____

15. Describe the purposes of iMovie software.

_____

Review Questions

1. What is one advantage of using an Apple computer compared to using a PC?

_____

2. For what type of user do you think the Apple applications are intended?

_____

3. Why do you think it is easier for Apple to provide compatibility between hardware and the operating system than it is for Microsoft or Linux?

_____

_____

4. For what type of user is the iMac intended?

_____

_____

Lab 23.9 Examine a Macintosh

Objective

The objective of this lab is to help you become familiar with an Apple Macintosh computer. After completing this lab, you should be able to:

➤ Explain the differences between a Macintosh and a PC

➤ Identify differences between the Mac operating system and Windows

Materials Required

➤ Macintosh computer with OS 9 or OS X

➤ Workgroup of 2–4 students

Activity Background

In this lab you will take a look at a Macintosh computer. You will use the Mac's graphical user interface (GUI) to find files and launch applications, noting the main differences in the way a Mac and a Windows PC accomplish these tasks. You will also note the strengths and weaknesses of both operating systems.

As you know, a mouse on a Windows system has at least two buttons, and may include other features, such as wheels, that are devoted to specific tasks. If you prefer, you can use keystroke shortcuts in Windows to perform tasks through the keyboard instead of using the mouse. For some people, these keystrokes are more efficient than clicking a mouse. And even if you normally use the mouse, you can always use the keyboard shortcuts if the mouse happens to fail. By contrast, most Mac mouse devices have only one button. Others have no button at all (in which case pressing the entire mouse has the same effect as pressing a button). When using a Mac, then, you have to use the keyboard in combination with the mouse to perform tasks that could be performed using only the mouse in Windows. In this lab you will have a chance to experience these differences for yourself.

Estimated completion time: **45 minutes**

ACTIVITY

In Windows 9x and later, the quickest way to view the properties of an object is to open Windows Explorer, right–click the object, and then click Properties in the shortcut menu. Alternatively, you can highlight the object in My Computer and press Alt+F+R. A Macintosh mouse, however, has no right mouse button. Follow these instructions to view the properties of an object on a Mac:

1. Highlight a desktop icon using the arrow keys.

2. Press and hold the **Apple** key, press the **i** key, and then release both keys. An Info window opens, displaying information on that object. Close the window by clicking the box at the upper-left corner in OS 9 or by clicking the **X** box in OS X.

3. Use the mouse alone to highlight the same object on the desktop.

4. Click **File** on the menu bar at the top of the desktop and then click **Get Info** (in OS 9) or **Show Info** (in OS X). Close the window.

In Windows, each open window has its own menu bar. With a Mac, all open windows share the same menu bar at the top of the desktop. This menu bar changes its options according to which window is selected. When no applications are open, the Finder menu bar is displayed as shown in Figure 23-1.

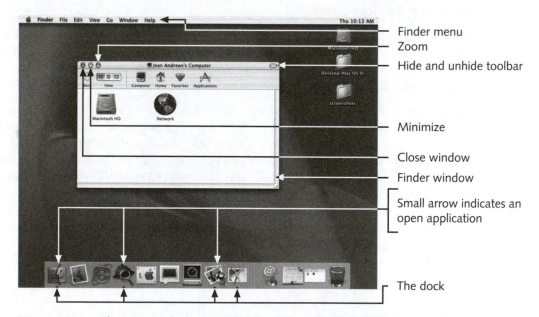

Figure 23-1 The Mac X desktop with a Finder window showing

Experiment with the Mac menu bar by following these steps:

1. Click **File** on the Finder menu and then click **Find**. This opens Sherlock, which is like the Windows Find or Search features.

2. Examine the menu bar, and notice that it has changed to display commands related to Sherlock.

The icons at the top of the Sherlock window indicate different places that Sherlock can look for information. By default, the hard drive is selected, indicating that Sherlock is ready to search for files or folders (see Figure 23-2). You'll use Sherlock now to search for a Web browser.

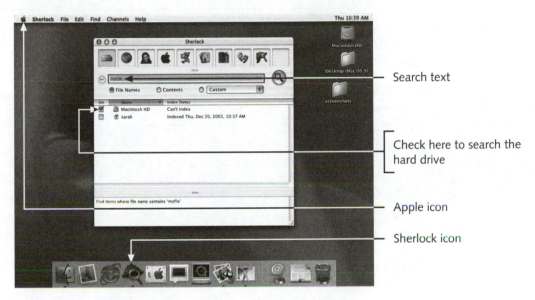

Figure 23-2   Use Sherlock to search for files and folders

Follow these steps:

1. In the field below the hard drive symbol, type **Explorer**. Make sure the **File Names** option button is selected, and check the box next to the hard drive in the field below.

2. Click the **magnifying glass icon** to start the search. The results are displayed in the same field where you checked the box next to the hard drive. (If you don't see "Explorer" in the list of results, begin again with step 1, only this time type "Netscape".)

3. Double-click the **Internet Explorer** (or **Netscape**) icon to launch your browser and note that, once again, the menu bar has changed to offer options for the active application.

In Windows 9x and later, the taskbar displays buttons for all open applications. You can switch to an application by clicking its icon in the taskbar. Mac OS X has a feature called the Dock that functions much like the taskbar in Windows, which you can see at the bottom of the screen in Figure 23-1. (This feature is not included in Mac OS 9.) If you are working on a Mac OS X computer, you can experiment with the Dock feature by performing the following steps. If you are using a Mac OS 9 computer, simply read these steps instead.

1. Click the **Internet Explorer** (or **Netscape**) icon on the left side of the Dock. Internet Explorer opens, and the menu bar at the top of the screen changes to show options for this application. Record the options that the menu bar offers for Internet Explorer.

   _____

   _____

2. Click the **Sherlock** icon on the left side of the Dock. Sherlock is maximized, and the menu bar changes again. Record the options that the menu bar offers for Sherlock.

   _____

   _____

3. Minimize both Sherlock and the Web browser. Notice that these two icons on the right side of the Dock have small arrows pointing to them, indicating open applications. (These arrows are shown in Figure 23-2.) The menu bar should still reflect the last application that was active, not necessarily the last one you minimized.

4. Move your mouse over the icons on the Dock and describe what happens.

   _____

   _____

5. Click the **Sherlock** icon on the right of the Dock. The Sherlock window and menu options are restored.

Review Questions

1. When using a Mac, why do you have to rely more on keyboard/mouse combinations than when using a PC?

   _____

   _____

2. What Mac feature is similar to the Find or Search feature of Windows?

   _____

3. Does each window on a Mac include its own menu bar? Explain.

   _____

   _____

23

4. What Mac OS X feature performs much the same function as the Windows taskbar?

_____

5. What is the quickest way to view the properties of an object on a Mac?

_____

_____

LAB 23.10 DOWNLOAD AND INSTALL SHAREWARE ON A MAC

Objectives

The goal of this lab is to help you download and install a Shareware utility on a Mac. After completing this lab, you will be able to:

➤ Locate Shareware utilities for a Mac

➤ Download and install a utility

➤ Use the utility that you downloaded

Materials Required

This lab will require the following:

➤ Macintosh computer with OS 9 or OS X

➤ Internet access

Activity Background

Despite the similarities between the Macintosh and Windows environments, there are significant differences between the file structures and the interfaces. Thus, you can't always assume that just because you know how to perform a task on a PC that you also know how to perform it on a Macintosh. For example, installing a software program on a Mac is different from installing software on a Windows computer. In this lab, you will research available Shareware utilities for the Mac. Then you will download a program, install it on a Mac, and use it.

Estimated completion time: **30 minutes**

ACTIVITY

Follow these instructions to download and install a Shareware utility on a Mac:

1. Open Internet Explorer or another browser and go to *www.cnet.com*.

2. Click the **Downloads** link at the top of the page. (The same link is also included in the body of the page.)

3. The Downloads page opens, offering downloads for your operating system (Mac OS in this case). In the middle of the page, note the links for the categories of downloads available. List those categories here.

_____

_____

_____

_____

_____

4. Locate, download, and install one of the following:
   - Mac operating system update
   - Free browser
   - Game
   - Calendar for the Dock
   - Utility that allows you to read Microsoft Word documents on your Mac
   - Other (list here)

_____

_____

The following steps offer general instructions for downloading software on the Mac. The procedure may be slightly different on your Mac.

1. Navigate the categories and subcategories on the CNet site until you find the name of the utility you want to download.

2. Click the name of the utility you want to download. The next Web page provides additional information about the selected utility.

3. Click **Download Now**.

4. A message is displayed indicating that the download site is being contacted. When your computer connects to the download site, the Mac's Download Manager launches, showing the progress of the download, including the estimated time that the download will take. When the download is complete, minimize the Download Manager and your Web browser.

Most installation files are downloaded to the Mac desktop by default. Now that the download is complete and you have minimized open windows, you should be able to see the program files you downloaded on the desktop. (Depending on the utility you downloaded, more than one file might have been installed.) You can move the file later by using a Finder window to open the folder you want to store the downloaded file in and then dragging the installation file to that folder. For now, you will focus on installing the utility.

1. Double-click the installation file on your desktop and follow the directions to install the utility. (Depending on the size of the utility, it might have been downloaded as a compressed file. In that case, you will have to double-click the file to expand before the actual installation program appears on your desktop. Once the installation program appears, you can double-click it.)

2. After the program is installed, open it and verify that it is working.

3. Download and install additional utilities. Check with your instructor to see how many you should download and install.

4. Use Sherlock to search the hard drive for all files associated with the utilities you installed. Record the name of each utility, the names of files associated with the utilities, and their locations:

_____

_____

_____

_____

_____

Review Questions

1. What program or programs did you choose to install and why?

_____

_____

_____

_____

2. In labs in other chapters, you downloaded and installed utilities for Windows. What differences did you notice between that process and the process for downloading and installing a utility on a Mac?

_____

_____

_____

_____

3. Describe the differences between the general procedure given in this lab and the actual steps required to download and install the utility:

_____

_____

_____

_____

4. After you installed each utility, where was the shortcut for launching the utility located?

_____

5. What problems, if any, did you experience during the process of downloading and installing the program, and what did you do to solve them?

_____

_____

_____

_____

Lab 23.11 Investigate Linux

Objectives

The goal of this lab is to find information about Linux. After completing this lab, you will be able to:

➤ Research Linux on the Linux Web site (*www.linux.org*)

➤ Compare Linux with other operating systems

➤ Use the Linux tutorial on the Linux Web site

Materials Required

This lab will require the following:

➤ Internet access

Activity Background

Unix is a popular OS used to control networks and to support applications used on the Internet. Linux is a scaled-down version of Unix that is provided, in basic form, free of charge and includes open access to the programming code of the OS. Linux can be used both as a server platform and a desktop platform, but its greatest popularity has come in the server market.

In this lab, you will search the *www.linux.org* site for general information on Linux. You will also survey the Linux tutorial.

Estimated completion time: **60 minutes**

ACTIVITY

1. Open your browser and go to *www.linux.org*. Spend a few minutes exploring the site on your own and then return to the main page.

2. Click the **General Info** link (on the navigation bar). Using the information on the "What is Linux" page, answer the following:

   ■ What is the current, full-featured version of Linux?

   _____

   ■ Who is credited with inventing the Linux kernel?

   _____

   ■ How is Linux licensed? Read the GNU General Public License. Give a brief description of the terms and conditions of this license.

   _____

   _____

   ■ How much does Linux cost?

   _____

For an operating system to be useful, there must be applications written for it. Suppose a small business is interested in using Linux on its desktop computers. Will this business be able to run common business-type applications on its Linux desktops? To find out, click the **Applications** link (on the navigation bar). The types of applications are listed by category. Search this page and its links to answer the following questions:

1. Will the business be able to send faxes from a Linux machine?

_____

2. List two Web browsers suitable for Linux.

_____

3. How many antivirus software packages are available for Linux? List at least two.

_____

_____

4. Searching under Office and Word Processor, list at least three word-processing applications available for Linux.

_____

_____

_____

5. How many accounting applications are available for Linux? List at least two and tell where you found them.

_____

_____

_____

Now you can continue exploring the Linux Web site. Follow these steps to compare Linux to other operating systems:

1. Click the **Documentation** link on the navigation bar.
2. Read about the Linux Documentation Project.

Use the information displayed on the Linux Web site to answer the following questions:

1. Give a brief description of the Linux Documentation Project.

_____

_____

2. Who is responsible for writing documentation for the Linux Operating System?

_____

_____

Next, you will explore the Web site's Linux tutorial. Follow these steps:

1. Return to the Home page, scroll down to display the heading **Linux 101**, and then click **more** at the bottom of that section.

2. Scroll down, and then click **Getting Started with Linux**. Browse through this tutorial and answer the following questions.

3. What are the distributions (flavors) of Linux and how are they categorized?

_____

_____

4. Can you install Linux on a computer that has another operating system already installed? Print the Web page supporting your answer.

_____

5. When preparing to install Linux, what is a good computer-use practice?

_____

_____

Continue exploring the Web site by completing the following:

1. Click the **Distributions** link. A link to the source code for Linux kernels is available on this page. Notice the Distribution search area. When searching for a distribution of Linux, if you do not narrow your search, you will return a large number of distributions.

2. Select **English** from the **Language** drop-down list.

3. Select **Mainstream/General Public** from the **Category** drop-down list.

4. Select **Intel compatible** from the **Platform** list and click **Go**. How many distributions do you see listed?

_____

5. Browse through the list, looking for SCO/Caldera Open Linux, Mandrake Linux, and Red Hat. Which distribution appears to be easiest to use? What is its intended purpose?

_____

_____

6. Can Linux be used on systems other than those that run Intel-compatible processors? Print the Web page supporting your answer.

_____

Review Questions

1. What is the least amount of money that you will pay for Linux?

_____

2. Why might a company not want to use Linux on its desktop computers?

_____

_____

_____

3. What is one advantage of using Linux on a desktop rather than a Windows operating system?

_____

_____

_____

4. Based on what you learned from the Linux Web site, how do you think companies that provide Linux make the most profit?

_____

_____

LAB 23.12 EXPLORE THE GNOME ENVIRONMENT IN LINUX

Objectives

The goal of this lab is to help you become familiar with a Linux GUI operating environment. After completing this lab, you will be able to:

➤ Identify and use the main features of GNOME, a Linux GUI

➤ Describe differences between GNOME and Windows

Materials Required

This lab will require the following:

➤ Linux PC with GNOME installed (or another Linux GUI, if necessary)

Activity Background

Linux and Unix rely more heavily on the command prompt than do Windows and the Mac OS. There are, however, several GUI operating environments available for Linux. One common Linux GUI is GNOME.

There are noticeable similarities between GNOME and Windows, such as the presence of menus and windows. However, whereas Windows 9x and later Windows versions are true operating systems, GNOME is an operating environment that, in its relationship to the underlying OS, is closer to the earlier Windows 3.x. The menus and other features of the GNOME and the modern Windows interfaces also differ significantly. In this lab, you will explore the GNOME operating environment and note some of the differences between it and Windows. Note that if you don't have access to GNOME, you can perform this lab using another Linux GUI instead.

ACTIVITY

1. Boot up your Linux computer. During the boot process, text on the screen shows which components are being loaded and whether each process succeeds or fails. Depending on your installation of Linux, whether other operating systems are installed on the machine, and which startup options are selected during installation, you may have to choose to launch GNOME from a startup menu. (This startup menu will look similar to the one you saw in Lab 16.4, where you installed Recovery Console on Windows XP.) If you encounter such a startup menu, record the options on that menu here:

   _____

   _____

   _____

   _____

2. The GUI begins to load, and a logon screen appears. Type **root**, press **Enter**, and then enter the password, if required. You are now logged on as the root user with administrative privileges. (You can also use the logon provided to you by your instructor.)

3. Wait for the GUI to load completely.

4. Before opening any programs, take a minute or two to familiarize yourself with the GUI's general appearance. List at least three similarities and three differences between GNOME and Windows.

   _____

   _____

   _____

   _____

   _____

   _____

5. In the bottom-left corner on the toolbar, look for a button labeled Start (or something similar). Click this button and explore the menus it offers. Find and open the following applications, taking notes about how you opened each application.

- Word-processing program

_____

- Command prompt

_____

- A view that will allow you to explore the computer's file structure

_____

- A utility similar to Windows' Control Panel that allows you to change system settings and display properties

_____

- A game

_____

6. Once you have several windows open, practice using some of the applications and switching between them, making notes about similarities and differences with corresponding functions in Windows.

_____

_____

_____

_____

_____

_____

Review Questions

1. Which is more closely related to the underlying operating system, GNOME or the Windows GUI? Explain your answer.

_____

_____

2. Did your familiarity with Windows help you learn how to use GNOME? Why or why not?

_____

_____

3. How did the menus in GNOME work differently from the menus in Windows?

_____

_____

4. Do you find GNOME or Windows easier to use? Explain your answer.

_____

_____

5. Name at least three features of GNOME that offer functionality that is not included in Windows.

_____

_____

LAB 23.13 USE THE VI EDITOR IN LINUX

Objectives

The goal of this lab is to help you use the Linux vi editor. After completing this lab, you will be able to:

➤ Open the vi editor and create and save a memo

➤ Use commands from within the vi editor to manipulate text

Materials Required

This lab will require the following:

➤ A computer with Linux installed

Activity Background

Like Windows, most distributions of Linux offer at least one simple GUI word processing program. Linux also provides the vi editor, which you can use to work with text documents in a command interface. The vi editor name comes from the fact that it is a visual text editor that was, at one time, the most popular Unix text editor. It is still used with shells that don't allow the use of the arrow, Delete, or Backspace keys. The vi editor can be used in insert mode, which allows you to enter text, or in command mode, which allows you to enter commands to perform editing tasks. In this lab, you will learn how to create and use commands on a text file in the vi editor. All of these commands are case-sensitive.

| Estimated completion time: **30 minutes** |

ACTIVITY

Follow these steps to open the vi editor and create a document:

1. Boot up your Linux computer. If you boot to a command prompt, skip to step 3.

2. If you boot to a GUI locate and open a terminal window. (This is similar to opening a command-prompt window from within Windows.)

3. Type **vi mymemo** at the command prompt and press **Enter**. This command opens the vi editor and at the same time creates an empty text document called mymemo.

4. At this point, when you first open the vi editor, you are in Command mode, which means that anything you type will be interpreted as a Command by the vi editor. Type **i** to switch to Insert mode. (You will not see the command on the screen, and you do not need to press Enter to execute it. The command automatically switches you to insert mode.) The word INSERT at the bottom of the screen indicates that you are now in Insert mode.

5. Type the first two sentences of step 4 as the text for your memo. If your shell (the component of Linux that enables the user to interact with the OS) supports it, practice using the arrow keys to move the cursor through the text, up, down, left, and right, one character at a time. Table 23-7 shows the commands to use if your shell does not support the arrow keys, as well as other common vi editor commands.

Table 23-7   vi editor commands

Command	Alternate	Description
Ctrl+B	Pg up	Back one screen
Ctrl+F	Pg down	Forward one screen
Ctrl+U		Up half a screen
Ctrl+D		Down half a screen
k	Up arrow	Up one line
j	Down arrow	Down one line
h	Left arrow	Left one character
l	Right arrow	Right one character
w		Forward one word
b		Back one word
0 (zero)		Beginning of the current line
$		End of the current line
nG		Line specified by number n
H		Upper-left corner of screen
L		Last line on the screen

6. To switch back to Command mode, press the **Esc** key.

Now you are ready to enter commands to manipulate your text.

1. Type **H** to move the cursor to the upper-left corner of the screen. You must use an uppercase H, because all these commands are case-sensitive.

2. Type **w** repeatedly (make sure to use lowercase) until you reach the beginning of the word "first."

3. Type **dw** to delete the word "first." To delete one character at a time, you would use x; to delete an entire line, you would use dd.

4. Practice using some of the other commands listed in Table 23-7 that you have not already used in this lab. Switch between Insert and Command modes as necessary.

5. To save the file and exit the vi editor, type **:x** and press **Enter**. The file is saved and the vi editor closes.

Review Questions

1. Were any of the commands or keystrokes you tried to use within the vi editor not supported by your shell? If so, list them.

_____

_____

2. What do you see at the bottom of the screen when you are in Insert mode? In Command mode?

_____

_____

3. Assume that you are in Insert mode in the vi editor. List in order the commands you would use to switch to Command mode, move to the fourth word in the third line, type the text "new words," and move to the last line in the text.

_____

_____

_____

_____

_____

4. Assume you are in the vi editor working with your document mymemo. List in order the commands you would use to exit the vi editor, save the document, and open the vi editor to work with a new document called mylist.

_____

_____

_____

_____

5. What are the advantages and disadvantages of working with text in the vi editor as opposed to a GUI word processing program?

_____

_____

_____

LAB 23.14 USE LINUX COMMANDS

Objectives

The goal of this lab is to help you learn to use some Linux commands. After completing this lab, you will be able to:

➤ Use common Linux commands to work with files

Materials Required

This lab will require the following:

➤ A computer with Linux installed

Activity Background

In Lab 23.12, you learned about GNOME, which is a Linux GUI. When working with Linux or Unix, it is necessary to know how to use some common commands, as these operating systems rely heavily on the command prompt. In this lab, you will use the Linux command prompt to create and work with a file.

> Estimated completion time: **30 minutes**

ACTIVITY

The shells file in the /etc directory contains a list of the shells available on a Linux system. Each shell incorporates slightly different support for programming and scripting languages, as well as keystrokes. The directions in this lab are for the bash shell. To determine whether you are using the bash shell (and to switch to it if necessary), do the following:

1. At a command prompt, type **echo $shell** and press **Enter**. If you see the output /bin/bash, you are using the bash shell.

2. If you are not using the bash shell, type **bash** and press **Enter** to change to the bash shell.

Follow these steps to view a list of available shells:

1. Type **cat /etc/shells** and press **Enter**.

2. A list of available shells appears. Notice that all these shells are stored in the /bin directory. Type **clear** and press **Enter**. What happens?

_____

_____

3. Type **cat –n /etc/shells** and press **Enter**. What happens?

_____

_____

Next, you will save the list of shells to a file. Follow these steps:

1. Go to the root directory by typing **cd /** and pressing **Enter**.

2. Type **cat /etc/shells > available_shells** and press **Enter**.

3. Notice that no command output appears on the screen, because the output has been saved to the new file available_shells. (The file is created when the command is entered.) To view the contents of the file, type **cat available_shells** and press **Enter**.

The file was saved in the root directory because that's the directory you were in when you created it. It is not a good idea to store data files in the root directory, so follow these steps to create a new directory and move the available_shells file to it:

1. Type **mkdir myfiles** and press **Enter**. This creates a new directory named myfiles under the current directory, which is root. (If you wanted to delete the directory later, you would use the command rmdir.)

2. Type **cd myfiles** to change from the current directory to the new directory.

3. Type **mv /available_shells .** and press **Enter**. (Don't overlook the period at the end of the command line; type it, too.) The period in the command line indicates that you mean the current directory. The complete command copies the file from the root directory to the current directory, which is /myfiles. The source directory is the root and the destination directory is /myfiles.

4. Type **ls** to see the contents of the myfiles directory. The available_shells file is listed.

Now that you have learned how to create a file and a directory and how to move a file, compose and execute commands that will do the following:

1. Make the root directory the current directory. What command did you use?

_____

2. Use the cat command to view the contents of the /bin directory. What command did you use?

_____

3. Use the cat command to send the output to a file. What command did you use?

_____

4. Move the file from the root directory to the /myfiles directory. What command did you use?

_____

5. You can also produce a list of the /bin directory in a file that is initially created in the /myfiles directory, eliminating the need to move the file. List the commands required to do that, and then execute the commands.

_____

_____

_____

_____

_____

6. Remove the /myfiles directory and all its contents. What command (or commands) did you use?

_____

_____

_____

Review Questions

1. What command would you use to create a file in the /myfiles directory that lists the contents of your user file, which is located in the home directory? (Assume that your user file is called yourname.)

_____

_____

2. What is the function of the clear command?

_____

_____

3. What is the function of the −n option that you used with the cat command, and how is it helpful?

_____

_____

4. From the root directory, what command would you use to create a directory called importantfiles? What command would you use to delete the directory?

_____

_____

_____

_____

24
TROUBLESHOOTING AND MAINTENANCE FUNDAMENTALS

Labs included in this chapter

➤ Lab 24.1 Produce Help Desk Procedures

➤ Lab 24.2 Flash BIOS

➤ Lab 24.3 Troubleshoot General Computer Problems

➤ Lab 24.4 Troubleshoot Hypothetical Situations

➤ Lab 24.5 Critical Thinking: Update Motherboard Drivers

The following grid shows the correlation between the labs in this chapter and the A+ Guides to Hardware and Software.

A+ Guide to Managing and Maintaining Your PC, Fifth Edition	A+ Guide to Hardware, Third Edition	A+ Guide to Software, Third Edition
Lab 24.1 Produce Help Desk Procedures	Chapter 16	
Lab 24.2 Flash BIOS	Chapter 16	
Lab 24.3 Troubleshoot General Computer Problems	Chapter 16	
Lab 24.4 Troubleshoot Hypothetical Situations	Chapter 16	
Lab 24.5 Critical Thinking: Update Motherboard Drivers	Chapter 16	

LAB 24.1 PRODUCE HELP DESK PROCEDURES

Objectives

The goal of this lab is to demonstrate the process of setting up help desk troubleshooting procedures. After completing this lab, you will be able to:

➤ Identify problems that would prevent users from browsing the network

➤ Decide which problems can be solved over the telephone

➤ Decide which problems require administrative intervention

➤ Create a support matrix for telephone instruction

Materials Required

This lab will require the following:

➤ Windows 9x or Windows 2000/XP operating system

➤ PC connected to a working TCP/IP network

➤ Two workgroups with 2–4 students in each group

Activity Background

When a company sets up a help desk for computer users, it establishes a set of procedures to address common troubleshooting situations. These procedures should include instructions that the average user can be expected to carry out with telephone support. In this lab, you will design and create help desk procedures for one common problem: the inability to connect to a network. In this lab, assume that you are working at the company help desk. Assume that if you cannot solve the problem, you will escalate the problem to the network administrator or to another technician who will actually go to the computer that has the problem.

Estimated completion time: **60 minutes**

ACTIVITY

1. Assume that your company network is designed according to the following parameters. (Note that your instructor might alter these parameters so they more closely resemble the parameters of your working network.)

   ■ Ethernet LAN is using only a single subnet

   ■ TCP/IP is the only protocol

   ■ Workgroup name is ATLGA

   ■ DHCP server assigns IP information

2. Assume that all users on your company network use computers with the following parameters. (Note that your instructor might alter these parameters so they more closely resemble your PC.)

- Pentium III 750 MHz

- Windows XP operating system

- Internal NIC

- Category 5 cabling with RJ-45 connectors

3. As a group, discuss the various reasons a user might not be able to connect to the network, and then make a list of the four most common reasons. List the source of these problems below. Consider both hardware and software problems. In your list, include at least one problem that is difficult to solve over the phone by talking to the user, requiring, instead, that the network administrator or another technician actually go to the computer to solve the problem. Order the four problems from the least difficult to solve to the most difficult to solve. List the one problem that requires administrator intervention at the bottom of the list.

- Source of Problem 1:

  _____

- Source of Problem 2:

  _____

- Source of Problem 3:

  _____

- Source of Problem 4 (requires administrator or another technician to get involved):

  _____

For each problem, describe the symptoms as a user would describe them:

- Symptoms of Problem 1:

  _____

  _____

- Symptoms of Problem 2:

  _____

  _____

- Symptoms of Problem 3:

  _____

  _____

- Symptoms of Problem 4 (requires administrator or another technician intervention):

  _____

  _____

As a group, decide how to solve each of the problems. On separate pieces of paper, list the steps required to verify and resolve the problems. (Such a list of steps is sometimes referred to as a procedure, support matrix, or job aid.) Double-check the steps by testing them on your computer. (In real life, you would actually test your steps using a computer attached to the network you are supporting.) When making your list of steps, allow for alternatives, based on how the user responds to your questions. For example, you might include one list of steps for situations in which the user says others on the network are visible in My Network Places and another list of steps for situations in which the user says no remote computers can be seen in My Network Places. Well-written help desk procedures ensure that the help desk worker knows exactly what steps to perform; this in turn results in quicker and more confident user support. For any problem that cannot be solved by the procedure, the last step should be for the help desk personnel to notify the administrator. In your procedure, include questions to the user where appropriate. As you work, you might find it helpful to use a diagram or flowchart of the questions asked and decisions made.

An example of one step that involves a question is:

➤ **Question:** Is your computer on?

➤ **Answer:** Yes, go to step 3; No, go to step 2

Now test your help desk procedures by using them on another workgroup. Follow these steps:

1. Introduce one of your four problems to a PC connected to a network.

2. Have someone from another workgroup sit at your PC. The remainder of these steps refer to this person as "the user."

3. Sit with your back to this person so you cannot see what he or she is doing. Place your step-by-step procedures in front of you, either on paper or on screen. (It's helpful if you can sit at a PC that is connected to the network, so that you can perform the same steps you ask the user to perform. But make sure you cannot see the other PC or see what the user is doing.)

4. The user should attempt to access the network and then "call" your help desk for assistance.

5. Follow your procedure to solve the problem.

6. Revise your procedure as necessary.

7. Test all four help desk procedures.

Review Questions

1. Can all users' computer problems be resolved with help desk support? Explain.

_____

_____

2. After you first design and write your help desk procedures to resolve problems, what should you do next?

_____

_____

3. How should help desk procedures address complex problems that require administrative intervention?

_____

_____

_____

4. How should you alter your procedures based on the technical experience of your users? Explain.

_____

_____

_____

_____

5. Why do you need to consider what the network and computer are like when creating your procedures?

_____

_____

_____

6. What has been your experience when calling a help desk? How well did the technician walk you through the process of solving your problem?

_____

_____

Lab 24.2 Flash BIOS

Objectives

The goal of this lab is to help you examine the process of flashing BIOS. After completing this lab, you will be able to:

➤ Gather motherboard information

➤ Gather BIOS string information

➤ Research correct BIOS update information

➤ Record current BIOS settings

➤ Flash your BIOS, if permitted by your instructor

Materials Required

This lab will require the following:

➤ Windows 9x or Windows 2000/XP operating system

➤ Motherboard documentation or SANDRA software installed in Lab 1.3

➤ Internet access

➤ Blank floppy disk

Activity Background

The BIOS on a motherboard controls many of the basic input/output functions of the system. The BIOS programming can be updated by downloading the latest update from the BIOS or motherboard manufacturer's Web site and then following specific procedures to update (or flash) the BIOS. Flashing a computer's BIOS is necessary when troubleshooting an unstable motherboard. You may also need to flash a computer's BIOS to provide support for new hardware (such as a processor, hard drive, or CD-ROM drive) or an operating system that you are about to install. For example, before upgrading your operating system to Windows 2000/XP Professional, you could update your BIOS to add support for ACPI power management. In this lab you will gather information about your system, including what BIOS you are using and how to flash the BIOS. If you instructor permits, you will also flash your BIOS.

Estimated completion time: **45 minutes**

24

ACTIVITY

Before making hardware, software, or BIOS changes to a system, it's important to know your starting point so that, if problems occur, you will know whether the problems already existed or you created them by what you did to the system. Do the following:

1. Verify that your computer can successfully boot to a Windows desktop with no errors.

2. Does the PC boot without errors?

   _____

It's critical that when flashing the BIOS you use the correct BIOS update. Using the wrong BIOS update can render your system inoperable. Follow these steps to gather information on the motherboard chip set and BIOS:

1. Use motherboard documentation or SANDRA to find and record the following:

   - Motherboard manufacturer:

     _____

   - Motherboard model number and version/revision:

     _____

   - Chip set manufacturer:

     _____

   - Chip set model number and version/revision:

     _____

2. Next, you need to record the BIOS string and manufacturer information that are displayed during the boot process. To make it possible to record this information, for an older PC, turn off the PC, unplug your keyboard and then turn on the PC. In most cases, the very first screen will contain video BIOS information from the video card and will be identified by "VGA BIOS" or "Video BIOS." Ignore this screen and wait for the next screen, which indicates the start of POST. At this point, because you unplugged the keyboard, POST will stop and report the error about a missing keyboard. This freezes the screen so you can read the BIOS information. For a newer PC, turn off the PC and then turn on the PC while pressing the Pause/Break key, which causes POST to halt.

3. The BIOS manufacturer and version can usually be found at the top left of the POST screen. You may also see a release date, which is useful in determining whether newer versions of the BIOS are available. The motherboard identification string will usually be located at the bottom left of the screen and usually

contains dozens of characters. It is important to verify that this string is correct so that the exact BIOS update is obtained. Record your information below.

- BIOS manufacturer and version:

  _____

- BIOS release date, if provided:

  _____

- Motherboard identification string:

  _____

If you have a name-brand PC that does not identify BIOS information during the boot process, you should be able to locate BIOS information on the manufacturer's Web site by computer model number and serial number. Also, some newer computers will not halt the boot process if the keyboard is missing. Alternatively, you can go to CMOS setup and look for the BIOS identifying information on the CMOS main menu screen.

Using the information you gathered, you can search the Web to determine what files you will need to update your BIOS.

1. First, search the motherboard manufacturer's Web site and then the BIOS manufacturer's Web site's support section for information on updating your BIOS. Alternatively, search by motherboard model number or BIOS version number. Download the files required to update your BIOS or, if your computer is running the latest version of the BIOS, download the files required to refresh your existing BIOS. Answer the following questions:

   - Did you download files to update or refresh your BIOS?

     _____

   - Which manufacturer provided the BIOS: the BIOS manufacturer or motherboard manufacturer?

     _____

   - What is the name of the file you downloaded?

     _____

   - What is the release date of the latest version?

     _____

2. Search the manufacturer's Web site for the steps required to flash your BIOS. Print this procedure so you can use it during the upgrade. Does the procedure call for an additional BIOS utility or Flash utility? If so, download this utility as well. Research Flash utilities on *www.wimsbios.com*. Wim's BIOS is an excellent Web site for researching BIOS information in general. Print information on what BIOS utilities are available.

3. The next step is to record any changes you have previously made to CMOS settings. Generally, when BIOS is updated, settings are returned to their default state, so you will probably need to return the settings to their present state after you have flashed BIOS. In addition, you might need to manually input settings for all hard drives (or allow these settings to be detected automatically). Record any settings that you know you changed, as well as any hard drive settings that might have to be reconfigured after you update the BIOS. Also, record any additional settings specified by your instructor.

■ Hard drive information:

_____

_____

■ Settings you have changed:

_____

_____

_____

_____

■ Settings specified by your instructor:

_____

_____

_____

_____

4. At this point, if your update procedures require the use of a bootable floppy, verify that the boot order allows you to boot from drive A before drive C.

5. Prepare to update your BIOS. Decompress any files, double-check procedures, read any readme.txt files included in the upgrade files (which often contain last-minute adjustments to the procedure), and create the upgrade boot disk, if necessary.

6. If your instructor permits, follow the BIOS update procedure to update your BIOS. During the procedure, if you are given the opportunity to save your old BIOS, do so. This will make it possible to return to the previous BIOS version if you encounter problems with the new BIOS.

7. Reboot, verify CMOS settings, and verify that the computer will boot to a Windows desktop successfully.

Review Questions

1. At what point in the boot process is BIOS information displayed?

   _____

2. How can you freeze the screen during POST so that you can read the BIOS information?

   _____

   _____

3. Why is it so important to record BIOS and motherboard information correctly?

   _____

   _____

4. What files might contain last-minute changes to the upgrade procedures?

   _____

5. In what state are CMOS settings usually placed after a BIOS update?

   _____

6. If given the opportunity during the update, what should you always do and why?

   _____

   _____

Lab 24.3 Troubleshoot General Computer Problems

Objectives

The goal of this lab is to troubleshoot and remedy general computer problems. After completing this lab, you will be able to:

➤ Diagnose and solve problems with various hardware devices

➤ Document the troubleshooting process

Materials Required

This lab will require the following:

➤ Windows 98 or Windows 2000/XP operating system

➤ Windows 98 or Windows 2000/XP installation CD or installation files stored in another location

➤ Drivers for all devices

➤ PC toolkit with ground strap

➤ Workgroup partner

Activity Background

In previous labs, you have learned to troubleshoot problems in specific subsystems of a PC. This lab takes a comprehensive approach to troubleshooting an entire system, where the problem might relate to any subsystem. Troubleshooting a general problem is no different from troubleshooting a specific subsystem. You simply apply your troubleshooting techniques to a larger range of possibilities.

Estimated completion time: **120 minutes**

ACTIVITY

1. Verify that your computer and your partner's computers are working by verifying that the system runs smoothly and that all drives are accessible. Browse the network and connect to a Web site.

2. Randomly pick one of the following problems and introduce it to your PC:

   - For PCs that have SIMMs installed, move the RAM to a different SIMM slot.

   - Change the boot sequence to boot from a nonexistent device.

   - If both the mouse and the keyboard have PS/2 connectors, switch the connectors at the case.

   - Using Add/Remove Hardware, install a nonexisting device.

   - Remove the data cable from the primary master hard drive.

   - Change the display settings to two colors that are hard to read.

   - Install the wrong type SIMM or DIMM or the wrong number of SIMMs or DIMMs on the motherboard. Or, for a system that uses SIMMs, remove one SIMM. Be sure to store all memory modules in an anti-static bag while they are outside the case.

   - Unplug the monitor from the video adapter.

   - Add drive B in BIOS, but do not install a second floppy drive.

   - In BIOS, manually add information for a fictitious hard disk drive.

   - Unplug the network cable from the wall or hub.

   - Connect the floppy drive to the drive B connector on the data cable (the one without the twist).

3. Troubleshoot your partner's PC while your partner troubleshoots your computer. Verify that you can accomplish all the tasks that you could before the computer was sabotaged.

4. On a separate sheet of paper, answer these questions:

   ■ What is the initial symptom of a problem as a user would describe it?

   _____

   _____

   ■ How did you discover the source of the problem?

   _____

   _____

   _____

   ■ How did you resolve the problem?

   _____

   _____

   _____

   _____

   ■ If you were working at a help desk and someone called with this problem, could the problem have been solved over the phone or would it have required a visit from a technician? Explain your answer.

   _____

   _____

5. Return to your computer and repeat steps 2 through 4. Continue until you have solved all the problems listed in step 2. For each problem, make sure to answer the questions listed in step 4.

Review Questions

1. Which problems caused the computer to halt during the boot process?

   _____

   _____

   _____

2. What problem was the most difficult to repair? Why?

   _____

   _____

   _____

3. Of those problems that *allowed* the computer to boot, which problem was easiest to detect? Why?

   _____

   _____

   _____

4. Of those problems that *prevented* the computer from booting, which problem was easiest to detect? Why?

   _____

   _____

   _____

LAB 24.4 TROUBLESHOOT HYPOTHETICAL SITUATIONS

Objectives

The goal of this lab is to help you think through the troubleshooting process using hypothetical situations. After completing this lab, you will be able to:

➤ Evaluate a troubleshooting situation

➤ Determine a likely source of a problem

➤ Explain how to verify the source of a problem

➤ Briefly explain a problem and the procedure required to remedy it

Materials Required

This lab will require the following:

➤ Workgroup of 2–4 students

Activity Background

One way to sharpen your troubleshooting skill is to think through the process of solving hypothetical problems. This lab will present situations that, while common, should present a challenge for your workgroup.

To complete this lab, imagine that you are in charge of repairs at a small computer shop. As part of your job, you first need to describe the symptoms of the problem on the repair work order and explain your initial guess or opinion as to the source of the problem. You must then write a short summary on the work order explaining what you did to repair the computer. The explanations you write on the work order should be as clear and precise as possible. Customers who know something about computers will appreciate your careful explanations. And even if the customer does not fully understand, a detailed work order will help assure the customer that you did a thorough job.

Estimated completion time: **30 minutes**

ACTIVITY

1. A customer installed a new 20 GB hard drive and complains that it will not work. He claims that he called the manufacturer's technical support, who walked him through BIOS setup. When he rebooted, POST did recognize the hard drive but Windows still did not. The customer then became frustrated and decided to bring the computer to you.

   ■ What are the possible sources of the problem?

   _____

   _____

   _____

   _____

   ■ What would you do to find out how to resolve the problem?

   _____

   _____

2. A customer brings in a computer and says that when she turns on the computer it will not boot. She says that a screen appears with an error message regarding something about the operating system. The customer claims that she has never modified the system, but that she does have children who use the computer and may have changed something inadvertently.

When you boot the system, you get an invalid system disk error and you can hear the hard drive spin up when power is applied. You suspect that the BIOS settings are incorrect and that the hard drive is not being recognized. You successfully detect the hard drive using the BIOS autodetection feature. In standard CMOS setup you notice that the date and time are also incorrect, so you reset them. You save your changes and reboot. The system reboots to Windows. You test the system for 10 minutes, leave it on and come back to it after an hour, and it is still functioning correctly. You call the customer and tell her that you have fixed the situation and she can come and pick it up the next day. Then you shut the system off and eventually leave work.

The next day the customer comes in, and when you demonstrate that you have fixed the problem, you see the invalid system disk message again.

- What do you suspect the problem is?

- How long will it probably take you to fix it?

3. A customer brings in a computer. The customer was trying to install a new U. S. Robotics modem, but the modem will not work, even after trying several different ways to install the drivers for the new modem. When you boot and check Device Manager, you see two instances of U.S. Robotics modems, neither of which are functioning correctly. You also see one instance of a modem made by Creative Labs, which is reportedly functioning correctly. When you physically check the modem card, only the U.S. Robotics modem is present in the computer.

- What is the source of the problem?

■ What steps would you take to install the U.S. Robotics modem?

_____

_____

_____

_____

_____

4. A customer brings in a computer with a new external modem and says that the computer is working fine but that the modem does not work. The customer wants you to get the modem to work with his computer. The customer says he tried attaching the external modem on both serial ports but to no avail. You decide to test the modem on a separate system and you find that it functions correctly. On the customer's computer, you check the Ports Group in Device Manager and only the parallel port is present.

■ What is likely the problem?

_____

■ What will you do to correct it?

_____

_____

5. A customer brings in a system and claims that it does not work after a thunderstorm. You open the case and immediately notice a burning smell. You test each component in a test system and find no functional components. You call and report the sad news to the customer. The customer is upset about the system but even more upset about the loss of important information on the hard drive for which he has no backup.

■ What information or recommendation can you give the customer about what he can do now and what he should do in the future to safeguard important data?

_____

_____

_____

_____

- What advice can you give the customer about protecting his hardware?

_____

_____

_____

6. A customer wanted to upgrade his processor to a faster one. He checked with the motherboard manufacturer and discovered that his motherboard supports a faster processor. When the client installed the new processor, the system booted and the POST reported that the processor is only running at two-thirds of its potential. Windows works and the computer functions normally but at a slower clock speed.

- What is the likely problem?

_____

- How would you solve the problem?

_____

Review Questions

1. How could a properly functioning hard drive, which is recognized by BIOS, fail to show up in Windows?

_____

_____

2. What device maintains CMOS settings even if the computer is totally unplugged from AC power?

_____

3. What Control Panel applet will let the inexperienced user forcibly install an incorrect device or non-existent device? What Windows feature will let you remove devices?

_____

_____

4. Suppose that the COM ports were enabled in BIOS. How could they be disabled in Windows, thereby preventing a modem from using a COM port?

_____

_____

_____

5. How, besides coming in through the roof and directly striking the computer, might lightning destroy a computer?

LAB 24.5 CRITICAL THINKING: UPDATE MOTHERBOARD DRIVERS

Objectives

The goal of this lab is to help you update the drivers for motherboard components. After completing this lab, you will be able to:

➤ Identify a motherboard and its embedded devices

➤ Search a motherboard's manufacturer's Web site for updated drivers

➤ Download all applicable drivers for a motherboard

➤ Install drivers

➤ Document the process of updating motherboard drivers

Materials Required

This lab will require the following:

➤ Windows 98 or Windows 2000/XP operating system

➤ Motherboard documentation or SANDRA software installed in Lab 1.3

➤ Internet access

➤ PC toolkit with ground strap (if necessary)

➤ Blank floppy disk (if necessary)

Activity Background

Like other devices, components on the motherboard use drivers to interact with the operating system. These drivers may be updated from time to time to resolve newly discovered bugs or to conform to newly implemented industry standards. However, know that if the motherboard is working properly and performance is acceptable, you should not update the drivers because, when doing so, you might introduce new problems. In this lab, you will use your experience researching and installing drivers to install all available drivers for the components embedded on your motherboard.

Estimated completion time: **90 minutes**

ACTIVITY

1. Using procedures learned in previous labs, provide information below:
   ■ Motherboard manufacturer:

24

■ Motherboard model:

_____

2. Using procedures learned in previous labs, identify the components on your motherboard and record the information in Table 24-1. In the Included? column, enter Yes or No for whether a component is included on the motherboard. Enter the version number of each component, if you have that information.

Table 24-1

Component	Included?	Version number (if available)
CPU type		
Chip set		
IDE controller		
AGP controller		
Embedded audio		
Embedded NIC/LAN		
Embedded modem		
Embedded video		
Other		
Other		

3. Research the motherboard manufacturer's Web site for driver updates and documentation for performing the updates.

4. Download any necessary files, including any documentation. List the files you downloaded and the purpose of each file in Table 24-2.

Table 24-2

Downloaded file	Purpose of the file

5. Print any documentation describing how to perform the updates.

6. Update the drivers.

7. Briefly explain how you updated the drivers.

_____

_____

_____

_____

_____

Review Questions

1. What is an embedded device?

_____

_____

2. If your motherboard documentation covers different models of motherboards, some with more embedded components than others, how can you definitely determine which model is installed in your computer?

_____

_____

3. What embedded device controls non-SCSI hard drives?

_____

4. If you connect your monitor to a PCI video card in an expansion slot, would downloading and installing drivers for embedded video or for an AGP controller likely resolve any problems related to video performance? Explain.

_____

_____

_____

5. Why would you want to update motherboard drivers? Give two reasons.

_____

_____

6. When would you not want to update the motherboard drivers?

_____

_____

GLOSSARY

This glossary defines terms related to managing and maintaining a personal computer.

100BaseT — An Ethernet standard that operates at 100 Mbps and uses STP cabling. *Also called* Fast Ethernet. Variations of 100BaseT are 100BaseTX and 100BaseFX.

10Base2 — An Ethernet standard that operates at 10 Mbps and uses small coaxial cable up to 200 meters long. *Also called* ThinNet.

10Base5 — An Ethernet standard that operates at 10 Mbps and uses thick coaxial cable up to 500 meters long. *Also called* ThickNet.

80 conductor IDE cable — An IDE cable that has 40 pins but uses 80 wires, 40 of which are ground wires designed to reduce crosstalk on the cable. The cable is used by ATA/66, ATA/100, and ATA/133 IDE drives.

802.11b — *See* IEEE 802.11b.

access point (AP) — A device connected to a LAN that provides wireless communication so that computers, printers, and other wireless devices can communicate with devices on the LAN.

ACPI (Advanced Configuration and Power Interface) — Specification developed by Intel, Compaq, Phoenix, Microsoft, and Toshiba to control power on notebooks and other devices. Windows 98 and Windows 2000/XP support ACPI.

active matrix — A type of video display that amplifies the signal at every intersection in the grid of electrodes, which enhances the pixel quality over that of a dual-scan passive matrix display.

active partition — The primary partition on the hard drive that boots the OS. Windows NT/2000/XP calls the active partition the "system partition."

active terminator — A type of terminator for single-ended SCSI cables that includes voltage regulators in addition to the simple resistors used with passive termination.

adapter address — *See* MAC address.

adapter card — A small circuit board inserted in an expansion slot used to communicate between the system bus and a peripheral device. *Also called* an interface card.

administrator account — In Windows NT/2000/XP, an account that grants to the administrator(s) rights and permissions to all hardware and software resources, such as the right to add, delete, and change accounts and to change hardware configurations.

Advanced Options menu — A Windows 2000/XP menu that appears when you press F8 when Windows starts. The menu can be used to troubleshoot problems when loading Windows 2000/XP.

Advanced SCSI Programming Interface (ASPI) — A popular device driver that enables operating systems to communicate with a SCSI host adapter. (The "A" originally stood for Adaptec.)

Advanced Transfer Cache (ATC) — A type of L2 cache contained within the Pentium processor housing that is embedded on the same core processor die as the CPU itself.

AirPort — The term Apple computers use to describe the IEEE 802.11b standard.

alternating current (AC) — Current that cycles back and forth rather than traveling in only one direction. In the United States, the AC voltage from a standard wall outlet is normally between 110 and 115 V. In Europe, the standard AC voltage from a wall outlet is 220 V.

ammeter — A meter that measures electrical current in amps.

ampere or **amp (A)** — A unit of measurement for electrical current. One volt across a resistance of one ohm will produce a flow of one amp.

antivirus (AV) software — Utility programs that prevent infection or scan a system to detect and remove viruses. McAfee Associates' VirusScan and Norton AntiVirus are two popular AV packages.

ASCII (American Standard Code for Information Interchange) — A popular standard for writing letters and other characters in binary code. Originally, ASCII characters were seven bits, so there were 127 possible values. ASCII has been expanded to an 8-bit version, allowing 128 additional values.

AT — A form factor, generally no longer produced, in which the motherboard requires a full-size case. Because of their dimensions and configuration, AT systems are difficult to install, service, and upgrade. *Also called* full AT.

AT command set — A set of commands that a PC uses to control a modem and that a user can enter to troubleshoot the modem.

ATAPI (Advanced Technology Attachment Packet Interface) — An interface standard, part of the IDE/ATA standards, that allows tape drives, CD-ROM drives, and other drives to be treated like an IDE hard drive by the system.

ATX — The most common form factor for PC systems presently in use, originally introduced by Intel in 1995. ATX motherboards and cases make better use of space and resources than did the AT form factor.

autodetection — A feature on newer system BIOS and hard drives that automatically identifies and configures a new drive in the CMOS setup.

Autoexec.bat — A startup text file once used by DOS and used by Windows to provide backward-compatibility. It executes commands automatically during the boot process and is used to create a 16-bit environment.

Automated System Recovery (ASR) — The Windows XP process that allows you to restore an entire hard drive volume or logical drive to its state at the time the backup of the volume was made.

Automatic Private IP Address (APIPA) — An IP address in the address range 169.254.x.x, used by a computer when it cannot successfully lease an IP address from a DHCP server.

autorange meter — A multimeter that senses the quantity of input and sets the range accordingly.

Baby AT — An improved and more flexible version of the AT form factor. Baby AT was the industry standard from approximately 1993 to 1997 and can fit into some ATX cases.

backup — An extra copy of a file, used in the event that the original becomes damaged or destroyed.

bandwidth — In relation to analog communication, the range of frequencies that a communications channel or cable can carry. In general use, the term refers to the volume of data that can travel on a bus or over a cable stated in bits per second (bps), kilobits per second (Kbps), or megabits per second (Mbps). *Also called* data throughput or line speed.

bank — An area on the motherboard that contains slots for memory modules (typically labeled bank 0, 1, 2, and 3).

baseline — The level of performance expected from a system, which can be compared to current measurements to determine what needs upgrading or tuning.

basic disk — A way to partition a hard drive, used by DOS and all versions of Windows, that stores information about the drive in a partition table at the beginning of the drive. *Compare to* dynamic disk.

batch file — A text file containing a series of OS commands. Autoexec.bat is a batch file.

binary number system — The number system used by computers; it has only two numbers, 0 and 1, called binary digits, or bits.

binding — The process by which a protocol is associated with a network card or a modem card.

BIOS (basic input/output system) — Firmware that can control much of a computer's input/output functions, such as communication with the floppy drive and the monitor. *Also called* ROM BIOS.

bit (binary digit) — A 0 or 1 used by the binary number system.

bits per second (bps) — A measure of data transmission speed. For example, a common modem speed is 56,000 bps, or 56 Kbps.

blue screen — A Windows NT/2000/XP error that displays against a blue screen and causes the system to halt. *Also called* a stop error.

Bluetooth — A standard for wireless communication and data synchronization between devices, developed by a group of electronics manufacturers and overseen by the Bluetooth Special Interest Group. Bluetooth uses the same frequency range as IEEE 802.11b but does not have as wide a range.

BNC connector — A connector used with thin coaxial cable. Some BNC connectors are T-shaped and called T-connectors. One end of the T connects to the NIC, and the two other ends can connect to cables or end a bus formation with a terminator.

boot loader menu — A startup menu that gives the user the choice of which operating system to load such as Windows 98 or Windows XP, which are both installed on the same system, creating a dual boot.

boot partition — The hard drive partition where the Windows NT/2000/XP OS is stored. The system partition and the boot partition may be different partitions.

boot record — The first sector of a floppy disk or logical drive in a partition; it contains information about the disk or logical drive. On a hard drive, if the boot record is in the active partition, then it is used to boot the OS. *Also called* boot sector.

boot sector — *See* boot record.

boot sector virus — An infectious program that can replace the boot program with a modified, infected version of the boot command utilities, often causing boot and data retrieval problems.

Boot.ini — A Windows NT/2000/XP hidden text file that contains information needed to build the boot loader menu.

bootable disk — For DOS and Windows, a floppy disk that can upload the OS files necessary for computer startup. For DOS or Windows 9x, it must contain the files Io.sys, Msdos.sys, and Command.com.

bootstrap loader — A small program at the end of the boot record that can be used to boot an OS from the disk or logical drive.

broadband — A transmission technique that carries more than one type of transmission on the same medium, such as cable modem or DSL.

brownouts — Temporary reductions in voltage, which can sometimes cause data loss.

buffer — A temporary memory area where data is kept before being written to a hard drive or sent to a printer, thus reducing the number of writes to the devices.

bus — The paths, or lines, on the motherboard on which data, instructions, and electrical power move from component to component.

bus speed — The speed, or frequency, at which the data on the motherboard is moving.

byte — A collection of eight bits that is equivalent to a single character. When referring to system memory, an additional error-checking bit might be added, making the total nine bits.

cabinet file — A file with a .cab extension that contains one or more compressed files and is often used to distribute software on disk. The Extract command is used to extract files from the cabinet file.

cable modem — A technology that uses cable TV lines for data transmission, requiring a modem at each end. From the modem, a network cable connects to a NIC in the user's PC.

capacitor — An electronic device that can maintain an electrical charge for a period of time and is used to smooth out the flow of electrical current. Capacitors are often found in computer power supplies.

CardBus — The latest PCMCIA specification. It improves I/O speed, increases the bus width to 32 bits, and supports lower-voltage PC Cards, while maintaining backward compatibility with earlier standards.

cards — Adapter boards or interface cards placed into expansion slots to expand the functions of a computer, allowing it to communicate with external devices such as monitors or speakers.

carrier — A signal used to activate a phone line to confirm a continuous frequency; used to indicate that two computers are ready to receive or transmit data through modems.

CCITT (Comité Consultatif International Télégraphique et Téléphonique) — An international organization that was responsible for developing standards for international communications. This organization has been incorporated into the ITU. *See also* ITU.

CD (change directory) command — A command given at the command prompt that changes the default directory, for example CD \Windows.

CDFS (Compact Disc File System) — The 32-bit file system for CD discs and some CD-R and CD-RW discs that replaced the older 16-bit mscdex file system used by DOS. *See also* Universal Disk Format (UDF).

CD-R (CD-recordable) — A CD drive that can record or write data to a CD. The drive may or may not be multisession, but the data cannot be erased once it is written.

CD-RW (CD-rewritable) — A CD drive that can record or write data to a CD. The data can be erased and overwritten. The drive may or may not be multisession.

central processing unit (CPU) — The heart and brain of the computer, which receives data input, processes information, and executes instructions. *Also called* a microprocessor or processor.

chain — A group of clusters used to hold a single file.

child directory — *See* subdirectory.

chip creep — A condition in which chips loosen because of thermal changes.

chip set — A group of chips on the motherboard that controls the timing and flow of data and instructions to and from the CPU.

CHS (cylinder, head, sector) mode — The traditional method by which BIOS reads from and writes to hard drives by addressing the correct cylinder, head, and sector. *Also called* normal mode.

circuit board — A computer component, such as the main motherboard or an adapter board, that has electronic circuits and chips.

clean install — An installation of an OS on a new hard drive or on a hard drive that has a previous OS installed, but without carrying forward any settings kept by the old OS, including information about hardware, software, or user preferences. A fresh installation.

client/server — A computer concept whereby one computer (the client) requests information from another computer (the server).

client/server application — An application that has two components. The client software requests data from the server software on the same or another computer.

clock speed — The speed, or frequency, expressed in MHz, that controls activity on the motherboard and is generated by a crystal or oscillator located somewhere on the motherboard.

clone — A computer that is a no-name Intel- and Microsoft-compatible PC.

cluster — One or more sectors that constitute the smallest unit of space on a disk for storing data. Files are written to a disk as groups of whole clusters. *Also called* a file allocation unit.

CMOS (complementary metal-oxide semiconductor) — The technology used to manufacture microchips. CMOS chips require less electricity, hold data longer after the electricity is turned off, are slower, and produce less heat than TTL chips. The configuration, or setup, chip is a CMOS chip.

CMOS configuration chip — A chip on the motherboard that contains a very small amount of memory, or RAM—enough to hold configuration, or setup, information about the computer. The chip is powered by a battery when the PC is turned off. *Also called* CMOS setup chip or CMOS RAM chip.

CMOS setup — (1) The CMOS configuration chip. (2) The program in system BIOS that can change the values in the CMOS RAM.

CMOS setup chip — *See* CMOS configuration chip.

coaxial cable — Networking cable used with 10-Mbps Ethernet ThinNet or ThickNet.

cold boot — *See* hard boot.

combo card — An Ethernet card that contains more than one transceiver, each with a different port on the back of the card, to accommodate different cabling media.

Command.com — Along with Msdos.sys and Io.sys, one of the three files that are the core components of the real-mode portion of Windows 9x. Command.com provides a command prompt and interprets commands.

comment — A line or part of a line in a program that is intended as a remark or comment and is ignored when the program runs. A semicolon or an REM is often used to mark a line as a comment.

compact case — A type of case used in low-end desktop systems. Compact cases follow either the NLX, LPX, or Mini LPX form factor. They are likely to have fewer drive bays, but they generally still provide for some expansion. *Also called* low-profile or slimline cases.

compressed drive — A drive whose format has been reorganized to store more data. A compressed drive is really not a drive at all; it's actually a type of file, typically with a host drive called H.

computer name — Character-based host name or NetBIOS name assigned to a computer.

Config.sys — A text file used by DOS and supported by Windows 9x that lists device drivers to be loaded at startup. It can also set system variables to be used by DOS and Windows.

console — A centralized location from which to execute commonly used tools.

continuity — A continuous, unbroken path for the flow of electricity. A continuity test can determine whether internal wiring is still intact, or whether a fuse is good or bad.

conventional memory — Memory addresses between 0 and 640K. *Also called* base memory.

cooler — A combination cooling fan and heat sink mounted on the top or side of a processor to keep it cool.

C-RIMM (Continuity RIMM) — A placeholder RIMM module that provides continuity so that every RIMM slot is filled.

cross-linked clusters — Errors caused when more than one file points to a cluster, and the files appear to share the same disk space, according to the file allocation table.

crossover cable — A cable used to connect two PCs into the simplest network possible. Also used to connect two hubs.

CVF (compressed volume file) — The file on the host drive of a compressed drive that holds all compressed data.

data bus — The lines on the system bus that the CPU uses to send and receive data.

data cartridge — A type of tape medium typically used for backups. Full-sized data cartridges are $4 \times 6 \times \frac{3}{8}$ inches in size. A minicartridge is only $3\frac{1}{4} \times 2\frac{1}{2} \times \frac{3}{8}$ inches in size.

data line protector — A surge protector designed to work with the telephone line to a modem.

data path size — The number of lines on a bus that can hold data, for example, 8, 16, 32, and 64 lines, which can accommodate 8, 16, 32, and 64 bits at a time.

data throughput — *See* bandwidth.

DC controller — A card inside a notebook that converts voltage to CPU voltage. Some notebook manufacturers consider the card to be an FRU.

DCE (Data Communications Equipment) — The hardware, usually a dial-up modem, that provides the connection between a data terminal and a communications line. *See also* DTE.

default gateway — The gateway a computer on a network will use to access another network unless it knows to specifically use another gateway for quicker access to that network.

default printer — The printer Windows prints to unless another printer is selected.

defragment — To "optimize" or rewrite a file to a disk in one contiguous chain of clusters, thus speeding up data retrieval.

desktop — The initial screen that is displayed when an OS has a GUI interface loaded.

device driver — A program stored on the hard drive that tells the computer how to communicate with an input/output device such as a printer or modem.

DHCP (Dynamic Host Configuration Protocol) server — A service that assigns dynamic IP addresses to computers on a network when they first access the network.

diagnostic cards — Adapter cards designed to discover and report computer errors and conflicts at POST time (before the computer boots up), often by displaying a number on the card.

diagnostic software — Utility programs that help troubleshoot computer systems. Some Windows diagnostic utilities are CHKDSK and SCANDISK. PC-Technician is an example of a third-party diagnostic program.

dial-up networking — A Windows 9x and Windows NT/2000/XP utility that uses a modem and telephone line to connect to a network.

differential cable — A SCSI cable in which a signal is carried on two wires, each carrying voltage, and the signal is the difference between the two. Differential signaling provides for error checking and greater data integrity. *Compare to* single-ended cable.

digital certificate — A code used to authenticate the source of a file or document or to identify and authenticate a person or organization sending data over the Internet. The code is assigned by a certificate authority such as VeriSign and includes a public key for encryption. *Also called* digital ID or digital signature.

digital ID — *See* digital certificate.

digital signature — *See* digital certificate.

DIMM (dual inline memory module) — A miniature circuit board used in newer computers to hold memory. DIMMs can hold up to 2 GB of RAM on a single module.

DIP (dual inline package) switch — A switch on a circuit board or other device that can be set on or off to hold configuration or setup information.

direct current (DC) — Current that travels in only one direction (the type of electricity provided by batteries). Computer power supplies transform AC to low DC.

Direct Rambus DRAM — A memory technology by Rambus and Intel that uses a narrow, very fast network-type system bus. Memory is stored on a RIMM module. *Also called* RDRAM or Direct RDRAM.

Direct RDRAM — *See* Direct Rambus DRAM.

directory table — An OS table that contains file information such as the name, size, time, and date of last modification, and cluster number of the file's beginning location.

disk cache — A method whereby recently retrieved data and adjacent data are read into memory in advance, anticipating the next CPU request.

disk cloning — *See* drive imaging.

disk compression — Compressing data on a hard drive to allow more data to be written to the drive.

disk imaging — *See* drive imaging.

Disk Management — A Windows 2000/XP utility used to display, create, and format partitions on basic disks and volumes on dynamic disks.

disk quota — A limit placed on the amount of disk space that is available to users. Requires a Windows 2000/XP NTFS volume.

disk thrashing — A condition that results when the hard drive is excessively used for virtual memory because RAM is full. It dramatically slows down processing and can cause premature hard drive failure.

Display Power Management Signaling (DPMS) — Energy Star standard specifications that allow for the video card and monitor to go into sleep mode simultaneously. *See also* Energy Star.

DMA (direct memory access) channel — A number identifying a channel whereby a device can pass data to memory without involving the CPU. Think of a DMA channel as a shortcut for data moving to/from the device and memory.

DMA transfer mode — A transfer mode used by devices, including the hard drive, to transfer data to memory without involving the CPU.

DNS server — A computer that can find an IP address for another computer when only the domain name is known.

docking station — A device that receives a notebook computer and provides additional secondary storage and easy connection to peripheral devices.

domain — In Windows NT/2000/XP, a logical group of networked computers, such as those on a college campus, that share a centralized directory database of user account information and security for the entire domain.

domain controller — A Windows NT/2000 computer that holds and controls a database of (1) user accounts, (2) group accounts, and (3) computer accounts used to manage access to the network.

domain name — A unique, text-based name that identifies a network.

DOS box — A command window.

Dosstart.bat — A type of Autoexec.bat file that is executed by Windows 9x in two situations: when you select Restart the computer in MS-DOS mode from the shutdown menu or when you run a program in MS-DOS mode.

dot pitch — The distance between the dots that the electronic beam hits on a monitor screen.

Double Data Rate SDRAM (DDR SDRAM) — A type of memory technology used on DIMMs that runs at twice the speed of the system clock.

doze time — The time before an Energy Star or "Green" system will reduce 80 percent of its activity.

Dr. Watson — A Windows utility that can record detailed information about the system, errors that occur, and the programs that caused them in a log file. Windows 9x names the log file \Windows\ Drwatson\WatsonXX.wlg, where XX is an incrementing number. Windows 2000 names the file \Documents and Settings\user\Documents\ DrWatson\Drwtsn32.log. Windows XP calls the file Drwatson.log.

drive imaging — Making an exact image of a hard drive, including partition information, boot sectors, operating system installation, and application software to replicate the hard drive on another system or recover from a hard drive crash. *Also called* disk cloning and disk imaging.

drop height — The height from which a manufacturer states that its drive can be dropped without making the drive unusable.

DSL (Digital Subscriber Line) — A telephone line that carries digital data from end to end and can be leased from the telephone company for individual use. DSL lines are rated at 5 Mbps, about 50 times faster than regular telephone lines.

DTE (Data Terminal Equipment) — Both the computer and a remote terminal or other computer to which it is attached. *See also* DCE.

dual boot — The ability to boot using either of two different OSs, such as Windows 98 and Windows XP.

dual-scan passive matrix — A type of video display that is less expensive than an active-matrix display and does not provide as high-quality an image. With dual-scan display, two columns of electrodes are activated at the same time.

dual-voltage CPU — A CPU that requires two different voltages, one for internal processing and the other for I/O processing.

DVD (digital video disc or **digital versatile disk)** — A faster, larger CD format that can read older CDs, store over 8 GB of data, and hold full-length motion picture videos.

dynamic disk — A way to partition one or more hard drives, introduced with Windows 2000, in which information about the drive is stored in a database at the end of the drive. *Compare to* basic disk.

dynamic IP address — An assigned IP address that is used for the current session only. When the session is terminated, the IP address is returned to the list of available addresses.

dynamic RAM (DRAM) — The most common type of system memory, it requires refreshing every few milliseconds.

dynamic volume — A volume type used with dynamic disks for which you can change the size of the volume after you have created it.

ECC (error-correcting code) — A chip set feature on a motherboard that checks the integrity of data stored on DIMMs or RIMMs and can correct single-bit errors in a byte. More advanced ECC schemas can detect, but not correct, double-bit errors in a byte.

ECHS (extended CHS) mode — *See* large mode.

ECP (Extended Capabilities Port) — A bidirectional parallel port mode that uses a DMA channel to speed up data flow.

EDO (extended data out) — A type of RAM that can be 10 to 20 percent faster than conventional RAM because it eliminates the delay before it issues the next memory address.

EEPROM (electrically erasable programmable ROM) — A type of chip in which higher voltage may be applied to one of the pins to erase its previous memory before a new instruction set is electronically written.

EIDE (Enhanced IDE) — A standard for managing the interface between secondary storage devices and a computer system. A system can support up to six serial ATA and parallel ATA EIDE devices or up to four parallel ATA IDE devices such as hard drives, CD-ROM drives, and Zip drives.

electromagnetic interference (EMI) — A magnetic field produced as a side effect from the flow of electricity. EMI can cause corrupted data in data lines that are not properly shielded.

electrostatic discharge (ESD) — Another name for static electricity, which can damage chips and destroy motherboards, even though it might not be felt or seen with the naked eye.

Emergency Repair Disk (ERD) — A Windows NT record of critical information about your system that can be used to fix a problem with the OS. The ERD enables restoration of the Windows NT registry on your hard drive.

Emergency Repair Process — A Windows 2000 process that restores the OS to its state at the completion of a successful installation.

emergency startup disk (ESD) — *See* rescue disk.

Emm386.exe — A DOS and Windows 9x utility that provides access to upper memory for 16-bit device drivers and other software.

Encrypted File System (EFS) — A way to use a key to encode a file or folder on an NTFS volume to protect sensitive data. Because it is an integrated system service, EFS is transparent to users and applications and is difficult to attack.

encryption — The process of putting readable data into an encoded form that can only be decoded (or decrypted) through use of a key.

Energy Star — "Green" systems that satisfy the EPA requirements to decrease the overall consumption of electricity. *See also* Green Standards.

enhanced BIOS — A system BIOS that has been written to accommodate large-capacity drives (over 504 MB, usually in the gigabyte range).

EPP (Enhanced Parallel Port) — A parallel port that allows data to flow in both directions (bidirectional port) and is faster than original parallel ports on PCs that allowed communication only in one direction.

EPROM (erasable programmable ROM) — A type of chip with a special window that allows the current memory contents to be erased with special ultraviolet light so that the chip can be reprogrammed. Many BIOS chips are EPROMs.

error correction — The ability of a modem to identify transmission errors and then automatically request another transmission.

Ethernet — The most popular LAN architecture that can run at 10 Mbps (ThinNet or ThickNet), 100 Mbps (Fast Ethernet), or 1 Gbps (Gigabit Ethernet).

expansion bus — A bus that does not run in sync with the system clock.

expansion card — A circuit board inserted into a slot on the motherboard to enhance the capability of the computer.

expansion slot — A narrow slot on the motherboard where an expansion card can be inserted. Expansion slots connect to a bus on the motherboard.

extended memory — Memory above 1024K used in a DOS or Windows 9x system.

extended partition — The only partition on a hard drive that can contain more than one logical drive.

external command — Commands that have their own program files.

faceplate — A metal plate that comes with the motherboard and fits over the ports to create a well-fitted enclosure around them.

Fast Ethernet — *See* 100BaseT.

FAT (file allocation table) — A table on a hard drive or floppy disk that tracks the clusters used to contain a file.

FAT12 — The 12-bit-wide, one-column file allocation table for a floppy disk, containing information about how each cluster or file allocation unit on the disk is currently used.

fault tolerance — The degree to which a system can tolerate failures. Adding redundant components, such as disk mirroring or disk duplexing, is a way to build in fault tolerance.

field replaceable unit (FRU) — A component in a computer or device that can be replaced with a new component without sending the computer or device back to the manufacturer. Examples: power supply, DIMM, motherboard, floppy disk drive.

file allocation unit — *See* cluster.

file extension — A three-character portion of the filename that is used to identify the file type. In command lines, the file extension follows the filename and is separated from it by a period, for example, Msd.exe, where exe is the file extension.

file system — The overall structure that an OS uses to name, store, and organize files on a disk. Examples of file systems are FAT32 and NTFS.

file virus — A virus that inserts virus code into an executable program file and can spread wherever that program is executed.

filename — The first part of the name assigned to a file. In DOS, the filename can be no more than eight characters long and is followed by the file extension. In Windows, a filename can be up to 255 characters.

firewall — Hardware or software that protects a computer or network from unauthorized access.

FireWire — *See* IEEE 1394.

firmware — Software that is permanently stored in a chip. The BIOS on a motherboard is an example of firmware.

flash ROM — ROM that can be reprogrammed or changed without replacing chips.

flat panel monitor — A desktop monitor that uses an LCD panel.

FlexATX — A version of the ATX form factor that allows for maximum flexibility in the size and shape of cases and motherboards. FlexATX is ideal for custom systems.

flow control — When using modems, a method of controlling the flow of data to adjust for problems with data transmission. Xon/Xoff is an example of a flow control protocol.

folder — *See* subdirectory.

forced perfect terminator (FPT) — A type of SCSI active terminator that includes a mechanism to force signal termination to the correct voltage, eliminating most signal echoes and interference.

forgotten password floppy disk — A Windows XP disk created to be used in the event the user forgets the user account password to the system.

form factor — A set of specifications on the size, shape, and configuration of a computer hardware component such as a case, power supply, or motherboard.

formatting — Preparing a hard drive volume or floppy disk for use by placing tracks and sectors on its surface to store information (for example, FORMAT A:).

fragmentation — The distribution of data files on a hard drive or floppy disk such that they are stored in noncontiguous clusters.

fragmented file — A file that has been written to different portions of the disk so that it is not in contiguous clusters.

FTP (File Transfer Protocol) — The protocol used to transfer files over a TCP/IP network such that the file does not need to be converted to ASCII format before transferring it.

full AT — *See* AT.

fully qualified domain name (FQDN) — A host name and a domain name such as *jsmith.amazon.com*. Sometimes loosely referred to as a domain name.

gateway — A computer or other device that connects networks.

GDI (Graphics Device Interface) — A Windows 9x component that controls screens, graphics, and printing.

General Protection Fault (GPF) — A Windows error that occurs when a program attempts to access a memory address that is not available or is no longer assigned to it.

Gigabit Ethernet — The newest version of Ethernet. Gigabit Ethernet supports rates of data transfer up to 1 gigabit per second but is not yet widely used.

gigahertz (GHz) — One thousand MHz, or one billion cycles per second.

global user account — Sometimes called a domain user account, the account is used at the domain level, created by an administrator, and stored in the SAM (security accounts manager) database on a Windows 2000 or Windows 2003 domain controller.

graphics accelerator — A type of video card that has an on-board processor that can substantially increase speed and boost graphical and video performance.

Green Standards — A computer or device that conforms to these standards can go into sleep or doze mode when not in use, thus saving energy and helping the environment. Devices that carry the Green Star or Energy Star comply with these standards.

ground bracelet — A strap you wear around your wrist that is attached to the computer case, ground mat, or another ground so that ESD is discharged from your body before you touch sensitive components inside a computer. *Also called* static strap, ground strap, or ESD bracelet.

group profile — A group of user profiles. All profiles in the group can be changed by changing the group profile.

guard tone — A tone that an answering modem sends when it first answers the phone, to tell the calling modem that a modem is on the other end of the line.

Guest user — A user who has limited permissions on a system and cannot make changes to it. Guest user accounts are intended for one-time or infrequent users of a workstation.

handshaking — When two modems begin to communicate, the initial agreement made as to how to send and receive data.

hard boot — Restart the computer by turning off the power or by pressing the Reset button. *Also called* a cold boot.

hard copy — Output from a printer to paper.

hard drive — The main secondary storage device of a PC, a small case that contains magnetic coated platters that rotate at high speed.

hard drive controller — The firmware on a circuit board mounted on or inside the hard drive housing that controls access to a hard drive. Older hard drives used firmware on a controller card that connected to the drive by way of two cables, one for data and one for control.

hard drive standby time — The amount of time before a hard drive shuts down to conserve energy.

hardware — The physical components that constitute the computer system, such as the monitor, the keyboard, the motherboard, and the printer.

hardware address — *See* MAC address.

hardware cache — A disk cache that is contained in RAM chips built right on the disk controller. *Also called* a buffer.

hardware interrupt — An event caused by a hardware device signaling the CPU that it requires service.

hardware profile — A set of hardware configuration information that Windows keeps in the registry. Windows can maintain more than one hardware profile for the same PC.

HCL (hardware compatibility list) — The list of all computers and peripheral devices that have been tested and are officially supported by Windows NT/2000/XP (see *www.microsoft.com/whdc/hcl/default.mspx*).

HD-DVD (high-density or **high-definition DVD)** — A new DVD standard that supports high-definition video encoding using blue or violet lasers. HD-DVD discs cannot be read by regular DVD drives.

head — The top or bottom surface of one platter on a hard drive. Each platter has two heads.

heat sink — A piece of metal, with cooling fins, that can be attached to or mounted on an integrated chip (such as the CPU) to dissipate heat.

hertz (Hz) — Unit of measurement for frequency, calculated in terms of vibrations, or cycles per second. For example, for 16-bit stereo sound, a frequency of 44,000 Hz is used. *See also* megahertz.

hexadecimal notation (hex) — A numbering system that uses 16 digits, the numerals 0-9, and the letters A-F. Hexadecimal notation is often used to display memory addresses.

hibernation — A notebook OS feature that conserves power by using a small trickle of electricity. Before the notebook begins to hibernate, everything currently stored in memory is saved to the hard drive. When the notebook is brought out of hibernation, open applications and their data are returned to their state before hibernation.

hidden file — A file that is not displayed in a directory list. Whether to hide or display a file is one of the file's attributes kept by the OS.

high memory area (HMA) — The first 64K of extended memory.

High Voltage Differential (HVD) — A type of SCSI differential signaling requiring more expensive hardware to handle the higher voltage. HVD became obsolete with the introduction of SCSI-3.

high-level formatting — Formatting performed by means of the DOS or Windows Format program (for example, FORMAT C:/S creates the boot record, FAT, and root directory on drive C and makes the drive bootable). *Also called* operating system formatting.

Himem.sys — The DOS and Windows 9x memory manager extension that allows access to memory addresses above 1 MB.

hive — Physical segment of the Windows NT/2000/XP registry that is stored in a file.

host — Any computer or other device on a network that has been assigned an IP address. *Also called* node.

host adapter — The circuit board that controls a SCSI bus supporting as many as seven or 15 separate devices. The host adapter controls communication between the SCSI bus and the PC.

host bus — *See* system bus.

host drive — Typically drive H on a compressed drive. *See* compressed drive.

host name — A name that identifies a computer, printer, or other device on a network.

hot-pluggable — *See* hot-swappable.

hot-swappable — A device that can be plugged into a computer while it is turned on and the computer will sense the device and configure it without rebooting, or the device can be removed without an OS error. *Also called* hot-pluggable.

HTML (HyperText Markup Language) — A markup language used for hypertext documents on the World Wide Web. This language uses tags to format the document, create hyperlinks, and mark locations for graphics.

HTTP (HyperText Transfer Protocol) — The protocol used by the World Wide Web.

HTTPS (HTTP secure) — A version of the HTTP protocol that includes data encryption for security.

hub — A network device or box that provides a central location to connect cables.

hypertext — Text that contains links to remote points in the document or to other files, documents, or graphics. Hypertext is created using HTML and is commonly distributed from Web sites.

i.Link — *See* IEEE 1394.

I/O addresses — Numbers that are used by devices and the CPU to manage communication between them. *Also called* ports or port addresses.

I/O controller card — An older card that can contain serial, parallel, and game ports and floppy drive and IDE connectors.

IBM-compatible PC — A computer that uses an Intel (or compatible) processor and can run DOS and Windows.

IDE (Integrated Drive Electronics or **Integrated Device Electronics)** — A hard drive whose disk controller is integrated into the drive, eliminating the need for a controller cable and thus increasing speed as well as reducing price. *See also* EIDE.

IEEE 1284 — A standard for parallel ports and cables developed by the Institute for Electrical and Electronics Engineers and supported by many hardware manufacturers.

IEEE 1394 — Standards for an expansion bus that can also be configured to work as a local bus. It is expected to replace the SCSI bus, providing an easy method to install and configure fast I/O devices. *Also called* FireWire and i.Link.

IEEE 1394.3 — A standard, developed by the 1394 Trade Association, that is designed for peer-to-peer data transmission and allows imaging devices to send images and photos directly to printers without involving a computer.

IEEE 802.11b — An IEEE specification for wireless communication and data synchronization that competes with Bluetooth. *Also called* Wi-Fi. Apple Computer's version of 802.11b is called AirPort.

infestation — Any unwanted program that is transmitted to a computer without the user's knowledge and that is designed to do varying degrees of damage to data and software. There are a number of different types of infestations, including viruses, Trojan horses, worms, and logic bombs.

information (.inf) file — Text file with an .inf file extension, such as Msbatch.inf, that contains information about a hardware or software installation.

infrared transceiver — A wireless transceiver that uses infrared technology to support some wireless devices such as keyboards, mice, and printers. A motherboard might have an embedded infrared transceiver, or the transceiver might plug into a USB or serial port. The technology is defined by the Infrared Data Association (IrDA). *Also called* an IrDA transceiver or infrared port.

initialization files — Configuration information files for Windows. System.ini is one of the most important Windows 9x initialization files.

inkjet printer — A type of ink dispersion printer that uses cartridges of ink. The ink is heated to a boiling point and then ejected onto the paper through tiny nozzles.

Institute of Electrical and Electronics Engineers (IEEE) — A nonprofit organization that develops standards for the computer and electronics industries.

internal command — Commands that are embedded in the Command.com file.

Internet Connection Firewall (ICF) — Windows XP software designed to protect a PC from unauthorized access from the Internet.

Internet Connection Sharing (ICS) — A Windows 98 and Windows XP utility that uses NAT and acts as a proxy server to manage two or more computers connected to the Internet.

Internet service provider (ISP) — A commercial group that provides Internet access for a monthly fee. AOL, Earthlink, and CompuServe are large ISPs.

intranet — A private network that uses the TCP/IP protocols.

Io.sys — Along with Msdos.sys and Command.com, one of the three files that are the core components of the real mode portion of Windows 9x. It is the first program file of the OS.

IP address — A 32-bit address consisting of four numbers separated by periods, used to uniquely identify a device on a network that uses TCP/IP protocols. The first numbers identify the network; the last numbers identify a host. An example of an IP address is 206.96.103.114.

IrDA transceiver — *See* infrared transceiver.

IRQ (interrupt request) line — A line on a bus that is assigned to a device and is used to signal the CPU for servicing. These lines are assigned a reference number (for example, the normal IRQ for a printer is IRQ 7).

ISA (Industry Standard Architecture) slot — An older slot on the motherboard used for slower I/O devices, which can support an 8-bit or a 16-bit data path. ISA slots are mostly replaced by PCI slots.

ISDN (Integrated Services Digital Network) — A digital telephone line that can carry data at about five times the speed of regular telephone lines. Two channels (telephone numbers) share a single pair of wires.

ITU (International Telecommunications Union) — The international organization responsible for developing international standards of communication. Formerly CCITT.

JPEG (Joint Photographic Experts Group) — A graphical compression scheme that allows the user to control the amount of data that is averaged and sacrificed as file size is reduced. It is a common Internet file format. Most JPEG files have a .jpg extension.

jumper — Two wires that stick up side by side on the motherboard and are used to hold configuration information. The jumper is considered closed if a cover is over the wires and open if the cover is missing.

key — (1) In encryption, a secret number or code used to encode and decode data. (2) In Windows, a section name of the Windows registry.

keyboard — A common input device through which data and instructions may be typed into computer memory.

LAN (local area network) — A computer network that covers only a small area, usually within one building.

laptop computer — *See* notebook.

large mode — A mode of addressing information on hard drives that range from 504 MB to 8.4 GB, addressing information on a hard drive by translating cylinder, head, and sector information to break the 528-MB hard drive barrier. *Also called* ECHS mode.

large-capacity drive — A hard drive larger than 504 MB.

Last Known Good configuration — In Windows NT/2000/XP, registry settings and device drivers that were in effect when the computer last booted successfully. These settings can be restored during the startup process to recover from errors during the last boot.

LBA (logical block addressing) mode — A mode of addressing information on hard drives in which the BIOS and operating system view the drive as one long linear list of LBAs or addressable sectors, permitting drives to be larger than 8.4 GB (LBA 0 is cylinder 0, head 0, and sector 1).

Limited user — Windows XP user accounts known as Users in Windows NT/2000, which have read-write access only on their own folders, read-only access to most system folders, and no access to other users' data.

line speed — *See* bandwidth or modem speed.

LMHosts — A text file located in the Windows folder that contains NetBIOS names and their associated IP addresses. This file is used for name resolution for a NetBEUI network.

local bus — A bus that operates at a speed synchronized with the CPU frequency. The system bus is a local bus.

local I/O bus — A local bus that provides I/O devices with fast access to the CPU.

local printer — A printer connected to a computer by way of a port on the computer. *Compare to* network printer.

local profile — User profile that is stored on a local computer and cannot be accessed from another computer on the network.

local user account — A user account that applies only to a local computer and cannot be used to access resources from other computers on the network.

logical drive — A portion or all of a hard drive partition that is treated by the operating system as though it were a physical drive. Each logical drive is assigned a drive letter, such as drive C, and contains a file system. *Also called* a volume.

logical geometry — The number of heads, tracks, and sectors that the BIOS on the hard drive controller presents to the system BIOS and the OS. The logical geometry does not consist of the same values as the physical geometry, although calculations of drive capacity yield the same results.

lost allocation units — *See* lost clusters.

lost clusters — File fragments that, according to the file allocation table, contain data that does not belong to any file. The command CHKDSK/F can free these fragments. *Also called* lost allocation units.

low insertion force (LIF) socket — A socket that requires the installer to manually apply an even force over the microchip when inserting the chip into the socket.

Low Voltage Differential (LVD) — A type of differential signaling that uses lower voltage than does HVD, is less expensive, and can be compatible with single-ended signaling on the same SCSI bus.

low-level formatting — A process (usually performed at the factory) that electronically creates the hard drive tracks and sectors and tests for bad spots on the disk surface.

low-profile case — *See* compact case.

LPX — A form factor in which expansion cards are mounted on a riser card that plugs into a motherboard. The expansion cards in LPX systems are mounted parallel to the motherboard, rather than perpendicular to it as in AT and ATX systems.

MAC (Media Access Control) address — A 6-byte hexadecimal hardware address unique to each NIC card and assigned by the manufacturer. The address is often printed on the adapter. An example is 00 00 0C 08 2F 35. *Also called* a physical address, an adapter address, or a hardware address.

main board — *See* motherboard.

Master Boot Record (MBR) — The first sector on a hard drive, which contains the partition table and a program the BIOS uses to boot an OS from the drive.

material safety data sheet (MSDS) — A document that explains how to properly handle substances such as chemical solvents; it includes information such as physical data, toxicity, health effects, first aid, storage, disposal, and spill procedures.

megahertz (MHz) — One million Hz, or one million cycles per second. *See also* hertz (Hz).

memory — Physical microchips that can hold data and programming, located on the motherboard or expansion cards.

memory address — A number assigned to each byte in memory. The CPU can use memory addresses to track where information is stored in RAM. Memory addresses are usually displayed as hexadecimal numbers in segment/offset form.

memory bus — *See* system bus.

memory dump — The contents of memory saved to a file at the time an event halted the system. Support technicians can analyze the dump file to help understand the source of the problem.

memory extender — For DOS and Windows 9x, a device driver named Himem.sys that manages RAM, giving access to memory addresses above 1 MB.

memory paging — In Windows, swapping blocks of RAM memory to an area of the hard drive to serve as virtual memory when RAM is low.

memory-resident virus — A virus that can stay lurking in memory even after its host program is terminated.

microATX — A recent version of the ATX form factor. MicroATX addresses some new technologies that have been developed since the original introduction of ATX.

MicroDIMM — A type of memory module used on sub-notebooks that has 144 pins and uses a 64-bit data path.

microprocessor — *See* central processing unit (CPU).

Microsoft Management Console (MMC) — A utility to build customized consoles. These consoles can be saved to a file with an .msc file extension.

Mini PCI — The PCI industry standard for desktop computer expansion cards, applied to a much smaller form factor for notebook expansion cards.

Mini-ATX — A smaller ATX board that can be used with regular ATX cases and power supplies.

minicartridge — A tape drive cartridge that is only 3¼ × 2½ × ⅜ inches. It is small enough to allow two drives to fit into a standard 5½-inch drive bay of a PC case.

Mini-LPX — A smaller version of the LPX motherboard.

MMX (Multimedia Extensions) — Multimedia instructions built into Intel processors to add functionality such as better processing of multimedia, SIMD support, and increased cache.

modem — From MOdulate/DEModulate. A device that modulates digital data from a computer to an analog format that can be sent over telephone lines, then demodulates it back into digital form.

modem eliminator — *See* null modem cable.

modem speed — The speed at which a modem can transmit data along a phone line, measured in bits per second (bps). *Also called* bandwidth or line speed.

monitor — The most commonly used output device for displaying text and graphics on a computer.

motherboard — The main board in the computer, *also called* the main board or system board. The CPU, ROM chips, SIMMs, DIMMs, RIMMs, and interface cards are plugged into the motherboard.

motherboard bus — *See* system bus.

motherboard mouse — *See* PS/2-compatible mouse.

mouse — A pointing and input device that allows the user to move a cursor around a screen and select programs with the click of a button.

MP3 — A method to compress audio files that uses MPEG level 1. It can reduce sound files as low as a 1:24 ratio without losing much sound quality.

MPEG (Moving Pictures Experts Group) — A processing-intensive standard for data compression for motion pictures that tracks movement from one frame to the next and stores only the data that has changed.

Msdos.sys — In Windows 9x, a text file that contains settings used by Io.sys during booting. In DOS, the Msdos.sys file was a program file that contained part of the DOS core.

multicasting — A process in which a message is sent by one host to multiple hosts, such as when a video conference is broadcast to several hosts on the Internet.

multimeter — A device used to measure the various components of an electrical circuit. The most common measurements are voltage, current, and resistance.

multiplier — The factor by which the bus speed or frequency is multiplied to get the CPU clock speed.

multiscan monitor — A monitor that can work within a range of frequencies and thus can work with different standards and video cards. It offers a variety of refresh rates.

name resolution — The process of associating a NetBIOS name or host name to an IP address.

narrow SCSI — One of the two main SCSI specifications. Narrow SCSI has an 8-bit data bus. The word "narrow" is not usually included in the names of narrow SCSI devices.

NAT (Network Address Translation) — A process that converts private IP addresses on a LAN to the proxy server's IP address before a data packet is sent over the Internet.

NetBEUI (NetBIOS Extended User Interface) — A fast, proprietary Microsoft networking protocol used only by Windows-based systems, and limited to LANs because it does not support routing.

NetBIOS (Network Basic Input/Output System) — An API protocol used by some applications to communicate over a NetBEUI network. NetBIOS has largely been replaced by Windows Sockets over a TCP/IP network.

network adapter — *See* network interface card.

network drive map — Mounting a drive to a computer, such as drive E, that is actually hard drive space on another host computer on the network.

network interface card (NIC) — An expansion card that plugs into a computer's motherboard and provides a port on the back of the card to connect a PC to a network. *Also called* a network adapter.

network operating system (NOS) — An operating system that resides on the controlling computer in the network. The NOS controls what software, data, and devices a user on the network can access. Examples of an NOS are Novell Netware and Windows 2000 Server.

network printer — A printer that any user on the network can access, through its own network card and connection to the network, through a connection to a standalone print server, or through a connection to a computer as a local printer, which is shared on the network. *Compare to* local printer.

NLX — A low-end form factor that is similar to LPX but provides greater support for current and emerging processor technologies. NLX was designed for flexibility and efficiency of space.

node — *See* host.

noise — An extraneous, unwanted signal, often over an analog phone line, that can cause communication interference or transmission errors. Possible sources are fluorescent lighting, radios, TVs, lightning, or bad wiring.

nonparity memory — Eight-bit memory without error checking. A SIMM part number with a 32 in it (4 x 8 bits) is nonparity.

nonvolatile — Refers to a kind of RAM that is stable and can hold data as long as electricity is powering the memory.

normal mode — *See* CHS mode.

notebook — A portable computer that is designed for travel and mobility. Notebooks use the same technology as desktop PCs, with modifications for conserving voltage, taking up less space, and operating while on the move. *Also called* a laptop computer.

NTFS (NT file system) — The file system for the Windows NT/2000/XP operating systems. NTFS cannot be accessed by other operating systems such as DOS. It provides increased reliability and security in comparison to other methods of organizing and accessing files. There are several versions of NTFS that might be compatible.

Ntldr (NT Loader) — In Windows NT/2000/XP, the OS loader used on Intel systems.

NTVDM (NT virtual DOS machine) — An emulated environment in which a 16-bit DOS application resides within Windows NT/2000/XP with its own memory space or WOW (Win16 on Win32).

null modem cable — A cable that allows two data terminal equipment (DTE) devices to communicate in which the transmit and receive wires are cross-connected and no modems are necessary.

octet — Term for each of the four 8-bit numbers that make up an IP address. For example, the IP address 206.96.103.114 has four octets.

ohm (Ω) — The standard unit of measurement for electrical resistance. Resistors are rated in ohms.

on-board ports — Ports that are directly on the motherboard, such as a built-in keyboard port or on-board serial port.

operating system (OS) — Software that controls a computer. An OS controls how system resources are used and provides a user interface, a way of managing hardware and software, and ways to work with files.

operating system formatting — *See* high-level formatting.

P1 connector — Power connection on an ATX motherboard.

P8 connector — One of two power connectors on an AT motherboard.

P9 connector — One of two power connectors on an AT motherboard.

page fault — An OS interrupt that occurs when the OS is forced to access the hard drive to satisfy the demands for virtual memory.

page file — *See* swap file.

Pagefile.sys — The Windows NT/2000/XP swap file.

page-in — The process in which the memory manager goes to the hard drive to return the data from a swap file to RAM.

page-out — The process in which, when RAM is full, the memory manager takes a page and moves it to the swap file.

pages — 4K segments in which Windows NT/2000/XP allocates memory.

parallel ATA (PATA) — An older IDE cabling method that uses a 40-pin flat data cable or an 80-conductor cable and a 40-pin IDE connector. *See also* serial ATA.

parallel port — A female 25-pin port on a computer that can transmit data in parallel, 8 bits at a time, and is usually used with a printer. The names for parallel ports are LPT1 and LPT2.

parity — An error-checking scheme in which a ninth, or "parity," bit is added. The value of the parity bit is set to either 0 or 1 to provide an even number of ones for even parity and an odd number of ones for odd parity.

parity error — An error that occurs when the number of 1s in the byte is not in agreement with the expected number.

parity memory — Nine-bit memory in which the ninth bit is used for error checking. A SIMM part number with a 36 in it (4 × 9 bits) is parity. Older PCs almost always use parity chips.

partition — A division of a hard drive that can be used to hold logical drives.

partition table — A table at the beginning of the hard drive that contains information about each partition on the drive. The partition table is contained in the Master Boot Record.

passive terminator — A type of terminator for single-ended SCSI cables. Simple resistors are used to provide termination of a signal. Passive termination is not reliable over long distances and should only be used with narrow SCSI.

patch — An update to software that corrects an error, adds a feature, or addresses security issues. *Also called* an update or service pack.

patch cable — A network cable that is used to connect a PC to a hub.

path — (1) A drive and list of directories pointing to a file such as C:\Windows\command. (2) The OS command to provide a list of paths to the system for finding program files to execute.

PC Card — A credit-card-sized adapter card that can be slid into a slot in the side of many notebook computers and is used for connecting to modems, networks, and CD-ROM drives. *Also called* PCMCIA Card.

PC Card slot — An expansion slot on a notebook computer, into which a PC Card is inserted. *Also called* a PCMCIA Card slot.

PCI (Peripheral Component Interconnect) bus — A bus common on Pentium computers that runs at speeds of up to 33 MHz or 66 MHz, with a 32-bit-wide or 64-bit-wide data path. PCI-X, released in September 1999, enables PCI to run at 133 MHz. For some chip sets, it serves as the middle layer between the memory bus and expansion buses.

PCMCIA (Personal Computer Memory Card International Association) Card — *See* PC Card.

PCMCIA Card slot — *See* PC Card slot.

PDA (Personal Digital Assistant) — A small, hand-held computer that has its own operating system and applications.

peer-to-peer network — A network of computers that are all equals, or peers. Each computer has the same amount of authority, and each can act as a server to the other computers.

peripheral devices — Devices that communicate with the CPU but are not located directly on the motherboard, such as the monitor, floppy drive, printer, and mouse.

physical address — *See* MAC address.

physical geometry — The actual layout of heads, tracks, and sectors on a hard drive. *See also* logical geometry.

PIF (program information file) — A file used by Windows to describe the environment for a DOS program to use.

pin grid array (PGA) — A feature of a CPU socket whereby the pins are aligned in uniform rows around the socket.

Ping (Packet Internet Groper) — A Windows and Unix command used to troubleshoot network connections. It verifies that the host can communicate with another host on the network.

pinout — A description of how each pin on a bus, connection, plug, slot, or socket is used.

PIO (Programmed I/O) transfer mode — A transfer mode that uses the CPU to transfer data from the hard drive to memory. PIO mode is slower than DMA mode.

pixel — A small spot on a fine horizontal scan line. Pixels are illuminated to create an image on the monitor.

Plug and Play (PnP) — A standard designed to make the installation of new hardware devices easier by automatically configuring devices to eliminate system resource conflicts (such as IRQ or I/O address conflicts). PnP is supported by Windows 9x, Windows 2000, and Windows XP.

polling — A process by which the CPU checks the status of connected devices to determine if they are ready to send or receive data.

port — (1) As applied to services running on a computer, a number assigned to a process on a computer so that the process can be found by TCP/IP. *Also called* a port address or port number. (2) Another name for an I/O address. *See also* I/O address. (3) A physical connector, usually at the back of a computer, that allows a cable from a peripheral device, such as a printer, mouse, or modem, to be attached.

port address — *See* port or I/O addresses.

port number — *See* port.

port replicator — A device designed to connect to a notebook computer to make it easy to connect the notebook to peripheral devices.

port settings — The configuration parameters of communications devices such as COM1, COM2, or COM3, including IRQ settings.

port speed — The communication speed between a DTE (computer) and a DCE (modem). As a general rule, the port speed should be at least four times as fast as the modem speed.

POST (power-on self test) — A self-diagnostic program used to perform a simple test of the CPU, RAM, and various I/O devices. The POST is performed by startup BIOS when the computer is first turned on and is stored in ROM-BIOS.

power scheme — A feature of Windows XP support for notebooks that allows the user to create groups of power settings for specific sets of conditions.

power supply — A box inside the computer case that supplies power to the motherboard and other installed devices. Power supplies provide 3.3, 5, and 12 volts DC.

power-on password — A password that a computer uses to control access during the boot process.

primary partition — A hard disk partition that can contain only one logical drive.

primary storage — Temporary storage on the motherboard used by the CPU to process data and instructions. Memory is considered primary storage.

printer — A peripheral output device that produces printed output to paper. Different types include dot matrix, ink-jet, and laser printers.

printer maintenance kit — A kit purchased from a printer manufacturer that contains the parts, tools, and instructions needed to perform routine printer maintenance.

private IP address — An IP address that is used on a private TCP/IP network that is isolated from the Internet.

process — An executing instance of a program together with the program resources. More than one process can be running for a program at the same time. One process for a program happens each time the program is loaded into memory or executed.

processor — *See* central processing unit (CPU).

processor speed — The speed, or frequency, at which the CPU operates. Usually expressed in GHz.

product activation — The process that Microsoft uses to prevent software piracy. For example, once Windows XP is activated for a particular computer, it cannot be installed on another computer.

program — A set of step-by-step instructions to a computer. Some are burned directly into chips, whereas others are stored as program files. Programs are written in languages such as BASIC and C++.

program file — A file that contains instructions designed to be executed by the CPU.

protected mode — An operating mode that supports preemptive multitasking, the OS manages memory and other hardware devices, and programs can use a 32-bit data path. *Also called* 32-bit mode.

protocol — A set of rules and standards that two entities use for communication.

Protocol.ini — A Windows initialization file that contains network configuration information.

proxy server — A server that acts as an intermediary between another computer and the Internet. The proxy server substitutes its own IP address for the IP address of the computer on the network making a request, so that all traffic over the Internet appears to be coming from only the IP address of the proxy server.

PS/2-compatible mouse — A mouse that plugs into a round mouse PS/2 port on the motherboard. *Also called* a motherboard mouse.

public IP address — An IP address available to the Internet.

RAID (redundant array of inexpensive disks or **redundant array of independent disks)** — Several methods of configuring multiple hard drives to store data to increase logical volume size and improve performance, or to ensure that if one hard drive fails, the data is still available from another hard drive.

RAM (random access memory) — Memory modules on the motherboard containing microchips used to temporarily hold data and programs while the CPU processes both. Information in RAM is lost when the PC is turned off.

RAM drive — An area of memory that is treated as though it were a hard drive but works much faster than a hard drive. The Windows 9x startup disk uses a RAM drive. *Compare to* virtual memory.

RDRAM — *See* Direct Rambus DRAM.

read/write head — A sealed, magnetic coil device that moves across the surface of a disk either reading data from or writing data to the disk.

real mode — A single-tasking operating mode whereby a program has 1024K of memory addresses, has direct access to RAM, and uses a 16-bit data path. Using a memory extender (Himem.sys) a program in real mode can access memory above 1024K. *Also called* 16-bit mode.

Recovery Console — A Windows 2000/XP command interface utility and OS that can be used to solve problems when Windows cannot load from the hard drive.

registry — A database that Windows uses to store hardware and software configuration information, user preferences, and setup information.

re-marked chips — Chips that have been used and returned to the factory, marked again, and resold. The surface of the chips may be dull or scratched.

rescue disk — A floppy disk that can be used to start up a computer when the hard drive fails to boot. *Also called* emergency startup disk (ESD) or startup disk.

resistance — The degree to which a device opposes or resists the flow of electricity. As the electrical resistance increases, the current decreases. *See* ohm and resistor.

resistor — An electronic device that resists or opposes the flow of electricity. A resistor can be used to reduce the amount of electricity being supplied to an electronic component.

resolution — The number of pixels on a monitor screen that are addressable by software (example: 1024 x 768 pixels).

restore point — A snapshot of the Windows Me/XP system state, usually made before installation of new hardware or applications.

RIMM — A type of memory module developed by Rambus, Inc.

RJ-11 — A phone line connection found on modems, telephones, and house phone outlets.

RJ-45 connector — A connector used with twisted-pair cable that connects the cable to the NIC.

ROM (read-only memory) — Chips that contain programming code and cannot be erased.

ROM BIOS — *See* BIOS.

root directory — The main directory created when a hard drive or disk is first formatted. In Linux, it's indicated by a forward slash. In DOS and Windows, it's indicated by a backward slash.

routable protocol — A protocol that can be routed to interconnected networks on the basis of a network address. TCP/IP is a routable protocol but NetBEUI is not.

SCAM (SCSI Configuration AutoMatically) — A method of configuring SCSI device settings that follows the Plug and Play standard. SCAM makes installation of SCSI devices much easier, provided that the devices are SCAM-compliant.

SCSI (Small Computer System Interface) — A fast interface between a host adapter and the CPU that can daisy chain as many as seven or 15 devices on a single bus.

SCSI ID — A number from 0 to 15 assigned to each SCSI device attached to the daisy chain.

SDRAM II — *See* Double Data Rate SDRAM (DDR SDRAM).

secondary storage — Storage that is remote to the CPU and permanently holds data, even when the PC is turned off, such as a hard drive.

sector — On a disk surface one segment of a track, which almost always contains 512 bytes of data.

sequential access — A method of data access used by tape drives, whereby data is written or read sequentially from the beginning to the end of the tape or until the desired data is found.

serial ATA (SATA) — An ATAPI cabling method that uses a narrower and more reliable cable than the 80-conductor cable. *See also* parallel ATA.

serial ATA cable — An IDE cable that is narrower and has fewer pins than the parallel IDE 80-conductor cable.

serial mouse — A mouse that uses a serial port and has a female 9-pin DB-9 connector.

serial port — A male 9-pin or 25-pin port on a computer system used by slower I/O devices such as a mouse or modem. Data travels serially, one bit at a time, through the port. Serial ports are sometimes configured as COM1, COM2, COM3, or COM4.

service pack — *See* patch.

SFC (System File Checker) — A Windows tool that checks to make sure Windows is using the correct versions of system files.

shadow RAM or shadowing ROM — ROM programming code copied into RAM to speed up the system operation, because of the faster access speed of RAM.

shielded twisted-pair (STP) cable — A cable that is made of one or more twisted pairs of wires and is surrounded by a metal shield.

shortcut — An icon on the desktop that points to a program that can be executed or to a file or folder.

SIMM (single inline memory module) — A miniature circuit board used in older computers to hold RAM. SIMMs hold 8, 16, 32, or 64 MB on a single module.

simple volume — A type of dynamic volume used on a single hard drive that corresponds to a primary partition on a basic disk.

single-ended (SE) cable — A type of SCSI cable in which two wires are used to carry a signal, one of which carries the signal itself; the other is a ground for the signal. *Compare to* differential cable.

single-voltage CPU — A CPU that requires one voltage for both internal and I/O operations.

slack — Wasted space on a hard drive caused by not using all available space at the end of clusters.

sleep mode — A mode used in many "Green" systems that allows them to be configured through CMOS to suspend the monitor or even the drive, if the keyboard and/or CPU have been inactive for a set number of minutes. *See also* Green Standards.

slimline case — *See* compact case.

snap-ins — Components added to a console using the Microsoft Management Console.

SO-DIMM (small outline DIMM) — A type of memory module used in notebook computers that uses DIMM technology and can have either 72 pins or 144 pins.

soft boot — To restart a PC without turning off the power, for example, in Windows XP by clicking Start, Turn Off Computer, and Restart. *Also called* warm boot.

soft power — *See* soft switch.

soft switch — A feature on an ATX system that allows an OS to power down the system and allows for activity such as a keystroke or network activity to power up the system. *Also called* soft power.

software — Computer programs, or instructions to perform a specific task. Software may be BIOS, OSs, or applications software such as a word-processing or spreadsheet program.

software cache — Cache controlled by software whereby the cache is stored in RAM.

SO-RIMM (small outline RIMM) — A 160-pin memory module used in notebooks that uses Rambus technology.

spacers — *See* standoffs.

SPI (SCSI Parallel Interface) — The part of the SCSI-3 standard that specifies how SCSI devices are connected.

spooling — Placing print jobs in a print queue so that an application can be released from the printing process before printing is completed. Spooling is an acronym for simultaneous peripheral operations online.

staggered pin grid array (SPGA) — A feature of a CPU socket whereby the pins are staggered over the socket to squeeze more pins into a small space.

standby time — The time before a "Green" system will reduce 92 percent of its activity. *See also* Green Standards.

standoffs — Round plastic or metal pegs that separate the motherboard from the case, so that components on the back of the motherboard do not touch the case.

startup BIOS — Part of system BIOS that is responsible for controlling the PC when it is first turned on. Startup BIOS gives control over to the OS once it is loaded.

startup disk — *See* rescue disk.

startup password — *See* power-on password.

static electricity — *See* electrostatic discharge.

static IP address — An IP address permanently assigned to a workstation.

static RAM (SRAM) — RAM chips that retain information without the need for refreshing, as long as the computer's power is on. They are more expensive than traditional DRAM.

stop error — An error severe enough to cause the operating system to stop all processes. *See also* blue screen.

streaming audio — Downloading audio data from the Internet in a continuous stream of data without first downloading an entire audio file.

subdirectory — A directory or folder contained in another directory or folder. *Also called* a child directory or folder.

subnet mask — A group of four numbers (dotted decimal numbers) that tell TCP/IP if a remote computer is on the same or a different network.

surge suppressor or surge protector — A device or power strip designed to protect electronic equipment from power surges and spikes.

suspend time — The time before a "Green" system will reduce 99 percent of its activity. After this time, the system needs a warm-up time so that the CPU, monitor, and hard drive can reach full activity.

swap file — A file on the hard drive that is used by the OS for virtual memory. *Also called* a page file.

synchronous DRAM (SDRAM) — A type of memory stored on DIMMs that runs in sync with the system clock, running at the same speed as the motherboard.

synchronous SRAM — SRAM that is faster and more expensive than asynchronous SRAM. It requires a clock signal to validate its control signals, enabling the cache to run in step with the CPU.

Sysedit — The Windows System Configuration Editor, a text editor generally used to edit system files.

system BIOS — BIOS located on the motherboard.

system board — *See* motherboard.

system bus — The bus between the CPU and memory on the motherboard. The bus frequency in documentation is called the system speed, such as 400 MHz. *Also called* the memory bus, motherboard bus, front-side bus, local bus, or host bus.

system clock — A line on a bus that is dedicated to timing the activities of components connected to it. The system clock provides a continuous pulse that other devices use to time themselves.

system disk — Windows terminology for a bootable disk.

system partition — The active partition of the hard drive containing the boot record and the specific files required to load Windows NT/2000/XP.

system resource — A channel, line, or address on the motherboard that can be used by the CPU or a device for communication. The four system resources are IRQ, I/O address, DMA channel, and memory address.

System Restore — A Windows Me/XP utility, similar to the ScanReg tool in earlier versions of Windows, that is used to restore the system to a restore point. Unlike ScanReg, System Restore cannot be executed from a command prompt.

system state data — In Windows 2000/XP, files that are necessary for a successful load of the operating system.

System Tray — An area to the right of the taskbar that holds the icons of small applets launched at startup.

System.ini — A text configuration file used by Windows 3.x and supported by Windows 9x for backward-compatibility.

TAPI (Telephony Application Programming Interface) — A standard developed by Intel and Microsoft that can be used by 32-bit Windows communications programs for communicating over phone lines.

TCP/IP (Transmission Control Protocol/ Internet Protocol) — The suite of protocols that supports communication on the Internet. TCP is responsible for error checking, and IP is responsible for routing.

telephony — A term describing the technology of converting sound to signals that can travel over telephone lines.

terminating resistor — The resistor added at the end of a SCSI chain to dampen the voltage at the end of the chain.

termination — A process necessary to prevent an echo effect of power at the end of a SCSI chain, resulting in interference with the data transmission.

ThickNet — *See* 10Base5.

ThinNet — *See* 10Base2.

TIFF (Tagged Image File Format) — A bitmapped file format used to hold photographs, graphics, and screen captures. TIFF files can be rather large and have a .tif file extension.

top-level domain — The highest level of domain names, indicated by a suffix that tells something about the host. For example, .com is for commercial use and .edu is for educational institutions.

tower case — The largest type of personal computer case. Tower cases stand vertically and can be as high as two feet tall. They have more drive bays and are a good choice for computer users who anticipate making significant upgrades.

trace — A wire on a circuit board that connects two components or devices.

track — One of many concentric circles on the surface of a hard drive or floppy disk.

training — *See* handshaking.

translation — A technique used by system BIOS and hard drive controller BIOS to break the 504-MB hard drive barrier, whereby a different set of drive parameters are communicated to the OS and other software than that used by the hard drive controller BIOS.

TSR (terminate-and-stay-resident) — A program that is loaded into memory and remains dormant until called on, such as a screen saver or a memory-resident antivirus program.

UART (universal asynchronous receiver-transmitter) chip — A chip that controls serial ports. It sets protocol and converts parallel data bits received from the system bus into serial bits.

unattended installation — A Windows NT/ 2000/XP installation that is done by storing the answers to installation questions in a text file or script that Windows NT/2000/XP calls an answer file so that the answers do not have to be typed in during the installation.

Universal Disk Format (UDF) file system — A file system for optical media used by all DVD discs and some CD-R and CD-RW discs.

unshielded twisted-pair (UTP) cable — A cable that is made of one or more twisted pairs of wires and is not surrounded by a metal shield.

upgrade install — The installation of an OS on a hard drive that already has an OS installed in such a way that settings kept by the old OS are carried forward into the upgrade, including information about hardware, software, and user preferences.

upper memory — In DOS and Windows 9x, the memory addresses from 640K up to 1024K, originally reserved for BIOS, device drivers, and TSRs.

upper memory block (UMB) — In DOS and Windows 9x, a group of consecutive memory addresses in RAM from 640K to 1MB that can be used by 16-bit device drivers and TSRs.

URL (Uniform Resource Locator) — An address for a resource on the Internet. A URL can contain the protocol used by the resource, the name of the computer and its network, and the path and name of a file on the computer.

USB (universal serial bus) port — A type of port designed to make installation and configuration of I/O devices easy, providing room for as many as 127 devices daisy-chained together.

USB host controller — Manages the USB bus. If the motherboard contains on-board USB ports, the USB host controller is part of the chipset. The USB uses only a single set of resources for all devices on the bus.

user account — The information, stored in the SAM database, that defines a Windows NT/ 2000/XP user, including username, password, memberships, and rights.

user profile — A personal profile about a user that enables the user's desktop settings and other operating parameters to be retained from one session to another.

User State Migration Tool (USMT) — A Windows XP utility that helps you migrate user files and preferences from one computer to another to help a user makes a smooth transition from one computer to another.

V.92 — The latest standard for data transmission over phone lines that can attain a speed of 56 Kbps.

value data — In Windows, the name and value of a setting in the registry.

VCACHE — A built-in Windows 9x 32-bit software cache that doesn't take up conventional memory space or upper memory space as SMARTDrive did.

VESA (Video Electronics Standards Association) VL bus — An outdated local bus used on 80486 computers for connecting 32-bit adapters directly to the local processor bus.

video card — An interface card installed in the computer to control visual output on a monitor. Also called display adapter.

virtual device driver (VxD or VDD) — A Windows device driver that may have direct access to a device. It might depend on a Windows component to communicate with the device itself.

virtual memory — A method whereby the OS uses the hard drive as though it were RAM. *Compare to* RAM drive.

virtual real mode — An operating mode that works similarly to real mode provided by a 32-bit OS for a 16-bit program to work.

virus — A program that often has an incubation period, is infectious, and is intended to cause damage. A virus program might destroy data and programs or damage a disk drive's boot sector.

virus signature — A set of distinguishing characteristics of a virus used by antivirus software to identify the virus.

volatile — Refers to a kind of RAM that is temporary, cannot hold data very long, and must be frequently refreshed.

volt (V) — A measure of potential difference in an electrical circuit. A computer ATX power supply usually provides five separate voltages: +12V, -12V, +5V, -5V, and +3.3V.

voltage — Electrical differential that causes current to flow, measured in volts. *See also* volt.

voltage regulator module (VRM) — A device embedded or installed on the motherboard that regulates voltage to the processor.

voltmeter — A device for measuring electrical AC or DC voltage.

volume — *See* logical drive.

VRAM (video RAM) — RAM on video cards that holds the data that is being passed from the computer to the monitor and can be accessed by two devices simultaneously. Higher resolutions often require more video memory.

VxD — *See* virtual device driver.

wait state — A clock tick in which nothing happens, used to ensure that the microprocessor isn't getting ahead of slower components. A 0-wait state is preferable to a 1-wait state. Too many wait states can slow down a system.

WAN (wide area network) — A network or group of networks that span a large geographical area.

warm boot — *See* soft boot.

watt (W) — The unit used to measure power. A typical computer may use a power supply that provides 200W.

wattage — Electrical power measured in watts.

WFP (Windows File Protection) — A Windows 2000/XP tool that protects system files from modification.

wide SCSI — One of the two main SCSI specifications. Wide SCSI has a 16-bit data bus. *See also* narrow SCSI.

Wi-Fi — *See* IEEE 802.11b.

wildcard — A * or ? character used in a command line that represents a character or group of characters in a filename or extension.

Win.ini — The Windows initialization file that contains program configuration information needed for running the Windows operating environment. Its functions were replaced by the registry beginning with Windows 9x, which still supports it for backward compatibility with Windows 3.x.

Win386.swp — The name of the Windows 9x swap file. Its default location is C:\Windows.

wireless LAN (WLAN) — A type of LAN that does not use wires or cables to create connections, but instead transmits data over radio or infrared waves.

workgroup — In Windows, a logical group of computers and users in which administration, resources, and security are distributed throughout the network, without centralized management or security.

worm — An infestation designed to copy itself repeatedly to memory, on drive space or on a network, until little memory or disk space remains.

WRAM (window RAM) — Dual-ported video RAM that is faster and less expensive than VRAM. It has its own internal bus on the chip, with a data path that is 256 bits wide.

zero insertion force (ZIF) socket — A socket that uses a small lever to apply even force when you install the microchip into the socket.

zone bit recording — A method of storing data on a hard drive whereby the drive can have more sectors per track near the outside of the platter.